Rot515

Pd/MX

o/p £9

A GRAMSCI READ.

CU00798502

A GRAMSCI READER

Selected Writings 1916-1935

edited by
DAVID FORGACS

LAWRENCE AND WISHART
LONDON

Lawrence and Wishart Limited
99a Wallis Road
London E9 5LN

Introduction © Eric Hobsbawm, 1999

Annotation and selection
© David Forgacs, 1988
Translations from *Selections from Prison Notebooks*,
© Quintin Hoare and Geoffrey Nowell-Smith, 1971;
from *Selections from Political Writings (1910-1920)*,
© Lawrence and Wishart, 1977; from *Selections from
Political Writings (1921-1926)*, © Quintin Hoare, 1978;
from *Selections from Cultural Writings*, © Lawrence and
Wishart, 1986; previously unpublished material, © David
Forgacs, 1988 and © Lawrence and Wishart, 1988

All rights reserved. Apart from any fair dealing
for the purpose of private study, research,
criticism or review, no part of this publication,
may be reproduced, stored in a retrieval system,
or transmitted, in any form or by any means,
electronic, electical, chemical, mechanical,
optical, photocopying, recording or otherwise,
without the prior permission of the copyright
owner.

ISBN 978-0-85315-892-9

Typeset by
Derek Doyle & Associates, Liverpool
Printed in Great Britain by
the MPG Books Group, Bodmin and King's Lynn

Contents

INTRODUCTION

The international fortunes of Gramsci's work have fluctuated with the changes of fashion on the intellectual left. Thus in the 1960s the vogue for Althusser in Latin America largely blocked the way for Gramsci, although in France itself Althusser's prominence also gave publicity to the then barely known Italian, whom he both praised and criticised. The element of fashion was particularly evident inasmuch as the reception of Gramsci coincided largely with the heyday of the 'new lefts' of the 1960s and 1970s, whose capacity to consume an eclectic mix made of mutually incompatible intellectual ingredients was considerable.

The element of fashion was even more evident in the 1990s, when former leftists transformed into neo-liberals no longer cared to be reminded of anything that recalled old enthusiasms. This could be witnessed in post-1991 Russia where the heritage of marxist ideas is under a serious attack.

It is equally evident that Gramsci could not have become a major figure on the world intellectual scene but for the determination of his comrade and admirer Palmiro Togliatti to preserve and publish his writings, and to give them a central place in Italian communism. Under the conditions of Stalinism this was by no means an inevitable choice, especially given the known heterodoxy of Gramsci, even though the line of the Seventh World Congress of the International made it a little less risky. Whatever the subsequent criticism of Togliatti's own views on Gramsci, his concern after Gramsci's death 'to remove him from the misfortunes of the present and safeguard him for the future life of the party' (P. Spriano, *Gramsci in carcere e il partito*, Rome 1988), and his insistence on Gramsci's centrality from the moment of his return to Italy, were the foundations of Gramsci's subsequent fortunes. The editorial deficiencies and omissions of the early post-war years were the price paid for making Gramsci known; in retrospect a price worth paying. Thanks to Togliatti's determination, and the new prestige of the PCI, at least the *Lettere* were published in a number of countries, including some 'people's democracies' before the death of Stalin. Where the local communist parties failed to do so, no one else did. Though excellent English translations were almost immediately made, it took decades actually to find publishers for the *Lettere* in Britain and the USA.

Even so, apart from a few foreigners with personal memories of the Italian Resistance and personal friendships on the post-war Italian left, the *Rezeptionsgeschichte* of Gramsci begins with the twentieth Congress of the CPSU. For two decades it was part of the attempt by the international communist movement to emancipate itself from the heritage both of Stalin and the Communist International. Within the 'socialist camp' this was reflected in the almost immediate official acknowledgement of Gramsci as a political thinker as well as a martyr – as witness the publication of a three-volume selection from his works in the USSR in 1957-1959, the Soviet presence at the first Gramsci *Convegno* in 1958 and the substantial and implicitly reformist Soviet delegation to the second (1967). Eventually, of course, Gramsci was to make his way into the academic literature.

More precisely, Gramsci attracted attention outside Italy primarily as a communist thinker who provided a marxist strategy for countries in which the October Revolution might have been an inspiration, but could not be a model, that is to say for socialist movements in non-revolutionary environments and situations. The prestige and success of the Italian Communist Party in the years between the Yalta Memorandum and the death of Enrico Berlinguer naturally spread the influence of a thinker generally considered as the inspirer of its strategies. Gramsci undoubtedly reached the peak of his international prominence in the years of 'eurocommunism' of the 1970s, and receded somewhat in the 1980s – except perhaps in the German Federal republic, where he was discovered rather late, and interest in him was at its height in the first half of the 1980s.

The international discussion on Gramsci, it seems, remained largely separate from and independent of the vigorous Italian debate on the country's greatest marxist thinker. This is not surprising. Foreigners inevitably read some national thinker, however universal in his or her interests, in a different manner from readers in their own culture, and when the thinker is, like Gramsci, so closely concerned with his national reality, foreign and national readings are even more likely to diverge. In any case several of the issues most hotly debated in Italy were not so much arguments about Gramsci as arguments for (or more usually against) some phase of the policy of the PCI. These were not always of major interest to non-specialists outside. Nevertheless, it is relevant to note that what has influenced foreign readers is the text of Gramsci's writings rather than the literature of criticism and interpretation that has accumulated around them in his own country. That is to say, it is the Gramsci of the era when the first major selections of his work became widely available in translation or, at the earliest, when the first important local 'Gramscians' appeared on the intellectual scene to introduce the as yet untranslated thinker. Essentially, we may say that the non-Italian Gramsci-reception was that of the Gramsci of the 1960s-1970s.

The international reception of Gramsci has therefore been, and still remains, subject to the fluctuating fortunes of the political left. And it will, and must, continue to be so to some extent. For Gramsci was par excellence the philosopher of political praxis. Most of the luminaries of what has been called 'western marxism' can be read, as it were, as academics, which many of them were or could have been: Lukacs, Korsch, Benjamin, Althusser, Marcuse and others. They wrote at one or two removes from the concrete political realities even when, like Henri Lefebvre, they were at one time or another plunged into them as political organisers. Gramsci cannot be separated from these realities, since even his widest generalisations are invariably concerned with the investigation of the practical conditions for transforming the world by politics in the *specific* circumstances in which he wrote. Unlike Lenin but like Marx, he was a born intellectual, a man almost physically excited by the sheer attraction of ideas. Not for nothing was he the only genuine marxist theorist who was also the leader of a marxist mass party (if we leave aside the much less original Otto Bauer). One of the reasons why historians, marxist and even non-marxist, have found him so rewarding is precisely his refusal to leave the terrain of concrete historical, social and cultural realities for abstraction and reductionist theoretical models.

It is therefore likely that Gramsci will continue to be read mainly for the light his writings throw on politics, in his own words, the 'body of practical rules for research and detailed observations useful for awakening an interest in effective reality and for stimulating more rigorous and more vigorous political insights'. I do not believe that those looking for such insights will only be found on the left, although for evident reasons those who share Gramsci's objectives are most likely to look to him for guidance. Yet, while one hopes that Gramsci may still be a guide to successful political action for the left, it is already clear that his international influence has penetrated beyond the left, and indeed beyond the sphere of instrumental politics.

It may seem trivial that an Anglo-saxon reference work can – I quote the entry in its entirety – reduce him to a single word: 'Antonio Gramsci (Italian political thinker, 1891-1937) see under HEGEMONY' (A. Bullock and O. Stallybrass (eds), *The Fontana Dictionary of Modern Thought*, London 1977). It may be absurd that an American journalist quoted by Buttigieg believes that the concept of 'civil society' was introduced into modern political discourse by Gramsci alone. Yet the acceptance of a thinker as a permanent classic is often indicated just by such superficial references to him by people who patently know little more about him than that he is 'important'.

Fifty years after his death Gramsci had become 'important' in this manner even outside Italy, where his status in national history and national culture was recognised almost from the beginning. It is now recognised in most parts of the globe. Indeed, the flourishing historical school of 'subaltern studies' centred in Calcutta suggests that Gramsci's influence is still expanding. He has survived the political conjunctures which first gave him international prominence. He has survived the European communist movement itself. He has demonstrated his independence of the fluctuations of ideological fashion. Who now expects another vogue for Althusser, any more than for Spengler? He has survived the enclosure in academic ghettos which looks like being the fate of so many other thinkers of 'western marxism'. He has even avoided becoming an 'ism'.

What the future fortunes of his writings will be, we cannot know. However, his permanence is already sufficiently sure, and justifies the continuing study of his writings.

E. J. Hobsbawm

NOTE ON THE TEXT

Most of the writings included here are to be found in one of the four existing volumes published in Britain by Lawrence and Wishart and in the United States by International Publishers (with the exception of the last, of which the American imprint is by Harvard University Press): *Selections from the Prison Notebooks*, edited and translated by Quintin Hoare and Geoffrey Nowell-Smith, 1971 (henceforth abbreviated as SPN); *Selections from Political Writings (1910-1920)*, selected and edited by Quintin Hoare, translated by John Mathews, 1977 (abbreviated as SPW I); *Selections from Political Writings (1921-26)*, translated and edited by Quintin Hoare, 1978 (abbreviated as SPW II); *Selections from Cultural Writings*, edited by David Forgacs and Geoffrey Nowell-Smith, translated by William Boelhower, 1985 (abbreviated as SCW). Although I have sought to include as many important texts and passages as possible, with one or two exceptions I have deliberately left out or cut passages which require a specialized knowledge (historical, philosophical, literary). Where such passages seemed indispensable I have included them and put a note, although I have generally tried to keep notes to a minimum and to confine detailed explanations to the introductions heading each section. I have however used a few notes to cross-refer to passages in other texts. Some notes have been transcribed from the existing English editions; others are new.

Each item (text) in this book is identified by both an Arabic numeral and a separate title. Titles enclosed in square brackets have been supplied by me where Gramsci either did not give one or where the existing one is inappropriate (for instance some of the prison notes have only general headings). At the foot of each text I have indicated, using the appropriate abbreviation followed by page numbers, where it is to be found in one of the four volumes mentioned. Where no previous translation exists the text is marked * and its published Italian source is indicated. In Part One this source is given in the form of abbreviated title followed by page numbers. The three editions cited here are: CT = *Cronache*

14

torinesi, 1913-1917, CF = *La Città futura, 1917-1918* and NM = *Il nostro Marx, 1918-1919*, all edited by Sergio Caprioglio, Einaudi, Turin, respectively 1980, 1982 and 1984. In Part Two an Italian source in the prison notebooks is given in all cases. This takes the form of a notebook (Q = *quaderno*) number and a paragraph (§) number, following the numbering of *Quaderni del carcere* edited by Valentino Gerratana, 4 volumes, Turin 1975. New translations are mine, except for VI, 4, 6 and 7, which are by Derek Boothman. The biographical outline in the prefatory material is based on the ones in CT and Gerratana's edition, as above.

As for dates of the writings, all texts in Part One carry a date of first publication or original composition. In Part Two I have not attempted to date individual texts, since a given draft in the prison notebooks cannot always be dated more accurately than by its year of composition and many of the later notes are in any case revised versions of earlier drafts. However, the following dates of composition of the individual notebooks drawn on in this volume will give readers a rough guide (the dating is that given in Gerratana's critical edition): Q 3: 1930; Q 5, 6 and 7: 1930-32; Q 8: 1931-32; Q 10: 1932-35; Q 11: 1932-33; Q 12: 1932; Q 13: 1932-34; Q 14: 1932-35; Q 15: 1933; Q 16: 1933-34; Q 19 and 21: 1934-35; Q 22, 23 and 24: 1934; Q 26, 27 and 29: 1935.

In most places the text given here follows exactly that of the earlier English editions, but six kinds of variant reading will be found.

1. I have made *cuts*, marked by [...], in some texts. This is partly for reasons of space (in the case of a long text), partly in order to remove specific references (e.g. to Italian political figures) that seemed dispensable in an edition of this kind. Every cut involves an editorial judgement, and it may be that some readers will disapprove of some of my judgements. Where this occurs, I can only refer them to the uncut version in the other editions. I had originally intended to include only uncut texts in this edition, but I soon realized that if I did so I should either have had to include many fewer texts than I wanted or else leave out for lack of space such fundamental writings as 'The Lyons Theses', 'Some Aspects of the Southern Question' and the prison notes on the Risorgimento and intellectuals. Some texts have been substantially reduced, but in many cases the cuts are minor ones.

2. At a few points there are *additional* passages. Where these

run to more than few lines I have enclosed them in angled brackets < >. In one case (I.4), the passage in question was cut from Gramsci's original newspaper article by the press censor. It was published for the first time in NM after Caprioglio found the original printers' proof seized by the censor in the State Archive at Turin. It was therefore not available to the translator of SPW I.

3. The *internal order of paragraphs* within some of the notes in Part Two differs from that in SPN and passages which appeared as footnotes in that edition appear here integrated into the main body of the text. In this respect I have followed the text of the critical edition, which reproduces Gramsci's manuscript notebooks more exactly. For the same reason, there are a few cases where what appears as a single note in SPN appears here as two notes or even three, and occasionally the other way round.

4. The *order of notes* themselves in Part Two does not correspond, on the whole, to the sequences in SPN. Like the earlier Italian editions, SPN did not generally follow Gramsci's manuscript arrangement. I have consequently felt free to regroup the notes, with respect to SPN, in an order that both seemed to make more sense for the particular thematic arrangements of this edition and to correspond as far as possible to the order of composition by year of their first drafts (the translations are however, with one exception (VIII.6), all of second drafts or unique drafts).

5. I have made some minor *emendations* to the translations in the few cases where the existing translation seemed to me either incorrect or unclear. Translations have been checked against the critical editions, where these have now appeared.

6. There are a few variants of *style* introduced to resolve inconsistencies between the four volumes: for instance the word 'state' appears here with a lower-case initial throughout, 'Communist', 'Socialist' and 'Fascist' (when they refer to political parties) have an initial capital, the forms 'II' and 'III', used as ordinals, are written out as 'Second' and 'Third', main quotations are in single rather than double inverted commas and most spellings in '-ise' have been amended to '-ize'.

CHRONOLOGICAL OUTLINE

1891

Antonio Gramsci born in Ales (province of Cagliari, Sardinia) on 22 January, fourth of seven children.

1897

His father, Francesco, a civil servant, is accused of administrative irregularity and suspended from office. He is subsequently tried and sentenced to five years' imprisonment.

1903-05

Gramsci is obliged to work, because of the family's straitened circumstances, in the local tax office. Around 1905 his elder brother Gennaro, doing military service in Turin, starts sending him *Avanti!*, the organ of the Italian Socialist Party (PSI).

1908-11

Moves to Cagliari to complete his school studies. Lives with Gennaro (now a PSI activist) and has his first contacts with the socialist movement. Also becomes involved with Sardinian regionalist politics. He first reads Karl Marx's writings in this period.

1911

Wins a scholarship to University of Turin. Meets Palmiro Togliatti and Angelo Tasca, also students in Turin. Particularly interested in linguistics.

1913

Becomes involved in PSI activity in Turin.

1915

Withdraws from university courses without graduating and devotes himself full time to working for the socialist press – the Turin office of *Avanti!* and the local Socialist weekly *Il Grido del*

Popolo (The People's Cry). He continues working part-time on a thesis in linguistics until 1918.

1917

February. Edits single issue of *La Città futura*, newspaper of the regional youth movement of the PSI.

April. First articles in support of Lenin and the Russian revolution.

August. Food riots and anti-war protests in Turin. Many local PSI leaders arrested in subsequent wave of repression.

September. Becomes secretary of provisional executive of Turin PSI and acting editor of *Il Grido del Popolo*.

December. Publishes article 'The Revolution against *Capital*' in support of the Bolsheviks and against a determinist Marxism.

1918

Il Grido del Popolo ceases publication. With Togliatti and others, launches a Turin edition of *Avanti!*

1919

May. Gramsci, Togliatti and Tasca launch the weekly *L'Ordine Nuovo* (The New Order).

June. Publishes in *L'Ordine Nuovo* the article 'Workers' Democracy' calling for the internal commissions in the workplace to be developed as 'organs of proletarian power, replacing the capitalist'. Translates many articles dealing with factory councils and the shop stewards' movement.

October. Meets Sylvia Pankhurst in Turin. A series of her 'Letters from England', translated by Togliatti, appears in *L'Ordine Nuovo*.

November–December. Factory council movement develops in Turin.

1920

April. Unofficial general strike in Turin (not supported by PSI or socialist trade union (CGL) leaders) involving over 200,000 workers.

July–August. Gramsci and *L'Ordine Nuovo* group approve the setting up of 'factory communist groups', later to be the local nuclei of the Communist Party. Second Congress of Communist

International (Comintern) in Petrograd sets conditions ('21 points') for membership. Lenin praises Gramsci's motion 'For a renewal of the Socialist Party' amid the dissent of the Italian delegation.

September. Occupation of the factories. 500,000 workers involved in northern industrial cities. Gramsci's article 'Red Sunday'. CGL votes against occupation being turned into revolution. Movement collapses.

November. Participates at PSI Congress in Imola where communist fraction is formed.

1921

January. Gramsci and others set up institute of Proletarian Culture in Turin, affiliated to Soviet Proletkult. Livorno congress of PSI. Motion of communist fraction wins a third of the votes. Fraction secedes to form Communist Party of Italy (PCdI). General secretary is Amadeo Bordiga.

December. Comintern launches 'united front' policy of working-class unity between Communists and Socialists at both party and trade union level. Policy opposed by PCdI.

1922

March. Second Congress of PCdI, Rome. 'Rome Theses' opposing united front policy approved by a large majority.

May. Gramsci, designated PCdI representative to Comintern, leaves for Moscow in poor health. He will not return to Italy for two years.

June. Begins to participate in Comintern activities but is taken ill. Spends several months in a Moscow sanatorium where he meets his future wife, Julia Schucht.

October. 'March on Rome'. Mussolini takes power.

November-December. Fourth Congress of Comintern deals with 'Italian question' and recommends fusion of PCdI with PSI. Majority of PCdI is opposed to the recommendation but accepts it out of discipline. Fusion however will never take place.

1923

February. Bordiga and several other Communist leaders arrested. Togliatti enters Executive Committee.

April-June. Bordiga from prison launches appeal to party to oppose Comintern line on the issue of fusion with PSI. Gramsci refuses to sign. Nucleus of new leading group of party (Togliatti, Gramsci, Umberto Terracini) begins to form.

December. Gramsci is transferred from Moscow to Vienna to maintain links between PCdI and other European Communist parties.

1924

February. First issue of *L'Unità* appears, joint daily paper of PCdI and 'Third Internationalist' fraction of PSI (latter will fuse with PCdI in August).

April. General election. Gramsci elected parliamentary deputy.

May. Returns to Italy. Clandestine party conference in Como. Gramsci elected to Executive Committee, opposes Bordiga's policies. He subsequently becomes the new General Secretary.

June. Fascists murder opposition deputy Giacomo Matteotti. Gramsci calls for general strike and working-class anti-fascist unity against legalistic protest of other opposition parties.

August. Julia Schucht gives birth to her and Gramsci's first child, Delio.

August-September. Comintern calls for 'Bolshevization' of Communist parties: application of united front policy, slogan of 'workers' and peasants' government', restructuring of party organization on the basis of workplace cells.

1925

January. Fascist 'exceptional laws' introduced.

October. Julia with Delio joins Gramsci in Rome. She works at the Soviet Embassy.

1926

January. Third Congress of PCdI, Lyons. Drafts with Togliatti the main congress document ('Lyons Theses') which is overwhelmingly approved (90.8 per cent), a victory for the new leading group over the Bordiga opposition.

July. Julia, now expecting a second child, leaves Italy because of the deteriorating political climate.

August. Second son, Giuliano, born to Julia in Moscow. Gramsci will only ever see photographs of him.

October. Gramsci writes a letter to the Central Committee of the Bolshevik Party expressing anxiety about the inner-party struggle (between the Stalin-Bukharin majority and the Trotsky-Zinoviev-Kamenev Joint Opposition) and its effect on the international movement. He nevertheless declares his support for the majority. The letter is sent to Togliatti in Moscow, who withholds it, though he shows it to Bukharin. Drafts 'Some Aspects of the Southern Question'.

November. Arrested with other Communist deputies, in violation of parliamentary immunity. Imprisoned first in Rome, then (December) transferred to exile on the island of Ustica (off Sicily) where he briefly shares a house with Bordiga and others. To enable Gramsci to read during his imprisonment, his friend Piero Sraffa, the Marxist economist based in Cambridge, opens an unlimited account on his behalf at a bookshop in Milan.

1927

January. Transferred from Ustica to prison in Milan to await trial.

March. First plan of prison notebooks communicated in a letter to his sister-in-law, Tatiana Schucht, acting as an intermediary, in this instance, for Piero Sraffa. Four subjects outlined: history of Italian intellectuals, theatre of Pirandello, comparative linguistics and popular literature.

October. A letter from Piero Sraffa publicizing Gramsci's plight and attacking 'the methods of Fascism' appears in the *Manchester Guardian* on 21 October.

1928

May. Transferred to Rome. Tried with other Communist leaders before Special Tribunal. The prosecuting attorney Michele Isgrò allegedly says of Gramsci: 'For twenty years we must stop this brain from working.'

June. Sentenced to 20 years and 8 months.

July. Sent to a special prison in Turi (near Bari, in the south) because of his ill health. At first he shares a cell with five other prisoners, then he obtains permission for a cell on his own.

1929

January. Granted permission to write in his cell. He begins with translation exercises.

February. Begins to write the first 'notebook', a school exercise
book.
March. Outlines new plan of prison research to Tatiana Schucht:
nineteenth-century Italian history, history of intellectual groups,
theory and history of historiography, Americanism and Fordism.
The notebooks of this first period (1929-31) are miscellanies
containing writings on several themes.

1930
Internal crisis in PCdI leadership as a result of Togliatti's
acceptance of Comintern 'Third Period' policy of 'class against
class'. Three leading members who oppose the policy (Leonetti,
Tresso, Ravazzoli) are expelled. Gramsci tells his brother
Gennaro, sent by Togliatti to visit him, that he disagrees with the
Third Period line and the expulsion of the three. Gennaro does not
report this back to Togliatti, for fear that his brother too might
suffer recrimination. Gramsci is subsequently criticized and
ostracized by fellow Communists in prison for his opposition to the
view that an immediately revolutionary situation would result
from an imminent fall of Fascism and his suggested slogan of the
constituent assembly for the transitional period.

1931
Gramsci's health deteriorates. On 3 August he coughs up blood in
the night. A second period of notebook writing (1931-34) begins in
which he rewrites and regroups earlier drafts and arranges notes
more thematically.

1932
Revised plan of the notebooks set out in Notebook 8 under ten
groupings: Intellectuals and education, Machiavelli, Encyclopaedic notions and cultural themes, Introduction to the study of
philosophy and critical notes on Bukharin's *Popular Manual of
Sociology*, Catholics, 'Past and present' (miscellany), Italian
Risorgimento, Literature and popular literature, 'Lorianism',
Journalism.
  An attempt, supported by Gramsci, gets underway to obtain his
release through an exchange of prisoners with the Soviet Union,
where his wife and two children are living. The Soviet authorities
approach the Italian government without success.

August. Gramsci writes to Tatiana: 'I have reached a point where my strength to resist is about to collapse completely, with what consequences I do not know.'

November. As a result of the government's amnesty provisions for the tenth anniversary of the Fascist 'revolution', Gramsci's sentence is commuted to 12 years and 4 months.

December. Gramsci's mother dies. His relatives withhold the news from him.

1933

March. Gramsci collapses in his cell. For two weeks he is tended night and day by fellow prisoners. He is examined by a doctor, Professor Arcangeli, who certifies 'Gramsci cannot survive for long in present conditions: I consider it necessary for him to be transferred to a civil hospital or a clinic, unless he can be granted conditional liberty.' Gramsci refuses to submit a plea for mercy to the Fascist authorities.

May–June. Arcangeli's statement is published in *L'Humanité*. In Paris a committee for Gramsci's release and that of other victims of Fascism is set up, headed by Henri Barbusse and Romain Rolland.

December. Gramsci is transferred to a clinic in Formia (between Rome and Naples). Here in a third period of writing (1934-35), despite his deteriorating health, he begins to transcribe, revise and regroup earlier drafts of notes in a series of 'special' notebooks on particular themes.

1934

October. Gramsci submits a request for conditional release. The request is granted (25 October). He is allowed to go out of the clinic but is too weak to leave. The Fascist authorities block his request to be transferred to a clinic elsewhere, suspecting plans for his escape.

1935

August. After a further deterioration, Gramsci is transferred to a clinic in Rome.

1936

He resumes his correspondence with his wife and children. He considers returning to Sardinia to convalesce, but fears such a withdrawal would put him in a position 'of complete isolation, of an

even more pronounced intellectual degradation than at present, of
the complete or almost complete erasure of certain forms of expectation which in the past few years, although they may have tormented me, have also given my life a certain content' (letter to
Julia, summer 1936).

1937
April. The period of conditional release ends and Gramsci is now
legally free. But he is too ill to move. On 25 April he has a cerebral
haemorrhage and he dies on 27 April.
June. First extracts of the prison letters (dealing with Croce)
published in Paris in PCdI periodical *Lo Stato Operaio*.
July. Tatiana Schucht deposits manuscript prison notebooks, which
she had removed along with Gramsci's other effects after his death,
in a safe at the Banca Commerciale in Rome. A year later she has
them despatched to Moscow. They are passed on to Togliatti.

1945
After the liberation from Nazi-Fascist occupation, further extracts
from the prison letters and the first extracts from the notebooks
appear in the PCI press.

1947
218 of the prison letters published in a first edition (*Lettere dal
carcere*, Einaudi, Turin). A number of references to Bordiga and
Trotsky have been excised.

1948-51
First edition of the prison notebooks (*Quaderni del carcere*). The
manuscript notebooks are rearranged thematically by the editor
Felice Platone into six volumes: *Il materialismo storico e la filosofia
di Benedetto Croce* (1948), *Gli intellettuali e l'organizzazione della
cultura* (1949), *Il Risorgimento* (1949), *Note sul Machiavelli, sulla
politica e sullo Stato moderno* (1949), *Letteratura e vita nazionale*
(1950), *Passato e presente* (1951).

1954-74
The bulk of Gramsci's writings from the period 1913-26 are edited
and published at various intervals between these dates.

1957

The first selection of Gramsci's works, *The Modern Prince and Other Writings*, is published in English.

1971

Selections from Prison Notebooks makes a wide range of Gramsci's writings available to an English-language readership for the first time.

1975

Critical edition of the prison notebooks edited by Valentino Gerratana in four volumes (three volumes of text, one of critical apparatus). The notebooks are arranged in chronological order according to when they were commenced and, apart from some internal restorations of chronological order, are published in exact accordance with the manuscript. All drafts are included.

1980

A multi-volume critical edition of the pre-prison writings, arranged in chronological sequence, begins to appear in Italy.

PART ONE: WRITINGS 1916-1926

I SOCIALISM AND MARXISM 1917-1918

Introduction

When Gramsci joined the Italian Socialist Party (PSI) in 1913 it was divided, like other European social-democratic parties, into a 'reformist' right and a 'revolutionary' left. The reformists envisaged a 'legal' transition to socialism through parliamentary majorities and reforms, trade union gains, extension of the co-operative movement and occupancy of the local state. From the turn of the century they had supported the group of parliamentary Liberals around Giovanni Giolitti (Prime Minister for most of the decade before the First World War), a central plank of whose political strategy had been the formation of an alliance between representatives of north Italian skilled labour and northern capital. This alliance rested on concessions to the moderate wing of the labour movement, including social reforms, together with the continuing economic and political subjugation of the underdeveloped south to the industrialized north. The left, known in Italy as 'maximalists' from their support for the party's maximum (revolutionary) programme, was a more heterogeneous set of fractions. During and after the First World War they held the PSI leadership (formally separate from the parliamentary party) and controlled its newspaper *Avanti!*. They did not believe in a parliamentary road to socialism, although most of them were prepared to use parliament as a platform for revolutionary propaganda. They adopted a position of 'intransigence' (refusal to participate in coalition governments with bourgeois parties), were fiercely anti-Giolittian and attacked the reformists for their 'collaborationism'.

Gramsci's political sympathies with Sardinia (economically part of the south) and his experience of Turin's unique concentration of heavy industry and its well organized and combative labour movement made him highly critical of reformism, whose leadership was mainly northern middle-class and whose typical power bases were among the skilled craft workers of Milan and the co-operative movement of central Italy. But though he was squarely on the 'intransigent revolutionary' left of the party and worked on the local page of *Avanti!*, he did not share either the anarchistic rebelliousness or the 'economic catastrophism' which were the typical hallmarks of maximalism. Rather he absorbed a heterogeneous culture, strongly anti-positivist, in which elements of idealism and voluntarism (Croce, Sorel, Bergson) were mixed in with elements of Marxism. He was concerned, as one of his university teachers was later to recall, with 'how thinking makes one act ... how and why one can act with ideas ... *how ideas become practical forces*'. (Fiori 1970: 93). The outbreak of revolution in Russia in February 1917 had a galvanizing effect on Gramsci's thinking. Already in April he was writing that the revolution 'must naturally lead to a socialist regime' (SPW I, p. 28) and when the Bolsheviks (to whom he referred initially as 'maximalists') took power in November he wrote of 'the revolution against Karl Marx's *Capital*', seeing it as a revolution in defiance of orthodox predictions and consequently against the 'positivistic incrustations' of Second International orthodoxy which had turned Marxism into a gradual unfolding of impersonal economic 'laws'. The revolution vindicated for Gramsci a more authentic Marxism, one which was about the 'collective popular will'. In 'Our Marx' (1918) he characterizes Marxism as being neither about the force of ideas in themselves nor about an impersonal and mechanical fatalism of economic development. It has to do, rather, with people becoming conscious of objective reality and with ideas finding the instrument of their realization in the material forces of production and in a disciplined working-class movement. It is about revolutionary action, not about what he calls, alluding to the vision of socialism typically projected in the propaganda of the reformists, 'cordial fraternity' and 'tender declarations of respect and love'.

These early writings are in many ways remarkable for the clarity with which they adumbrate themes of Gramsci's later work. Three arguments in particular stand out. The first is the moral argument about discipline as a means towards self-advancement and collective liberation (see 'Discipline'): a characteristically Gramscian emphasis which will recur in later discussions of the need for members of a revolutionary movement to overcome both 'passivity' (or 'inertia') and individual rebelliousness. Secondly, there is the opposition to any 'mechanical' or 'economistic' interpretation of the base-superstructure paradigm – in other words to an interpretation which reduces the complex political and ideological spheres to an underlying economic foundation. Attacking the view that the Bolshevik revolution had forced a radical political solution on economically immature conditions, he writes here ('Utopia'): 'It is not the economic structure [base] which directly determines political activity, but rather the way in which that structure and the so-called laws which govern its development are interpreted... Events... depend on the wills of a great many people [and] on the knowledge a minority possesses concerning those wills.' Thirdly, there is a view of the state which avoids 'class instrumentalism', i.e. Gramsci does not reduce the state to the expression or instrument of an already unified social class. He sees the mature bourgeois state rather as an arena in which conflicts between competing fractions of the bourgeoisie are regulated and the dominance of one fraction over the others is secured ('Class Intransigence and Italian History'). Moreover he avoids a static characterization of the 'state in general' and deals with the peculiarities and recent transformations of the Italian state in particular. He stresses its *antiquated* character in relation to the modern bourgeois state, a reflection of the *immaturity* of Italian capitalism, of the persistence of pre-capitalist economic forms and the quasi-colonial subjugation of the south of Italy to northern capital. The task of the Socialists, Gramsci argues, should not be to seek to perpetuate this bourgeois form of state, as the reformists ('collaborationists') were doing. Rather, the state needed to be replaced by a socialist state whose role would be limited to that of organizing production and exchange.

1 Discipline

In one of the stories in *The Jungle Book* Rudyard Kipling shows discipline at work in a strong bourgeois society. Everyone obeys in the bourgeois state. The mules in the battery obey the battery sergeant, the horses obey the soldiers who ride them. The soldiers obey the lieutenant, the lieutenants obey the regimental colonels; the regiments obey a brigadier general; the brigades obey the viceroy of the Indias. The viceroy obeys Queen Victoria (still alive when Kipling was writing). The queen gives an order: the viceroy, the brigadier generals, the colonels, the lieutenants, the soldiers, the animals, all move in unison and go off to the conquest. The protagonist of the story says to a native who is watching a parade: 'Because you cannot do likewise, you are our subjects.'[1]

Bourgeois discipline is the only force which keeps the bourgeois aggregation firmly together. Discipline must be met with discipline. But whereas bourgeois discipline is mechanical and authoritarian, socialist discipline is autonomous and spontaneous. If you accept socialist discipline it means you are a socialist or you want to be so more fully, joining the youth movement if you are young. And whoever is a socialist or wants to become one does not obey: he commands himself, he imposes a rule of life on his impulses, on his disorderly aspirations. It would be strange if, while one too often obeys without a murmur a discipline that one does not understand and does not feel, we were not able to act according to a course of conduct that we ourselves have helped prescribe and keep rigidly consistent. For this is what autonomous disciplines are like: the very life, the very thought of the person who observes them. The discipline imposed on citizens by the bourgeois state makes them into subjects, people who delude themselves that they exert an influence on the course of events. The discipline of the Socialist Party makes the subject into a citizen: a citizen who is now rebellious, precisely because he has become conscious of his personality and feels it is shackled and cannot freely express itself in the world.

La Città futura, 11 February 1917.*

(CF, 19-20)

2 The Revolution Against *Capital*

The Bolshevik Revolution is now definitively part of the general revolution of the Russian people. The maximalists [Bolsheviks] up until two months ago were the active agents needed to ensure that events should not stagnate, that the drive to the future should not come to a halt and allow a final settlement – a bourgeois settlement – to be reached. Now these maximalists have seized power and established their dictatorship, and are creating the socialist framework within which the revolution will have to settle down if it is to continue to develop harmoniously, without head-on confrontations, on the basis of the immense gains which have already been made.

The Bolshevik Revolution consists more of ideologies than of events. (And hence, at bottom, we do not really need to know more than we do.) This is the revolution against Karl Marx's *Capital*. In Russia, Marx's *Capital* was more the book of the bourgeoisie than of the proletariat. It stood as the critical demonstration of how events should follow a predetermined course: how in Russia a bourgeoisie had to develop, and a capitalist era had to open, with the setting-up of a Western-type civilization, before the proletariat could even think in terms of its own revolt, its own class demands, its own revolution. But events have overcome ideologies. Events have exploded the critical schemas determining how the history of Russia would unfold according to the canons of historical materialism. The Bolsheviks reject Karl Marx, and their explicit actions and conquests bear witness that the canons of historical materialism are not so rigid as one might have thought and has been believed.

And yet there is a fatality even in these events, and if the Bolsheviks reject some of the statements in *Capital*, they do not reject its invigorating, immanent thought. These people are not 'Marxists', that is all; they have not used the works of the Master to compile a rigid doctrine of dogmatic utterances never to be questioned. They live Marxist thought – that thought which is eternal, which represents the continuation of German and Italian idealism, and which in the case of Marx was contaminated by positivist and naturalist incrustations. This thought sees as the dominant factor in history, not raw economic facts, but man, men in societies, men in relation to one another, reaching agreements with one another, developing through these contacts (civilization) a collective, social will; men coming to understand economic facts, judging them and adapting them to their will until this becomes the driving force of the economy and moulds objective reality, which lives and moves and comes to resemble a current of volcanic lava that can be channelled wherever and in whatever way the will determines.

Marx foresaw the foreseeable. But he could not foresee the European war, or rather he could not foresee that the war would

last as long as it has or have the effects it has had. He could not
foresee that in the space of three years of unspeakable suffering
and miseries, this war would have aroused in Russia the collective
popular will that it has aroused. *In normal times* a lengthy process
of gradual diffusion through society is needed for such a collective
will to form; a wide range of class experience is needed. Men are
lazy, they need to be organized, first externally into corporations
and leagues, then internally, within their thought and their will in a
ceaseless continuity and multiplicity of external stimuli. This is
why, *under normal conditions*, the canons of Marxist historical
criticism grasp reality, capture and clarify it. *Under normal
conditions* the two classes of the capitalist world create history
through an ever more intensified class struggle. The proletariat is
sharply aware of its poverty and its ever-present discomfort and
puts pressure on the bourgeoisie to improve its living standards. It
enters into struggle, and forces the bourgeoisie to improve the
techniques of production and make it more adapted to meeting the
urgent needs of the proletariat. The result is a headlong drive for
improvement, an acceleration of the rhythm of production, and a
continually increasing output of goods useful to society. And in
this drive many fall by the wayside, so making the needs of those
who are left more urgent; the masses are forever in a state of
turmoil, and out of this chaos they develop some order in their
thoughts, and become ever more conscious of their own potential,
of their own capacity to shoulder social responsibility and become
the arbiters of their own destiny.

This is what happens under normal conditions. When events are
repeated with a certain regularity. When history develops through
stages which, though ever more complex and richer in significance
and value, are nevertheless similar. But in Russia the war
galvanized the people's will. As a result of the sufferings
accumulated over three years, their will became as one almost
overnight. Famine was imminent, and hunger, death from hunger,
could claim anyone, could crush tens of millions of men at one
stroke. Mechanically at first, then actively and consciously after
the first revolution, the people's will became as one.

Socialist propaganda put the Russian people in contact with the
experience of other proletariats. Socialist propaganda could bring
the history of the proletariat dramatically to life in a moment: its
struggles against capitalism, the lengthy series of efforts required

to emancipate it completely from the chains of servility that made it so abject and to allow it to forge a new consciousness and become a testimony today to a world yet to come. It was socialist propaganda that forged the will of the Russian people. Why should they wait for the history of England to be repeated in Russia, for the bourgeoisie to arise, for the class struggle to begin, so that class consciousness may be formed and the final catastrophe of the capitalist world eventually hit them? The Russian people – or at least a minority of the Russian people – has already passed through these experiences in thought. It has gone beyond them. It will make use of them now to assert itself just as it will make use of Western capitalist experience to bring itself rapidly to the same level of production as the Western world. In capitalist terms, North America is more advanced than England, because the Anglo-Saxons in North America took off at once from the level England had reached only after long evolution. Now the Russian proletariat, socialistically educated, will begin its history at the highest level England has reached today. Since it has to start from scratch, it will start from what has been perfected elsewhere, and hence will be driven to achieve that level of economic maturity which Marx considered to be a necessary condition for collectivism. The revolutionaries themselves will create the conditions needed for the *complete and full* achievement of their goal. And they will create them faster than capitalism could have done. The criticisms that socialists have made of the bourgeois system, to emphasize its imperfections and its squandering of wealth, can now be applied by the revolutionaries to do better, to avoid the squandering and not fall prey to the imperfections. It will at first be a collectivism of poverty and suffering. But a bourgeois regime would have inherited the same conditions of poverty and suffering. Capitalism could do no more *immediately* than collectivism in Russia. In fact today it would do a lot less, since it would be faced *immediately* by a discontented and turbulent proletariat, a proletariat no longer able to support on behalf of others the suffering and privation that economic dislocation would bring in its wake. So even in absolute, human terms, socialism now can be justified in Russia. The hardships that await them after the peace will be bearable only if the proletarians feel they have things under their own control and know that by their efforts they can reduce these hardships in the shortest possible time.

One has the impression that the maximalists at this moment are the spontaneous expression of a *biological* necessity – that they *had* to take power if the Russian people were not to fall prey to a horrible calamity; if the Russian people, throwing themselves into the colossal labours needed for their own regeneration, were to feel less sharply the fangs of the starving wolf; if Russia were not to become strewn with the corpses of savage beasts that had torn each other to pieces.

Signed a.g., *Avanti!*, 24 December 1917.
SPWI, 34-7

3 Our Marx

Are we Marxists? Do Marxists exist? Stupidity, thou alone art immortal. The question will probably be taken up again over the next few days, the period around Marx's centenary, and will bring forth rivers of ink and idiocy. Wild mumblings and stylistic affectation are the incorruptible heritage of man. Marx did not write a nice little doctrine, he is not a Messiah who left a string of parables laden with categorical imperatives, with absolute, unquestionable norms beyond the categories of time and space. The only categorical imperative, the only norm: 'Workers of the world, unite!' The duty of organizing, the propagation of the duty to organize and associate, should therefore be what distinguishes Marxists from non-Marxists. Too little and too much: who in this case would not be a Marxist?

And yet that is how it is. Everyone is a bit of a Marxist, without being aware of it. Marx was great, his action was fecund, not because he invented from nothing, not because he extracted an *original* vision of history from his imagination, but because in him the fragmentary, the incomplete, the immature became maturity, system, awareness. His personal awareness can become everyone's, it has already become that of many people: because of this Marx is not just a scholar, he is a man of action; he is great and fecund in action as in thought, his books have transformed the world, just as they have transformed thought.

Marx signifies the entry of intelligence into the history of humanity, the reign of awareness.

His work falls in exactly the same period as the great battle between Thomas Carlyle and Herbert Spencer on the role of man in history.

Carlyle: the hero, the great individual, the mystical synthesis of a spiritual communion, leads the destinies of humanity towards an unknown, evanescent goal in the chimerical land of perfection and saintliness.

Spencer: nature, evolution, mechanical and inanimate abstraction. Man: atom of a natural organism, one which obeys a law that is abstract as such, but which becomes historically concrete in individuals: immediate utility.

Marx plants himself squarely in history with the solid bearing of a giant. He is neither a mystic nor a positivist metaphysician. He is a historian, he is an interpreter of the documents of the past, of all the documents, not just a part of them.

This was the intrinsic defect of histories, of research into human events: to have examined and taken into account only a part of the documents. And this part was selected not by the historical will but by partisan prejudice, even if it was unconscious and in good faith. What this research aimed at was not truth, precision, the integral recreation of the life of the past, but the highlighting of a particular activity, the bearing out of a prior hypothesis. History was a domain solely of ideas. Man was considered as spirit, as pure consciousness. Two erroneous consequences derived from this conception: the ideas that were borne out were often merely arbitrary, fictitious. The facts that were given importance were anecdote, not history. If history was written, in the real sense of the word, it was due to the brilliant intuition of single individuals, not to a systematic and conscious scientific activity.

With Marx, history continues to be the domain of ideas, of spirit, of the conscious activity of single or associated individuals. But ideas, spirit, take on substance, lose their arbitrariness, they are no longer fictitious religious or sociological abstractions. Their substance is in the economy, in practical activity, in the systems and relations of production and exchange. History as that which happens is pure practical (economic and moral) activity. An idea becomes real not because it is logically in conformity with pure truth, pure humanity (which exists only as a plan, as a general ethical goal of mankind), but because it finds in economic reality its justification, the instrument with which it can be carried out. In order to know with precision what the historical ends of a country, a society, a social grouping are, one must know first of all what systems and relations of production and exchange obtain in that country, that society. Without this knowledge one will be able to write partial monographs, dissertations which are useful for the history of culture, one will pick up secondary reflections, distant consequences, but one will not be doing history, practical activity will not be disclosed in all its solid compactness.

Idols crumble from their altar, divinities see the clouds of perfumed incense disperse. Man acquires awareness of objective reality, he masters the secret which lies behind the real unfolding of events. Man knows himself, he knows how much his individual will can be worth, and how it can be made more powerful in that, by obeying, by disciplining itself to necessity, it finally dominates necessity itself, identifying it with its own ends. Who knows himself? Not man in general, but he who undergoes the yoke of necessity. The search for the substance of history, the identification of that substance in the system and the relations of production and exchange, leads one to discover how human society is split into two classes. The class which owns the instruments of production already necessarily knows itself, it has a consciousness, albeit confused and fragmentary, of its power and its mission. It has individual ends and it attains them through its capacity to organize, coldly, objectively, without worrying whether its road is paved with bodies reduced by hunger or corpses on battlefields.

The organizing of real historical causality takes on the value of a revelation for the other class, it becomes an ordering principle for the huge flock without a shepherd. The flock acquires awareness of itself, of the task which it must now carry out in order to assert itself as a class, becomes conscious that its individual ends will remain purely arbitrary, pure words, empty and inflated wishes, until it possesses the tools, until these wishes have become will.

Voluntarism? The word is meaningless, or it is used with the meaning of arbitrary will. Will, in a Marxist sense, means awareness of ends, which in turn means exact knowledge of one's own power and the means to express it in action. It therefore means, in the first place, that the class become distinct and individuated, compactly organized and disciplined to its own specific ends, without wavering or being deflected. It means an impulse acting in a straight line towards the maximum destination, without jaunts into the green meadows on the wayside to drink a glass of cordial fraternity, softened by the greenery and by tender declarations of respect and love.

But the phrase 'in a Marxist sense' is pointless; it can give rise to equivocations and fatuous showerings of words. Marxist, in a Marxist sense ... the terms are worn like coins that have passed through too many hands.

Karl Marx is for us a master of spiritual and moral life, not a shepherd wielding a crook. He is the stimulator of mental laziness, the arouser of good energies which slumber and which must wake up for the good fight. He is an example of intense and tenacious work to attain the clear honesty of ideas, the solid culture necessary in order not to talk in a void, about abstractions. He is a monolithic bloc of knowing and thinking humanity, who does not look at his tongue in order to speak, who does not put his hand on his heart in order to feel, but who constructs iron syllogisms which encircle reality in its essence and dominate it, which penetrate people's minds, which bring the sedimentations of prejudice and fixed ideas crumbling down and strengthen the moral character.

Karl Marx is not, for us, the infant whimpering in the cradle or the bearded man who frightens priests. He is none of the anecdotal episodes of his biography, no brilliant or gauche gesture of his outward human animality. He is a broad and serene thinking brain, he is an individual moment in the anxious search that humanity has been conducting for centuries to acquire consciousness of its being and its becoming, to grasp the mysterious rhythm of history and disperse the mystery, to be stronger in its thinking and to act better. He is a necessary and integral part of our spirit, which would not be what it is if he had not lived, had not thought, had not sent sparks of light flying from the collision with his passions and his ideas, his sufferings and his ideals.

In glorifying Karl Marx on the centenary of his birth, the international proletariat is glorifying itself, its conscious strength, the dynamism of its aggressiveness of conquest which undermines the rule of privilege and prepares for the final struggle which will crown all its efforts and all its sacrifices.

Signed Antonio Gramsci, *Il Grido del Popolo*, 4 May 1918.*
(NM, 3-7)

4 Class Intransigence and Italian History

[...]

Class, state, parties

What does the state represent from the socialist point of view? The state is the economic-political organization of the bourgeois class. The state is the bourgeois class in its modern, concrete expression. The bourgeois class is not a unified entity outside the state. As a result of the working of free competition, new groups of capitalist producers are constantly forming to fulfil the regime's economic capacity. Each one of these groups yearns to remove itself from the bloody struggle of competition through recourse to monopoly. The state's function is to find a juridical settlement to internal class disputes, to clashes between opposed interests; thereby it unifies different groupings and gives the class a solid and united external appearance. Competition between groupings is concentrated at the point of government, of state power. The government is the prize for the strongest bourgeois party or grouping; the latter's strength wins for it the right to regulate state power, to turn it in any particular direction and to manipulate it at any time in accordance with its economic and political programme.

The bourgeois parties and the Socialist Party have utterly different attitudes to the state.

The bourgeois parties are either the representatives of categories of producers, or they are simply a swarm of 'coachman-flies' who make not the slightest impact on the framework of the state, but drone their speeches and suck the honey of favouritism.

The Socialist Party is not a sectional, but a class organization: its morphology is quite different from that of any other party. It can only view the state, the network of bourgeois class power, as its antagonistic likeness. It cannot enter into direct or indirect competition for the conquest of the state without committing suicide, without losing its nature, without becoming a mere political faction that is estranged from the historical activity of the proletariat, without turning into a swarm of 'coachman-flies' on the hunt for a bowl of blancmange in which to get stuck and perish ingloriously. The Socialist Party does not conquer the state, it replaces it; it replaces the regime, abolishes party government and replaces free competition by the organization of production and exchange.

Does Italy have a class state?

In discussions and polemics, words are too frequently superimposed on historical reality. When speaking of Italy we use words like capitalists, proletarians, states, parties as if they represented social entities which had reached the peak of their historical development, or a level of maturity comparable to that achieved in the economically advanced countries. But in Italy capitalism is in its infancy, and the law is in no way adapted to the real situation. The law is a modern excrescence on an ancient edifice. It is not the product of economic evolution, but of international political mimicry, of the intellectual evolution of jurisprudence, not of the instruments of labour.

Giuseppe Prezzolini drew attention to this recently in connection with the polemic over 'democracy'.[2] Behind a façade of democratic institutions, the Italian state has retained the substance and framework of a despotic state (the same can be said of France). There exists a bureaucratic, centralist regime, founded on the tyrannical Napoleonic system, with the express aim of crushing and containing any spontaneous drive or movement. Foreign affairs are conducted in the highest secrecy – not only are discussions not public, but even the terms of treaties are kept from those whom they nevertheless affect. The army (until the war made the antiquated system untenable) had a career structure; it was not the nation in arms. There is a state religion, supported financially and in other ways by the state; there is no separation of church and state nor equality of all religions. Schools are either non-existent, or the teachers, who come from a restricted number of needy folk, given the paltriness of the wages, are not equal to the demands of national education. The suffrage was restricted right up until the last elections, and even today is still far from giving the nation the capacity to express its will.

Free competition, the essential principle of the capitalist bourgeoisie, has not yet touched the most important aspects of national affairs. So we have a position where political forms are mere arbitrary superstructures – they lack any effectiveness, and achieve nothing. The seats of power are still confused and interdependent; there are no large parties organized by the agrarian and industrial bourgeoisies.

<Parliament is, in reality, subordinated to the executive power, it has no effective capacity of control. The parliamentary deputies are no more than the messenger boys of local groups of peasants or the third estate who go up to the capital to request particular privileges, as in a full-blooded feudal regime, not to establish the rule of law.>

Hence the class state, in which the effectiveness of the principle of free competition culminates, with great parties representing the vast interests of the different sectors of production, does not exist. What has existed has been the dictatorship of one man [Giolitti], the representative of the narrow political interests of Piedmont, who in order to keep the country united, has imposed on Italy a centralized and despotic system of colonial domination. The system is collapsing; new bourgeois forces have arisen and are growing stronger – ever more insistently they are demanding recognition of their interests. Interventionism is a contingent phenomenon, and so is pacifism – the war will not last forever. But what is in imminent danger is the despotic Giolittian state, the entire mass of parasitic interests encrusted upon this old state, and the old enfeebled bourgeoisie which sees its super-privileges threatened by the agitation of bourgeois youth wanting its place in the government, wanting to be part of the free play of political competition. Provided no new event cuts off its evolution, this new bourgeois generation will undoubtedly rejuvenate the state and throw out all the traditional dross. For a democratic state is not the product of a kind heart or a liberal education; it is a necessity of life for large-scale production, for busy exchange, for the concentration of the population in modern, capitalist cities.
[...]

The function of the proletariat

Just as the Socialist Party, the organization of the proletarian class, cannot enter into competition for conquest of the government without losing its intrinsic value and turning into a swarm of coachman-flies, so too it cannot collaborate with any organized bourgeois parliamentary grouping without causing harm, without creating pseudo-facts that will have to be undone and corrected. The political decadence which class collaboration brings is due to the spasmodic expansion of a bourgeois party which is not satisfied with merely clinging to the state, but also makes use of the party which is antagonistic to the state. It thus becomes a hircocervus, a historical monster devoid of will or particular aims, concerned only with its possession of the state, to which it is encrusted like rust. State activity is reduced to mere legalities, to the formal settling of disputes, and never touches the substance; the state becomes a gypsy caravan held together by bits and pieces of wood – a mastodon on four tiny wheels.

If it wishes to maintain and secure its position as the executive organ of the proletariat, the Socialist Party must itself observe and make everyone else respect the method of the fiercest intransigence. And if the bourgeois parties wish to form a government from their own forces, they will have to evolve, put themselves in contact with the country, bring their sectional disputes to an end and acquire a distinctive political and economic structure. If they are unwilling to do so, then, since no party is capable of standing on its own, a permanent and dangerous crisis will arise: a crisis in which the proletariat, firm and tightly-knit, will accelerate its rise and evolution.

Intransigence is not inertia, since it forces others to move and act.[3] It is not based on stupidities, as *La Stampa* so cleverly insinuates. It is a principled policy, the policy of a proletariat that is conscious of its revolutionary mission as accelerator of the capitalist evolution of society, as a reagent clarifying the chaos of bourgeois production and politics and forcing modern states to carry through their natural mission as dismantlers of the feudal institutions that still, after the collapse of the former societies, survive and hinder historical development.

Intransigence is the only way in which the class struggle can be expressed. It is the only evidence we have that history is developing and creating solid, substantial achievements, not 'privileged', arbitrary 'syntheses' cooked up by mutual agreement between a thesis and an antithesis who have thrown in their lots together, like the proverbial fire and water.

The supreme law of capitalist society is free competition between all social forces. Merchants compete for markets, bourgeois groupings compete for the government, the two classes compete for the state. Merchants seek to create monopolies behind protective legislation. Each bourgeois grouping would like to monopolize the government, and to be able to make exclusive use of the spell-bound energies of the class that is outside governmental competition. Intransigents are free-traders. They do not want barons – whether sugar and steel barons or barons in government. The law of freedom must be allowed unrestricted operation; it is intrinsic to bourgeois activity, the chemical reagent that is continually dissolving its cadres and forcing them to improve and perfect themselves. The powerful Anglo-Saxon bourgeois cadres acquired their modern productive capacity through the implacable play of free competition. The English state has evolved and been purged of its noxious elements through the free clash of bourgeois social forces that finally constituted themselves into the great historic parties, the Liberals and Conservatives. Indirectly from this clash the proletariat has gained cheap bread, and a substantial series of rights guaranteed by law and custom: the right to assemble, the right to strike, an individual security which in Italy remains a chimerical myth.

Class struggle is not a puerile dream – it is an act that is freely determined upon and an inner necessity of the social order. To obstruct its clear course, arbitrarily, by pre-established syntheses hatched by impenitent pipe-dreamers, is a puerile mistake, a historical waste of time. The non-Giolittian parties now in power (quite apart from the fact of the war, which is contingency – and already proving too much for the political capacity of the small nations' ruling classes) are unconsciously carrying out the task of dismantling the feudal, militarist despotic state that Giovanni Giolitti perpetuated in order to make it the instrument of his dictatorship. The Giolittians can feel the monopoly slipping from their grasp. Let them move, by God, let them struggle, let them call on the country to judge. But no, they would rather make the proletariat do their moving for them, or better still, they would like to make the socialist deputies vote.

So intransigence is inertia, is it? Movement, however, is never just a physical act; it is intellectual as well. Indeed, it is always intellectual before becoming physical – except for puppets on a string. Take away from the proletariat its class consciousness, and what have you? Puppets dancing on a string!

Unsigned, *Il Grido del Popolo*, 18 May 1918.
SPWI, 38-47

5 Utopia

Political constitutions are necessarily dependent on economic
structure, on forms of production and exchange. By simply
enunciating this formula, many people believe they resolve every
economic and political problem, believe they are in a position to
impart lessons to right and to left and to judge events with
certainty – coming to the conclusion, for example, that Lenin is a
utopian, and the unfortunate Russian proletarians are prey to an
utterly utopian illusion, so that a terrible awakening implacably
awaits them.

The truth is that no two political constitutions are the same, just
as no two economic structures are the same. The truth is that the
formula is anything but the arid expression of a glaringly obvious
natural law. Between the premisses (economic structure) and the
consequence (political constitution) the relations are anything but
simple and direct; and the history of a people is not documented
by economic facts alone. The unravelling of the causation is a
complex and involved process. To disentangle it requires nothing
short of a profound and wide-ranging study of every intellectual
and practical activity. This sort of study is possible only after the
events have settled into a definite continuity, i.e. long, long after
the facts have occurred. The academic may be able to state with
certainty that a particular political constitution will not emerge
victorious (will not exist on a permanent basis) unless it is attached
indissolubly and intrinsically to a particular economic structure –
but his statement will have no value other than as a general
indication. And while the facts are actually unfolding how could he
possibly know what pattern of dependency would be established?
The unknowns are more numerous than the facts which can be
ascertained and verified, and every single one of these unknowns
could upset the eventual conclusion. History is not a mathematical
calculation; it does not possess a decimal system, a progressive
enumeration of equal quantities amenable to the four basic
operations, the solution of equations and the extraction of roots.
Quantity (economic structure) turns into quality because it
becomes an instrument for action in men's hands – men whose
worth is to be seen not only in terms of their weight, their size and
the mechanical energy they derive from their muscles and nerves,
but in the fact that they have a mind, that they suffer, understand,

rejoice, desire and reject. In a proletarian revolution, the unknown variable 'humanity' is more mysterious than in any other event. The common mentality of the Russian proletariat, as of other proletariats in general, has never been studied, and perhaps it was impossible to study it. The successful or unsuccessful outcome of the revolution will give us reliable documentary evidence on its capacity to make history. For the moment we can do nothing but wait.

Those who do not wait, but seek to come at once to a definitive judgement, have other aims – current political aims, to be achieved among the people to whom their propaganda is directed. The assertion that Lenin is a utopian is not a cultural fact, nor a historical judgement; it is a political act with immediate consequences. To state so bluntly that political constitutions, etc., etc., is not a statement of doctrine, but an attempt to arouse a particular mentality, to direct action one way rather than another.

In life no act remains without consequences, and to believe in one theory rather than another has its own particular impact on action. Even an error leaves traces of itself, to the extent that its acceptance and promulgation can *delay* (but certainly not prevent) the attainment of an end.

This is a proof that it is not the economic structure which directly determines political activity, but rather the way in which that structure and the so-called laws which govern its development are interpreted. These laws have nothing in common with natural laws – even granting that natural laws too have no objective, factual existence, but are the constructs of our intelligence, designed to facilitate study and teaching.

Events do not depend on the will of a single individual, nor on that even of a numerous group. They depend on the wills of a great many people, revealed through their doing or not doing certain acts and through their corresponding intellectual attitudes. And they depend on the knowledge a minority possesses concerning those wills, and on the minority's capacity to channel them more or less towards a common aim, after having incorporated them within the powers of the state.

Why do the great majority of individuals perform only certain actions? Because they have no social goal other than the

1 Socialism and Marxism 1917-1918

preservation of their own physiological and moral integrity. It therefore comes about that they adapt to circumstances and mechanically repeat certain gestures which, through their own experience or through the education they have received (the outcome of others' experience), have proved themselves to be suitable for attaining the desired goal: survival. This similarity in the activity of the majority induces a similarity in its effects, so giving a certain structure to economic activity: there arises the concept of law. Only the pursuit of a higher goal can destroy this adaptation to the environment. If the human goal is no longer mere survival, but a particular standard of survival, then greater efforts are expended and, depending on the dissemination of the higher human goal, the environment is successfully transformed and new hierarchies are established. These hierarchies are different from those which currently exist to regulate the relations between individuals and the state, and gradually come to replace them on a permanent basis as the higher human goal is more and more generally attained.

Anyone who posits these pseudo-laws as absolutes lying outside individual will, rather than as a psychological adaptation to the environment due to the weakness of individuals (to their not being organized, and hence ultimately to the uncertainty of the future), is incapable of seeing that psychology can change, weakness can become strength. Yet such things do happen, and the law, or pseudo-law, is broken. Individuals abandon their solitary existence and associate together. But how does this association come about? It too is conceived only in terms of the absolute law, of normality – and if, through stupidity or prejudice, the law is not immediately obvious, then judgement is decreed and sentence passed: utopia, utopians.

Lenin is thus a utopian. From the time of the Bolshevik revolution to the present day, the Russian proletariat has been utterly utopian in its outlook, and a terrible awakening implacably awaits it.

If one were to apply to Russian history the abstract, general schemas constructed to follow the stages of the normal development of economic and political activity in the Western world, then one's conclusion could not be otherwise. But every historical phenomenon is 'individual'; development is governed by a rhythm of 'freedom'; research should not concentrate on generic necessity, but on the particular. The causal process must be studied strictly within the context of the Russian events, and not from an abstract and generic perspective.

In the Russian events, there undoubtedly exists a relationship of necessity, and it is a relationship of capitalist necessity. The war was the economic condition, the way of organizing practical daily life, that determined the development of the new state and made the dictatorship of the proletariat necessary: *the war that backward Russia had to fight in the same ways as the more advanced capitalist states.*

In patriarchal Russia those concentrations of individuals that occur in an industrialized society – and which are a necessary condition if proletarians are to recognize each other, to organize and acquire an awareness of their own class strength which could be used to attain a universal human goal – could not occur. A country of extensive agriculture isolates individuals and prevents any uniform and widespread awareness: it makes impossible proletarian social units and the concrete class consciousness that gives people an indication of their own strength and the will to establish a regime legitimized on a permanent basis by that strength.

The war represents the maximum concentration of economic activity in a few hands (the leaders of the state); and to it there corresponds a maximum concentration of individuals in the barracks and trenches. Russia at war was truly the country of utopia: with barbarian invaders, the state sought to wage a war demanding technology, organization, spiritual resistance – all of which could be achieved only by a people welded together intellectually and physically by factories and machines. The war was utopia, and patriarchal Tsarist Russia collapsed under the extreme strain of the effort which it had chosen to assume and that which was imposed upon it by a battle-hardened enemy. But the conditions created artificially by the all-embracing power of the despotic state brought about the necessary consequences: the broad masses of socially isolated individuals thrust together in a small geographical area developed new feelings and an unprecedented human solidarity. The weaker they had felt in their former state of isolation and the more they had bowed before despotism, the greater was the revelation of their existing collective strength and the more tenacious and adventurous was their will to preserve it, and to build upon it the new society.

Despotic discipline was liquidated; a period of chaos ensued. Individuals sought to organize themselves, but how? And how were they to preserve this human unity that had grown out of suffering?

Here the philistine comes forward and replies: the bourgeoisie had to restore order, because it has always happened in that way – a patriarchal and feudal economy has always been followed by a bourgeois economy and a bourgeois political constitution. The philistine sees no salvation outside the pre-established schemas; he conceives of history as simply a natural organism passing through fixed and predictable stages of growth. If you plant an acorn, you can be sure of getting an oak shoot, and of having to wait a certain number of years for the tree to grow and give fruit. But history is not an oak tree, and men are not acorns.

Whereabouts in Russia was the bourgeoisie that was capable of fulfilling this task? And if it is a natural law that the bourgeoisie should prevail, how come the law did not operate in this instance?

This particular bourgeoisie has not been seen. A few bourgeois tried to take charge and were crushed. Did they have to win, did they have to take charge, even though they were few in numbers, incapable and weak? But with what holy chrism were these unfortunates anointed to have to triumph even in defeat? Is historical materialism then just a reincarnation of legitimism, of divine right?

Anyone who finds Lenin utopian, who states that the attempt to establish a proletarian dictatorship in Russia is a utopian attempt, cannot be a conscious socialist, and cannot have acquired his culture through study of the doctrine of historical materialism. He is a Catholic, he is bogged down in Holy Writ. It is he who is the real utopian.

Utopianism consists, in fact, in not being able to conceive of history as a free development, in seeing the future as a pre-fashioned commodity, in believing in pre-established plans. Utopianism is philistinism, of the kind Heinrich Heine mocked. The reformists are the philistines and utopians of socialism, just as the protectionists and nationalists are the philistines and utopians of the capitalist bourgeoisie. Heinrich von Treitschke is the fore-most exponent of German philistinism (the German state-worshippers are his spiritual heirs), just as Auguste Comte and Hippolyte Taine represent French philistinism and Vincenzo Gioberti the Italian variety. These are the people who preach national historic missions, or believe in individual vocations; all of them are people who mortgage the future and seek to imprison it within their pre-established schemas, people who do not conceive of divine freedom, and are for ever groaning about the past because things have turned out so *badly*.

They do not conceive of history as free development – the birth and free integration of free energies – which is quite different from natural evolution, just as man and human associations are different from molecules and molecular aggregates. They have not learnt that freedom is the inner force in history, exploding every pre-established schema. The philistines of socialism have degraded and soiled the socialist doctrine, and they become ridiculously angry with anyone who in their eyes does not respect it.

In Russia the free expression of individual and combined energies has swept aside the obstacles of pre-established words and plans. The bourgeoisie sought to impose its hegemony and failed. Accord-ingly the proletariat has taken over the direction of political and economic life and is establishing its own order. Its own order, not socialism, since socialism is not conjured up through a magical *fiat*. Socialism is a historical process, a development from one social stage to another that is richer in collective values. The proletariat is establishing its own order, it is constructing the political institutions which will ensure the autonomy of this development, which will place its power on a permanent footing.

Dictatorship is the fundamental institution guaranteeing free-dom, through its prevention of *coups de main* by factious minori-ties. It is a guarantee of freedom, since it is not a method to be perpetuated, but a transitional stage allowing the creation and consolidation of the permanent organisms into which the dictator-ship, having accomplished its mission, will be dissolved.

After the revolution Russia was not yet free, for there existed no guarantees of freedom, for freedom had not been organized.

The problem was to create a hierarchy, but one which was open, which could not harden into a class- and caste-order.

From the mass, from number, it was necessary to attain oneness, so that a social unity existed, so that authority was only spiritual authority.

The living nuclei of this hierarchy are the Soviets and the popular parties. The Soviets are the basic organizations to be integrated and developed, and the Bolsheviks become the government party precisely because they maintain that state power should rest upon and be controlled by the Soviets.

Out of the Russian chaos these elements of order are crystallizing; the new order has begun. A hierarchy is being constituted: from disorganized and suffering masses one moves up to the organized workers and peasants, then the Soviets, then the Bolshevik Party and finally one man: Lenin. It is a hierarchical gradation based on prestige and trust, which formed spontaneously and is maintained through free choice.

Where is the utopia in this spontaneity? Utopia is authority, not spontaneity; and it is utopia to the extent that it becomes careerism, a caste system, and claims to be eternal. Freedom is not utopia, because it is a basic aspiration; the whole history of mankind consists of struggles and efforts to create social institutions capable of ensuring a maximum of freedom.

Once this hierarchy has been formed, it develops its own logic. The Soviets and the Bolshevik Party are not closed organisms; they are continually being integrated with one another. It is in this that freedom holds sway, that freedom is guaranteed. They are not castes, but organisms in a continuous state of development. They represent the development of consciousness, represent the capacity of Russian society to become organized.

All workers can take part in the Soviets, and all workers can exert their influence in modifying the Soviets and bringing them closer into line with what is wanted and needed. The direction being taken by Russian political life at the moment is tending to coincide with that taken by the country's moral life, by the universal spirit of the Russian people. There is continual movement between the hierarchical levels: an uncultivated individual gets a chance to improve himself in the discussion over the election of his representative to the Soviet – he himself could be the representative. He controls these organs because he has them constantly under review and near to hand in the community. He acquires a sense of social responsibility, and becomes a citizen who is active in deciding the destiny of his country. Power and awareness are passed on, through the agency of this hierarchy, from one person to many: society is such as has never before appeared in history.

This is the *élan vital* of the new Russian history. In what way is it utopian? Where is the pre-established plan that people want to bring into operation, even against the grain of economic and political conditions? The Russian revolution is the triumph of freedom; its organization is based on spontaneity, not on the dictates of a 'hero' who imposes himself through violence. It is a continuous and systematic elevation of a people, following the lines of a hierarchy, and creating for itself one by one the organs that the new social life demands.

But is it then not socialism? ... No, it is not socialism in the ridiculous sense that these philistines with their grandiose blueprints give the word. It is a human society developing under the leadership of the proletariat. Once the majority of the proletariat is organized, social life will be richer in socialist content than it is at present and the process of socialization will be continually intensified and perfected. Socialism is not established on a particular day – it is a continuous process, a never-ending development towards a realm of freedom that is organized and controlled by the majority of the citizens, the proletariat.

Signed A. G., *Avanti!*, 25 July 1918
SPWI, 48-55

II WORKING-CLASS EDUCATION AND CULTURE

Introduction

Questions of education and culture were always of central importance to Gramsci. His early educational thinking revolves around the problem of how working-class people can become intellectually autonomous. If this can be achieved they can lead their own movement without having to delegate decision-making to 'career intellectuals'. They can then be capable of acting as a ruling class.

Educational opportunity and provision for working-class and peasant children, despite some progressive reforms in the Giolitti period, remained woefully inadequate in Italy during the early years of the century. The state school system was badly under-resourced. Teachers were poorly paid and demoralized. Compulsory schooling ended at the age of nine. Post-primary education since the 1859 Casati Act had been divided into three main streams: *ginnasio* and *liceo* (akin to the American junior high and high school), *scuola tecnica* or *professionale* (for the lower professions and white-collar jobs) and *scuola normale* (where primary teachers were trained). The upper tiers (*liceo* and university) received a disproportionate amount of the funding and the system as a whole discriminated against children from the working class. In addition illiteracy rates in Italy were among the highest in Europe, rising steeply as one moved from the larger towns to rural areas and from north to south. The 1911 census recorded illiteracy rates for people over the age of six as 11 per cent in Piedmont, 13 per cent in Lombardy, 37 per cent in Tuscany, 58 per cent in Sardinia, and 70 per cent in Calabria.

The Italian labour movement, and notably the reformist wing of the PSI, had responded to this situation since the 1890s by making education a central plank of its programme. The Socialists set up their own evening and day schools for both adults and children, and campaigned in and outside parliament for the eradication of illiteracy and for the introduction of compulsory, free, lay education – the last of these in order to check the educational influence of the Catholic Church. By and large, however, and despite progressive intentions, the reformists' conception of socialist education reproduced a bourgeois-paternalistic model of teaching as the dissemination of a body of knowledge to the unenlightened masses and the 'elevation' of this mass to 'culture'. In many cases, moreover, the content of what was taught was either a simplified socialist propaganda, a literature of moral and political edification, or it was identical to the traditional curriculum.

Gramsci's approach is in many ways more radical. He starts from the assumption that 'everybody is already cultured' but in a primordial and undisciplined way (SCW, p. 25). He begins, in other words, not from the point of view of the teacher but from that of the learner, and he emphasizes that the learning process is a movement towards self-knowledge, self-mastery and thus liber-ation. Education is not a matter of handing out 'encyclopaedic knowledge' but of developing and disciplining the awareness which the learner already possesses. Gramsci consequently criticizes the Popular Universities (often PSI-sponsored, similar to university extension in Britain and the *universités populaires* in France) for dispensing 'bits of knowledge' without taking account of the different needs and background of a working-class public. He also repeatedly criticizes as paternalistic the reduction of socialist ideas into a simple language and argues that complex ideas cannot be vulgarized without falsifying their meaning: workers active in a political movement have to make the effort necessary to grasp them (see for instance 'Culture and Class Struggle' in SCW, pp. 31-4). In the political party, education plays a central role for Gramsci because through it working-class members can develop a critical understanding of their own situation and of the revolutionary task and so liberate themselves from their dependence on an upper stratum of intellectuals who tend to deflect their class demands towards reformist solutions.

Two further themes represented here indicate the direction of Gramsci's thinking on education and culture at this time. The first is his twin vindication of a kind of school which can form a modern proletariat ('Schools of Labour') and of a school able to provide workers with an education in the humanities rather than just vocational training ('Men or Machines?'). These two positions, which appear to be at odds with one another, are perhaps reconciled in his vision of a 'new educational tradition' emerging in post-revolutionary Russia, one in which the working class fuses 'manual labour and intellectual labour' (see 'Questions of Culture'). A 'common school' in which a broad general education is offered prior to specialization was always central to Gramsci's conception. It is these ideas which he will later expand in 'Americanism and Fordism' and in the prison notes on education (see Sections IX and X below) when he talks of the need to found 'new relations between intellectual and industrial work' and to create 'a psycho-physical nexus of a new type'.

The second theme is that of revolutionary culture. Writing in 1921, Gramsci maintains that the Italian avant-garde movement Futurism is revolutionary because of its 'productivism' and its iconoclastic hostility to the mummified traditions of bourgeois art ('Marinetti the Revolutionary?'). Although Gramsci himself was later to modify this judgement quite radically (compare 'A Letter to Trotsky on Futurism' in SCW, pp. 52-4), the 1921 article remains striking for its contrast with contemporary conceptions of socialist culture as edification or as a proletarian 'inheritance' of bourgeois culture and it reveals Gramsci's affinity with pro-avant-garde Soviet positions of the time.

Certain aspects of Gramsci's educational outlook – notably his recurrent emphasis on discipline, his defence of the traditional curriculum, his insistence on the virtues of 'sweating at' grammar and logic in order to learn to think critically – have been described as 'conservative' and have been the object of criticism from several quarters. There is certainly some justification in this view. Gramsci's educational writings do constitute a problematic legacy for the left. But their conservative aspects need to be understood both in relation to the culture of Gramsci's time and to his own experience as a 'scholarship boy' from Sardinia. They also need to be weighed against the radical democratic and liberatory aspects which are present in his educational thinking as a whole and which emerge clearly in these early pieces.

1 Socialism and Culture

A short time ago an article by Enrico Leone came to our attention, where in that nebulous and convoluted style he all too often indulges in he repeated a few commonplaces on culture and intellectualism in relation to the proletariat, opposing to them *practice* and the *historical fact* that the working class is building its future with its own hands.[1] We believe it would not be unproductive to return to this theme, one which has been aired before in *Il Grido* [*del Popolo*] and which in the youth federation's *Avanguardia* received a more rigidly doctrinal treatment in the polemic between Bordiga from Naples and our own Tasca.[2]

Let us recall two passages. The first comes from a German Romantic, Novalis (who lived from 1772 to 1801), and says: 'The supreme problem of culture is that of gaining possession of one's transcendental self, of being at one and the same time the self of oneself. Thus it should not surprise us that there is an absence of feeling or complete understanding of others. Lacking a perfect comprehension of ourselves, we can never really hope to know others.'

The other, which we summarize, is from Giambattista Vico, who (in the 'First Corollary concerning the speech in poetic characters of the first nations' in his *Scienza Nuova*) gives a political interpretation of the famous dictum of Solon which Socrates subsequently made his own in relation to philosophy: 'Know thyself'. Vico maintains that in this dictum Solon wished to admonish the plebeians, who believed themselves to be of *bestial origin* and the nobility to be of *divine origin*, to reflect on themselves and see that they had the *same human nature as the nobles* and hence should claim to be *their equals in civil law*. Vico then points to this consciousness of human equality between plebeians and nobles as the basis and historical reason for the rise of the democratic republics of antiquity.

We have not chosen these two fragments entirely at random. In them we believe the writers touch upon, though admittedly in a vaguely expressed and defined manner, the limits and principles governing the correct comprehension of the concept of culture even in relation to socialism.

We need to free ourselves from the habit of seeing culture as encyclopaedic knowledge, and men as mere receptacles to be stuffed full of empirical data and a mass of unconnected raw facts, which have to be filed in the brain as in the columns of a dictionary, enabling their owner to respond to the various stimuli from the outside world. This form of culture really is harmful, particularly for the proletariat. It serves only to create maladjusted people, people who believe they are superior to the rest of humanity because they have memorized a certain number of facts and dates and who rattle them off at every opportunity, so turning them almost into a barrier between themselves and others. It serves to create the kind of weak and colourless intellectualism that Romain Rolland has flayed so mercilessly, which has given birth to a mass of pretentious babblers who have a more damaging effect on social life than tuberculosis or syphilis germs have on the beauty and physical health of the body. The young student who knows a little Latin and history, the young lawyer who has been successful in wringing a scrap of paper called a degree out of the laziness and lackadaisical attitude of his professors – they end up seeing themselves as different from and superior to even the best skilled workman, who fulfils a precise and indispensable task in life and is a hundred times more valuable in his activity than they are in theirs. But this is not culture, but pedantry, not intelligence, but intellect, and it is absolutely right to react against it.

Culture is something quite different. It is organization, discipline of one's inner self, a coming to terms with one's own personality; it is the attainment of a higher awareness, with the aid of which one succeeds in understanding one's own historical value, one's own function in life, one's own rights and obligations. But none of this can come about through spontaneous evolution, through a series of actions and reactions which are independent of one's own will – as is the case in the animal and vegetable kingdoms where every unit is selected and specifies its own organs unconsciously, through a fatalistic law of things. Above all, man is mind, i.e. he is a product of history, not nature. Otherwise how could one explain the fact, given that there have always been exploiters and exploited, creators of wealth and its selfish consumers, that socialism has not yet come into being? The fact is that only by degrees, one stage at a time, has humanity acquired consciousness of its own value and won for itself the right to throw off the patterns of organization imposed on it by minorities at a previous period in history. And this consciousness was formed not

under the brutal goad of physiological necessity, but as a result of
intelligent reflection, at first by just a few people and later by a
whole class, on why certain conditions exist and how best to
convert the facts of vassalage into the signals of rebellion and
social reconstruction. This means that every revolution has been
preceded by an intense labour of criticism, by the diffusion of
culture and the spread of ideas amongst masses of men who are at
first resistant, and think only of solving their own immediate
economic and political problems for themselves, who have no ties
of solidarity with others in the same condition. The latest example,
the closest to us and hence least foreign to our own time, is that of
the French Revolution. The preceding cultural period, called the
Enlightenment, which has been so misrepresented by the facile
critics of theoretical reason, was not in any way or at least was not
entirely a flutter of superficial encyclopaedic intellectuals
discoursing on anything and everything with equal imperturbabi-
lity, believing themselves to be men of their time only if they had
read the *Encyclopédie* of D'Alembert and Diderot; in short it was
not solely a phenomenon of pedantic and arid intellectualism, the
like of which we see before our eyes today, exhibited most fully in
the Popular Universities of the lowest order. The Enlightenment
was a magnificent revolution in itself and, as De Sanctis acutely
notes in his *History of Italian Literature*, it gave all Europe a
bourgeois spiritual International in the form of a unified
consciousness, one which was sensitive to all the woes and
misfortunes of the common people and which was the best possible
preparation for the bloody revolt that followed in France.

In Italy, France and Germany, the same topics, the same
institutions and same principles were being discussed. Each new
comedy by Voltaire, each new pamphlet moved like a spark along
the lines that were already stretched between state and state,
between region and region, and found the same supporters and the
same opponents everywhere and every time. The bayonets of
Napoleon's armies found their road already smoothed by an
invisible army of books and pamphlets that had swarmed out of
Paris from the first half of the eighteenth century and had prepared
both men and institutions for the necessary renewal. Later, after
the French events had welded a unified consciousness, a
demonstration in Paris was enough to provoke similar disturbances in Milan, Vienna and the smaller centres. All this seems

natural and spontaneous to superficial observers, yet it would be incomprehensible if we were not aware of the cultural factors that helped to create a state of mental preparedness for those explosions in the name of what was seen as a common cause.

The same phenomenon is being repeated today in the case of socialism. It was through a critique of capitalist civilization that the unified consciousness of the proletariat was or is still being formed, and a critique implies culture, not simply a spontaneous and naturalistic evolution. A critique implies precisely the self-consciousness that Novalis considered to be the purpose of culture. Consciousness of a self which is opposed to others, which is differentiated and, once having set itself a goal, can judge facts and events other than in themselves or for themselves but also in so far as they tend to drive history forward or backward. To know oneself means to be oneself, to be master of oneself, to distinguish oneself, to free oneself from a state of chaos, to exist as an element of order – but of one's own order and one's own discipline in striving for an ideal. And we cannot be successful in this unless we also know others, their history, the successive efforts they have made to be what they are, to create the civilization they have created and which we seek to replace with our own. In other words, we must form some idea of nature and its laws in order to come to know the laws governing the mind. And we must learn all this without losing sight of the ultimate aim: to know oneself better through others and to know others better through oneself.

If it is true that universal history is a chain made up of the efforts man has exerted to free himself from privilege, prejudice and idolatry, then it is hard to understand why the proletariat, which seeks to add another link to that chain, should not know how and why and by whom it has been preceded, or what advantage it might derive from this knowledge.

Signed Alfa Gamma, Il Grido del Popolo,
29 January 1916. SPWI, 10-13

2 Schools of Labour

Returning to his professorial chair at the Sorbonne after the war of 1870, Gaston Paris, with that liberty of spirit characteristic of sovereign minds, wove a magnificent eulogy of German universities, which had moulded the character and the energy of the new Germany, and he proposed to his pupils and colleagues as an example of how to achieve the transformation of France the model of its abhorred rival.

After more than forty years it has taken a new and terrible war to direct attention back to the school, to the education system as a whole, and make people realize that an enormous disproportion exists in our country between the mass of those who study the liberal arts and those who study the art of production, of labour. Many people are ashamed even to quote the figures, to set out the statistics. The state, with that blindness characteristic of the backward Latin bourgeoisies who hate anything new, has turned its attention exclusively to the creation in the middle categories of the petty bourgeoisie of a legion of lawyers, doctors and white-collar workers with a leaving certificate from the *liceo*, or the technical school. It has done nothing to give the proletariat, the enormous mass of citizens who form the backbone and the vital force of the nation, the chance to improve themselves, raise themselves up, acquire that professional culture from which spring the forces that animate industry, commerce and agriculture.

The school of labour has been sacrificed to the school of the service professions and occupations. The bureaucracy has murdered production. The minister, Casati, who fifty years ago drafted the legislation on Italian education with wide criteria that could have borne fruit, did not find successors able to adapt the law to new circumstances, although its dispositions lent themselves to such adaptation. The technical school also became a factory for white-collar workers, even though Casati, who had planned it, had seen its aim as 'to give young people who intend to dedicate themselves to specific careers in public service, industry and commerce and in the conduct of agricultural affairs the appropriate general and specific education'. Casati was concerned that lessons should be imparted 'with respect to their practical results, and particularly to the applications that can be made of them in the natural and economic conditions of the state'. But the production of new wealth derived no benefit at all from all these dispositions: the spheres of administration and distribution expanded enormously at the expense of all the rest. Now, after the lessons of the war, people are realizing that it is not enough to know how to administer and distribute, but that one needs especially to produce. A country's potential comes from the wealth it produces, and the way it produces, not from the tittle-tattle of its lawyers and the clever inventions of its geniuses. The genius is too bizarre a product, too much beyond the control of any will, for plans to be based on him. Assiduous work, small-scale competence, the spread of a professional culture: these alone can become indices of well-being, diplomas of historical merit.

Italy lacks schools of labour. The little that has been done is due to chance, to the blind impulse of a necessity which throws up, alongside solid organisms, useless, unhealthy, harmful ones as well. In Italy labour, despite the essays schoolchildren are given to write, is not held in civil or social esteem. A chief technician is considered inferior to a lawyer, a mechanic inferior to a professor. The state makes 50 million lire available for the high schools and only 2.5 million for professional schools. Every high-school student costs the state about 1000 lire a year, according to former education minister Rava. And yet, while for every thirty vice-magistrate's jobs there are 300 applicants and 15 who are suitably qualified, our workshops are forced to import technical personnel, commerce falls into the hands of foreigners, and money, in the form of savings, leaves the country, and instead of increasing the nation's wealth and spreading well-being and jobs in our territory, it serves only to worsen the exchange rate, stimulate base egoism and atrocious jingoistic enthusiasms.

It is the proletariat which must demand, which must impose the school of labour. Everything which serves to intensify, to improve production is of particular interest to socialism and the proletariat. We must be in agreement on a plan whereby our industries and Italian commerce employ Italian skilled labour and where this should be equal in value and competence to the best skilled labour of other countries. No exclusions for the purposes of economic war, no protectionism even for the proletariat, but honest competition of abilities, contest for a greater exploitation of the products of the mind, so that everyone is given all the means necessary for their own inner improvement, for the valorization of their own good qualities. The proletariat must constrain the state to cut out of the national organism many universities, suppurating sores which produce prattlers and misfits, as well as many *licei* and *ginnasi* which cost a fortune and give neither culture nor dignity. It must replace these old producers of administrators incapable of administering with schools of labour, out of which can swarm the new generation of producers, who will give the country fewer sonnets and novels and more machines and factory chimneys.

Unsigned, Avanti!, 18 July 1916.* (CT, 440-2)

3 Men or Machines?

The brief discussion which was held at the last council meeting between our comrades and some representatives of the majority, on the subject of vocational education programmes, deserves some comment, however brief and succinct.[3] Comrade Zini's observations ('There is still a conflict between the humanistic and vocational camps over the issue of popular education: we must endeavour to reconcile these currents, without forgetting that a worker is above all a man, who should not be denied the possibility of exploring the widest realms of the spirit, by being enslaved from his earliest youth to the machine') and Councillor Sincero's attacks against philosophy (philosophy finds people opposed to it especially when it states truths that strike at vested interests) are not just isolated polemical episodes: they are necessary clashes between people representing fundamentally opposed interests.

1. Our party has still not settled on a concrete educational programme that is in any way different from traditional ones. Until now we have been content to support the general principle of the need for culture, whether it be at an elementary, or secondary-technical or higher level, and we have campaigned in favour of this principle and propagated it with vigour and energy. We can state that the reduction in illiteracy in Italy is due not so much to the law on compulsory education, as to the intellectual awakening, the awareness of certain spiritual needs that socialist propaganda has succeeded in arousing amongst the ranks of the proletariat in Italy. But we have gone no further than that. Education in Italy is still a rigidly *bourgeois* affair, in the worst sense of the word. Middle and high schools, which are state-run and hence financed from state revenues, i.e. direct taxes paid by the proletariat, can only be attended by the children of the bourgeoisie, who alone enjoy the economic independence needed

for uninterrupted study. A proletarian, no matter how intelligent, no matter how fit to become a man of culture, is forced either to squander his qualities on some other activity, or else to become a rebel and autodidact – i.e. (apart from some notable exceptions) a mediocrity, a man who cannot give all he could have given had he been completed and strengthened by the discipline of school. Culture is a privilege. Education is a privilege. And we do not want it to be so. All young people should be equal before culture. The state should not be financing out of everybody's money the education even of mediocre and gormless children of wealthy parents while it excludes the able and intelligent children of proletarians. Middle and high schools should be only for those who can demonstrate that they are worthy of it. And if it is in the public interest that such forms of education should exist, preferably supported and regulated by the state, then it is also in the public interest that they should be open to all intelligent children, regardless of their economic potential. Collective sacrifice is justified only when it benefits those who are most deserving. Therefore, this collective sacrifice should serve especially to give the most deserving children that economic independence they need if they are to devote their time to serious study.

2. The proletariat, which is excluded from the middle and high schools as a result of the present social conditions – conditions which ensure that the division of labour between men is unnatural (not being based on different capacities) and so retards and is inimical to production – has to fall back on the parallel educational system: the technical and vocational colleges. As a result of the anti-democratic restrictions imposed by the state budget, the technical colleges, which were set up along democratic lines by the Casati ministry, have undergone a transformation that has largely destroyed their nature. In most cases they have become mere superfetations of the classical schools, and an innocent outlet for the petty bourgeois mania for finding a secure job. The continually rising entrance fees, and the particular prospects they open up in practical life, have turned these schools too into a privilege. Anyway, the overwhelming majority of the proletariat is automatically excluded from them on account of the uncertain and precarious life which the wage-earner is forced to lead – the sort of life which is certainly not the most propitious for fruitfully following a course of study.

3. What the proletariat needs is an educational system that is

open to all. A system in which the child is allowed to develop and mature and acquire those general features that serve to develop character. In a word, a humanistic school, as conceived by the ancients, and more recently by the men of the Renaissance. A school which does not mortgage the child's future, a school that does not force the child's will, his intelligence and growing awareness to run along tracks to a predetermined station. A school of freedom and free initiative, not a school of slavery and mechanical precision. The children of proletarians too should have all possibilities open to them; they should be able to develop their own individuality in the optimal way, and hence in the most productive way for both themselves and society. Technical schools should not be allowed to become incubators of little monsters aridly trained for a job, with no general ideas, no general culture, no intellectual stimulation, but only an infallible eye and a firm hand. Technical education too helps a child to blossom into an adult – so long as it is educative and not simply informative, simply passing on manual techniques. Councillor Sincero, who is an industrialist, is being too meanly bourgeois when he protests against philosophy.

Of course, meanly bourgeois industrialists might prefer to have workers who were more machines than men. But the sacrifices which everyone in society willingly makes in order to foster improvements and nourish the best and most perfect men who will improve it still more – these sacrifices must bring benefits to the whole of society, not just to one category of people or one class.

It is a problem of right and of force. The proletariat must stay alert, to prevent another abuse being added to the many it already suffers.

Unsigned, Avanti!, 24 December 1916.
SPWI, 26-7

4 The Popular University

I have in front of me the programme for the Popular University (*Università Popolare*) for the first period 1916-17. Five courses: three devoted to natural sciences, one to Italian literature, one to philosophy. Six lectures on various subjects: only two have titles giving some guarantee of seriousness. I sometimes wonder why it has not been possible in Turin to develop a solid institution for the popularization of culture, why the Popular University has remained the poor thing it is and has been unable to win the public's attention, respect and love, why it has not succeeded in forming a public of its own.

The answer is not easy, or it is too easy. There are clearly problems with organization and with the criteria which inform the university. The best response should be to do better, to show concretely that it is possible to do better and to gather a public round a cultural heat source, provided it is alive and really gives off heat. In Turin the Popular University is a cold flame. It is neither a university, nor popular. Its directors are amateurs in matters of cultural organization. What causes them to act is a mild and insipid spirit of charity, not a live and fecund desire to contribute to the spiritual raising of the multitude through teaching. As in vulgar charitable institutes, they distribute food parcels which fill the stomach, perhaps cause some indigestion, but then leave no trace, bring about no change in people's lives. The directors of the Popular University know that the institution they run has to cater for a specific category of people who have not been able to follow regular studies at school. And that is all. They are not bothered about how this category of people might be drawn most effectively to the world of knowledge. They find a model in the existing cultural institutions: they copy it, they worsen it. They reason something like this: people who attend courses at the Popular University are the same age and have the same general background as people who go to the state universities; so let us give them a surrogate of the latter. And they ignore everything else. They do not consider the fact that the state universities are a natural point of arrival of a whole activity of previous work; they do not consider that when a student arrives at university he has passed through the experience of high school and this has disciplined his spirit of research, has bolstered his amateurish impulsiveness with a methodical approach. In other words he has been through a process of *becoming*, he has been made alert gradually and gently, falling into error and pulling himself up, taking wrong turns and getting back on course. These directors do not understand that bits of *knowledge*, plucked out from all this previous activity of individual research, are nothing other than dogmas, absolute truths. They do not understand that the Popular University, as they run it, is reduced to a form of theological teaching, a new version of the Jesuit schools, where knowledge is presented as something definitive, self-evident and unquestionable. Not even the universities are like this. There is now a common conviction that a truth is fecund only when one has made an effort to master it, that it does not exist in and for itself but has been a conquest of the spirit, and that each individual must reproduce in himself that state of anxiety which the scholar passed through before arriving at it. This is why the truly magisterial teachers give great importance in their teaching to the history of their subject. Taking one's audience through the series of attempts, efforts and successes through which men had to pass in order to attain the present state of knowledge has far more educational value than a schematic exposition of the knowledge itself. It forms the scholar, it gives his mind that elasticity of methodical doubt which makes an amateur into a serious person, which purifies curiosity (in the popular sense of the word) and turns it into a healthy and fecund stimulus towards ever increasing and more perfect knowledge. The author of these notes speaks partly out of personal experience. The courses he remembers most vividly from when he started at university were those where the lecturer made him feel the active effort of research over the centuries to bring the research method to perfection. In the natural sciences, for instance, we were shown all the effort it cost to liberate the human spirit from prejudices and *a priori* religious or philosophical notions in order to arrive at the conclusion that sources of water originate from atmospheric precipitations and not from the sea. In philology we saw how the historical method was arrived at through the trials and errors of traditional empiricism and how, for example, the criteria and convictions that guided Francesco De Sanctis in writing his history of Italian literature were nothing other than truths which had emerged through tiring research, truths which liberated the spirit from the sentimental and rhetorical dross that had polluted the study of literature in the past. And so on for the other subjects. This was the most living part of studying: this spirit of re-creation, which enabled encyclopaedic items of information to be assimilated and fused them into a flame burning with new individual life.

Teaching done in this way becomes an act of liberation. It has the fascination of all vital things. It needs particularly to demonstrate its effectiveness in the Popular Universities, whose audiences lack precisely that intellectual preparation one needs in order to arrange the individual items of one's studies into an organized whole. For them, particularly, what is most effective and interesting is the history of research, the history of this immense epic of the human spirit which slowly, patiently, tenaciously takes possession of truth, conquers truth. How from error one arrives at scientific truth. This is the road that everyone must follow. To show how it has been followed by others is the lesson that produces the best results. And it is, besides, a lesson in modesty, which avoids the formation of those irritating know-it-alls who believe they have plumbed the depths of the universe when their memories are fortunate enough to pigeon-hole a few dates and some random bits of knowledge.

But the Popular Universities, like that of Turin, prefer to run useless and unwieldy courses on 'The Italian Soul in the Art of Literature in Recent Generations' or give lectures on 'The European Conflagration as Judged by Vico', where more care is taken to impress than to teach effectively, and the pretentious little lecturer outstrips the efforts of the modest teacher, who at least knows he is talking to uneducated people.

Unsigned, *Avanti!*, 29 December 1916.* (CT, 673-6)

5 Illiteracy

Why are there still so many illiterate people in Italy? Because in Italy there are too many people who restrict their lives to their village and their family. They do not feel a need to learn the Italian language because dialect will do for their local and family life, because all their life of relationships is filled up with conversations in dialect. Literacy is not a need, and it therefore becomes a torment, something imposed by the wielders of power. In order for it to become a need, the general life would have to acquire greater fervour, it would have to draw in an ever increasing number of citizens and therefore make the sense of need arise spontaneously, out of the necessity for reading and writing and for the Italian language. Socialist propaganda has done more towards literacy than all the laws on compulsory schooling. The law is an imposition: it can oblige you to go to school but it cannot oblige you to learn, or, once you have learned, not to forget. Socialist propaganda directly arouses a sharp sense of not being just an individual within a little circle of immediate interests (the local community and the family), but a citizen of a wider world, with whose other citizens one needs to exchange ideas, hopes and sufferings. Culture, literacy, has thus acquired a purpose, and for as long as this purpose remains alive in people's consciousness, love of knowledge will be a compelling force. It is a sacrosanct truth, of which the Socialists can be proud: illiteracy will disappear completely only when socialism has made it disappear, because socialism is the only ideal which can make citizens, in the best and fullest sense of the word, out of all the Italians who at present live exclusively on their little personal interests, humans born only to consume the fruits of the earth.

La Città futura, 11 February 1917.* (CF, 17)

6 The Problem of the School

[...]

The problem of the school (like any other problem which concerns a general activity of the state, a necessary function in society) must be studied as part of the sphere of action of the state of workers' and peasants' councils.[4] We are aiming to stimulate a mentality of construction, of comrades already ideally organized in the state of the Councils, already ideally active and at work in evoking all the organs of the new social life. The educational propaganda conducted so far by the Socialists has been largely negative and critical: it could not have been otherwise. Today, after the positive experiences of our Russian comrades, it can and must be otherwise if we want to ensure that their experiences have not been in vain for us. We must develop these experiences critically, paring away from them what is specific to Russia, dependent on the particular conditions in which the Soviet Republic found Russian society when it came to power. We must pick out and establish what in them is of permanent necessity to communist society, dependent on the needs and aspirations of the class of workers and peasants exploited to the same degree in all parts of the globe.

The problem of the school is at once both technical and political.

In a parliamentary-democratic state there can be no technical and political solution to the problem of the school. Ministers of education are placed in office because they belong to a political party, not because they know how to administer and direct the educational function of the state. It cannot even in all honesty be claimed that the bourgeois class moulds the school to its own ends of domination. If this were to happen, it would mean that the bourgeois class had an educational programme and was carrying it out with single-minded energy: the school would then be a living thing. This is not the case. The bourgeoisie, as the class which controls the state, takes no interest in the school. It lets the bureaucrats make or destroy it as they are able and allows the education ministers to be chosen according to the caprice of political competition, through partisan intrigue, so as to attain a happy balance of parties in the cabinet. In these conditions the technical study of the educational problem is a pure exercise of mental chess, a matter of intellectual gymnastics rather than a serious and concrete contribution to the problem itself: when, that is, it is not a tiresome lamentation and rehashing of old banalities about the excellence of the educative role of the state, the benefits of education, etc.

In the state of the Councils, the school will represent one of the most important and essential of public activities. Indeed, to the development and success of the school is linked the development of the communist state, the advent of a democracy in which the dictatorship of the proletariat is absorbed. The present generation will be educated into the practice of the social discipline necessary for the realization of communist society, with assemblies and direct participation in deliberation and the administration of the socialist state. The school will have the task of rearing the new generations, those who will enjoy the fruits of our sacrifices and efforts, those who will reap, after the transitional period of national proletarian dictatorships, the fullness of life and development of international communist democracy. How will the communist schools carry out this task? How should the educative function of the state be organized in the overall system of the Councils? What administrative duty will need to be carried out by the primary and secondary teachers' union? How will universities and polytechnics be transformed and co-ordinated in the general cultural activity? Once the constitution is changed and the fundamental principles of the law have been altered, what character should the Faculty of Law possess? Our review numbers among its subscribers and readers a strong contingent of young students, artists and teachers of different levels who have the ability and the training to pose these problems critically and try to solve them. We appeal to their good will, to the active desire they feel for useful co-operation towards the advent of the new order of communism.

Unsigned, *L'Ordine Nuovo*, 27 June 1919. SCW, 39-40

7 [Questions of Culture]

The proletarian revolution cannot but be a total revolution. It consists in the foundation of new modes of labour, new modes of production and distribution that are peculiar to the working class in its historical determination in the course of the capitalist process. This revolution also presupposes the formation of a new set of standards, a new psychology, new ways of feeling, thinking and living that must be specific to the working class, that must be created by it, that will become 'dominant' when the working class becomes the dominant class. The proletarian revolution is essentially the liberation of the productive forces already existing within bourgeois society. These forces can be identified in the economic and political fields; but is it possible to start identifying the latent elements that will lead to the creation of a proletarian civilization or culture? Do elements for an art, philosophy and morality (standards) specific to the working class already exist? The question must be raised and it must be answered. Together with the problem of gaining political and economic power, the proletariat must also face the problem of winning intellectual power. Just as it has thought to organize itself politically and economically, it must also think about organizing itself culturally. Although through such organizations it is not yet going to be possible (no more than in the economic and political sectors) to obtain positive creative results before the system of bourgeois domination has been broken up, it should still be possible to pose the fundamental questions and outline the most characteristic features of the development of the new civilization. According to our Russian comrades, who have already set up an entire network of organizations for 'Proletarian Culture' (Proletkult), the mere fact that the workers raise these questions and attempt to answer them means that the elements of an original proletarian civilization already exist, that there are already proletarian forces of production of cultural values, just as the fact that the workers create class organizations in order to carry out their cultural activity means that these values too, unlike in the bourgeois period, will be created by the working class on the basis of organization.

Do the workers have their own 'conception of the world'? The conception of the world specific to the working class today is that of critical communism which bases historical development on the class struggle. Yet because of this very conception of the world, the working class knows that its conquest of political and economic power will mark the end of the period of class-divided societies. Will there no longer be historical development, will the machine of progress be broken once classes have been abolished and the class struggle suppressed? Many workers have undoubtedly asked this question, just as some of them have undoubtedly felt anxiety because they have been unable to find an answer. The working class, therefore, has its own 'metaphysical needs' which are proper to it alone. Even a bourgeois can conceive the world from the standpoint of the class struggle, but since he cannot but imagine this struggle as perpetual, he does not ask himself, 'And after the abolition of classes?' The abolition of the class struggle does not mean the abolition of the need to struggle as a principle of development. There will still be the struggle against the brute forces of nature, and this struggle will be applied on a scale never before seen. But what notions, what particular ways of seeing, thinking and feeling does this form of struggle, which does not set living beings against each other, presuppose in order for one to imagine the same conquering spirit in people, the same expansive energy that one finds today in the class struggle?

On this basis, then, we can begin to think that in the fullness of its autonomous historical life the working class will also have its own original conception of the world, some of whose fundamental features can already be delineated.

Tomorrow, like today, the school will undoubtedly be a crucible where the new spirits will be forged. Indeed, tomorrow the school will be immensely more important than it is now. In the various educational organizations (near home or at the workplace) in Russia, one studies up to the age of fifty. In the way schools have been organized in Russia, a Marxist principle has been applied in practice: the dominant class reflects in its social life the relations that characterize its particular modes of existence. The Russian school reflects the way of studying characteristic of the working class. The worker studies and works; his labour is study and study is labour. In order to become a specialist in his work, the worker on average puts in the same number of years that it takes to get a specialized degree. The worker, however, carries out his studies in the very act of doing immediately productive work. Industrial progress tends to annihilate the 'studies' proper to the worker in that it tends to destroy specialized trades. Having become dominant, the working class wants manual labour and intellectual labour to be joined in the schools and thus creates a new educational tradition.

One can easily foresee that when the working class wins its liberty, it will bring to the light of history new complexes of linguistic expressions even if it will not radically change the notion of beauty. The existence of Esperanto, although it does not demonstrate much in itself and has more to do with bourgeois cosmopolitanism than with proletarian internationalism, shows nevertheless, by the fact that the workers are strongly interested in it and manage to waste their time over it, that there is a desire for and a historical push towards the formation of verbal complexes that transcend national limits and in relation to which current national languages will have the same role as dialects now have.

For those who have the will to solve them or to try to solve them, there are an endless number of problems of this order. Is it a waste of time to be concerned with these problems? Our Russian comrades say that not only is it not a waste of time but that, on the contrary, if the working class is not concerned with them, it means that it has not yet reached that stage of revolutionary development in which it truly understands the full implications of the notion of 'ruling class'. In order to help in this field too the working classes that have not yet liberated themselves from the political yoke of the bourgeoisie, our Russian comrades want to establish relations between the Proletkult and the proletarian cultural organizations that already exist in embryonic form throughout the world.

Unsigned, *Avanti!*, 14 June 1920. SCW, 41-3

8 Marinetti the Revolutionary?

This incredible, enormous, colossal event has happened, which, if
divulged, threatens completely to destroy all the prestige and
reputation of the Communist International: during the Second
Congress in Moscow, comrade Lunacharsky, in his speech to the
Italian delegates (a speech given, mark you, in Italian, excellent
Italian even; so that any suspicion of a dubious interpretation must
a priori be rejected), said that in Italy there lives a revolutionary
intellectual by the name of Filippo Tommaso Marinetti. The
philistines of the workers' movement are extremely shocked. It is
now certain that to the insults of being called 'Bergsonian
voluntarists, pragmatists and spiritualists' will be added the more
deadly one of 'Futurists! Marinettians!'[5] Since such a fate awaits
us, let us see if we can raise ourselves to a self-awareness of our
new intellectual position.

Many groups of workers looked kindly towards Futurism
(before the European war). It happened very often (before the
war) that groups of workers would defend the Futurists from the
attacks of cliques of professional 'artists' and 'littérateurs'. This
point established, this historical observation made, the question
automatically arises: 'In this attitude of the workers was there an
intuition (here we are with the word intuition: Bergsonians,
Bergsonians) of an unsatisfied need in the proletarian field?' We
must answer: 'Yes. The revolutionary working class was and is
aware that it must found a new state, that by its tenacious and
patient labour it must elaborate a new economic structure and
found a new civilization.' It is relatively easy to outline right from
this moment the shape of the new state and the new economic
structure. In this absolutely practical field, we are convinced that
for a certain time the only possible thing to do will be to exercise
an iron-like power over the existing organization, over that
constructed by the bourgeoisie. From this conviction comes the
stimulus to struggle for the conquest of power and from it comes
the formula by which Lenin has characterized the workers' state:
'For a certain time the workers' state cannot be other than a
bourgeois state without the bourgeoisie.'[6]

The battlefield for the creation of a new civilization is, on the
other hand, absolutely mysterious, absolutely characterized by the
unforeseeable and the unexpected. Having passed from capitalist

power to workers' power, the factory will continue to produce the same material things that it produces today. But in what way and under what forms will poetry, drama, the novel, music, painting and moral and linguistic works be born? It is not a material factory that produces these works. It cannot be reorganized by a workers' power according to a plan. One cannot establish its rate of production for the satisfaction of immediate needs, to be controlled and determined statistically. Nothing in this field is foreseeable except for this general hypothesis: there will be a proletarian culture (a civilization) totally different from the bourgeois one and in this field too class distinctions will be shattered. Bourgeois careerism will be shattered and there will be a poetry, a novel, a theatre, a moral code, a language, a painting and a music peculiar to proletarian civilization, the flowering and ornament of proletarian social organization. What remains to be done? Nothing other than to destroy the present form of civilization. In this field, 'to destroy' does not mean the same as in the economic field. It does not mean to deprive humanity of the material products that it needs to subsist and to develop. It means to destroy spiritual hierarchies, prejudices, idols and ossified traditions. It means not to be afraid of innovations and audacities, not to be afraid of monsters, not to believe that the world will collapse if a worker makes grammatical mistakes, if a poem limps, if a picture resembles a hoarding or if young men sneer at academic and feeble-minded senility. The Futurists have carried out this task in the field of bourgeois culture. They have destroyed, destroyed, destroyed, without worrying if the new creations produced by their activity were on the whole superior to those destroyed. They have had confidence in themselves, in the impetuosity of their youthful energies. *They have grasped sharply and clearly that our age, the age of big industry, of the large proletarian city and of intense and tumultuous life, was in need of new forms of art, philosophy, behaviour and language.* This sharply revolutionary and absolutely *Marxist* idea came to them when the Socialists were not even vaguely interested in such a question, when the Socialists certainly did not have as precise an idea in politics and economics, when the Socialists would have been frightened (as is evident from the current fear of many of them) by the thought that it was necessary to shatter the machine of bourgeois power in the state and the factory. In their field, the field of culture, the Futurists are revolutionaries. In this field it is likely to be a long time before the working classes will manage to do anything more creative than the Futurists have done. When they supported the Futurists, the workers' groups showed that they were not afraid of *destruction*, certain as they were of being able to create poetry, paintings and plays, like the Futurists; these workers were supporting historicity, the possibility of a proletarian culture created by the workers themselves.

Unsigned, *L'Ordine Nuovo*, 5 January 1921. SCW, 49-51

III FACTORY COUNCILS AND SOCIALIST DEMOCRACY

Introduction

In 1919 the situation in Italy was characterized by acute labour conflicts and a weak state. Both the industrial bourgeoisie and the labour movement had emerged strengthened after the war. Strike activity reached unprecedented levels and took on an increasingly political character. The model of Soviet Russia was powerful. In 1919 came the conquest of an eight-hour day and a national minimum wage. In the summer there were widespread street riots against the high cost of living.

It was in this year that Gramsci and a handful of others (Palmiro Togliatti, Umberto Terracini, Angelo Tasca) set up in Turin a weekly newspaper *L'Ordine Nuovo* (The New Order). From June 1919 its animating idea – largely Gramsci's inspiration – was that of the factory council. The point was to transform the factory workshop committees (*commissioni interne*) that had emerged during the war into assemblies of elected delegates which would be capable of taking over the means of production at the point of production, fulfilling simultaneously, on the model of the Russian soviets, the economic role of direct workers' management of the plant and the political function of democratic self-government. These factory councils would in turn elect delegates to a ward committee (*comitato rionale*) whose function would be to co-ordinate all workers in a given area and become democratic committees for the whole community. Similar organizations were to be developed among the peasantry.

By the end of 1919 the *Ordine Nuovo* proposals had been adopted by the 16,000-strong Turin branch of FIOM, the metalworkers' union, and by the local section of the PSI. The formation of factory councils in the city's big engineering plants (Fiat, Lancia, etc.) frightened the employers into a lock-out in March 1920. The workers responded in April with a general strike involving over 200,000 people – the action, explicitly about the political principle of workers' control in the factories, was widely considered to have been the high point in Turin of the 'two red years' (*biennio rosso*) of 1919-20. The strike was defeated, not only because of a well organized response by the employers, who sent in troops and hired volunteer strike-breakers, but also because the leaders of the PSI and CGL, the reformist trade union confederation, refused to back it.

In September 1920 came the occupation of factories throughout Northern Italy, most notably in Milan, Turin and Genoa. The occupation followed the breakdown of negotiations over a new national wage agreement in the engineering industry. The occupied factories carried on production under workers' control while the police and army – although they surrounded the factories – did not intervene. Prime Minister Giolitti deliberately refrained from ordering the troops to break the occupation, preferring a more tactical approach. He set up a committee to study the problem and promised to introduce a parliamentary bill establishing workers' control over industry, thus giving the reformists a semblance of satisfaction and taking the ground away from the revolutionaries. The PSI and CGL leaders met in Milan from 9 to 11 September, and decided by 591,245 votes to 409,569, with 93,623 abstentions, to limit the aims of the workers' action to winning recognition by the factory owners of trade union control in the plants. The factories were evacuated and work was resumed for the owners on 4 October 1920.

The end of the occupation of the factories marked a turning-point in the class struggle in Italy. By January 1921 a concerted employers' counter-offensive was underway, with increased workplace discipline, victimizations and sackings of the leaders of the 1920 actions. There was also now an increasing alignment between employers – their confidence in the government further weakened by Giolitti's refusal to use a heavy hand – and the rising Fascist movement. The factory councils were ultimately destroyed in the course of the Fascist reaction.

The idea of the factory councils drew both on contemporary Communist sources – Lenin's ideas on 'dual power' and those of Rosa Luxemburg and the Spartakist periodical *Arbeiter Rat* (Workers' Council) – as well as on revolutionary syndicalism: Georges Sorel's writings in France, the shop stewards' movement in Britain and the Industrial Workers of the World ('Wobblies') in the United States and elsewhere. These syndicalist elements in the factory council movement were criticized within the PSI both from the right (the reformists and the CGL) and from the left. For example, Amadeo Bordiga, leader of the other main communist fraction within the PSI, said the movement was a form of economic gradualism and predicted that the councils would, like trade unions, be 'reabsorbed' by the employers as corporatist organizations. He also accused the *Ordine Nuovo* group of underemphasizing the central role of a tightly disciplined political party in leading the revolution.

Gramsci later accepted some of these criticisms. He said that at the time he had not sufficiently connected the factory council movement to the party, whose role was left somewhat nebulous. He wrote in 1925 that the *Ordine Nuovo* group's concentration on mass action had 'placed it in a position of inferiority within the general organization of the party'. He was also self-critical of the group for not having organized during the *biennio rosso* a national faction within the PSI which could have broken the grip of the reformists in the party and the trade unions and prevented its own political isolation (see SPW II, p. 189). He nevertheless asserted that there was an essential difference between factory councils and trade unions and repudiated Bordiga's emphasis on strict party leadership from above *at the expense of* the mobilization and organization of the working class from below. It was this emphasis on working-class autonomy and socialist democracy which constituted the most original and powerful aspect of the factory councils movement.

By contrast, one of the major limitations of the movement and a key reason for its defeat, as Gramsci would later argue, was its relative geographical isolation. The movement was confined to the industrial north and, although it did seem able to build an alliance with the peasantry in Piedmont in April 1920, it failed to forge political links with the poor peasants of the south. The *Ordine Nuovo* group emphasized the importance of building a platform of common action with the peasants (see Gramsci's article 'Workers and Peasants' in Section IV) but this platform was not constructed at a national level. This was one of the principal sources of the movement's vulnerability in the face of the employers' counter-offensive and the rise of Fascism. The lesson of its defeat was to underlie one of the main areas of Gramsci's strategic rethinking from 1923 onwards.

1 Workers' Democracy

An urgent problem today faces every socialist with a keen sense of the historical responsibility that rests on the working class and on the party representing the critical and active consciousness of the mission of this class.

How are the immense social forces unleashed by the war to be harnessed? How are they to be disciplined and given a political form which has the potential to develop normally and continuously into the skeleton of the socialist state in which the dictatorship of the proletariat will be embodied? How can the present be welded to the future, so that while satisfying the urgent necessities of the one we may work effectively to create and 'anticipate' the other?

The aim of this article is to stimulate thought and action. It is an invitation to the best and most conscious workers to reflect on the problem and collaborate – each in the sphere of his own competence and activity – towards its solution, focusing the attention of their comrades and associations on it. Only common solidarity in a work of clarification, persuasion and mutual education will produce concrete constructive action.

The socialist state already exists potentially in the institutions of social life characteristic of the exploited working class. To link these institutions, co-ordinating and ordering them into a highly centralized hierarchy of competences and powers, while respecting the necessary autonomy and articulation of each, is to create a genuine workers' democracy here and now – a workers' democracy in effective and active opposition to the bourgeois state, and prepared to replace it here and now in all its essential functions of administering and controlling the national heritage.

The workers' movement today is led by the Socialist Party and the Confederation of Labour [CGL]. But for the great mass of workers, the exercise of the social power of the party and Confederation is achieved indirectly, by prestige and enthusiasm, authoritarian pressure and even inertia. The party's influence grows daily, spreading to previously unexplored popular strata; it wins consent and a desire to work effectively for the advent of communism among groups and individuals hitherto absent from the political struggle. These disorderly and chaotic energies must be given a permanent form and discipline. They must be absorbed, organized and strengthened. The proletarian and semi-proletarian class must be transformed into an organized society that can educate itself, gain experience and acquire a responsible consciousness of the obligations that fall to classes achieving state power.

It will take the Socialist Party and the trade unions years, even decades of effort to absorb the whole of the working class. These two institutions will not be identified immediately with the proletarian state. In fact, in the Communist Republics, they have continued to exist independently of the state, with the party functioning as a driving force, and the unions as instruments for supervision and the achievement of limited reforms. The party must carry on its role as the organ of communist education, as the furnace of faith, the depository of doctrine, the supreme power harmonizing the organized and disciplined forces of the working class and peasantry and leading them towards the ultimate goal. It is just because it must strictly carry out this task that the party cannot throw open its doors to an invasion of new members who are not accustomed to the exercise of responsibility and discipline.

But the social life of the working class is rich in the very institutions and activities which need to be developed, fully organized and co-ordinated into a broad and flexible system that is capable of absorbing and disciplining the entire working class.

The workshop with its internal commissions, the socialist clubs, the peasant communities – these are the centres of proletarian life we should be working in directly.

The internal commissions are organs of workers' democracy which must be freed from the limitations imposed on them by the entrepreneurs, and infused with new life and energy. Today the internal commissions limit the power of the capitalist in the factory and perform functions of arbitration and discipline. Tomorrow, developed and enriched, they must be the organs of proletarian power, replacing the capitalist in all his useful functions of management and administration.

The workers should proceed at once to the election of vast assemblies of delegates, chosen from their best and most conscious comrades, under the slogan: 'All power in the workshop to the workshop committees' together with its complement: 'All state power to the Workers' and Peasants' Councils'.

The communists organized in the party and the ward clubs would thus be presented with a vast field for concrete, revolutionary propaganda. The clubs, in agreement with the urban party sections, should carry out a survey of the working-class forces in their area, and become the seat of the ward council of workshop delegates, the ganglion co-ordinating and centralizing all the proletarian energies in the ward. The electoral system could vary according to the size of the workshops: the aim, however, should be to elect one delegate for every fifteen workers, divided into categories (as is done in English factories) and ending up, through a series of elections, with a committee of factory delegates representing every aspect of work (manual workers, clerical workers, technicians). The ward committee should also seek to incorporate delegates from other categories of workers living in the ward: waiters, cab-drivers, tramwaymen, railwaymen, road-sweepers, private employees, clerks and others.

The ward committee should be an expression of *the whole of the working class* living in the ward, an expression that is legitimate and authoritative, that can enforce a spontaneously delegated discipline that is backed with powers, and can order the immediate and complete cessation of all work throughout the ward.

The ward committees would grow into urban commissariats, controlled and disciplined by the Socialist Party and the craft federations.

Such a system of workers' democracy (integrated with corresponding peasants' organizations) would give the masses a permanent structure and discipline. It would be a magnificent school of political and administrative experience and would involve the masses down to the last man, accustoming them to tenacity and perseverance, and to thinking of themselves as an army in the field which needs a strict cohesion if it is not to be destroyed and reduced to slavery.

Each factory would make up one or more of the regiments of this army, which would have to have its own NCOs, its own liaison services, officer corps and general staff, with all powers being delegated by free election and not imposed in an authoritarian manner. Meetings held inside the factory, together with ceaseless propaganda and persuasion by the most conscious elements, should effect a radical transformation of the worker's mentality, should make the masses better equipped to exercise power, and finally should diffuse a consciousness of the rights and obligations of comrade and worker that is both concrete and effective, because spontaneously generated from living historical experience.

As we said above, these brief proposals are put forward only to stimulate thought and action. Every aspect of the problem deserves special study, detailed elucidation, coherent extension and integration. But the concrete and complete solution to the problems of socialist living can only arise from communist practice: collective discussion, which sympathetically alters men's consciousness, unifies them and inspires them to industrious enthusiasm. To tell the truth, to arrive together at the truth, is a communist and revolutionary act. The formula 'dictatorship of the proletariat' must cease to be a mere formula, a flourish of revolutionary rhetoric. Whoever wills the end, must will the means. The dictatorship of the proletariat represents the establishment of a new, proletarian state, which channels the institutional experiences of the oppressed class and transforms the social activity of the working class and peasantry into a widespread and powerfully organized system. This state cannot be improvised: the Russian Bolshevik communists laboured for eight months to broadcast and concretize their slogan: 'All power to the Soviets' – and the Russian workers had been familiar with Soviets since 1905. Italian communists must treasure this Russian experience and economize on time and effort: the work of reconstruction itself will demand so much time and effort that every day and every act should be dedicated to it.

Unsigned, but written in collaboration with Palmiro Togliatti
L'Ordine Nuovo, 21 June 1919. SPWI, 65-8

2 Conquest of the State

Capitalist concentration, determined by the mode of production, produces a corresponding concentration of working human masses. This is the fact that underlies all the revolutionary theses of Marxism, that underlies the conditions of the new proletarian way of life, the new communist order destined to replace the bourgeois way of life and the disorder of capitalism arising from free competition and class struggle.

In the sphere of general capitalist activity, the worker too operates on the level of free competition; he is an individual and a citizen. But the starting conditions in the struggle are not the same for everyone, at the same time. The existence of private property places the social minority in a privileged position and makes the struggle uneven. The worker is continuously exposed to the most deadly hazards: the bare necessities of his life, his culture, the life and future of his family, are all exposed to the sudden consequences of a shift in the labour market. So the worker attempts to free himself from the sphere of competition and individualism. The principles of combination and solidarity become paramount for the working class; they transform the mentality and way of life of the workers and peasants. Organs and institutions embodying these principles arise; they are the basis upon which the process of historical development that leads to communism in the means of production and exchange begins.

The principle of combination can and must be seen as the central feature of the proletarian revolution. The emergence and development of the Socialist Party and the trade unions in the period preceding this present one (what we might call the period of the First and Second Internationals, or the period of recruitment) was dependent upon this historical tendency.

The development of these proletarian institutions and of the whole proletarian movement in general was not, however, autonomous. It was not constrained wholly by laws inherent in the living conditions and historical experience of the exploited working class. In fact, the laws of historical development were laid down by the property-owning class organized in the state. The state has always been the protagonist of history. In its organs the power of the propertied class is centralized. Within the state, the propertied class forges its own discipline and unity, over and above the disputes and clashes of competition, in order to keep intact its privileged position in the supreme phase of competition itself: the class struggle for power, for pre-eminence in the leadership and ordering of society.

In this period the proletarian movement was merely a function of capitalist free competition. Proletarian institutions developed in the way they did not through inner necessity, but through external influences: under the formidable pressure of events and compulsions dependent upon capitalist competition. In this lies the origin of the inner conflicts, the deviations, the hesitations, the compromises that characterized the whole of the proletarian movement's existence prior to the current period, and which have now culminated in the bankruptcy of the Second International.

Some of the currents in the socialist and proletarian movement had emphasized trade-union organization as the essential feature of the revolution, and directed their propaganda and activity accordingly. At one stage, the syndicalist movement appeared in the light of the true interpreter of Marxism, the true interpreter of reality.

The error of syndicalism consists in this: it assumes that the present form and functions of the trade unions are permanent and represent the perennial form of the principle of combination, when in fact they have been imposed on the unions and not proposed by them, and so cannot have a constant and predictable line of development. Syndicalism, while presenting itself as the initiator of a 'spontaneist', libertarian tradition, was in fact one of the many disguises of the Jacobin and abstract spirit.

This was the origin of the errors of the syndicalist current, which did not succeed in replacing the Socialist Party in the task of educating the working class for the revolution. The workers and peasants felt that, so long as the propertied class and the democratic-parliamentary state are dictating the laws of history, any attempt to remove oneself from the sphere of operation of these laws is inane and ridiculous. There is no denying the fact that within the general configuration of an industrial society, each man can actively participate in affairs and modify his surroundings only to the extent that he operates as an individual and citizen, as a member of the democratic-parliamentary state. The liberal experience is not worthless and can only be transcended after it has been experienced. The apoliticism of the apoliticals was merely a degeneration of politics: to reject the state and fight against it is just as much a political act as to take part in the general historical activity that is channelled into Parliament and the municipal councils, the popular institutions of the state. The quality of the political act varies. The syndicalists worked outside of reality, and hence their politics were fundamentally mistaken. On the other hand, the parliamentary socialists worked in close contact with events, and while they could make mistakes (and indeed, they committed many mistakes, and grievous ones too), they made no mistake in the direction their activity took and so they triumphed in the 'competition'; the broad masses, the people who objectively modify social relations through their intervention, favoured the Socialist Party. Notwithstanding all its mistakes and shortcomings, the party did succeed, in the final analysis, in accomplishing its mission: namely, to transform the proletariat into something whereas before it had been nothing, to give it an awareness, to point the liberation movement firmly and enthusiastically in the direction corresponding in its general lines to the process of historical development of human society.

The gravest error of the socialist movement was akin to that of the syndicalists. Participating in the general activity of human society within the state, the socialists forgot that their role had to be essentially one of criticism, of antithesis. Instead of mastering reality, they allowed themselves to be absorbed by it.

Marxist communists should be characterized by what may be called a 'maieutic' mentality. Their activity does not consist in throwing themselves into the course of events determined by bourgeois competition, but in a critical biding of their time. History is a continuous process of development, and hence is essentially unpredictable. But this does not mean that 'everything' is unpredictable in the process of development of history; that history, in other words, is the domain of arbitrariness and irresponsible caprice. History is at once freedom and necessity. The institutions in whose development and activity history is embodied emerged and continue to exist because they have a task and a mission to accomplish. There emerged and developed particular objective conditions for the production of material wealth and for men's intellectual awareness. If these objective conditions, which by virtue of their mechanical nature are almost mathematically commensurable, change, then there is a corresponding change in the totality of relations that regulate and inform human society and a change in the degree of men's awareness. The social configuration is transformed; traditional institutions are impoverished and become inadequate to their task, obstructive and lethal. If man's intelligence were incapable of discerning rhythm or establishing a process in the course of history, then civilized life would be impossible. Political genius can be recognized precisely by this capacity to master the greatest possible number of concrete conditions necessary and sufficient to determine a process of development; by the capacity, therefore, to anticipate both the immediate and distant future and on the basis of this intuition to prescribe a state's activity and hazard the fortunes of a people. In this sense Karl Marx was by far the greatest of contemporary political geniuses.

The Socialists have simply accepted, and frequently in a supine fashion, the historical reality produced by capitalist initiative. They have acquired the same mistaken mentality as the liberal economists: they believe in the perpetuity and fundamental perfection of the institutions of the democratic state. In their view, the form of these democratic institutions can be corrected, touched up here and there, but in fundamentals must be respected. An example of this narrow-minded conceit is evident in Filippo Turati's Minoan judgment that Parliament stands in relation to the Soviet like the city to the barbarian horde.[1]

Now the modern formula of the 'conquest of the state' arises precisely from this mistaken conception of historical development, from the old game of compromise and from the 'cretinous' tactics of parliamentarism.

We, on the other hand, remain convinced, in the light of the revolutionary experiences of Russia, Hungary and Germany, that the socialist state cannot be embodied in the institutions of the capitalist state. We remain convinced that with respect to these institutions, if not with respect to those of the proletariat, the socialist state must be a fundamentally new creation. The institutions of the capitalist state are organized in such a way as to facilitate free competition: merely to change the personnel in these institutions is hardly going to change the direction of their activity. The socialist state is not yet communism, i.e. the establishment of a practice and an economic way of life that are communal; but it is the transitional state whose mission is to suppress competition via the suppression of private property, classes and national economies. This mission cannot be accomplished by parliamentary democracy. So the formula 'conquest of the state' should be understood in the following sense: replacement of the democratic parliamentary state by a new type of state, one that is generated by the associative experience of the proletarian class.

And here we come back to our starting point. We said that the institutions of the socialist and proletarian movement in the period prior to this present one did not develop autonomously, but in response to the general configuration of human society under the sway of the sovereign laws of capitalism. The war turned the strategic conditions of the class struggle upside down. The capitalists have lost their pre-eminence; their freedom is limited; their power is reduced to a minimum. Capitalist concentration has reached its maximum possible level, with the achievement of a global monopoly of production and exchange. The corresponding concentration of the working masses has given the revolutionary proletarian class an unprecedented power.

The traditional institutions of the movement have become incapable of containing such a flowering of revolutionary activity. Their very structure is inadequate to the task of disciplining the forces which have become part of the conscious historical process. These institutions are not dead. Born in response to free competition, they must continue to exist until the last remnant of competition has been wiped out, until classes and parties have been completely suppressed and national proletarian dictatorships have been fused in the Communist International. But beside these institutions, new, state-oriented institutions must arise and develop – the very institutions which will replace the private and public institutions of the parliamentary-democratic state. The very institutions which will replace the person of the capitalist in his administrative functions and his industrial power, and so achieve the autonomy of the producer in the factory. Institutions capable of taking over the management of all the functions inherent in the complex system of relations of production and exchange that link the various workshops of a factory together to form a basic economic unit, link together the various activities of the agricultural industry, and through horizontal and vertical planning have to construct the harmonious edifice of the national and international economy, liberated from the obstructive and parasitical tyranny of the private property-owners.

Never has the drive and revolutionary enthusiasm of the Western European proletariat been more vigorous. It seems to us, however, that a lucid and precise awareness of the end is not accompanied by a comparably lucid and precise awareness of the means that are needed at the present moment to achieve that end. The conviction has already taken root in the masses that the proletarian state is embodied in a system of workers', peasants' and soldiers' Councils. But the tactical conception which will objectively ensure that this state comes into being is not yet evident. So a network of proletarian institutions must be set up without delay, a network rooted in the consciousness of the broad masses, one that can depend on their discipline and permanent support, a network in which the class of workers and peasants, in their totality, can adopt a form that is rich in dynamism and in future growth possibilities. It is certain that if a mass movement with a revolutionary character were to develop today, in the present conditions of proletarian organization, all it would achieve would be a purely formal correction of the democratic state. The outcome would simply be increased powers for the Chamber of Deputies (via a constituent assembly) and the arrival in power of the bungling, anti-communist Socialists. The forces of the democratic state and of the capitalist class are still immense: we must not blind ourselves to the fact that capitalism survives mainly through the activity of its sycophants and lackeys, and this scurvy race is certainly far from extinct.

To sum up, the creation of the proletarian state is not a thaumaturgical act: it is itself a process of development. It presupposes a preparatory period involving organizing and propaganda. Greater emphasis and powers must be given to the proletarian factory institutions that already exist, comparable ones must be set up in the villages, they must be composed of communists conscious of the revolutionary mission these institutions must accomplish. Otherwise all our enthusiasm, all the faith of the working masses, will not succeed in preventing the revolution from degenerating pathetically into a new parliament of schemers, talkers and irresponsibles, nor in avoiding the necessity to make further and more dreadful sacrifices to bring about a proletarian state.

Unsigned, *L'Ordine Nuovo*, 12 July 1919. SPWI, 73-8

3 To the Workshop Delegates
of the Fiat Centro and Brevetti Plants

The new form which the internal commission has assumed in your plants with the election of workshop delegates, together with the discussions that led up to and accompanied this transformation, have not passed unnoticed amongst the workers and bosses of Turin. On the one hand, the workers in other plants in the city and province are preparing to follow your lead. On the other hand, the owners and their direct agents, the managers of the great industrial enterprises, are watching the movement with mounting interest: they are asking themselves and asking you what can be the ultimate goal of all this, what can be the programme that the Turin working class is pursuing.

We are well aware of the fact that our newspaper has played a substantial part in bringing this movement into existence. In its pages, not only has the question been examined from a theoretical and general point of view, but we have also brought together and analysed the results of experiences in other countries, to furnish material for the study of practical applications. We know, however, that our work has been of value to the extent that it has satisfied a need, and has helped to give concrete expression to an aspiration that was latent in the consciousness of the working masses. This is why we were so rapidly understood; this is why the transition from discussion to realization was effected so rapidly.

We believe that this need and this aspiration, whence the movement to renew working-class organization initiated by you draws its origins, are inscribed in reality; that they are a direct consequence of the point reached, in the process of its development, by the social and economic system based on private appropriation of the means of production and exchange. Today the worker on the shopfloor and the peasant in the fields, the English miner and the Russian moujik – all the workers of the whole world – are sensing more or less certainly, and experiencing more or less directly, that truth which studious men had foreseen, and about which they are growing more and more certain when they observe the events of this phase in the history of humanity. We have reached the point at which the working class, if it does not wish to fail in the task of reconstruction which is inherent in its actions and its will, must begin to organize itself positively and appropriately for the ends to be accomplished.

Now if it is true that the new society will be based on work and on co-ordination of the producers' energies, then tomorrow the workplaces where the producers live and function together will be the centres of the social organism and will have to take the place of the directive bodies of present-day society. In the early stages of the workers' struggle, organization along craft lines was most suitable for the purposes of defence, for the requirements of the struggle for immediate improvements in economic conditions and the work regime. So too today, when reconstructive aims are beginning to emerge and take on increasing coherence in the minds of the workers, it is essential that a factory organization should arise parallel to and in support of the craft one, as a true school for developing the reconstructive capacities of the workers.

The working masses must take adequate measures to acquire complete self-government, and the first step along this road consists in disciplining themselves, inside the workshop, in the strictest possible, yet autonomous, spontaneous and unconstrained manner. Nor can it be denied that the discipline which will be established along with the new system will lead to an improvement in production – but this is nothing but the confirmation of one of the theses of socialism: the more the productive human forces acquire consciousness, liberate themselves and freely organize themselves by emancipating themselves from the slavery to which capitalism would have liked to condemn them forever, the better does their mode of utilization become – a man will always work better than a slave. So to those who object that by this method we are collaborating with our opponents, with the owners of the factories, we reply that on the contrary this is the only means of letting them know in concrete terms that the end of their domination is at hand, since the working class is now aware of the possibility of *doing things itself*, and doing them well. Indeed from one day to the next it is acquiring an ever clearer certainty that it alone can save the entire world from ruin and desolation. Hence every action that you undertake, every battle that is waged under your leadership, will be illuminated by the light of that ultimate goal which is in all of your minds and intentions.

And so even the acts of apparently little importance in which the mandate conferred upon you is concretized will acquire an enormous value. Since you were elected by a workforce in which

there are still many unorganized elements, your first concern naturally will be to bring these into the ranks of the workers' organizations – a task which, moreover, will be facilitated by the fact that
these people will see in you their ready defenders, their guides, their
initiators into the life of the factory. You will show them through
example that a worker's strength lies wholly in union and solidarity
with his comrades.

You will also have the job of ensuring that the rules of work fixed
by the trade federations and accepted in the agreements are respected in the workshops; for in this area too, the slightest departure
from the established principles can constitute a grave threat to the
worker's rights and person – and you will be his inflexible and
tenacious defenders and guardians. And since you yourselves will
be living continuously on the job in the midst of the workers, you
will be in a position to know what modifications should be made in
the rules from time to time, as a result of technological progress or
the improved consciousness and capacity of the workers themselves. In this way a shop-floor *way of life* will be established, initial
germ of a true and effective labour legislation, i.e. laws which the
producers will enact and lay down for themselves. We feel sure that
the importance of all this does not escape you, and that it is equally
clear to all the workers who have promptly and enthusiastically
grasped the value and significance of the task you have set yourselves. The era of the active intervention of the labour forces themselves in the fields of technique and discipline has begun.

In the technical field you can, on the one hand, do an extremely
useful job of collecting precious data and factual material for both
the trade federations and the central directive bodies of the new
factory organizations. In addition, you will see to it that the
shop-floor workers acquire more and more skill, and that the petty
feelings of craft jealousy that still divide them are banished forever.
In this way you will prepare them for the day when they are no
longer working for the boss but for themselves, and will have to be
united and in solidarity if the strength of the great proletarian army,
whose first units they represent, is to be enhanced. Why could you
not set up, inside the factory, appropriate instruction departments,
real vocational schools, in which every worker, rousing himself
from the fatigue that brutalizes, may open his mind to knowledge of
the processes of production and so better himself?

Certainly, if all this is to be accomplished then discipline will be needed, but the discipline you will require from the working masses will be quite different from the kind imposed and demanded by the boss, who derived his strength from the property rights that gave him a position of privilege. You will derive your strength from another right, the right of labour: this has for centuries been an instrument in the hands of its exploiters, but today it is ready to redeem itself and govern itself on its own. Your power, as opposed to that of the bosses and their officials, represents not the forces of the past, but the free forces of the future – which await their hour and are preparing for it, in the knowledge that it will be the hour of redemption from all slavery.

And so the central organs that will be created for every group of workshops, every group of factories, every city and every region, right up to a supreme national Workers' Council, will pursue and broaden and intensify the job of controlling and preparing and organizing the whole class for the tasks of conquest and government.

We realize that the road will not be short or easy: many difficulties will arise and be placed in your path. To overcome them, you will have to draw on great ability, perhaps at times you will have to appeal to the strength of the organized working class, you will always have to be inspired and stimulated to action by a supreme faith in our cause. But what is most important, comrades, is that under your guidance and under the guidance of those who will follow your lead, the workers should acquire a deep certainty that now, secure in their goal, they are marching on the great road of the future.

Signed L'Ordine Nuovo, *L'Ordine Nuovo*, 13 September 1919
SPWI, 94-7

4 Unions and Councils

The trade union is not a predetermined phenomenon. It *becomes* a determinate institution, i.e. it takes on a definite historical form to the extent that the strength and will of the workers who are its members impress a policy and propose an aim that define it.

Objectively, the trade union is the form which labour as a commodity is bound to assume in a capitalist system, when it organizes itself in order to control the market. This form consists in an office staffed by functionaries, organizational technicians (when they can be called technicians), specialists (when they can be called specialists) in the art of concentrating and guiding the workers' forces in such a way as to establish a favourable balance between the working class and the power of capital.

The development of trade-union organization is characterized by two facts: 1. the union embraces an ever increasing number of workers; 2. the union concentrates and generalizes its scope until the movement's power and discipline is focused in a central office. This office becomes divorced from the masses it has regimented, and removes itself from the eddies and currents of fickle whims and foolish ambitions that are to be expected in the excitable broad masses. The union thus acquires the ability to negotiate agreements and take on responsibilities. In this way it obliges the employer to acknowledge a certain legality in his dealings with the workers, a legality that is conditional on his faith in the union's *solvency* and its capacity to secure respect for contracted obligations from the working masses.

The emergence of an industrial legality is a great victory for the working class, but it is not the ultimate and definitive victory. Industrial legality has improved the working class's standard of living but it is no more than a compromise – a compromise which had to be made and must be supported until the balance of forces favours the working class. If the trade-union officials regard industrial legality as a necessary, but not a permanently necessary compromise; if they deploy all the means at the union's disposal to improve the balance of forces in favour of the working class; and if they carry out all the spiritual and material preparatory work that will be needed if the working class is to launch at any particular moment a victorious offensive against capital and subject it to its law – then the trade union is a tool of revolution, and union discipline, even when used to make the workers respect industrial legality, is revolutionary discipline.

The relations which should prevail between the trade unions and Factory Councils need to be judged in the light of the following question: what is the nature and value of industrial legality?

The Council is the negation of industrial legality: it strives at all times to destroy it, to lead the working class to the conquest of industrial power and make it the source of industrial power. The union represents legality, and must aim to make its members respect that legality. The trade union is answerable to the industrialists, but only in so far as it is answerable to its own members: it guarantees to the worker and his family a continuous supply of work and wages, i.e. food and a roof over their heads. By virtue of its revolutionary spontaneity, the Factory Council tends to spark off the class war at any moment; while the trade union, by virtue of its bureaucratic form, tends to prevent class war from ever breaking out. The relations between the two institutions should be such that a capricious impulse on the part of the Councils could not result in a set-back or defeat for the working class; in other words, the Council should accept and assimilate the discipline of the union. They should also be such that the revolutionary character of the Council exercises an influence over the trade union, and functions as a reagent dissolving the union's bureaucracy and bureaucratism.

The Council strives at all times to break with industrial legality. The Council consists of the exploited and tyrannized masses who are obliged to perform servile labour: as such, it strives to universalize every rebellion and give a resolutive scope and value to each of its acts of power. The union, as an organization that is jointly responsible for legality, strives to universalize and perpetuate this legality. The relations between union and Council should create the conditions in which the break with legality, the working-class offensive, occurs at the most opportune moment for the working class, when it possesses that minimum of preparation that is deemed indispensable to a lasting victory.

The relations between unions and Councils cannot be stabilized by any other device than the following: the majority or a substantial number of the electors to the Council should be organized in unions. Any attempt to link the two institutions in a relation of hierarchical dependence can only lead to the destruction of both.

If the conception that sees the Councils merely as an instrument in the trade-union struggle takes material form in a bureaucratic discipline and a hierarchical structure in which the union has direct control over the Council, then the Council is sterilized as a force for revolutionary expansion – as a form of the actual development of the proletarian revolution, tending spontaneously to create new modes of production and labour, new modes of discipline and, in the end, a communist society. Since the rise of the Council is a function of the position that the working class has achieved in the sphere of production, and a historical necessity for the working class, any attempt to subordinate it hierarchically to the union would sooner or later result in a clash between the two institutions. The Council's strength consists in the fact that it is in close contact – indeed identified – with the consciousness of the working masses, who are seeking their autonomous emancipation and wish to put on record their freedom of initiative in the creation of history. The masses as a whole participate in the activity of the Council, and gain a measure of self-respect in the process. Only a very restricted number of members participate in the activity of the trade union; its real strength lies in this fact, but this fact is also a weakness that cannot be put to the test without running very grave risks.

If, moreover, the unions were to lean directly on the Councils, not to dominate them, but to become their higher form, then they would reflect the Council's own tendency to break at all times with industrial legality and unleash the final phase of the class war. The union would lose its capacity to negotiate agreements, and would lose its role as an agent to regulate and discipline the impulsive forces of the working class.

If its members establish a revolutionary discipline in the union, a discipline which the masses see as being necessary for the triumph of the workers' revolution and not as slavery to capital, this discipline will undoubtedly be accepted and made its own by the Council. It will become a natural aspect of the Council's activity. If the union headquarters becomes a centre for revolutionary preparation, and appears as such to the masses by virtue of the campaigns it succeeds in launching, the men who compose it and the propaganda it issues, then its centralized and absolutist character will be seen by the masses as a major revolutionary strength, as one more (and a very important) condition for the success of the struggle to which they are committed all the way.

In Italian conditions, the trade-union official sees industrial legality as a permanent state of affairs. Too often he defends it from the same perspective as the proprietor. He sees only chaos and wilfulness in everything that happens amongst the working masses. He does not universalize the worker's act of rebellion against capitalist discipline as rebellion; he perceives only the

A Gramsci Reader

physical act, which might in itself be trivial. Thus the story of the 'porter's raincoat' has been as widely disseminated and has been interpreted by stupid journalists in the same way as the myth of the 'socialization of women in Russia'. In these conditions, the trade-union discipline can be nothing other than a service rendered to capital; in these conditions any attempt to subordinate the Councils to the trade unions can only be judged as reactionary.

The communists would like the revolutionary act to be, as far as possible, a conscious and responsible act. Hence they would like to see the choice of the moment in which to launch the working-class offensive (to the extent that such a moment can be chosen) resting in the hands of the most conscious and responsible section of the working class – the section organized in the Socialist Party and playing the most active part in the life of the organization. For this reason, the communists could not possibly want the union to lose any of its disciplinary energy and systematic centralization.

By forming themselves into permanently organized groups within the trade unions and factories, the communists need to import into these bodies the ideas, theses and tactics of the Third International; they need to exert an influence over union discipline and determine its aims; they need to influence the decisions of the Factory Councils, and transform the rebellious impulses sparked off by the conditions that capitalism has created for the working class into a revolutionary consciousness and creativity. Since they bear the heaviest historical responsibility, the communists in the Party have the greatest interest in evoking, through their ceaseless activity, relations of interpenetration and natural interdependence between the various working-class institutions. It is these relations that leaven discipline and organization with a revolutionary spirit.

Unsigned, *L'Ordine Nuovo*, 12 June 1920. SPWI, 265-8

5 Red Sunday

The bourgeoisie's scribblers are writhing in fury, constrained as they are to acknowledge the activity of the working class in the occupied factories.[2] Working-class activity: initiatives by the working class in production, in internal order and in military defence! Social hierarchies have been smashed and historical values turned upside down. The 'executive' classes, the 'instrumental' classes, have become the 'controlling' classes. They have taken leadership over themselves and found in their own ranks their representatives: men to invest with the power of government; men who will take upon themselves all the functions that turn an elemental and mechanical aggregate into an organic whole, a living creature. All this has set the hacks of the bourgeoisie twisting in rage, believing as they do that the bourgeois class is divinely invested with powers of decision and historical initiative.

What the workers have done has an immense historical importance, and it needs to be understood in all its aspects by the working class. This is a day the workers will devote to thought, discussion and recapitulation of the events that have occurred: for the workers, one day like this is worth ten years of normal activity, normal propaganda and normal absorption of revolutionary notions and concepts.

What has happened in these past few days? The metalworkers' federation had called on the workers to engage in trade-union struggle to win wage improvements. The industrialists refused to acknowledge that there was any real validity in the workers' demands. Then the leaders of the organization, though they are not communists and sign manifestos against Bolshevik methods of emancipating the people, nevertheless, after examining the actual situation, found they had to transfer the struggle to a new domain – a domain where, if violence was not an immediate necessity, the study and organization of violence at once became a necessity. Meanwhile a new fact emerged at once from this new method of struggle. When the workers were fighting to improve their economic situation through strike action, their role in the struggle was limited to having faith in their distant leaders; it was limited to developing the virtues of solidarity and resistance, on the basis precisely of this generic faith. But if, in the course of the struggle, the workers occupy the factories with the intention of continuing production, the moral position of the masses at once takes on a different form and value. The trade-union leaders are no longer able to lead and disappear in the immensity of the membership; the masses are left to solve the problems of the factory on their own, with their own resources and their own men.

Under the capitalists, the factory was a miniature state, ruled over by a despotic lord. The lord had sole right to select the manual workers, clerks, foremen and specialists and distribute them among the workshops, offices and laboratories. The factory was a despotically organized state, with all power resting in the hands of the proprietor or his delegates. The multiplicity of states constituted by all the capitalist factories found united expression in the bourgeois state, which secured the discipline and obedience of the non-property-owning population by giving it a semblance of power and sovereignty; by summoning it every five or seven years to nominate its deputies to Parliament and the municipal councils. Today, after the workers' occupation, this despotic power in the factories has been smashed: the right to choose industrial executives has passed into the hands of the working class. Every factory has become an illegal state, a proletarian republic living from day to day, awaiting the outcome of events. But even if a great uncertainty still hangs over the future of these proletarian republics, given that the enemy forces have not revealed themselves and offer no hint as to their real intentions, the very fact that these republics 'live' has an importance and historical value out of all proportion. Life has a logic and inner energy of its own that goes beyond the will and whims of individuals. While these proletarian republics live, they will have to cope with all the problems that face any autonomous and independent power exercising its sovereignty over a delimited territory. The political capacity, the initiative and revolutionary creativity of the working class is now put to the test.

The first problem, the fundamental and unavoidable problem confronting the citizens of the factory-state is that of military defence. This problem arises in a novel form. The bourgeois state builds its army upon three social strata: the bourgeoisie, the petty bourgeoisie and the working people. The people provides the military mass, the big property-owning bourgeoisie and the aristocracy provide the upper ranks of the officers, while the petty bourgeoisie provides the junior commands. The same organization emerges in the capitalist army as in the capitalist factory, where the class of proprietors (or those assimilated to them through financial interests) has despotic command, the proletariat is the passive infantry-mass and the petty bourgeoisie fills the subordinate command posts.

In the factory-republic, there exists one class only, the proletariat: the class which provided the army and industry with a passive infantry-mass. Now the proletariat needs to create its own articulated, organized and disciplined army, an army that is capable of resisting the enemy forces and vanquishing them. The workers tend to see defence as an obligation incumbent upon all, and this conception hits the mark. But then they are led to conclude that everyone, without distinction, should at once fulfil this obligation – and this is a mistake. Military defence needs to be organized in a special corps, with its own commands and roles: the conception of hierarchy can no longer be applied to such a formation, as 'there exists one class only'. These formations should not be restricted in numbers, since defence may at any moment give way to attack and military initiative.

This problem of military initiative is linked to another: will not this multiplicity of proletarian republics, constituted by the factories occupied and controlled by the workers, be led necessarily – through the inner dialectic of historical development – to confederate themselves, form themselves into a unity and counterpose a central power of their own to the central power of the bourgeois state? Today the working class is confronted by the concrete problem of forming a city-wide Soviet. If such a Soviet is formed, it will need to have an armed force at its disposal. This force can and must be provided by regularly constituted and commanded factory brigades, that can be amalgamated, through a relay of commands, into an urban militia. But conversely, the creation of military nuclei in the factories raises the problem of the Soviet, since defence has no bounds and must proceed according to its own logic.

These problems should be discussed by the workers today in the factory general assemblies, the organs which express the power and sovereignty of the factory proletarian republics. The preparatory and propaganda work for the nomination of workers' deputies needs to be carried out in such a way that, at any given moment, when the march of events brings history to the pitch where the new and unexpected is bound to happen, the forms of the proletariat's power – as it struggles to emancipate itself – will spring from each individual factory or group of factories. And the same remarks apply to this particular revolutionary creation as to that of armed force.

Within the bourgeois state, the functions of supreme command (the government) are in the hands of the capitalists or the social class that is bound by financial interests to the proprietors. The subordinate posts – the role played by the national deputies – are in the hands of the petty bourgeoisie, which allows itself to be dominated economically and morally by the capitalists. The mass of the working people is manipulated politically to satisfy the material interests of the property-owners and the ideological ambitions of the petty bourgeois. To keep this hierarchy of classes intact, the state maintains that it is illegal for deputies to be bound by authoritative mandates. The bourgeoisie counts on the distractions of the surroundings, and on hints concerning the possibility of satisfying personal ambitions, to corrupt deputies – even when these are workers – if they are not bound by an imperative mandate. In the constitution of the proletarian central power, all these conditions are changed. There exists one class only, which elects its deputies from its own ranks, the electoral college being the factory and mandates being authoritative and binding. This means that the old hierarchies are smashed and the workers' power is built on a purely industrial and administrative basis. The anarchists should be the first to welcome this organization of power, since their ideals are given concrete expression.

Today, on the metalworkers' Red Sunday, the workers themselves must construct the first historic cell of the proletarian revolution that the general situation is generating with all the irresistible force of natural phenomena.

Unsigned, *Avanti!*, 5 September 1920. SPWI, 340-3

6 Political Capacity

Today, the metalworkers are to approve or reject, by referendum, the motion voted by the congress of their federation.[3] The result of this consultation of the workforce in the factories is not difficult to predict. The referendum is an exquisitely democratic and counter-revolutionary form; it serves to valorize the amorphous mass of the population and to crush the vanguards that lead those masses and give them political consciousness.

So the vanguard of the proletariat should not be demoralized or disorganized by this outcome of the revolutionary movement. Its quality as a vanguard will be verified by the strength of mind and political capacity it succeeds in demonstrating. Have the groups of workers which have been at the head of the movement in the last few days taken the exact measure of their powers to act and the forces of passive resistance that exist within the masses? Have they acquired a consciousness of their historical mission? Have they acquired a consciousness of the inner weaknesses which have been revealed in the solidity of the working class, weaknesses which are not individual, that do not modify our assessment of the revolutionary spirit of the proletariat in the present historical phase, but which can be traced to the general relations of a trade organization? Have they transformed their experiences into an active and operative consciousness? Have they become skilled in identifying the deepest hidden feelings that move the popular mind, and the negative feelings, the inhibiting forces that fatigue and immobilize the most generous and daring impulses?

The political capacity of the proletarian vanguard (and hence the real revolutionary capacity of the Italian working class) will be revealed by the attitudes that emerge from today's referendum. Many perils threaten the working class; these perils are not external, they are primarily internal. The greatest danger is the lack of a 'spirit of adaptation' to higher circumstances, a spirit of critical, conscious and deliberate adaptation, which cannot and must not be confused with opportunism. Rather, it is the lack of this spirit that leads the working class into opportunism – or, which comes to the same thing, to the triumph of the opportunists among the masses and the maintenance of the hierarchies that have brought the revolutionary movement to its present pass. The revolutionary vanguard needs to consider and analyse the events that have just taken place, not according to its own wishes, passions and will, but objectively, as external data to be subjected to political judgment, and as a historical movement susceptible to conscious extension and development. From a merely objective point of view, the working class can register a great step forward. As a mass guided and disciplined in the factory by its direct representatives, it has proved itself capable of industrial and political self-government. This fact, which should be elementary for revolutionary communists, has consequences of incalculable social importance. The middle classes of the population have compared the strength of the proletariat with the inadequacy of the entrepreneurial class. Half a century ago, the working class was still, as Marx put it, a *sack of potatoes*, a generic imponderable, an amorphous conglomeration of individuals without ideas, without will and without a unitary perspective. Today it is the entrepreneurial class that has become a *sack of potatoes*, an aggregate of the inept and the imbecile, without political capacity, without internal power. The revolutionary events of the past few days have illuminated this position of the two classes contending for the government of production and of society. The prejudice and follies which the capitalist-owned press had disseminated in public opinion have collapsed; the middle classes are lining up with the proletariat, convinced that this young and energetic class holds the key to civilization and human progress. From the test that both classes have had to undergo, the proletariat has emerged higher in public estimation, while capitalism has revealed even further its deficiencies and incapacity. This new political situation has definitely put forward the proletariat as a ruling class; it is a spring that drives it irresistibly towards the conquest of power.

Why then was this result not immediately attained? Or at least, why was no attempt made to attain it? The answer to this question must be sought in the tactics pursued until today, culminating in the referendum. The leaders of the proletarian movement base themselves on the 'masses', in other words they ask the prior permission of the masses before acting, consulting them in the forms and at the time they choose. But a revolutionary movement can only be based on the proletarian vanguard, and must be led without prior consultation, without the apparatus of representative assemblies. Revolution is like war; it must be minutely prepared by a working-class general staff, just as a war is by the army's general staff. Assemblies can only ratify what has already taken place, exalt the successful and implacably punish the unsuccessful. It is the task of the proletarian vanguard to keep the revolutionary spirit constantly awake in the masses, to create the conditions which keep them ready for action, in which the proletariat will respond immediately to the call for revolution. In the same way, the nationalists and imperialists, with their frantic preaching of patriotic vanities and hatred for foreigners, are trying to create the conditions in which the crowd will approve a war that has already been agreed on by the general staff of the army and by the diplomatic service. No war would ever break out if prior

permission had to be obtained from the masses to declare it;
parliaments approve wars because they know they have already
been inexorably decided, because they know that they will be
thrust inexorably aside if they oppose them. Similarly, no
revolutionary movement can be decreed by a workers' national
assembly. To call such an assembly is to confess in advance one's
disbelief in revolution; it amounts, therefore, to exercising a
prejudicial pressure against it.

The proletarian vanguard, which today is disillusioned and
threatened with dissolution, must ask itself whether it is not itself
responsible for this situation. It is a fact that in the General
Confederation of Labour there is no organized revolutionary
opposition, centralized enough to exercise control over the leading
offices and capable not only of replacing one man by another, but
one method by another, one aim by another and one will by
another. This is the real situation, which lamentations, curses and
oaths will not change, only tenacious and patient organizations
and preparation. It is thus essential that the groups of workers
which have been at the head of the masses accept reality as it is, in
order to alter it effectively. They must keep the masses firm and
united behind their programmes and slogans; they must become
capable of producing from among themselves an energetic general
staff, which is able to conduct a broad mass action with intelligence
and daring. Today, we have the referendum; its result must not be
the occasion for dismay and dissolution, but rather a warning of
the need for tighter, more disciplined and better organized action.
The emancipation of the proletariat is not a labour of small
account and of little men; only he who can keep his heart strong
and his will as sharp as a sword when the general disillusionment is
at its worst can be regarded as a fighter for the working class or
called a revolutionary.

Unsigned, *Avanti!*, 24 September 1920. SPWI, 347-9

7 Those Mainly Responsible

If in September 1920 the Turin communists had been anarchists
instead of communists, the factory occupation movement would
have had a very different outcome from the one it actually did
have: this is the essence of an article from Turin in *Umanità Nova*,

which reasserts our heavy responsibility for the failure to make a revolution.[4] What a pity! The Turin communists, in September 1920, were in fact communists and not anarchists. Even then, they believed that 'proletarian revolution' means and can only mean creation of a revolutionary government. Even then, they believed that a revolutionary government can only be created if there exists a revolutionary party, nationally organized, which is capable of leading a mass action towards this historically concrete objective.

The Turin communists belonged to the Italian Socialist Party, and were members of its Turin section; the reformist leaders of the General Confederation of Labour also belonged to that party and that section. The movement had been launched by the reformists. The weekly *L'Ordine Nuovo* of 15 August 1920 clearly shows that the Turin communists were opposed to the action initiated by FIOM – because of the way in which it had been initiated; because of the fact that it had not been preceded by any preparation; and because of the fact that it had no concrete aim. Given these concrete conditions, the movement could only culminate in a revolution on condition that the reformists continued to lead it. If the reformists, once the action had begun and taken on the dimensions and the character which it did, had led it forward to its logical conclusion, certainly the great majority of the proletariat, and broad layers of the petty bourgeoisie and peasantry as well, would have followed their slogans.

If, on the other hand, the Turin communists had begun the insurrection on their own initiative, Turin would have been isolated, proletarian Turin would have been pitilessly crushed by the armed forces of the state. In September 1920, Turin would not even have had the solidarity of the Piedmont region, as it had had in the previous April. The evil campaign which the trade-union officials and Serratian opportunists[5] had waged against the Turin communists after the April strike had had its effect, especially in Piedmont. The comrades from Turin could not even approach those from the region. Not a word of what they said was believed; they were always asked if they had an express mandate from the party leadership. The whole regional organization built up from Turin had completely fallen to pieces. The Turin correspondent of *Umanità Nova*, who perhaps knows the organizational efforts that were made in that period, certainly does not know many other things. The communists sought to put the Turin proletariat in the best conditions from the point of view of a probable insurrection. They knew, however, that elsewhere nothing was being done, nor any slogan being circulated. They knew that the union leaders responsible for the movement had no warlike intentions.

For a very brief period of time, three or four days, the union leaders were extremely favourable to an insurrection, they called wildly for an insurrection. Why? Apparently Giolitti, under pressure from the industrialists, who were openly threatening to overthrow the government by a military *pronunciamento*, wanted to go over from 'homoeopathy' to 'surgery'. He evidently made certain threats. The union leaders lost their heads. They wanted an 'outrage', a local massacre which would justify their reaching an agreement at national level in accordance with reformist traditions. Were we right or wrong to refuse to take part in this infamous game, which was to be played with the blood of the Turin proletariat? By dint of repeating from April onwards that the Turin communists were irresponsible hotheads, 'localists' and adventurers, the reformists had actually ended up by believing this – and by believing that we would lend ourselves to their game. They were not easy, those days of September 1920. In those days we acquired, perhaps belatedly, a precise and resolute conviction of the need for a split. How could men who mistrusted each other, who precisely at the moment of action saw that it was necessary to protect their backs from their own fellow-members, possibly remain together in the same party?

This was the situation, and we were not anarchists but communists, i.e. convinced of the need for a national party if the proletarian revolution was to have the least chance of a successful outcome. But even if we had been anarchists, would we have acted differently? There is a point of reference for answering this question: in September 1920 there did indeed exist anarchists in Italy, there existed a national anarchist movement. What did the anarchists do? Nothing. If we had been anarchists, we would not even have done what was done in Turin in September 1920 – i.e. carried out preparations that were certainly very considerable, seeing that they were accomplished by purely local effort, without assistance, without advice and without any national co-ordination.

If the anarchists reflect well upon the events of September 1920, they cannot fail to reach a single conclusion: the need for a strongly organized and centralized political party. Certainly the

Socialist Party, with its incapacity and its subordination to the trade-union officials, was responsible for the failed revolution. But precisely for that reason, there must exist a party which puts its national organization at the service of the proletarian revolution, and which – through discussion and through an iron discipline – prepares capable men who can see ahead, and who do not know hesitation or wavering.

Unsigned, *L'Ordine Nuovo*, 20 September 1921. SPWII, 68-70

8 Once Again on the Organic Capacities of the Working Class

Six years have passed since September 1920. In the intervening period, many things have changed among the working-class masses who in September 1920 occupied the factories in the metal-working industry. A notable part of the most active and combative workers, who in those years of heroic struggle represented the vanguard of the working class, are outside Italy. Marked with a triple cross on the black lists; after months and months of unemployment; after having tried every way (by changing trade, isolating themselves in small plants, etc., etc.) of remaining in their homeland to continue the revolutionary struggle, and to reconstruct each day the links which each day reaction was destroying; after unheard of sacrifices and sufferings – they were forced to emigrate. Six years are a long time. A new generation has already entered the factories: of workers who in 1920 were still adolescents or children, and who at most took part in political life by acting out in streets the war between the Red Army and the Polish Army, and by refusing to be the Polish one even in a game. Yet the occupation of the factories has not been forgotten by the masses, and this is true not just of the working-class masses but also of the peasant masses. It was the general test of the Italian revolutionary class, which as a class showed that it was mature; that it was capable of initiative; that it possessed an incalculable wealth of creative and organizational energies. If the movement failed, the responsibility cannot be laid at the door of the working class as such, but at that of the Socialist Party, which failed in its duty; which was incapable and inept; which was at the tail of the working class, not at its head.

The occupation of the factories is still on the agenda in the conversations and discussions which take place at the base, between vanguard elements and those who are more backward and passive, or between the former and class enemies. Recently, in a meeting of peasants and artisans in a village of Southern Italy (all sympathizers of our [Communist] party), after a brief report on the present situation two kinds of questions were raised by those present.

1. What is happening in Russia? How are the local authorities organized in Russia? How do they succeed in getting the workers and peasants to agree, given that the former want to buy foodstuffs cheap and the latter want to sell them at a decent price? Are the officers of the Red Army and the functionaries of the Soviet state like officers and functionaries in our country? Are they a different class, or are they workers and peasants?

2. Explain to us why we workers (an artisan was speaking, a blacksmith) abandoned the factories which we had occupied in September 1920. The gentry still say to us: 'Did you occupy the factories, yes or no? Why then did you abandon them? Certainly because without "capital" one cannot do anything. You sent away the capitalists and so the "capital" was not there, and you went bankrupt.' Explain the whole question to us, so that we will be able to reply. We know that the gentry are wrong, but we do not know how to put our arguments and often have to shut our mouths.

The revolutionary impact of the occupation of the factories was enormous, both in Italy and abroad. Why? Because the working masses saw in it a confirmation of the Russian revolution, in a Western country more industrially advanced than Russia, with a working class that was better organized, technically more skilled, and industrially more homogeneous and cohesive than was the Russian proletariat in October 1917. Are we capable of running production for ourselves, in accordance with our interests and a plan of our own? – wondered the workers. Are we capable of reorganizing production in such a way as to transfer society as a whole onto new tracks leading to the abolition of classes and economic equality? The test was positive, within the limits in which it took place and developed; within the limits in which the experiment could be carried through; in the sphere of the problems that were posed and resolved.

The experiment was limited, in general, to relations within the factory. Contacts between one factory and another were minimal from the industrial point of view; they occurred only for purposes of military defence, and even in this sense they were rather empirical and rudimentary.

The positive aspects of the occupation of the factories can be briefly resumed under the following headings.

1. Capacity for self-government of the mass of workers. In normal mass activity, the working class generally appears as a passive element awaiting orders. During struggles, strikes, etc., the masses are required to show the following qualities: solidarity, obedience to the mass organization, faith in their leaders, a spirit of resistance and sacrifice. But the masses are static, like an immense body with a tiny head.

The occupation of the factories required an unprecedented multiplicity of active, leading elements. Each factory had to put together its own government, which was invested at once with political and with industrial authority. Only a part of the technicians and white-collar employees remained at their posts; the majority deserted the plants. The workers had to choose from their own ranks technicians, clerks, managers, foremen, accountants, etc. etc. This task was performed brilliantly. The old management, when it took up its functions again, had no administrative difficulties to overcome. The normal functions of an enterprise had been kept up to date, in spite of the fact that the technical and administrative personnel was extremely limited and made up of 'crude, ignorant' workers.

2. Capacity of the mass of workers to maintain or exceed the capitalist order's level of production. The following occurred. The workforce was reduced – because a tiny proportion did desert their work; because a certain proportion was assigned to military defence; because a certain proportion was working to produce objects that were not precisely for current use, although they were very useful for the proletariat, and because workers had had to replace the majority of technicians and white-collar workers who had deserted – and in spite of all this, production kept up to the earlier level and often exceeded it. More cars were produced at Fiat than before the occupation, and the 'workers'' cars displayed to the public daily by proletarian Fiat were not among the least of the reasons for the undeniable sympathy which the occupation

enjoyed among the general population of the city of Turin, including among intellectuals and even tradesmen (who accepted the workers' goods as excellent currency).

3. Limitless capacity for initiative and creation of the working masses. An entire volume would be needed to cover this point fully. Initiative developed in every direction. In the industrial field, because of the need to resolve technical questions of industrial organization and production. In the military field, in order to turn every slight possibility into an instrument of defence. In the artistic field, through the capacity shown on Sundays to find ways of entertaining the masses by theatrical and other performances, in which *mise-en-scène*, production, everything was devised by the workers. It was really necessary to see with one's eyes old workers, who seemed broken down by decades upon decades of oppression and exploitation, stand upright even in a physical sense during the period of the occupation – see them develop creative activities; suggesting, helping, always active day and night. It was necessary to see these and other sights, in order to be convinced how limitless the latent powers of the masses are, and how they are revealed and develop swiftly as soon as the conviction takes root among the masses that they are arbiters and masters of their own destinies.

As a class, the Italian workers who occupied the factories revealed themselves to be up to their tasks and functions. All the problems which the needs of the movement posed for them to resolve were resolved brilliantly. They could not resolve the problems of re-stocking or communications, because the railways and merchant fleet were not occupied. They could not resolve the financial problems, because the institutes of credit and commercial firms were not occupied. They could not resolve the big national and international problems, because they did not conquer state power. These problems should have been confronted by the Socialist Party and by the unions, which instead capitulated shamefully, giving the immaturity of the masses as a pretext. In reality, it was the leaders who were immature and incapable, not the class. This was the reason why the Livorno split took place and a new party was created, the Communist Party.

[...]

Unsigned, *L'Unità*, 1 October 1926. SPWII, 417-20

IV COMMUNISM 1919–1924

Introduction

In January 1921 the Communist Party of Italy (PCdI) was formed out of a split at the Seventeenth PSI Congress in Livorno, the culmination of two years of acute inner-party conflict. It was an amalgamation of three main currents: a group of left maximalists and two communist fractions, one grouped around Amadeo Bordiga's Naples periodical *Il Soviet*, the other around the Turin *Ordine Nuovo* group. Together these groups carried a third of the delegates with them to found the new party, of which Bordiga became first general secretary. During his leadership in 1921-23 the new party held a course which was to prove politically disastrous at a time when Fascism achieved power in the state (1922) and struggled to consolidate it.

In December 1921 the Communist International (Comintern) launched the 'united front' policy. This called upon Communist parties to engage Socialists in common action at both party and trade union level. In Italy, this would have meant in practice a fusion between the Communists and a group of left-wing Socialists who were seeking affiliation to the Comintern. Fusion in early 1922 would probably have strengthened the left against Fascism, yet a majority of the PCdI, formed precisely out of a split with the Socialists, saw the united front policy as anathema and resisted it until the end of 1923. On the Fascist movement, Bordiga's position was that it was a symptom of capitalist crisis and that it would either collapse or be overthrown. He therefore saw a revolutionary confrontation in Italy as still on the agenda even after the Fascists came to power in October 1922. He argued that in these conditions the working class needed to be decisively led by a vanguard party rather than have its revolutionary will diluted by co-operation with Socialists. At the party's Second Congress at Rome in March 1922, a large majority approved Bordiga's theses on tactics opposing the united front policy (the text of the 'Rome Theses' is reproduced in SPW II, pp. 93-117).

From the autumn of 1923, however, a new leading group of the party began to form around Gramsci and Togliatti. Over the next two and a half years this group was to shift the party away from Bordiga's positions. It was to make a more particularized and accurate assessment of Fascism, develop a conception of the party as a potentially mass organization and become more tractable towards forms of united action and tactical alliance with other organizations.

Four points are perhaps particularly distinctive about Gramsci's political writing in this first period of PCdI activity from the Livorno Congress to his assumption of the party leadership in August 1924. The first is the centrality of the peasant question. For Gramsci the peasants, greatly radicalized at the end of the war, had to carry through a revolution in the underdeveloped south of Italy. The bourgeoisie had no interest in developing the south; on the contrary its interest lay in perpetuating the south's political and economic subordination. Hence agriculture could only be modernized under socialism. This meant an alliance of workers and peasants led by the Communists.

The second point is his attentiveness to a rapidly changing political situation, and his realistic assessment of shifts in the balance of class forces. The PSI, he argues, had failed to respond to the politicization of the peasantry and urban petty bourgeoisie at the end of the war. The peasants had therefore sought a political home instead in the new Catholic party – the PPI – and the petty bourgeoisie among the Fascists. These two political forces had consequently been strengthened at the expense of the parties of the left.

The third point concerns Gramsci's relations with the Comintern. Like Bordiga, he opposed the united front 'from above' (i.e. a formal fusion with the PSI left) and he criticized the centralism by which the Comintern decreed such policies without taking account of different national situations. But, unlike Bordiga, he did not want an open confrontation with the Comintern and after his residence in Moscow as PCdI representative (June 1922-December 1923) he gave increasing priority to disciplined internationalism while insisting on the need for a party strategy based on a rigorous reconnaissance of particular national conditions.

The fourth point concerns the nature of the party. Against the more orthodox conception of the vanguard party held by Bordiga,

Gramsci conceives of a dialectical movement between membership and leadership, in which the impulses of a mass democratic organization can be combined with clear leadership. This conception will be elaborated in the period leading up to the party's Lyons Congress in 1926 and theoretically developed in the prison notebooks in the discussion of democratic versus 'organic' (or bureaucratic) centralism.

1 The War in the Colonies

In a resolution adopted by the Fifth Congress of the Algerian Socialist Workers' Party, held at Constantine in 1902, these words were addressed to the French capitalists:

> If you declare yourselves to be incapable of carrying out this work (educating the indigenous population, giving it a consciousness and moral awareness), thus revealing your impotence, we have the right to ask you just what your intentions in this country are, and whether you have come simply to substitute French for Turkish tax-collectors.

This attitude of the indigenous peoples to the metropolitan countries was intensified considerably by the war. The war between capitalist imperialisms was quickly followed by the revolt of the colonies against the victorious imperialisms. During the war the colonies were exploited to an unprecedented degree, using inflexible and inhuman methods such as can be conceived only in periods of civilization as marvellous as that of capitalism. The indigenous peoples of the colonies were not even left their eyes for weeping; foodstuffs, raw materials, everything possible was combed from the colonies to sustain the resistance of the warring metropolitan peoples. This capitalist vice gripping the colonies worked wonderfully: millions and millions of Indians, Egyptians, Algerians, Tunisians and Tonkinese [Vietnamese] died from hunger or disease as a result of the devastation wrought on the wretched colonial economies by European capitalist competition. How could an Egyptian or Indian peasant make his prices competitive with the English or French or Italian state? Rice, wheat, cotton, wool – all this was secured for us Europeans, while the colonial peasant had to live on herbs and roots, had to subject himself to the harshest *corvée* labour in order to scrape a bare subsistence minimum, and had to suffer the raging of impetuous and untameable famines that rage in India like natural storms. For several years we Europeans have lived at the expense of the death of the coloured peoples: unconscious vampires that we are, we have fed off their innocent blood. As in Balzac's novel, the steaming plate of rice that was placed before our privileged mouths bore within its Hermetic numbers the death sentence of a distant human brother.[1]

But today flames of revolt are being fanned throughout the colonial world. This is the class struggle of the coloured peoples against their white exploiters and murderers. It is the vast irresistible drive towards autonomy and independence of a whole world, with all its spiritual riches. Connective tissues are being recreated to weld together once again peoples whom European domination seemed to have sundered once and for all. Out of its defeat, Turkey itself is regaining prestige, and seems to be setting an example to the world. For millions upon millions of human beings, the Anatolian shepherd is worth more than the Manchester cotton manufacturer; the Sultan is a beacon that beams brighter than any Liverpool shipowner. Armoured cars, tanks and machine-guns perform wonders on the dark skins of the Arab and Hindu peasants. But the extortions of capitalism are far more deadly than modern weapons: they kill women, children and old people through starvation and despair, by degrees, implacably. And those drowsy coloured peoples are now defying aeroplanes, machine-guns and tanks to win independence; to crush the monstrous vampire that feeds off their flesh and blood.

Signed A. G., *L'Ordine Nuovo*, 7 June 1919. SPWI, 59-60

2 Workers and Peasants

[...]

In the countries which are still backward in capitalist terms, like Russia, Italy, France and Spain, there is a clear separation between town and country, between workers and peasants. In agriculture, more or less feudal economic patterns have survived, together with a corresponding mentality. The idea of the modern liberal-capitalist state is still unknown. Economic and political institutions are not seen as historical categories, i.e. as categories having a beginning, then undergoing a process of development, and finally dissolving, after having created the conditions for a higher form of social system. Instead, they are seen as natural, perpetual, irreducible categories. In reality big landed property has remained impervious to free competition – and the modern state has respected its feudal essence, devising juridical formulae such as *fidei commissum*, which effectively perpetuate the investitures and privileges of the feudal regime. Hence the peasant still has the mentality of a glebe serf: he erupts in violent revolt against the 'gentry' every now and then, but he is incapable of seeing himself as a member of a collectivity (the nation for the land-holders, the class for the proletarians), nor can he wage a systematic and permanent campaign designed to alter the economic and political relations of society.

Under such conditions, the psychology of the peasants was inscrutable: their real feelings remained occult, entangled and confused in a system of defence against exploitation that was merely individualist, devoid of logical continuity, inspired largely by guile and feigned servility. Class struggle was confused with brigandage, with blackmail, with burning down woods, with the hamstringing of cattle, with the abduction of women and children, with assaults on the town hall – it was a form of elementary terrorism, without long-term or effective consequences. Objectively, therefore, the peasant's psychology was restricted to a tiny number of elemental feelings dependent upon the social conditions created by the democratic-parliamentary state. The peasant was left completely at the mercy of the landowners and their hangers-on and corrupt public officials; his principal concern was to defend himself physically from the assaults of the elements, and from the abuses and cruel barbarities of the landowners and public functionaries. The peasant has always lived outside the rule of law – he has never had a juridical personality, nor a moral individuality. He lives on as an anarchic element, an independent atom in a chaotic tumult, constrained only by his fear of the police and the devil. He had no understanding of organization, of the state, of discipline. Though patient and tenacious in his individual

efforts to wrest a lean harvest from nature and capable of making
unheard of sacrifices in his family life, he was impatient and
savagely violent in class struggle, incapable of setting himself a
general goal for action and pursuing it with perseverance and
systematic struggle.

Four years of the trenches and exploitation of his blood have
radically changed the peasant psychology. This change occurred
especially in Russia, and was one of the essential factors in the
revolution. What industrialism had not brought about in its normal
process of development was produced by the war. The war forced
those nations which were less advanced in capitalist terms, and
hence less endowed with technological equipment, to enrol all
available men and to oppose wave after wave of living flesh to the
war instruments of the Central Powers. For Russia, the war meant
that individuals who had previously been scattered over a vast
territory came into contact with each other. It meant that humans
were concentrated together uninterruptedly for years on end
under conditions of sacrifice, with the ever present danger of
death, and under a uniform and uniformly ferocious discipline.
The lengthy duration of such conditions of collective living had
profound psychological effects and was rich in unforeseen
consequences.

Selfish, individual instincts were blunted; a common, united
spirit was fashioned; feelings were universalized; the habit of
social discipline was formed. The peasants came to see the state in
all its complex grandeur, its measureless power, its intricate
construction. They came to see the world no longer as something
infinitely vast like the universe and as circumscribed and small as
the village bell-tower, but as a concrete reality consisting of states
and peoples, social strengths and weaknesses, armies and
machines, wealth and poverty. Links of solidarity were forged
which would have taken decades of historical experience and
intermittent struggles to form. Within four years, in the mud and
blood of the trenches, a spiritual world emerged that was avid to
form itself into permanent and dynamic social structures and
institutions.

In this way there emerged the Councils of military delegates on
the Russian front, and the peasant soldiers were able to play an
active part in the Soviets of Petrograd, Moscow and the other
industrial centres and so acquired a consciousness of the unity of

the working class. In this way too, as fast as the Russian army was demobilized and the soldiers returned to their jobs, the entire territory of the Empire, from the Vistula to the Pacific, became covered in a tight-knit network of local Councils, basic organs of the Russian people's reconstruction of their state. It was on this new psychology that the communist propaganda which radiated out from the industrial cities was based, and the same was true of the new social hierarchies freely advocated and accepted as a result of the experience of collective revolutionary living.

Historical conditions in Italy were not and are not very different from those in Russia. The problem of the class unification of the workers and peasants is expressed in identical terms: it will be achieved through the practice of the socialist state and will be based on the new psychology created by communal life in the trenches.

Italian agriculture must radically transform its procedures if it is to emerge from the crisis caused by the war. So much livestock was destroyed that machinery will have to be introduced: there will have to be a rapid transition to centralized industrial farming, with generously equipped technical institutions available. But a transformation of this order could not occur under a regime of private property without provoking a disaster: it will have to be effected by a socialist state, and in the interests of the peasants and workers combined in communist labour units. In the past, the introduction of machinery into the process of production has always provoked profound unemployment crises, only gradually overcome through the elasticity of the labour market. Today, labour conditions have been radically altered, and agrarian unemployment has already become an insoluble problem as a result of the virtual impossibility of emigrating. The industrial transformation of agriculture can only be achieved with the agreement of the poor peasants, via a dictatorship of the proletariat that is embodied in Councils of industrial workers and poor peasants.

Factory workers and poor peasants are the two driving forces of the proletarian revolution. For them, especially, communism is a vital necessity: its advent signifies life and liberty, while the continued existence of private property signifies the imminent danger of being crushed, of losing everything, including life itself. They are the revolution's irreducible element; they sustain revolutionary enthusiasm; they represent the iron will not to accept compromises, but to carry on implacably until everything has been accomplished, without either being demoralized by temporary and partial set-backs or manufacturing too many illusions as a result of easy victories.

They represent the backbone of the revolution, the iron battalions of the advancing proletarian army, which overturns obstacles by its sheer weight or lays siege to them with its human tides that demolish and corrode, through patient work and tireless sacrifice. For them, communism represents civilization: it stands for the system of historical conditions in which they will acquire a personality, a dignity, a culture, and through which they will become a spirit creating progress and beauty.

Any revolutionary work has a chance of succeeding only to the degree that it is based on the necessities of their life and on the needs of their culture. It is essential that the 'leaders' of the socialist and proletarian movement understand this. And it is essential that they see the urgency of the problem of giving this irrepressible revolutionary force the structure best adapted to its diffuse mentality.

In the backward conditions of the pre-war capitalist economy, there was no scope for the emergence and development of mass peasant organizations on a wide scale, in which the agricultural workers could acquire an organic conception of class struggle as well as the discipline needed to reconstruct the state after the capitalist catastrophe.

The spiritual advances made during the war, the communistic experiences accumulated over four years of bloody exploitation, undergone collectively, standing elbow to elbow in the muddy, bloody trenches – all this will be frittered away unless every individual is involved in organs of a new collective life. In the functioning and practice of these, the advances can be consolidated, the experiences developed and linked and directed consciously towards the accomplishment of a concrete historical goal. Organized in this way, the peasants will become an element of order and of progress; left to themselves, incapable as they are of waging any systematic and disciplined action, they will become a disordered rabble, a tumultuous horde driven to the cruellest barbarities by the unprecedented sufferings which are becoming ever more frighteningly evident.

The communist revolution is essentially a problem of organization and discipline. Given the actual objective conditions of Italian society, the protagonists of the revolution will be the industrial cities, with their tightly packed and homogeneous masses of factory workers. Hence we must devote maximum attention to the new life that the new form of class struggle is evoking within the factory and in the process of industrial production. But with the forces of the factory workers alone, the revolution will not be able to establish itself on a stable and widespread basis. The cities must be welded to the countryside; institutions of poor peasants must be set up in the countryside, on which the socialist state can be established and developed, and through which the socialist state will be able to foster the introduction of machinery and direct the immense process of transformation of the agrarian economy. In Italy this undertaking is not so difficult as it might seem. During the war, vast numbers of the rural population entered the urban factories; communist propaganda rapidly took root among them. They can now act as a bond between the town and countryside. They must be used to mount an intense propaganda campaign in the countryside, to destroy suspicion and resentment. Taking advantage of their profound understanding of the rural psychology and the confidence they inspire, they must be used precisely to begin the activity necessary to bring about the emergence and development of the new institutions that will draw the vast forces of the agricultural workers into the communist movement.

Unsigned, *L'Ordine Nuovo*, 2 August 1919. SPWI, 83-7

3 The Livorno Congress

The Livorno Congress is destined to become one of the most important historical events in contemporary Italian life.[2] At Livorno, the question whether the Italian working class has the capacity to form an autonomous class party from its own ranks will finally be resolved. The question whether the experiences of four years of imperialist war, and two years of misery for the productive forces all over the world, will succeed in making the Italian working class conscious of its historical mission will also be resolved.

The working class is both a national and an international class. It must place itself at the head of the working people struggling to emancipate themselves from the yoke of industrial and financial capitalism on both a national and international scale. The national task of the working class is determined by the process of development of Italian capitalism and its official expression, the bourgeois state. Italian capitalism came to power by following this line of development: it subjected the countryside to the industrial cities and central and southern Italy to the North. In the Italian bourgeois state, the question of relations between town and countryside is expressed not only as a question of the relations between the great industrial cities and the countryside immediately surrounding them, but also as a question of the relations between one part of the national territory and another – quite distinct and characteristic – part. Capitalism exercises its predominance and its exploitative practices in the following manner: within the factory, directly over the working class; but within the state, over broader layers of the Italian working people, made up of poor peasants and semi-proletarians. What is indisputable is that only the working class, by seizing political and economic power from the hands of the bankers and capitalists, is in a position to resolve the central problem of national life in Italy – the Southern problem. What is indisputable is that only the working class can bring the painful task of unification that the Risorgimento began to a successful conclusion. The bourgeoisie has unified the Italian people in terms of territory. The working class has the task of concluding this work of the bourgeoisie and unifying the Italian people in economic and spiritual terms. This can happen only by smashing the bourgeois state machine, which is constructed on the hierarchical dominance of industrial and financial capitalism over the nation's other productive forces. Such an event can happen only through the revolutionary efforts of the working class directly subjected to capitalism. It can only happen in Milan, Turin, Bologna, in the great industrial cities that generate those millions of threads which make up the network of industrial and finance capitalism's dominance over the rest of the country's productive forces. In Italy, as a result of the particular configuration of the country's economic and political structure, not only is it true that by emancipating itself the working class will emancipate all the other oppressed and exploited classes, but it is no less a fact that the only way these other classes will ever emancipate themselves is to enter into a close alliance with the working class, and to hold by this alliance through even the harshest sufferings and the cruellest trials.

The break between communists and reformists that will occur at Livorno will have the following special significance. The revolutionary working class will break with those degenerate socialist currents that have decayed into state parasitism. It will break with those currents that sought to exploit the position of superiority enjoyed by the North over the South in order to create proletarian aristocracies; that erected a co-operative protectionist system alongside the bourgeois protectionist system of tariffs (the legal expression of the predominance of industrial and financial capitalism over the other productive forces of the nation), in the belief that they could emancipate the working class behind the backs of the majority of the working people.

The reformists point to the socialism of Reggio Emilia as 'exemplary'; they expect us to believe that the whole of Italy and the whole world can become one great Reggio Emilia.[3] The revolutionary working class asserts its repudiation of such spurious forms of socialism. The emancipation of the workers cannot be secured through taking over a few privileges, through a workers' aristocracy or through parliamentary compromise and ministerial blackmail. The workers' emancipation can be secured only through an alliance between the industrial workers of the North and the poor peasants of the South – an alliance designed to smash the bourgeois state; found the workers' and peasants' state; and construct a new apparatus of industrial production that will serve the needs of agriculture, serve to industrialize the backward agriculture of Italy and hence raise the level of the national produce to the benefit of the working masses.

The Italian workers' revolution and the participation of the Italian working people in world affairs can come about only in the context of the world revolution. Already there exist the seeds of a world workers' government in the Executive Committee of the Communist International that emerged at the Second Congress. At

Livorno, the vanguard of the Italian working class, the communist fraction of the Socialist Party, will emphasize that disciplined loyalty to the first world government of the working class is necessary and unavoidable – indeed it will make this the central point of the Congress discussion. The Italian working class accepts a maximum of discipline, because it wants the working classes of all other nations to similarly accept and observe a maximum of discipline.

The Italian working class knows that the condition for its own self-emancipation, and for its ability to emancipate all the other classes exploited and oppressed by capitalism in Italy, is the existence of a system of world revolutionary forces all conspiring to the same end. The Italian working class is willing to help the other working classes in their efforts towards liberation, but it would also like some guarantee that the other classes will help it in its own efforts. This assurance can be given only by a powerfully centralized international authority, which enjoys the full and sincere confidence of all its members and is in a position to launch its forces with the same speed and precision that the world authority of capitalism achieves, on its own account and in the interests of the bourgeoisie.

Thus it should be obvious that the questions which are currently tormenting the Socialist Party, and which will be resolved at the Livorno Congress, are not simply internal party questions or personal conflicts between individuals. At Livorno, the destiny of the working people of Italy will be under discussion. At Livorno, a new era in the history of the Italian nation will begin.

Unsigned, *L'Ordine Nuovo*, 13 January 1921. SPWI, 375-7

4 Parties and Masses

[...]

Politically, the broad masses only exist insofar as they are organized within political parties. The changes of opinion which occur among the masses under pressure from the determinant economic forces are interpreted by the parties, which first split into tendencies and then into a multiplicity of new organic parties. Through this process of disarticulation, new association, and fusion of homogeneous entities, a more profound and intimate process of breakdown of democratic society is revealed. This leads to a definitive alignment of conflicting classes, for preservation or for conquest of power over the state and productive apparatus.

In the period which lasted from the armistice to the occupation of the factories, the Socialist Party represented a majority of the Italian working people, made up of three basic classes: the proletariat, the petty bourgeoisie and the poor peasants. Of these three classes, only the proletariat was essentially and therefore permanently revolutionary. The other two classes were 'occasionally' revolutionary: they were 'war socialists', who accepted the idea of revolution in general because of the sentiments of anti-governmental rebellion which germinated during the war. Since the Socialist Party was predominantly made up of petty-bourgeois and peasant elements, it could have made the revolution only in the first period after the armistice, when those sentiments of anti-government revolt were still alive and active. Furthermore, since the Socialist Party was predominantly made up of petty-bourgeois and peasant elements (whose mentality is not very different from that of urban petty bourgeois), it could not fail to waver and hesitate, without any clear or precise programme, without a line of march, and especially without an internationalist consciousness.

The occupation of the factories, basically proletarian, found the Socialist Party – only partially proletarian and already, under the first blows of Fascism, undergoing a crisis of consciousness in its other constitutive parts – unprepared. The end of the occupation of the factories threw the Socialist Party into total confusion. Its infantile and sentimental revolutionary beliefs were utterly confounded. The pains of war had been partly deadened (a revolution is not made because of memories of the past!). Bourgeois rule still appeared strong in the person of Giolitti and in the activity of the Fascists. The reformist leaders asserted that to think of communist revolution at all was insane. Serrati asserted that it was insane to think of communist revolution in Italy, in that period.[4] Only a minority of the party, made up of the most advanced and educated part of the industrial proletariat, did not change its communist and internationalist viewpoint; was not demoralized by what was occurring daily; and did not allow itself to be taken in by the bourgeois state's apparent strength and energy. Thus the Communist Party was born, first autonomous and independent organization of the industrial proletariat – the only class of the people that is essentially and permanently revolutionary.

The Communist Party did not at once become a party of the broadest masses. This proves only one thing: the conditions of great demoralization and dejection into which the masses had been plunged after the political failure of the occupation of the factories. In a great many leaders, faith was extinguished. What had previously been vaunted was now derided. The most intimate and sensitive feelings of the proletarian consciousness were vilely trampled on by these junior officers of the leadership, who had become sceptical, corrupted by repentance and remorse for their past of maximalist demagogy. The popular masses, who immediately after the armistice had aligned themselves around the Socialist Party, became dismembered, fluid, dispersed. The petty bourgeois who had sympathized with socialism now sympathized with Fascism. The peasants, now without support in the Socialist Party, tended to give their sympathies to the Popular Party.[5]

This confusion of the former forces of the Socialist Party with the Fascists on the one hand and the *popolari* on the other was not without its consequences. The Popular Party drew closer to the Socialist Party. In the parliamentary election, Popular 'open' slates in every constituency were filled with hundreds and thousands of names of Socialist candidates. In the municipal elections which have taken place in some country districts since the general election, the Socialists have often not put forward a minority slate but advised their supporters to vote for the Popular one. In Bergamo, this phenomenon took a sensational form: the *popolari* left-wingers split away from the Catholic organization and fused with the Socialists, founding a Chamber of Labour and a weekly newspaper respectively led and written by Socialists and *popolari* together.

Objectively, this process of Popular-Socialist *rapprochement* represents an advance. The peasant class is becoming united; acquiring consciousness and the idea of overall solidarity; breaking the religious carapace in the Popular camp; and breaking the carapace of petty-bourgeois anti-clerical culture in the Socialist camp. As a result of this tendency among its rural members, the Socialist Party is becoming further and further detached from the industrial proletariat, making it seem that the strong unitary bond which the Socialist Party appeared to have created between city and countryside is being broken. However, since this bond did not really exist, no real damage has derived from the new situation. On the contrary, a real advantage is becoming clear: the Popular Party is undergoing an extremely powerful swing to the left and becoming increasingly secular. The final result will be that its right wing, made up of big and medium landowners, will split off. In other words, it will decisively enter the field of the class struggle, with a consequent tremendous weakening of bourgeois rule.

The same phenomenon is beginning to appear in the Fascist camp. The urban petty bourgeoisie, politically strengthened by all the defectors from the Socialist Party, had sought after the armistice to put to advantage the skill in military organization and action which it had acquired during the war. The Italian war was led, in the absence of an effective general staff, by the junior officers, i.e. by the petty bourgeoisie. The disappointments suffered during the war aroused extremely powerful sentiments of anti-governmental rebellion in this class which, having lost the military unity of its cadres after the armistice, became fragmented among the various mass parties and infused them with the ferment of rebellion – but also with uncertainty, wavering and demagogy.

When the strength of the Socialist Party declined after the occupation of the factories, this class, with lightning speed, under pressure from that same general staff which had exploited it during the war, reconstructed its cadres militarily and organized itself on a national scale. Extremely swift evolution; extremely swift appearance of a constitutional crisis. The urban petty bourgeoisie, a toy in the hands of the general staff and the most retrograde forces in the government, allied itself with the landowners and broke the peasant organizations on their behalf. The Rome pact between Fascists and Socialists marked the halting-point of this blind and politically disastrous policy of the urban petty bourgeoisie, which came to understand that it was selling its 'birthright' for a mess of pottage.[6] If Fascism had gone on with punitive expeditions of the Treviso, Sarzana or Roccastrada type, the population would have risen *en masse*.[7] Moreover, even in the event of a popular defeat, it is certainly not the petty bourgeoisie who would have captured power, but rather the general staff and the big landowners. The Fascists are once again drawing closer to the Socialists; the petty bourgeoisie is seeking to break its links with large-scale landed property, and to have a political programme which ends up by strangely resembling that of Turati and D'Aragona.[8]

This is the present situation of the Italian popular masses – great confusion, replacing the artificial unity created by the war and personified by the Socialist Party. A great confusion which has found its points of dialectical polarization in the Communist Party, independent organization of the industrial proletariat; in the Popular Party, organization of the peasantry; and in Fascism, organization of the petty bourgeoisie. The Socialist Party, which from the armistice to the occupation of the factories represented the demagogic confusion of these three classes of the working people, is today the major exponent and the most notable victim of the process of disarticulation (towards a new, definitive order) which the popular masses of Italy are undergoing as a consequence of the breakdown of democracy.

Unsigned, *L'Ordine Nuovo*, 25 September 1921. SPW II, 71-4

5 What the Relations Should be Between the PCdI and the Comintern

Up till now, we have adopted an attitude towards the Comintern that has appeared equivocal. While we have proclaimed the utmost formal discipline and used language more appropriate for inferiors speaking to their superiors than for use between equals, we have acted in such a way as to give the impression that we were ready to do anything effectively to evade the directives established by the International Congresses and by the Executive Committee. It is a principle of orientation that has now become fundamental that every local attitude must have an international reflection, and can lead to an international process of organization, or at least a movement, that will bring about the emergence of factions within the Comintern. It is certain that the Executive will combat sharply any manifestation of such a kind. One procedure which the Executive regards as being of the highest importance is that there should always be unanimity in votes. This is not simply a formal question. From the entire experience of the Russian revolution it is clear that the absence of unanimity in important public votes produces quite specific attitudes among the broad masses: political enemies are polarized towards the minority, enlarging and generalizing its positions; they clandestinely publish manifestoes and programmes, etc., perhaps even signed by the oppositionists or by a group of their friends; and they carry out a whole agitational activity which may become extremely dangerous at a certain juncture. A defensive approach to such manoeuvres is unanimity in voting, which appears in the eyes of the public as an agreement reached and as proof of the most open unity. From this principle, which has become fundamental for the Communist parties in so far as they must take up positions today with an eye to tomorrow, there flow corollaries which are relevant to our attitudes too: for example, the assertion that we will observe discipline even if we are not convinced, the threat of resignations, etc. Indeed, this attitude is more dangerous in so far as it gives rise to, or can give rise to rumours and whisperings, and can lead to pseudo-revelations from behind the scenes which can have very grave repercussions in the international arena. It is therefore better to raise questions in their full dimensions in private discussions, upholding one's own point of view proudly and showing that one is also ready to struggle. Naturally, such questions can arise only within the limits of the statutes and of the decisions already taken by the various Congresses and Conferences.

We are in a questionable position, in view of the international situation. The tactic of the united front, laid down with considerable precision by the Russian comrades, both technically and in the general approach to its practical application, has *in no country* found the party or the men capable of concretizing it. Germany, where it seemed until recently that exemplary things had been achieved, has been strongly criticized. The great majority of the German party has not understood this tactic, and the minority is the expression of this widespread state of mind. The Frankfurt delegation sent to Amsterdam was only capable of pursuing a bureaucratic practice, and for that reason was recalled. Obviously, all this cannot be accidental. There is something not functioning in the international field as a whole, there is a weakness and inadequacy of leadership. The Italian question must be seen in this framework, not as something which depends on the ill-will of individuals and which can be modified by the good will of the first rough fellow who decides to become a Marcellus.[9] We must argue that we want to pose the problem to the other parties in this way, and must utilize whatever elements are available to us if there is a refusal to recognize our good will and correct conduct.

The present majority of the CP intends to defend to the last its position and historical role in Italy, where the unified Communist Party must be constituted with an ideological centre which is neither the traditional Socialist one nor a compromise with that. We are defending the future of the Italian revolution. The situation of the Socialist Party to a great extent depends upon a similar attitude in a group of Socialist leaders. They defend and will defend to the last and with every means their political profile and their future. We may have made mistakes and we are willing to amend them, but we are not willing to allow the centre of attraction and assimilation of new elements entering the Italian section of the Comintern to be shifted onto a new basis – represented by individuals who want to make a compromise with the Socialists on the fundamental issue.[10] The attitude of the Comintern and the activity of its representatives is bringing disintegration and corruption into the Communist ranks. We are determined to struggle against the elements who would liquidate our Party and against the corrupt elements. The situation of illegality and exile makes this obligatory. We do not want what happened in Hungary and in Yugoslavia to be repeated in Italy. If the Comintern too receives a few blows as we strike back, we should not be blamed for that: it is a mistake to ally oneself with untrustworthy elements.

Handwritten notes, probably written in Moscow in June 1923.
SPWII, 154-6

6 [Letter to Togliatti, Terracini and Others]

Vienna, 9 February 1924

[...] A new phase is beginning in the history not just of our party but of our country too. It is, therefore, necessary that we should enter a phase of greater clarity in relations within the party, and in relations between the party and the International. I do not want to run on too long. I will simply deal with a few points in the hope that they will suffice to illuminate also the questions left on one side.

One of the most serious errors which have characterized and continue to characterize our party's activity can be summed up in the same words as those used in the second of the theses on tactics: 'It would be wrong to see these two factors of consciousness and will as faculties which can be obtained from or should be demanded of individuals, since they are only realized through the integration of the activity of many individuals into a unitary collective organism.' This concept, correct if it refers to the working class, is mistaken and extremely dangerous if referred to the party. Before Livorno, it was the conception of Serrati, who maintained that the party as a whole was revolutionary even if socialists of various shapes and colours cohabited within it. At the congress where the Russian Social-Democrats split, this conception was upheld by the Mensheviks, who said it was the party as a whole that counted, not its individual members. So far as the latter were concerned, it was enough that they should declare themselves to be socialists. In our party, this conception has been partly responsible for the opportunist danger. For one cannot deny that the minority was born and won disciples as a result of the absence of discussion and polemic within the party, i.e. as a result of our failure to give importance to individual comrades or to seek to orient them a little more concretely than can be done through decrees and peremptory orders.

In our party, we have had another aspect of the danger to lament: the withering of all individual activity; the passivity of the mass of members; the stupid confidence that there is always somebody else who is thinking of everything and taking care of everything. This situation has had the most serious repercussions in the organizational field. The party has lacked the possibility of choosing, with rational criteria, the trustworthy elements to whom particular tasks could be assigned. The choice has been made empirically, according to the personal knowledge of individual leaders, and has most often fallen on elements who did not enjoy the confidence of the local organizations and therefore saw their work sabotaged. And it should be added that the work carried out has only been controlled to the most minimal extent, and that in the party there has therefore been produced a real separation between the membership and the leadership.

This situation still continues and seems to me to contain

innumerable dangers. In my stay in Moscow, I did not find a single one of the political exiles, though they came from every different part of Italy and were among the most active elements, who understood the position of our party or did not criticize the C[entral] C[ommittee] harshly (while, of course, observing fully the norms of discipline and obedience). The error of the party has been to have accorded priority in an abstract fashion to the problem of party organization, which in practice has simply meant creating an apparatus of functionaries who could be depended on for their orthodoxy towards the official view. It was believed, and it is still believed, that the revolution depends only on the existence of such an apparatus; and it is sometimes even believed that its existence can bring about the revolution.

The party has lacked any organic activity of agitation and propaganda, although this should have had all our attention and involved the formation of genuine specialists in this field. No attempt has been made to stimulate the masses, at every opportunity, to express themselves in the same direction as the Communist Party. Every event, every anniversary of a local or national or world-wide nature should have served to agitate the masses by means of the communist cells: putting through resolutions; distributing leaflets. This has not been accidental. The Communist Party has even been against the formation of factory cells. Any participation of the masses in the activity and internal life of the party, other than on big occasions and following a formal decree from the centre, has been seen as the result of a dialectical process, in which the spontaneous movement of the revolutionary masses and the organizing and directing will of the centre converge. It has been seen merely as something suspended in the air; something with its own autonomous and self-generated development; something which the masses will join when the situation is right and the crest of the revolutionary wave is at its highest point, or when the party centre decides to initiate an offensive and stoops to the level of the masses in order to arouse them and lead them into action. Naturally, since things do not work out in this way, areas of opportunistic infection have formed without the centre knowing anything about them. These have had their reflection in the parliamentary group, and subsequently, in a more organic form, in the minority.

This conception has had its influence on the fusion issue. The question that was always put to the Comintern was the following: 'Do you think that our party is still at the nebular stage, or that its formation has been completed?' The truth is that historically a party is never definitive and never will be. For it will become definitive only when it has become the whole population, in other words when it has disappeared. Until it disappears because it has achieved the ultimate aims of communism, it will pass through a whole series of transitory phases, and will from time to time absorb new elements in the two forms which are historically possible: through individual recruitment, or through the recruitment of smaller or larger groups. The situation was made even more difficult for our party, as a result of its disagreements with the Comintern. If the International is a world party, even taking this with many pinches of salt, it is obvious that the development of the party and the forms it can take depend on two factors and not just one. They depend, in other words, not just on the national Executive, but also and especially on the International Executive, which is the stronger. To repair the situation, to succeed in impressing the orientation which Amadeo [Bordiga] wants on the development of our party, it is necessary to conquer the International Executive, in other words to become the hub of a general opposition. Politically this is the result one arrives at, and it is natural that the International Executive should seek to break the back of the Italian Executive.

Amadeo has a whole theory about this, and in his system everything is logically coherent and consistent. He thinks that the tactic of the International reflects the Russian situation, i.e. was born on the terrain of a backward and primitive capitalist civilization. For him, this tactic is extremely voluntaristic and theatrical, because only with an extreme effort of will was it possible to obtain from the Russian masses a revolutionary activity which was not determined by the historical situation. He thinks that for the more developed countries of central and western Europe, this tactic is inadequate or even useless. In these countries, the historical mechanism functions according to all the approved schemes of Marxism. There exists the historical determinism which was lacking in Russia, and therefore the overriding task must be the organization of the party as an end in itself.

I think that the situation is quite different. Firstly, because the political conception of the Russian communists was formed on an international and not on a national terrain. Secondly, because in central and western Europe the development of capitalism has not only determined the formation of the broad proletarian strata, but also – and as a consequence – has created the higher stratum, the labour aristocracy, with its appendages in the trade-union bureaucracy and the social-democratic groups. The determination, which in Russia was direct and drove the masses onto the streets for a revolutionary uprising, in central and western Europe is complicated by all these political superstructures, created by the greater development of capitalism. This makes the action of the masses slower and more prudent, and therefore requires of the revolutionary party a strategy and tactics altogether more complex and long-term than those which were necessary for the Bolsheviks in the period between March and November 1917.

But the fact that Amadeo has this conception, and that he seeks to achieve its victory not merely on a national scale but also internationally, is one thing. He is a convinced man, and struggles with great skill and great elasticity to obtain his objective; to avoid compromising his theses; to postpone any Comintern sanctions which might prevent him from continuing until the historical period in which the revolution in western and central Europe deprives Russia of the hegemonic position it holds today. But that we, who are not convinced of the historical truth of this conception, should continue to ally ourselves with it politically and thereby give it the international status which it at present enjoys, is quite another thing. Amadeo approaches things from the viewpoint of an international minority, but we must approach things from the viewpoint of a national majority.

We cannot, therefore, wish the leadership of the party to be given to representatives of the minority on the grounds that they are in agreement with the International, even if after the discussion opened up by the manifesto the majority of the party remains with the present leaders. This in my view is the central point, which must determine our attitude politically. If we agreed with Amadeo's theses, of course, we ought to ask ourselves whether, having the majority of the party with us, it would be better to remain in the International, with a national leadership drawn from the minority, taking our time and waiting for a reversal of the situation to prove us correct theoretically; or

whether it would be better to break away. But if we do not agree
with the theses, to sign the manifesto means taking full responsibility for the following equivocal alternatives: either, if there is a
majority for Amadeo's theses, to accept a minority leadership – we
who do not agree with the theses, and could therefore resolve the
situation organically; or else to remain in a minority, when by virtue
of our ideas we are in agreement with the majority which would
align itself with the International. This would mean our political
liquidation; and to split from Amadeo after such a state of affairs
would appear extremely distasteful and odious.

Suggestions for our future work. I do not want to go very deeply
into this subject, because it would require a great deal of space to
deal with it adequately. I will content myself with a few suggestions.
The future work of the party will have to be renewed both organi-
zationally and politically.

In the organizational field, I think it is necessary to give a greater
role to the CC and make it do more work, in so far as this is possible
given the situation. I think it is necessary to establish more clearly
the relations which should exist between the various party bodies,
fixing more precisely and strictly the division of labour and the
allocation of responsibilities. Two new bodies and activities must be
created. A control commission, made up predominantly of old
workers, should in the last instance adjudicate litigious questions
which do not have immediate political repercussions, in other words
which do not require an immediate intervention by the Executive. It
should also keep the status of party members under continuous
review, through periodic checks. And an agitation and propaganda
committee should collect all such local and national material as is
necessary and useful for the party's agitational and propaganda
activity. It should study local situations, propose forms of agitation,
and compose leaflets and programmes to orient the work of the
local bodies. It should be based on a whole national organization,
whose constitutive nucleus will be the ward in the big urban centres
and the rural district in the countryside. It should begin its work by a
census of party members who should be divided up for organizational purposes according to their seniority and the posts which they
have held, the abilities they have shown, and of course their moral
and political talents.

A precise division of labour must be established between the

Executive and the Clandestine Bureau. Precise responsibilities and functions established, which cannot be violated without serious disciplinary sanctions. I think that this is one of the weakest sides of our party, demonstrating most clearly how the centralism installed has been more a bureaucratic formality and banal confusion of responsibilities and functions than a rigorous system of organization.

In the political field, it is necessary to draw up detailed theses on the Italian situation and the possible phases of its further development. In 1921-22, the party had the following official conception: that the advent of a fascist or military dictatorship was impossible. With great difficulty, I managed to get this conception removed from the theses and prevent it from being written down, securing basic modifications in theses 51 and 52 on tactics. Now, it seems to me that the party is falling into another error, closely linked to the previous one. Then, no importance was accorded to the silent, latent opposition to Fascism of the industrial bourgeoisie, and a social-democratic government was not thought possible, but only one of these three solutions: dictatorship of the proletariat (least probable); dictatorship of the general staff on behalf of the industrial bourgeoisie and the court; dictatorship of Fascism; this conception bound our political action and led us into many mistakes.

Now, once again, no account is being taken of the emerging opposition of the industrial bourgeoisie – especially that which is beginning to take shape in the South, with a more explicitly territorial character and thus presenting certain aspects of a national question. It is more or less believed that a proletarian revival can and must only benefit our party. I think, however, that if there is a revival our party will still be in a minority; that the majority of the working class will go with the reformists; and that the liberal-democratic bourgeois will still have a great deal to say. That the situation is actively revolutionary, I do not doubt; and that therefore within a given space of time our party will have the majority with it. But although this period will perhaps not be long chronologically, it will undoubtedly be packed with supplementary phases, which we will have to foresee with some accuracy in order to be able to manoeuvre and avoid making mistakes which would prolong the trials of the proletariat.

I believe, moreover, that the party should tackle in a practical sense certain problems which have never been confronted, and whose resolution has simply been left to such elements of the party as were directly affected by them. The problem of winning the Milanese proletariat is a national problem for our party, which should be solved with all means the party has at its disposal, rather than just with Milanese means. If we do not have with us, in a stable fashion, the overwhelming majority of the Milanese proletariat, we cannot carry out or keep going the revolution in Italy as a whole. It is, therefore, necessary to bring worker elements from other cities into Milan; to introduce them to work in the factories; to enrich the legal and clandestine organization in Milan with the best elements from all Italy. Thus, I think it is roughly speaking necessary to inject into the Milanese working class at least a hundred comrades willing to work themselves to death for the party.

Another problem of this kind is that of the seamen, closely linked to the problem of the military fleet. Italy lives from the sea; to fail to concern oneself with the problem of the seamen, as one of the most important questions and worthy of the party's maximum attention, would mean not to think concretely about revolution. When I think that for a long time the leader of our work among seamen was a boy like Caroti's son, it makes me shudder.[11] Another problem is that of the railwaymen, which we have always looked at from a purely trade-union point of view, whereas it transcends that definition and is a national political problem of the first order.

Fourth and last of these problems is that of the South, which we have misunderstood just as the Socialists did, considering that it could be solved within the normal framework of our general political activity. I have always been convinced that the South would become the grave of Fascism, but I also think that it will be the greatest reservoir and the marshalling-ground for national and international reaction if, before the revolution, we do not adequately study its problems and are not prepared for everything.

I think I have given you a fairly clear idea of my position, and of the differences which exist between it and what comes out from the manifesto. Since I think that to a great extent you are more in agreement with my position, on which we found ourselves together for some considerable time, I hope that you still have the possibility of deciding otherwise than you were on the point of doing.

With the most fraternal greetings.

Masci
SPWII, 196-203

V FASCIST REACTION AND COMMUNIST STRATEGY 1924–1926

Introduction

These writings date from the period of Gramsci's leadership of the PCdI (August 1924 to November 1926) and deal principally with three subjects: Fascism, developments in the Soviet Union and prospects for revolution in Italy.

In the summer of 1924 the Fascist movement was rocked by its first serious crisis since coming to power (see 'The Crisis of the Middle Classes' and 'Elements of the Situation'). Gramsci focused both on the immediate political crisis precipitated by the murder of the Socialist parliamentary deputy Giacomo Matteotti in June and on what he saw as a breakdown in the class alliance between the capitalists and petty bourgeoisie (the middle classes referred to in the first piece in this Section). Whereas in 1921-22 the middle classes had formed the mass base of the Fascist movement by making an alliance with the capitalists against the working class, they were now being economically squeezed by Fascism. This, Gramsci believed, would propel them towards an alliance with the proletariat.

The Matteotti murder generated a wave of popular protest and led to the formation by the other parliamentary parties (Liberals, Republicans, Catholics, Socialists) of an opposition known as the Aventine. The PCdI initially joined the opposition committee but withdrew when the other parties refused to back its demand for a general strike. Although some members of the party's right wing favoured a collaboration with the Aventine, the majority, including Gramsci, did not because they considered the Aventine's opposition feebly legalitarian, constrained within the limits of bourgeois democracy, and because they believed that after a phase of democratic transition the situation would turn to the advantage of the working class and be ripe for socialist revolution.

With hindsight it is easy to see that Gramsci's reading of the situation in 1924 overestimated the crisis of Fascism and underestimated the depth of its political and ideological resources.

One can also see that his attitude towards the legalitarian opposition was too sectarian under the circumstances, given that by the end of 1926 the Fascists had installed a dictatorship and outlawed all the opposition parties. Nonetheless he was quite correct in characterizing the immediate prospect for the left as 'democratic' rather than revolutionary – a characterization which was opposed by the left of the PCdI – and in recognizing the need to broaden the mass base of the anti-fascist opposition by applying the united front tactic.

Gramsci had acquired first-hand knowledge of the Russian situation during his time in Moscow and developments in the Soviet Union constituted an essential point of reference for his strategic thinking as leader of the Italian party. In 1924 Lenin's successors in the party leadership were becoming bitterly divided over the course of the revolution. Trotsky criticized both the bureaucratic stagnation of inner-party life and the New Economic Policy (NEP) for retarding socialism by entrenching a market economy in agriculture. He said the party was returning to the pre-1917 prejudice that the revolution had to pass through discrete phases and could not advance to socialism until capitalism had matured. He argued instead for the concept of 'permanent revolution': an uninterrupted transition from one phase to another sustained by a wave of revolutions abroad.

Gramsci initially seems to have judged the divisions among the Bolsheviks from Trotsky's viewpoint. He wrote to Togliatti and others from Vienna in February 1924: 'Demanding a greater intervention of the proletarian elements in the life of the party and a diminution in the powers of the bureaucracy, they [Trotsky and the left opposition] want basically to ensure the socialist and proletarian character of the revolution and prevent a gradual transition to that democratic dictatorship – carapace for a developing capitalism – which was still the programme of Zinoviev and Co. in November 1917.' (SPW II, p. 192). He was also alarmed by the ferocity of Stalin's criticisms of Trotsky. Writing to his wife he remarked 'I do not know Trotsky's article, nor Stalin's, ... I cannot understand the latter's attack which seems to me highly irresponsible and dangerous.' (*Duemila pagine di Gramsci*, ed. G. Ferrata and N. Gallo, Milan 1964, Vol.II, p. 29). He was to express similar anxieties again in 1926 (see 'Letter to the Central Committee of the CPSU') by which time the inner party crisis had become acute. By now, however, his political judgement of the opposition had changed. He had come to accept the pro-NEP positions of the majority (Stalin and Bukharin) against the positions of the joint opposition (Trotsky, Zinoviev, Kamenev). Yet his criticisms of the CPSU's handling of its internal divisions remained outspoken. Togliatti, who received Gramsci's letter in Moscow, did not forward it to the Central Committee, though he showed it to Bukharin (for his subsequent correspondence with Gramsci on this issue see SPW II, pp 432-40).

Soviet discussions of the 'agrarian question' as well as the formation in 1923 of the peasant international (Krestintern) and the Comintern's call for 'Bolshevization' – which included the building of Communist party cells in rural areas – all influenced Gramsci's decisive reorientation of PCdI policy around the slogans of a 'workers' and peasants' government' and a 'federal workers' and peasants' republic'. In particular he seems to have been influenced by Bukharin's conception of a 'bloc of workers and peasants'. Bukharin argued that, since the majority of the world's population were peasants, world revolution had to be based on alliances between the industrial proletariat and the colonial peasantry in which the former class exercised 'hegemony', i.e. leadership of the alliance. Bukharin put forward this conception against Trotsky's idea of proletarian dictatorship *over* the peasantry, which, he claimed, was couched in too narrowly 'Western' terms, i.e. in terms of the revolutionary possibilities of the advanced industrial countries only.

The innovative quality of Gramsci's positions within the PCdI in this period can perhaps be seen most clearly from its two most famous political documents: the Lyons Theses (written with Togliatti) and 'Some Aspects of the Southern Question', of which Gramsci left an unfinished draft at the time of his arrest in November 1926. The discussion, in the former, of Fascism and party strategy in relation to the peculiarities of the Italian situation and class structure is a model of concrete Marxist analysis. In the latter, Gramsci relates contemporary Soviet discussions of the worker and peasant alliance brilliantly to Italian conditions and adumbrates the themes of hegemony and the intellectuals which will become central to the prison notebooks.

1 The Crisis of the Middle Classes

[...]

Why has the crisis of the middle classes had more radical consequences in Italy than in other countries? Why has it created Fascism and carried it to the state power? Because in our country, given the scanty development of industry and the regional character of what industry there is, not only is the petty bourgeoisie very numerous, but it is also the only class that is 'territorially' national. The capitalist crisis, in the years following the war, had also taken the acute form of a collapse of the unitary state and thus encouraged the rebirth of a confusedly patriotic ideology, so that there was no other solution than the Fascist one – once the working class had in 1920 failed in its task of creating by its own means a state capable of also satisfying the unitary national needs of Italian society.

The Fascist regime is dying because it has not merely failed to halt, but has actually helped to accelerate the crisis of the middle classes initiated after the war. The economic aspect of this crisis consists in the ruin of small and medium firms: the number of bankruptcies has multiplied rapidly in the last two years. The monopoly of credit, the fiscal regime and legislation on rents have crushed the small commercial and industrial enterprise. A real transfer of wealth has taken place from the small and medium to the big bourgeoisie, without any development of the productive apparatus. The small producer has not even become proletarian. He is simply permanently hungry; a desperate man without prospects for the future. [...]

The Italian economic crisis can only be resolved by the proletariat. Only by participating in a European and world revolution can the Italian people regain the ability to utilize fully its human productive forces, and to restore development to the national productive apparatus. Fascism has merely delayed the proletarian revolution, it has not made it impossible. Indeed, it has helped to enlarge and enrich the terrain of the proletarian revolution, which after the Fascist experiment will be a truly popular one.

[...]

In what does the crisis of Fascism consist? To understand it, some say that it is first necessary to define the essence of Fascism.

But the truth is that there does not exist any essence of Fascism as such. The essence of Fascism in 1922-3 was provided by a particular system of relations of force that existed in Italian society. Today, this system has changed profoundly, and the 'essence' has evaporated to some extent. The characteristic feature of Fascism consists in the fact that it has succeeded in creating a mass organization of the petty bourgeoisie. It is the first time in history that this has happened. The originality of Fascism consists in having found the right form of organization for a social class which has always been incapable of having any cohesion or unitary ideology: this form of organization is the army in the field. The militia is thus the fulcrum of the National Fascist Party: one cannot dissolve the militia without also dissolving the party as a whole. There does not exist a Fascist Party that can turn quantity into quality; that is an apparatus for political selection of a class or a stratum. There only exists a mechanical aggregate, undifferentiated and impossible to differentiate from the point of view of intellectual and political capabilities, which only lives because it has acquired in the civil war an extremely strong *esprit de corps*, crudely identified with the national ideology. Outside the sphere of military organization, Fascism has not contributed and cannot contribute anything; and even in this sphere, what it can contribute is very relative.

The product of circumstances in this way, Fascism is not capable of realizing any of its ideological premises. Fascism today says that it aims to conquer the state: at the same time, it says that it aims to become a prevalently rural phenomenon. How the two assertions can be reconciled is hard to understand. To conquer the state, it is necessary to be capable of replacing the dominant class in those functions which have an essential importance for the government of society. In Italy, as in all capitalist countries, to conquer the state means first and foremost to conquer the factory; it means to have the capability of taking over from the capitalists in governing the country's productive forces. This can be done by the working class, it cannot be done by the petty bourgeoisie, which has no essential function in the productive field; which in the factory, as an industrial category, exercises a function that is mainly of a police nature, not a productive one. The petty bourgeoisie can conquer the state only by allying itself with the working class, only by accepting the programme of the working class: soviet system instead of parliament in the state organization; communism and not capitalism in the organization of the national and international economy.

[...]

What should be the political attitude and the tactics of our party in the present situation? The situation is 'democratic', because the broad working masses are disorganized, dispersed and fragmented into the undifferentiated people. Hence, whatever the immediate evolution of the crisis may be, we can only foresee an improvement in the political position of the working class, not a victorious struggle for power. The crucial task of our party consists in winning the majority of the working class. The phase which we are passing through is not that of a direct struggle for power, but rather a preparatory phase, of transition to the struggle for power; in short, a phase of agitation, propaganda and organization. This, of course, does not rule out the possibility that savage conflicts may take place. And it does not mean that our party must not at once prepare itself and be ready to confront these. Quite the contrary. But these conflicts too must be seen in the context of the transitional phase, as elements of propaganda and agitation for winning the majority. If there exist within our party fanatical groups and tendencies which want to force the situation, it will be necessary to struggle against these in the name of the entire party, in the name of the vital and permanent interests of the Italian proletarian revolution.

The Matteotti crisis has offered us many lessons in this respect. It has taught us that the masses, after three years of terror and oppression, have become very prudent and want to cut their coat according to their cloth. This prudence is called reformism, it is called maximalism, it is called 'opposition bloc'. It is destined to disappear, certainly, and in the not too distant future. But for the moment it exists, and can only be overcome if at all times, on every occasion and at every moment, although moving forward, we maintain contact with the working class as a whole. Thus, we must combat every rightist tendency which seeks a compromise with the opposition bloc, and which seeks to obstruct the revolutionary development of our tactics and our work of preparation for the next stage.

The first task of our party consists in equipping itself to become fitted for its historic mission. In every factory and every village there must exist a Communist cell, which represents the party and the International; which knows how to work politically; which shows initiative. Hence, it is necessary to struggle against a certain passivity which still exists among our comrades, and against the tendency to keep the ranks of the party narrow. On the contrary, we must become a great party, we must seek to draw into our organizations the greatest possible number of revolutionary workers and peasants, in order to educate them for struggle, form them into mass organizers and leaders, and raise their political level. The workers' and peasants' state can only be built if the revolution has many politically qualified elements at its disposal. The struggle for the revolution can be waged victoriously only if the broad masses are, in all their local formations, organized and led by solid and capable comrades. Otherwise we are really going back, as the reactionaries clamour, to the years 1919-20: in other words, to the years of proletarian impotence; to the years of maximalist demagogy; to the years of working-class defeat. We Communists do not want to go back to the years 1919-20 either.

The party must carry out an enormous amount of work in the trade-union field. Without big trade-union organizations, there is no way out of parliamentary democracy. [...]

The Communist Party represents the totality of the interests and aspirations of the working class: we are not a mere parliamentary party. Our party therefore carries on a genuine trade-union activity. It puts itself at the head of the masses also in the little daily struggles for wages, for working hours, for industrial discipline, for accommodation, for bread. Our cells must push the internal commissions to incorporate all proletarian activities within their operations. It is, therefore, necessary to create a broad factory movement that can develop until it gives birth to an organization of city-wide proletarian committees, elected directly by the masses. These committees, in the social crisis that is looming, can become the strongholds of the general interests of the entire working people. This real activity in the factories and villages will revive the trade union and give it back some content and effectiveness, if in parallel all the vanguard elements go back into the organization, for the struggle against the present reformist and maximalist leaders. Whoever keeps his distance from the trade unions today is an ally of the reformists, not a revolutionary militant. He will be able to produce anarchoid phrases, but he will not shift by a hair's breadth the iron conditions in which the real struggle is going on.

The extent to which the party as a whole, in other words the entire mass of members, succeeds in fulfilling its essential task of winning the majority of workers and transforming in a molecular fashion the bases of the democratic state, will also be the extent to which we shall advance along the path of revolution, and will permit us to pass on to a subsequent phase of development. The whole party, in all its bodies, but especially through its press, must work in a united way to secure the maximum benefit from each comrade's work. Today, we are forming up for the general struggle against the Fascist regime. We reply to the stupid campaigns of the opposition press by showing our real determination to overthrow, not merely the Fascism of Mussolini and Farinacci, but also the semi-fascism of Amendola, Sturzo and Turati.[1] To achieve this, it is necessary to reorganize the broad masses and become a great party: the only party in which the working population sees the expression of its political will; the citadel of its immediate and permanent historical interests.

L'Unità, 26 August 1924. SPWII, 255-66

2 The Italian Situation and the Tasks of the PCdI (Lyons Theses)

[...]

Analysis of the Italian Social Structure

4. Capitalism is the predominant element in Italian society, and the force which is decisive in determining its development. This fundamental fact means that there is no possibility of a revolution in Italy that is not the socialist revolution. In the capitalist countries, the only class which can accomplish a real, deep social transformation is the working class. Only the working class is capable of translating into action the changes of an economic and political character which are necessary, if the energies of our country are to have complete freedom and possibility to develop. The way in which it will accomplish this revolutionary function is related to the degree of development of capitalism in Italy, and to the social structure which corresponds to it.

5. Industrialism, which is the essential part of capitalism, is very weak in Italy. Its possibilities for development are limited, both because of the geographical situation and because of the lack of raw materials. It therefore does not succeed in absorbing the majority of the Italian population (4 million industrial workers exist side by side with 3½ million agricultural workers and 4 million peasants). To industrialism, there is counterposed an agriculture which naturally presents itself as the basis of the country's economy. The extremely varied conditions of the terrain, and the resulting differences in cultivation and in systems of tenancy, however, cause a high degree of differentiation among the rural strata, with a prevalence of poor strata, nearer to the conditions of the proletariat and more liable to be influenced by it and accept its leadership. Between the industrial and agrarian classes, there lies a fairly extensive urban petty bourgeoisie, which is of very great significance. It consists mainly of artisans, professionals and state employees.

6. The intrinsic weakness of capitalism compels the industrial class to adopt expedients to guarantee its control over the country's economy. These expedients are basically nothing more than a system of economic compromises between a part of the industrialists and a part of the agricultural classes, specifically the big landowners. One does not, therefore, find here the traditional economic struggle between industrialists and landowners, nor the rotation of ruling groups which this produces in other countries. The industrialists, in any case, do not need to defend against the landowners an economic policy ensuring a continuous flow of labour from the countryside into the factories, since this flow is guaranteed by the abundant poor rural population which is characteristic of Italy. The industrial-agrarian agreement is based on a solidarity of interests between certain privileged groups, at the expense of the general interests of production and of the majority of those who work. It produces an accumulation of wealth in the hands of the big industrialists, which is the result of a systematic plundering of whole categories of the population and whole regions of the country. The results of this economic policy have in fact been: to create a deficit in the economic budget; to halt economic development in entire regions (South, Islands); to block the emergence and development of an economy better fitted to the structure and resources of the country; growing poverty of

the working population; and the existence of a continuous stream of emigration, with the resulting demographic impoverishment.

7. Just as it does not naturally control the entire economy, so too the industrial class does not succeed in organizing single-handed the whole of society and the state. The construction of a national state is only made possible for it by the exploitation of factors of international politics (so-called Risorgimento). Its reinforcement and defence necessitate a compromise with the classes upon which industry exercises a limited hegemony: in particular, the landowners and petty bourgeoisie. Thence derives a heterogeneity and weakness of the entire social structure, and of the state which is its expression.

[...]

8. In Italy the relations between industry and agriculture, which are essential for the economic life of a country and for the determination of its political superstructures, have a territorial basis. In the North, agricultural production and the rural population are concentrated in a few big centres. As a result of this, all the conflicts inherent in the country's social structure contain within them an element which affects the unity of the state and puts it in danger. The solution of the problem is sought by the bourgeois and agrarian ruling groups through a compromise. None of these groups naturally possesses a unitary character or a unitary function. The compromise whereby unity is preserved is, moreover, such as to make the situation more serious. It gives the toiling masses of the South a position analogous to that of a colonial population. The big industry of the North fulfils towards them the function of the capitalist metropolis. The big landowners and even the middle bourgeoisie of the South, for their part, take on the role of those categories in the colonies which ally themselves to the metropolis in order to keep the mass of working people subjugated. Economic exploitation and political oppression thus unite to make of the working people of the South a force continuously mobilized against the state.

9. The proletariat has greater importance in Italy than in other European countries, even of a more advanced capitalist nature: it is comparable only to that which existed in Russia before the Revolution. This is above all related to the fact that industry, because of the shortage of raw materials, bases itself by preference on the labour force (specialized skilled workers). It is also related to the heterogeneity and conflicts of interest which weaken the

ruling classes. In the face of this heterogeneity, the proletariat appears as the only element which by its nature has a unificatory function, capable of co-ordinating the whole of society. Its class programme is the only 'unitary' programme: in other words, the only one whose implementation does not lead to a deepening of the conflicts between the various elements of the economy and of society, or to breaking the unity of the state. Alongside the industrial proletariat, there also exists a great mass of rural proletarians, centred above all in the Po Valley; these are easily influenced by the workers in industry, and hence easily mobilized for the struggle against capitalism and the state.

In Italy, there is a confirmation of the thesis that the most favourable conditions for the proletarian revolution do not necessarily always occur in those countries where capitalism and industrialism have reached the highest level of development, but may instead arise where the fabric of the capitalist system offers least resistance, because of its structural weakness, to an attack by the revolutionary class and its allies.

The Policy of the Italian Bourgeoisie

10. The aim which the Italian ruling classes set themselves from the origin of the unitary state onwards was to keep the great mass of the working people subjugated and prevent them from becoming – by organizing around the industrial and rural proletariat – a revolutionary force capable of carrying out a complete social and political transformation, and giving birth to a proletarian state. The intrinsic weakness of capitalism, however, compelled it to base the economic disposition of the bourgeois state upon a unity obtained by compromises between non-homogeneous groups. In a wide historical perspective, this system is clearly not adequate to its purpose. Every form of compromise between the different groups ruling Italian society in fact becomes an obstacle placed in the way of the development of one or other part of the country's economy. Thus new conflicts are produced and new reactions from the majority of the population; it becomes necessary to intensify the pressure on the masses; and the result is a more and more decisive tendency for them to mobilize in revolt against the state.

[...]

12. [...] The establishment of the industrial-agrarian dictator-

ship posed the problem of revolution in its real terms, determining its historical conditions. In the North, an industrial and rural proletariat emerged, while in the South the rural population, subjected to a 'colonial' system of exploitation, had to be held down with a stronger and stronger political repression. The terms of the 'Southern question' were laid down clearly in this period. And spontaneously – without the intervention of any conscious factor, and without the Socialist Party even drawing any indication from this fact for its strategy as the party of the working class – for the first time in this period there occurred a convergence of insurrectionary attempts by the Northern proletariat with a revolt of Southern peasants (Sicilian Fasci).[2]

[...]

14. The greatest economic concentration in the industrial field occurred in the post-war period. The proletariat reached its highest level of organization; and this corresponded to the maximum disintegration of the ruling classes and the state. All the contradictions inherent in the Italian social organism came to the surface with extreme violence, as a result of the reawakening to political life of even the most backward masses that was brought about by the war and its immediate consequences. As always, the advance of the industrial and agricultural workers was accompanied by a massive agitation of the peasant masses, both in the South and in the other regions. The great strikes and the occupation of the factories took place simultaneously with occupations of the land.

The resistance of the reactionary forces once again operated along traditional lines. The Vatican allowed a real party to be formed, alongside Catholic Action, which aimed to integrate the peasant masses into the framework of the bourgeois state by apparently satisfying their aspirations for economic redemption and political democracy. The ruling classes in their turn implemented in the grand style their plan to corrupt the working-class movement and destroy it from within, by dangling before the eyes of the opportunist leaders the possibility that a labour aristocracy might collaborate in government, in an attempted 'reformist' solution to the problem of the state (left government). But in a poor and disunited country like Italy, the appearance of a 'reformist' solution to the problem of the state inevitably provokes a disintegration of the cohesion of state and society; for this cannot resist the shock of the numerous groups into which the ruling classes themselves and the intermediate classes fragment. Each group has its own need for economic protection and political autonomy; and in the absence of a homogeneous class nucleus capable of imposing – through its dictatorship – a discipline of work and production on the whole country, routing and eliminating the capitalist and landowning exploiters, government is made impossible and the crisis of power is continuously open.

The defeat of the revolutionary proletariat in this decisive period was due to political, organizational, tactical and strategic deficiencies of the workers' party. As a consequence of these deficiencies, the proletariat did not succeed in placing itself at the head of the insurrection of the great majority of the population, and channelling it towards the creation of a workers' state. Instead, it was itself influenced by other social classes, which paralysed its activity. The victory of Fascism in 1922 must be seen, therefore, not as a victory won over the revolution, but as a consequence of the defeat suffered by the revolutionary forces through their own intrinsic weakness.

Fascism and its Policy

15. Fascism, as a movement of armed reaction which set itself the task of fragmenting and disorganizing the working class in order to immobilize it, fitted into the framework of traditional Italian ruling-class policies, and into capitalism's struggle against the working class. It was, therefore, favoured in its origins, in its organization and in its development by all the old ruling groups without exception – but especially by the landowners, who felt most threatened by the pressure of the rural populace. Socially, however, Fascism found its base in the urban petty bourgeoisie, and in a new rural bourgeoisie thrown up by a transformation of rural property in certain regions (phenomena of agrarian capitalism in Emilia; origin of a category of middlemen in the countryside; 'land grants'; new divisions of holdings). [...] In substance, Fascism merely modifies the programme of conservation and reaction which has always dominated Italian politics, through a different way of conceiving the process of unification of the reactionary forces. It replaces the tactic of agreements and compromises by the project of achieving an organic unity of all the bourgeoisie's forces in a single political organism under the control

of a single centre, which would simultaneously direct the party, the government and the state. This project corresponds to the determination to resist to the last against any revolutionary attack; it thus allows Fascism to win the support of the most decisively reactionary part of the industrial bourgeoisie and of the landowners.

16. The Fascist method of defending order, property and the state tends, even more than the traditional system of compromises and left policies, to shatter social cohesion and the political superstructures which go with it. The reactions which it provokes must be examined in relation to its application in both the economic and in the political field.

In the political field, first of all, the organic unity of the bourgeoisie in Fascism was not achieved immediately after the winning of power. Centres of a bourgeois opposition to the regime remain outside Fascism. [...]

Fascism is compelled to struggle very fiercely against these surviving groups, and to struggle even more fiercely against freemasonry, which it rightly considers as the organizing centre of all the traditional forces supporting the state. This struggle, which is the sign of a break in the bloc of conservative and anti-proletarian forces, whatever the intentions, may in certain circumstances favour the development and self-assertion of the proletariat as a third and decisive factor of the political situation.

In the economic field, Fascism acts as the instrument of an industrial and agrarian oligarchy, to concentrate control over all the wealth of the country in the hands of capitalism. This cannot fail to provoke discontent in the petty bourgeoisie, which believed that with the arrival of Fascism the hour of its rule had struck.

A whole series of measures are being adopted by Fascism to encourage a new industrial concentration (abolition of death duties; financial and fiscal policy; heightening of protectionism), and to these there correspond other measures favouring the landowners and directed against small and medium farmers (taxes; duty on grain; 'the battle for wheat'). The accumulation which these measures achieve is not an increase in the national wealth, but the plundering of one class in favour of another: in other words, that of the working and middle classes in favour of the plutocracy. The intention of favouring the plutocracy is shamelessly revealed in the plan to legalize the preference share system in the new commercial code; a little handful of financiers will in this way be enabled, without restriction, to dispose of vast masses of savings originating from the middle and petty bourgeoisie, and these categories will be stripped of the right to dispose of their wealth.

On the same level, but with bigger political consequences, must be placed the plan to unite the issuing banks, i.e. in practice to eliminate the two big Southern banks. [...] The elimination of the Southern banks as issuing banks will transfer this function to Northern big industry which controls, via the Banca Commerciale, the Bank of Italy. We shall thus see the 'colonial' economic exploitation and impoverishment of the South increased, and the slow process of detachment of the Southern petty bourgeoisie from the state accelerated.

The economic policy of Fascism is completed by the measures aimed at raising the value of the lira, stabilizing the trade balance, paying war debts and encouraging the intervention of Anglo-American capital in Italy. In all these fields, Fascism is carrying out the programme of the plutocracy [...] and of an industrial landowning minority, at the expense of the great majority of the population, whose conditions of life are being made progressively worse.

All the ideological propaganda and the political and economic activity of Fascism is crowned by its tendency to 'imperialism'. This tendency expresses the need felt by the industrial/landowning ruling classes of Italy to find outside the national domain the elements to resolve the crisis of Italian society. It contains the germs of a war which in appearance will be fought for Italian expansion, but in which Fascist Italy will in reality be an instrument in the hands of one of the imperialist groups which are striving for world domination.

17. As a consequence of Fascism's policies, deep reactions are provoked among the masses. The most serious phenomenon is the sharper and sharper detachment of the rural populations of the South and the Islands from the system of forces which rule the state. The old local ruling class [...] no longer exercises in a systematic fashion its function as a connecting link with the state. The petty bourgeoisie thus tends to draw closer to the peasantry. The system of exploitation and oppression of the Southern masses is being carried to extremes by Fascism; this facilitates the radicalization of the intermediate categories too, and poses the

Southern question in its true terms, as a question which will only
be resolved by the insurrection of the peasants allied to the
proletariat, in a struggle against both capitalists and landowners.

The middle and poor peasants of the other parts of Italy too are
taking on a revolutionary function, although in a slower fashion.
The Vatican – whose reactionary function has been taken over by
Fascism – no longer controls the rural populations completely
through the priests, Catholic Action and the Popular Party. There
is a part of the peasantry which has been reawoken to struggle in
defence of its own interests, precisely by the organizations
authorized and directed by the ecclesiastical authorities. Now,
under the economic and political pressure of Fascism, this element
is intensifying its own class orientation and beginning to feel that
its destiny cannot be separated from that of the working class. [...]

As for the proletariat, activity to shatter its forces is finding a
limit in the active resistance of the revolutionary vanguard, and in
a passive resistance of the broad masses, who remain
fundamentally class-conscious and give signs that they will begin to
move again, as soon as the physical pressure of Fascism is relaxed
and the stimuli of class interest make themselves more strongly
felt. The attempt via the Fascist unions to split their ranks can be
considered to have failed. The Fascist unions, changing their
programme, are now becoming direct instruments of reactionary
repression in the service of the state.

18. Fascism reacts to the dangerous shifts and new recruitment
of forces provoked by its policies, by subjecting the whole of
society to the weight of a military force and repressive system
which hold the population riveted to the mechanical fact of
production – without any possibility of having a life of its own,
expressing a will of its own, or organizing to defend its own
interests.

So-called Fascist legislation has no purpose other than to
consolidate this system and make it permanent. The new political
electoral law, the modifications to the administrative structure
with the introduction of the *podestà* in rural communes,[3] etc., are
designed to mark the end of any participation by the masses in the
country's political and administrative life. The control over
associations prevents any permanent 'legal' form of organization
of the masses. The new trade-union policy strips the Confederation of Labour and the class unions of any possibility of

negotiating agreements, in order to exclude them from contact with the masses who had been organized around them. The proletarian press is suppressed. The class party of the proletariat is reduced to a purely illegal existence. Physical violence and police persecution are utilized systematically, above all in the countryside, to strike terror and preserve a situation of emergency.

The result of this complex activity of reaction and repression is an imbalance between the real relationship of social forces and the relationship of organized forces, so that an apparent return to normality and stability in fact corresponds to an intensification of contradictions ready to break out at any instant in new ways.

18 *bis*. The crisis which followed the Matteotti assassination furnished an example of the possibility that the apparent stability of the fascist regime might be shaken from below, by the sudden outbreak of economic and political conflicts which have grown sharper without being noticed. At the same time, it furnished proof of the incapacity of the petty bourgeoisie in the present historical period to lead the struggle against industrial/landowning reaction to any outcome.

Motor Forces and Perspectives of the Revolution

19. The motor forces of the Italian revolution, as is now clear from our analysis, are in order of their importance the following:

(a)   the working class and the rural proletariat;
(b)   the peasantry of the South and the Islands [Sicily and Sardinia], and the peasantry in the other parts of Italy.

The development and speed of the revolutionary process cannot be predicted without an evaluation of subjective elements; i.e. of the extent to which the working class succeeds in acquiring its own political profile, a precise class consciousness and an independence from all the other classes; and of the extent to which it succeeds in organizing its own forces, i.e. in *de facto* exercising leadership over the other elements and above all in concretizing politically its alliance with the peasantry.

One may in general assert, basing oneself moreover upon Italian experience, that one will pass from the period of revolutionary preparation to an 'immediately' revolutionary period when the industrial and rural proletariat of the North has succeeded in regaining – thanks to the development of the objective situation, and through a series of specific and immediate struggles – a high level of organization and combativity.

As for the peasantry, that of the South and Islands must be included in the front line among the forces upon which the insurrection against the industrial/landowning dictatorship must rely, although one should not attribute to them decisive importance unless they are allied to the proletariat. The alliance between them and the workers is the result of a natural and deep historical process, encouraged by all the past experience of the Italian state. For the peasants of the other parts of Italy, the process of orientation towards an alliance with the proletariat is slower and will have to be encouraged by careful political activity on the part of the proletarian party. The successes already obtained in Italy in this field indicate, moreover, that the problem of breaking the alliance of the peasantry with the reactionary forces must be posed, to a great extent, in other western European countries too, as the problem of destroying the influence of Catholic organizations on the rural masses.

20. The obstacles to the development of the revolution do not derive only from Fascist pressure, but are also related to the variety of groups into which the bourgeoisie is divided. Each of these groups strives to exert an influence on a section of the working population, to prevent the influence of the proletariat being extended; or on the proletariat itself, to cause it to lose its profile and autonomy as a revolutionary class. In this way a chain of reactionary forces is created, which starts from Fascism and includes: anti-fascist groups which do not have a large mass base (Liberals); those which have a base among the peasants and petty bourgeoisie (democrats, war veterans, Popular Party, Republicans) and in part also among the workers (Reformist Party); and those which have a proletarian base, and tend to maintain the working-class masses in a condition of passivity and to induce them to follow the policies of other classes (Maximalist Party).[4] [...]

21. The possibility that action by so-called democratic anti-fascist groups might bring down the Fascist regime would only exist if these groups succeeded in neutralizing the activity of the proletariat, and in controlling a mass movement that would enable it to brake the latter's development. The function of the democratic bourgeois opposition is rather to collaborate with

Fascism, in preventing the reorganization of the working class and the realization of its class programme. In this sense, a compromise between Fascism and bourgeois opposition is in train, and will inspire the policies of every 'centre' formation which emerges from the ruins of the Aventine. The opposition will only be able to become once again the protagonist of the capitalist regime's defence activity, when Fascist repression itself no longer succeeds in preventing the unleashing of class conflict, and the danger of a proletarian insurrection, welded to a peasant war, appears grave and imminent. The possibility that the bourgeoisie and Fascism itself may resort to the system of reaction concealed by the appearance of a 'left government' must, therefore, be permanently present in our perspectives (division of functions between Fascism and democracy, *Theses of the Fifth World Congress*).

22. From this analysis of the factors of revolution and its perspectives, the tasks of the Communist Party can be deduced. The criteria for the Party's organizational and political activity must be related to the analysis from which the basic co-ordinates of its programme derive.

Fundamental Tasks of the Communist Party

23. Having victoriously resisted the reactionary wave which sought to engulf it (1923); having contributed with its own actions to marking a first halt in the process of dispersal of the working-class forces (1924 elections); having taken advantage of the Matteotti crisis to reorganize a proletarian vanguard which, with notable success; opposed the attempt to instal a petty-bourgeois predominance in political life (Aventine); and having laid the basis of a real peasant policy of the Italian proletariat – the party today finds itself in the phase of political preparation of the revolution.

Its fundamental task can be indicated by these three points:

(a) to organize and unify the industrial and rural proletariat for the revolution;

(b) to organize and mobilize around the proletariat all the forces necessary for the victory of the revolution and the foundation of the workers' state;

(c) to place before the proletariat and its allies the problem of insurrection against the bourgeois state and of the struggle for proletarian dictatorship, and to guide them politically and materially towards their solution, through a series of partial struggles.

The Construction of the Communist Party as a 'Bolshevik' Party

24. The organization of the proletarian vanguard in a Communist Party is the essential feature of our organizational activity. The Italian workers have learnt from their experience (1919-20) that where the leadership of a Communist Party, built as the party of the working class and as the party of revolution, is missing, no victorious outcome of the struggle to overthrow the capitalist order is possible. The construction of a Communist Party which really is the party of the working class and the party of revolution – in other words, which is a 'Bolshevik' party – is directly related to the following basic points:

(a)   the party's ideology;
(b)   its form of organization and degree of cohesion;
(c)   its capacity to operate in contact with the masses;
(d)   its strategic and tactical capacity.

[...]

The Party's Ideology

25. The Communist Party needs complete ideological unity in order to be able at all moments to fulfil its function as leader of the working class. Ideological unity is an element of the Party's strength and political capacity; it is indispensable, to make it into a Bolshevik Party. The basis of ideological unity is the doctrine of Marxism and Leninism, this last being understood as Marxist doctrine adapted to the problems of the period of imperialism and the start of the proletarian revolution (*Theses on Bolshevization* of the April 1925 Enlarged Executive meeting, numbers 4 and 6).

[...]

26. In spite of the beginnings of a struggle against rightist and centrist degenerations of the workers' movement, the danger of rightist deviations is present within the Communist Party of Italy. In the theoretical field, this danger is represented by the attempts to revise Marxism made by comrade Graziadei, in the guise of a

'scientific' refinement of some of the basic concepts of Marx's doctrine.[5] Graziadei's attempts certainly cannot lead to the creation of a current, and hence a faction, which endangers the ideological unity and the cohesion of the party. However, they imply a support for rightist currents and political deviations. In any case, they point to the need for the party to carry out a deep study of Marxism and to acquire a higher and more solid theoretical consciousness.

The danger that a right-wing tendency might be created is linked to the general situation in the country. The very repression exercised by Fascism tends to nourish the view that, since the proletariat cannot soon overturn the regime, the best tactic is one whose aim is, if not an actual bourgeois-proletarian bloc for the constitutional elimination of Fascism, at least a passivity of the revolutionary vanguard and non-intervention of the Communist Party in the immediate political struggle, thus allowing the bourgeoisie to use the proletariat as electoral troops against Fascism. This programme is expressed through the formula that the Communist Party must be the 'left wing' of an opposition of all the forces conspiring to bring down the Fascist regime. It is the expression of a profound pessimism concerning the revolutionary capacities of the working class.

The same pessimism and the same deviations lead to an incorrect interpretation of the nature and historical function of the social-democratic parties at the present time. They lead to forgetting that social democracy, although it still to a great extent conserves its social base in the proletariat, must so far as its ideology and the political function it fulfils are concerned be considered, not as a right wing of the working-class movement, but as a left wing of the bourgeoisie, and as such must be unmasked in the eyes of the masses.

The right-wing danger must be fought through ideological propaganda, by counterposing the revolutionary programme of the working class and its party to the right-wing programme, and by ordinary disciplinary means whenever the necessity arises.

27. There is a similar connection between the origins of the Party and the general situation in the country on the one hand, and the danger of a leftist deviation from Marxist and Leninist ideology on the other. This is represented by the ultra-left tendency led by comrade Bordiga. This tendency was formed in the specific situation of disintegration and programmatic,

organizational, strategic and tactical incapacity in which the Italian Socialist Party found itself from the end of the war up to the Livorno Congress. Its origin and fortunes are, moreover, related to the fact that, since the working class is a minority in the Italian working population, there is a constant danger that its party will be corrupted by infiltrations from other classes, and in particular from the petty bourgeoisie. The far left tendency reacted to this condition of the working class and to the situation in the Italian Socialist Party with a particular ideology, i.e. a conception of the nature of the Party and its function and tactics which conflicts with that of Marxism and Leninism.

(a) The far left, ignoring or under-estimating the Party's social content, defines it as an 'organ' of the working class, constituted through the synthesis of heterogeneous elements. In reality, when defining the party it is necessary above all to stress that it is a 'part' of the working class. The error in defining the party leads to an incorrect approach to organizational problems and problems of tactics.

(b) For the far left, the function of the Party is not to lead the class at all moments, striving to remain in contact with it through all changes in the objective situation, but to form and prepare cadres, who can lead the masses when the evolution of the situation has brought them to the party and made them accept the programmatic and principled positions it has fixed.

(c) As regards tactics, the far left maintains that these must not be determined on the basis of the objective situation and the position of the masses, in such a way as always to be in line with reality and provide a constant contact with the broadest layers of the working population; instead, they must be determined on the basis of formalistic concerns. [...] As a consequence, the situation of mass movements is only examined in order to check the line which has been deduced on the basis of formalistic and sectarian concerns. Thus, in determining the party's policy, the specific element is always missing; the unity and completeness of vision which characterizes our method of political enquiry (dialectic) is broken; the activity and the slogans of the party lose their effectiveness and value, remaining simply propaganda activity and propaganda slogans.

[...]

The Basis of Party Organization

29. All problems of organization are political problems. Their solution must enable the party to carry out its fundamental task of ensuring that the proletariat acquires complete political independence; giving it a physiognomy, a personality and a precise revolutionary consciousness; and preventing any infiltration or disintegrative influence from classes and elements which, even if they have interests contrary to capitalism, are not willing to take the struggle against the latter to its ultimate consequences.

First and foremost, there is a political problem: that of the basis for organization. The party organization must be constructed on the basis of production and hence of the workplace (cells). This principle is essential for the creation of a 'Bolshevik' party. It depends on the fact that the party must be equipped to lead the mass movement of the working class, which is naturally unified by the development of capitalism in accordance with the process of production. By locating the organizational basis in the place of production, the party performs an act of choice of the class on which it bases itself. It proclaims that it is a class party and the party of a single class, the working class.

[...]

It is certain that the Communist Party cannot be solely a party of workers. The working class and its party cannot do without intellectuals, nor can they ignore the problem of grouping around themselves and giving a lead to all those elements who, in one way or another, are driven to rebel against capitalism. Thus the Communist Party cannot close its doors to peasants; indeed it must contain peasants and use them to tighten the political bond between the proletariat and the rural classes. But it is necessary to reject vigorously, as counter-revolutionary, any conception which makes the party into a 'synthesis' of heterogeneous elements – instead of maintaining, without any concessions of this kind, that it is a part of the proletariat; that the proletariat must mark it with the imprint of its own organization; and that the proletariat must be guaranteed a leading function within the party itself.

30. There is no consistency in the practical objections to organization on the basis of production (cells), according to which this organizational structure would not allow us to transcend the competition between different categories of worker and would leave the

party at the mercy of functionarism. The practice of the factory movement (1919-20), has shown that only an organization adapted to the place and system of production makes it possible to establish a contact between the upper and lower strata of the working masses (skilled workers, unskilled workers and labourers), and to create bonds of solidarity which eliminate the basis for any phenomenon of 'labour aristocracy'.

[...]

Solidity of the Party Organization. Factionalism

31. The organization of a Bolshevik Party must at all moments in the life of the party be a centralized organization, led by the Central Committee not just in words but also in deed. An iron proletarian discipline must reign in its ranks. This does not mean that the party must be ruled from on high with autocratic methods. Both the Central Committee and the subordinate leading bodies are formed on the basis of election, and on the basis of a selection of capable elements carried out through the test of work and through the experience of the movement. This second element guarantees that the criteria for the formation of the local leading groups and of the central leading group are not mechanical, external and 'parliamentary', but correspond to a real process of formation of a homogeneous proletarian vanguard linked to the masses.

[...]

32. The centralization and cohesion of the party require that there should not exist organized groups within it which take on the character of factions. A Bolshevik Party is sharply differentiated in this respect from social-democratic parties, which contain a variety of groups, and in which factional struggle is the normal method of working out a political orientation and selecting a leading group. The Communist Parties and International emerged after a factional struggle waged inside the International. Establishing themselves as the parties and the world organization of the proletariat, they chose as the norm of their internal life and development, in place of factional struggle, the organic collaboration of all tendencies through participation in the leading bodies.

[...]

The Functioning of the Party Organization

34. A Bolshevik Party must be organized in such a way that it can function in contact with the masses, whatever the conditions may be. This principle takes on the greatest importance among us, because of the repression exercised by Fascism with the aim of preventing the real relation of forces from being translated into a relation of organized forces. Only with the greatest concentration and intensity of party activity can one succeed in neutralizing at least in part this negative factor, and in preventing it from hampering greatly the revolutionary process. [...]

Strategy and Tactics of the Party

35. The strategic and tactical capacity of the party is the capacity to organize and unify around the proletarian vanguard and the working class all the forces necessary for revolutionary victory; and to lead these in fact towards the revolution, taking advantage of objective circumstances and of the shifts in the balance of forces which they bring about, both among the working population and among the enemies of the working class. With its strategy and tactics, the party 'leads the working class' in major historical movements and day-to-day struggles alike. One form of leadership is linked to the other and conditioned by it.

36. The principle that the party leads the working class must not be interpreted in a mechanical manner. It is not necessary to believe that the party can lead the working class through an external imposition of authority. This is not true, either with respect to the period which precedes the winning of power, or with respect to the period which follows it. The error of a mechanical interpretation of this principle must be combated in the Italian party, as a possible consequence of the ideological deviations of the far left. For these deviations lead to an arbitrary, formal over-estimation of the party, so far as its function as leader of the class is concerned. We assert that the capacity to lead the class is related, not to the fact that the party 'proclaims' itself its revolutionary organ, but to the fact that it 'really' succeeds, as a part of the working class, in linking itself with all the sections of that class and impressing upon the masses a movement in the direction desired and favoured by objective conditions. Only as a

result of its activity among the masses will the party get the latter to recognize it as 'their' party (winning a majority); and only when this condition has been realized can it presume that it is able to draw the working class behind it. The need for this activity among the masses outweighs any party 'patriotism'.

37. The party leads the class by penetrating into all the organizations in which the working masses are assembled; and by carrying out, in and through these, a systematic mobilization of energies in line with the programme of the class struggle, and an activity aimed at winning the majority to Communist directives.

The organizations in which the party works, and which tend by their nature to incorporate the whole mass of workers, can never substitute for the Communist Party, which is the political organization of revolutionaries, in other words of the vanguard of the proletariat. This excludes any relationship of subordination, or of 'equality' between the mass organizations and the party [...]. The relationship between trade unions and party is a special one of leadership, which is realized through the activity which the Communists carry out inside the unions. The Communists organize themselves into fractions in the unions, and in all the mass formations, and participate in the front rank of the life of these formations and the struggles which they wage, upholding their party's programme and slogans there. Every tendency to separate oneself off from the life of those organizations, whatever they may be, in which it is possible to make contact with the working masses, is to be combated as a dangerous deviation, indicating pessimism and generating passivity.

38. In the capitalist countries, trade unions are the specific organs grouping the working masses. Activity in the unions must be considered essential for the accomplishment of the party's aims. The party which renounces the struggle to exercise its influence in the unions and to win leadership of them, *de facto* renounces winning the mass of workers and renounces the revolutionary struggle for power.

In Italy, activity in the unions takes on particular importance; for such activity makes it possible to work with greater intensity, and with better results, at that reorganization of the industrial and rural proletariat which must restore it to a predominant position *vis-à-vis* the other social classes. However, Fascist repression, and especially Fascism's new trade-union policy, are creating a quite particular state of affairs. [...] [The] party must manage to carry out activity to defend the class union and demand freedom for it; and at the same time it must encourage and stimulate the tendency to create representative mass organisms adapted to the system of production. With the class union's activity paralysed, defence of the workers' immediate interests tends to be carried out through a fragmentation of resistance and struggle – by factory, by category, by workplace, etc. The Communist Party must be able to follow all these struggles and exercise a real leadership over them: ensuring that the unitary and revolutionary character of class conflicts is not lost in them, and indeed taking advantage of them to aid the mobilization of the whole proletariat and its organization along a fighting front (Trade Union Theses).

39. The party leads and unifies the working class by taking part in all struggles of a partial nature, and by formulating and agitating around a programme of demands of immediate interest to the working class. Partial and limited actions are considered by it as necessary steps to achieving the progressive mobilization and unification of all the forces of the working class.

The party combats the conception according to which one should abstain from supporting or taking part in partial actions, because the problems which interest the working class can be solved only by the overthrow of the capitalist order and by a general action on the part of all the anti-capitalist forces. [...]

39 *bis*. It is an error to believe that immediate demands and partial actions can only have an economic character. With the deepening of the crisis of capitalism, the capitalist and landowning ruling classes are compelled, in order to preserve their power, to limit and suppress the proletariat's organizational and political freedoms. Consequently, the demand for these freedoms furnishes an excellent terrain for agitation and partial struggles which may lead to the mobilization of vast layers of the working population. All the legislation with which the Fascists in Italy suppress even the most elementary freedoms of the working class, must therefore provide the Communist Party with themes for agitating among the masses and mobilizing them. It will be the Communist Party's task to link each of the slogans it launches in this field with the general directives of its activity: in particular, with the practical demonstration of the impossibility for the regime installed by Fascism to undergo radical limitations and transformations in a 'liberal' and 'democratic' direction, without a mass struggle being unleashed against Fascism that will inevitably culminate in a civil

war. This conviction must be disseminated among the masses insofar as we succeed, linking the partial demands of a political character with those of an economic character, in transforming 'revolutionary democratic' movements into working-class, socialist revolutionary movements.

[...]

40. The task of uniting the forces of the proletariat and all the working class on a terrain of struggle is the 'positive' part of the united front tactic; in Italy, in the present circumstances, this is the party's fundamental task. Communists must see the unity of the working class as a concrete, real result to be achieved, in order to prevent capitalism from implementing its plan of permanently fragmenting the proletariat and making all revolutionary struggle impossible. They must be capable of working in every way to achieve this end. Above all, they must become capable of drawing close to the workers of other parties and those without a party, overcoming unwarranted hostility and incomprehension, and in all cases presenting themselves as the advocates of unity of the class in the struggle for its defence and liberation.

The 'united front' of anti-fascist and anti-capitalist struggle which the Communists are striving to create must aim at being an organized united front, i.e. at being based on bodies around which the masses as a whole can regroup and find a form. Such are the representative bodies which the masses themselves are tending to create today, from the factories and on the occasion of every struggle, since the possibilities for the trade unions to function normally began to be limited. The Communists must take account of this tendency among the masses and be capable of stimulating it, developing the positive elements which it contains and combating the particularist deviations to which it may give rise. The matter must be considered without fetishization of any particular form of organization, bearing in mind that our fundamental purpose is to achieve an ever-increasing mobilization and organic unity of forces. To accomplish this purpose, it is necessary to be able to adapt ourselves to every terrain offered us by reality; to make use of every agitational theme; and to stress one form of organization or another, depending on what is needed and depending on each one's possibilities for development [...].

42. The tactic of the united front as political activity (manoeuvre) designed to unmask so-called proletarian and revolutionary parties and groups which have a mass base, is closely

linked with the problem of how the Communist Party is to lead the masses and how it is to win a majority. In the form in which it has been defined by the World Congresses, it is applicable in all cases in which, because of the mass support of the groups against which we are fighting, frontal struggle against them is not sufficient to give us rapid and far-reaching results. The success of this tactic is related to the degree to which it is preceded or accompanied by an effective unification and mobilization of the masses, achieved by the party through action from below.

In Italy, the united front tactic must continue to be utilized by the party, insofar as it is still far from having won a decisive influence over the majority of the working class and the working population. [...]

43. While it advances its programme of immediate class demands, and concentrates its activity upon achieving the mobilization and unification of the working-class forces, the party – in order to facilitate the development of its own activity – may present intermediate solutions to general political problems, and put forward these solutions among the masses still supporting counter-revolutionary parties and formations. This presentation of, and agitation around, intermediate solutions – far removed both from the party's own slogans, and from the programme of inertia and passivity of the groups we wish to combat – allows us to assemble broader forces behind the party; to counterpose the words of the leaders of the counter-revolutionary mass parties to their real intentions; to push the masses towards revolutionary solutions; and to extend our influence (example: the 'Anti-parliament'). These intermediate solutions cannot all be foreseen, because they must in all cases be adapted to reality. But they must be such as to be able to constitute a bridge towards the party's slogans; and it must always be evident to the masses that if they were to be realized, this would lead to an acceleration of the revolutionary process and a beginning of wider struggles.

The presentation of, and struggle for, such intermediate solutions is the specific form of struggle which must be used against the so-called democratic parties – which are in reality one of the strongest props of the tottering capitalist order, and as such alternate in power with the reactionary groups – when these so-called democratic parties are linked to sizeable and decisive layers of the working population (as in Italy, in the first months of the Matteotti crisis), and when a serious reactionary danger is imminent (tactic adopted by the Bolsheviks towards Kerensky during the Kornilov coup).[6] In such cases, the Communist Party will obtain the best results by advancing the actual solutions which would be those of the so-called democratic parties, if they were in fact capable of waging a consistent struggle for democracy with all the means required by the situation. These parties, thus subjected to the test of deeds, will unmask themselves before the masses and lose their influence over them.

44. All the particular struggles led by the party, and its activities on every front to mobilize and unite the forces of the working class, must come together and be synthesized in a political formula which can be easily understood by the masses, and which has the greatest possible agitational value for them. This formula is the 'workers' and peasants' government'. It indicates even to the most backward masses the need to win power in order to solve the vital problems which interest them; and it provides the means to transport them onto the terrain of the more advanced proletarian vanguard (struggle for the dictatorship of the proletariat). In this sense, it is an agitational slogan, but only corresponds to a real phase of historical development in the same sense as the intermediate solutions dealt with in the preceding paragraph. The party cannot conceive of a realization of this slogan except as the beginning of a direct revolutionary struggle: i.e. of a civil war waged by the proletariat, in alliance with the peasantry, with the aim of winning power. The party could be led into serious deviations from its task as leader of the revolution if it were to interpret the workers' and peasants' government as corresponding to a real phase of development of the struggle for power: in other words, if it considered that this slogan indicated the possibility for the problem of the state to be resolved in the interests of the working class in any other form than the dictatorship of the proletariat.

Lyons, January 1926. SPWII, 340-75

3   [Letter to the Central Committee of the Soviet Communist Party]

[October 1926]

Dear comrades,

The Italian Communists and all the conscious workers of our country have always followed your discussions with the greatest attention. On the eve of every congress and every conference of the Russian Communist Party we were confident that, despite the sharpness of the polemics, the unity of the Russian party was not in danger. We were indeed confident that, having achieved a greater ideological and organizational homogeneity through such discussions, the party would be better prepared and equipped to overcome the multiple difficulties which attend the exercise of power in a workers' state. Today, on the eve of your Fifteenth Conference, we no longer have the confidence we had in the past. We cannot free ourselves from a sense of anguish. It seems to us that the present attitude of the opposition bloc and the sharpness of the polemics within the Communist Party of the USSR necessitate intervention by the fraternal parties. It is precisely by this conviction that we are motivated, in addressing this letter to you. It may be that the isolation in which our party is forced to exist has led us to exaggerate the dangers in connection with the internal situation in the Communist Party of the USSR. In any case, our judgement of the international repercussions of this situation is certainly not exaggerated, and as internationalists we wish to carry out our duty.

The present situation in our brother party in the USSR seems to us different and far more serious than in previous discussions, because today we see occurring, and deepening, a split in the Leninist central group which has always been the leading nucleus of the party and the International. A split of this kind, independently of the numerical results of the congress votes, can have the most serious repercussions, not only if the oppositional minority does not accept with the greatest loyalty the fundamental principles of revolutionary party discipline, but also if, in carrying on its polemics and its struggle, it goes beyond certain limits which are above all formal democracy.

One of Lenin's most precious lessons was that we should pay great attention to the opinions of our class enemies. Well, dear comrades, it is certain that the strongest press organs and statesmen of the international bourgeoisie are counting on this organic character of the conflict that exists within the fundamental nucleus of the Communist Party of the USSR: are counting on a split in our brother party, and are convinced that this must lead to the disintegration and slow death-agony of the proletarian dictatorship; that it will bring about the ruin of the revolution, which the invasions and the white-guard revolts did not succeed in

bringing about. The very coolness and circumspection with which
the bourgeois press today seeks to analyse Russian events, and the
fact that it seeks to avoid so far as it can the violent demagogy
which was more characteristic of it in the past, are symptoms
which should cause the Russian comrades to reflect and make
them more conscious of their responsibility.

For another reason too, the international bourgeoisie is counting
on a possible split or on a worsening of the internal crisis in the
Communist Party of the USSR. The workers' state has now existed
in Russia for nine years. It is certain that only a little minority, not
merely of the working classes but even of the Communist parties
themselves, in the other countries is capable of reconstructing in its
entirety the whole development of the revolution, and of finding
even in the details of which everyday life is made up in the Soviet
state the continuity of the red thread which leads to the general
perspective of the construction of socialism. This is true, not only in
those countries where freedom of association no longer exists and
freedom of the press has been totally suppressed or subjected to
unprecedented limitations, as in Italy (where the courts have confi-
scated and forbidden the printing of the books of Trotsky, Lenin,
Stalin, Zinoviev and most recently of the *Communist Manifesto* as
well), but also in those countries where our parties still have the
possibility of supplying their members and the masses in general
with an adequate documentation.

In these countries, the great masses cannot understand the
discussions which are taking place in the Communist Party of the
USSR, especially if they are as violent as the present one and
concern not some question of detail, but the political line of the
party in its entirety. Not just the working masses in general, but
even the mass of members within our parties see, and wish to see,
in the Republic of the Soviets and in the party which is in power
there, a single combat unit that is working in the general
perspective of socialism. Only in so far as the West European
masses see Russia and the Russian party from this point of view,
do they accept freely and as a historically necessary fact that the
CPSU should be the leading party in the International; only for
that reason are the Republic of the Soviets and the CPSU today a
formidable element of revolutionary organization and propulsion.

The bourgeois and social-democratic parties, for the same
reason, exploit the internal polemics and the conflicts which exist

within the CPSU. They want to combat this influence of the Russian revolution; to combat the revolutionary unity which is being forged around the CPSU throughout the world. Dear comrades, it is extremely significant that in a country like Italy – where the Fascist state and party organization succeeds in stifling every noteworthy manifestation of autonomous life on the part of the great mass of workers and peasants – it is significant that the Fascist papers, especially those in the provinces, are full of articles, technically well constructed for propaganda purposes, with the minimum of demagogy or insulting comment, in which an attempt is made to demonstrate with a manifest effort to achieve objectivity that now, as is proved by the best known leaders of the Joint Opposition in the CPSU themselves, the state of the Soviets is inexorably becoming a purely capitalist state, and that hence in the world duel between Fascism and Bolshevism, Fascism will come out on top. This campaign, if it shows that the Republic of the Soviets still enjoys limitless sympathy among the great mass of the Italian people, who in some regions have only received a trickle of illegal party literature for six years now, also shows that Fascism, which knows very well the real internal situation in Italy and has learnt to deal with the masses, is seeking to utilize the political stance of the Joint Opposition to break definitively the firm aversion of the workers to Mussolini's government, and to bring about a state of mind in which Fascism can appear at least as an ineluctable historical necessity, notwithstanding the brutalities and other ills which accompany it.

We believe that, in the entire International, our party is the one which feels most keenly the repercussions of the serious situation which exists in the CPSU. This is the case, not just for the reasons set out above, which are so to speak *external* ones, which relate to the general conditions of revolutionary development in our country. You know that all the parties of the International have inherited, both from the old social democracy and from the differing national traditions that exist in the various countries (anarchism, syndicalism, etc., etc.), a mass of prejudices and ideological features which represent the breeding-ground for all deviations, of both the right and the left. In the last years, but especially after the Fifth World Congress, our parties were beginning to achieve, through painful experience and through wearisome, exhausting crises, a secure Leninist stabilization; they were beginning to become true Bolshevik parties. New proletarian cadres were being created from below, from the factories. The intellectual elements were subjected to a rigorous selection process, and to a pitilessly strict test on the basis of their practical work, on the terrain of action. This reworking took place under the guidance of the CPSU as a united ensemble and of all the great leaders of the CPSU.

Well, the sharpness of the present crisis, and the threat of an open or latent split that it contains, is halting this process of development and elaboration; crystallizing right and left deviations; putting off once again the achievement of an organic unity of the world party of workers. It is upon this aspect, in particular, that we believe it is our duty as internationalists to call the attention of the most responsible comrades of the CPSU. Comrades, in these past nine years of world history you have been the organizing and propulsive element of the revolutionary forces in all countries. The function which you have fulfilled has no precedent to equal it in breadth and depth, in the entire history of humanity. But today you are destroying your work. You are degrading, and run the risk of annihilating, the leading function which the CPSU won through Lenin's contribution. It seems to us that the violent passion of Russian affairs is causing you to lose sight of the international aspects of Russian affairs themselves; is causing you to forget that your duties as Russian militants can and must be carried out only within the framework of the interests of the international proletariat.

The Political Bureau of the Italian Communist Party has studied with the greatest care and attention of which it was capable all the problems which are today under discussion in the CPSU. The questions which are posed for you today, may be posed for our party tomorrow. In our country too, the rural masses make up the majority of the working population. Moreover, all the problems inherent in the proletariat's hegemony will certainly present themselves in our country in a more complex and sharp form even than in Russia – because the density of the rural population in Italy is enormously greater; because our peasants have an extremely rich tradition of organization, and have always succeeded in making their specific mass weight felt very keenly in national political life; because the organizational apparatus of the Church has two thousand years of tradition behind it in our country, and has specialized in propaganda and in the organization of the peasants in a way which has no equal in other countries. If it is true that industry is more developed in our country, and the proletariat has a considerable material basis, it is also true that this industry does not have raw materials within the country and is therefore more exposed to crises. Hence, the proletariat will only be able to carry out its leading function if it is very rich in the spirit of sacrifice, and has freed itself completely from every residue of reformist or syndicalist corporativism.

From this realistic and we believe Leninist point of view, the Political Bureau of the Italian Communist Party has studied your discussions. Hitherto, we have expressed a party view only on the strictly disciplinary question of factions, since we wished to respect the request you made after your Fourteenth Congress not to take the Russian discussion into the other sections of the International. Now we declare that we consider basically correct the political line of the majority of the Central Committee of the CPSU, and that the majority of the Italian party will certainly take the same position, if it becomes necessary to pose the whole question. We do not wish, and we think it useless, to direct agitation or propaganda at you, or at the comrades of the Joint Opposition. We will not, therefore, make a list of all the specific questions with our opinion in the margin. We repeat that we are struck by the fact that the attitude of the opposition concerns the entire political line of the Central Committee, and touches the very heart of the Leninist doctrine and the political action of our Soviet party. It is the principle and practice of the proletariat's hegemony that are brought into question; the fundamental relations of alliance between workers and peasants that are disturbed and placed in danger: i.e. the pillars of the workers' state and the revolution.

Comrades, history has never seen a dominant class, in its entirety, experiencing conditions of living inferior to those of certain elements and strata of the dominated and subjected class. This unprecedented contradiction has been reserved by history as the destiny of the proletariat. In this contradiction lie the greatest dangers for the dictatorship of the proletariat, especially in those countries where capitalism has not had any great development or succeeded in unifying the productive forces. It is from this contradiction, which moreover already appears in certain forms in those capitalist countries where the proletariat has objectively reached a high social function, that reformism and syndicalism, the corporate spirit and the stratifications of the labour aristocracy are born.

Yet the proletariat cannot become the dominant class if it does not overcome this contradiction through the sacrifice of its corporate interests. It cannot maintain its hegemony and its dictatorship if, even when it has become dominant, it does not sacrifice these immediate interests for the general and permanent interests of the class. Certainly, it is easy to be demagogic in this sphere. It is easy to insist on the negative sides of the contradiction: 'Are you the ruler, o badly dressed and badly fed workers? Or is the Nepman[7] in his furs, with all the goods of the earth at his disposal, the real ruler?' Similarly the reformists, after a revolutionary strike which has increased the cohesion and discipline of the masses, but which as a result of its long duration has yet further impoverished the individual workers involved, say: 'What was the point of struggling? You are ruined and impoverished!' It is easy to be demagogic in this sphere, and it is hard not to be when the question has been posed in terms of corporate spirit and not in those of Leninism, the doctrine of the hegemony of the proletariat, which historically finds itself in one particular position and not in another.

For us, this is the essential element in your discussions; it is in this element that the root of the errors of the Joint Opposition, and the origin of the latent dangers contained in its activities, lie. In the ideology and practice of the Joint Opposition are born again, to the full, the whole tradition of social democracy and syndicalism which has hitherto prevented the Western proletariat from organizing itself as a leading class.

Only a firm unity and a firm discipline in the party which governs the workers' state can ensure proletarian hegemony under the regime of the New Economic Policy – i.e. amid the full development of the contradiction to which we have referred. But the unity and discipline in this case cannot be mechanical and enforced. They must be loyal and due to conviction, and not those of an enemy unit imprisoned or besieged, whose only thought is of escape or an unexpected sortie.

This, dearest comrades, is what we wished to say to you, with the spirit of brothers and friends, even if younger brothers. Comrades Zinoviev, Trotsky, Kamenev have contributed powerfully to educating us for the revolution; they have at times corrected us with great force and severity; they have been among our masters. To them especially we address ourselves, as those principally responsible for the present situation, because we like to feel certain that the majority of the Central Committee of the USSR does not intend to win a crushing victory in the struggle, and is disposed to avoid excessive measures. The unity of our brother party in Russia is necessary for the development and triumph of the world revolutionary forces. To this necessity, every Communist and internationalist must be prepared to make the greatest sacrifices. The damage caused by the error of a united party is easily mended; that caused by a split, or a prolonged condition of latent split, may easily be irreparable and fatal.

With communist greetings.

The Political Bureau of the PCdI

SPWII, 426-32

4 Some Aspects of the Southern Question

[...]

Here [...] is a passage from *L'Ordine Nuovo*, no. 3, January 1920, which sums up the viewpoint of the Turin communists [on the question of the Italian South]:

> The Northern bourgeoisie has subjugated the South of Italy and the Islands, and reduced them to exploitable colonies; by emancipating itself from capitalist slavery, the Northern proletariat will emancipate the Southern peasant masses enslaved to the banks and the parasitic industry of the North. The economic and political regeneration of the peasants should not be sought in a division of uncultivated or poorly cultivated lands, but in the solidarity of the industrial proletariat. This in turn needs the solidarity of the peasantry and has an 'interest' in ensuring that capitalism is not reborn economically from landed property; that Southern Italy and the Islands do not become a military base for capitalist counter-revolution. By introducing workers' control over industry, the proletariat will orient industry to the production of agricultural machinery for the peasants, clothing and footwear for the peasants, electrical lighting for the peasants, and will prevent industry and the banks from exploiting the peasants and subjecting them as slaves to the strongrooms. By smashing the factory autocracy, by smashing the oppressive apparatus of the capitalist state and setting up a workers' state that will subject the capitalists to the law of useful

labour, the workers will smash all the chains that bind the peasant to his poverty and desperation. By setting up a workers' dictatorship and taking over the industries and banks, the proletariat will swing the enormous weight of the state bureaucracy behind the peasants in their struggle against the landowners, against the elements and against poverty. The proletariat will provide the peasants with credit, set up co-operatives, guarantee security of person and property against looters and carry out public works of reclamation and irrigation. It will do all this because an increase in agricultural production is in its interests; because to win and keep the solidarity of the peasants is in its interests; because it is in its interests to orient industrial production to work which will promote peace and brotherhood between town and countryside, between North and South.[8]

That was written in January 1920. Seven years have gone by and we are seven years older politically too. Today, certain concepts might be expressed better. The period immediately following the conquest of state power, characterized by simple workers' control of industry, could and should be more clearly distinguished from the subsequent periods. But the important thing to note here is that the fundamental concept of the Turin communists was not the 'magical formula' of dividing the big estates, but rather the political alliance between Northern workers and Southern peasants, to oust the bourgeoisie from state power. Furthermore, precisely the Turin communists (though they supported division of the land, subordinated to the solidary action of the two classes) themselves warned against 'miraculist' illusions in a mechanical sharing out of the big estates. In the same article of 3 January, we find:

What can a poor peasant achieve by occupying uncultivated or poorly cultivated lands? Without machinery, without accommodation on the place of work, without credit to tide him over till harvest-time, without co-operative institutions to acquire the harvest (if – long before harvest time – the peasant has not hung himself from the strongest bush or the least unhealthy-looking wild fig in the undergrowth of his uncultivated land!) and preserve him from the clutches of the usurers – without all these things, what can a poor peasant achieve by occupying?

[...]
In the proletarian camp, the Turin communists had one undeniable 'merit': that of bringing the Southern question forcibly to the attention of the workers' vanguard, and identifying it as one

of the essential problems of national policy for the revolutionary proletariat. [...]

The Turin communists posed concretely the question of the 'hegemony of the proletariat': i.e. of the social basis of the proletarian dictatorship and of the workers' state. The proletariat can become the leading [*dirigente*] and the dominant class to the extent that it succeeds in creating a system of class alliances which allows it to mobilize the majority of the working population against capitalism and the bourgeois state. In Italy, in the real class relations which exist here, this means to the extent that it succeeds in gaining the consent of the broad peasant masses. But the peasant question is historically determined in Italy; it is not the 'peasant and agrarian question in general'. In Italy the peasant question, through the specific Italian tradition, and the specific development of Italian history, has taken two typical and particular forms – the Southern question and that of the Vatican. Winning the majority of the peasant masses thus means, for the Italian proletariat, making these two questions its own from the social point of view; understanding the class demands which they represent; incorporating these demands into its revolutionary transitional programme; placing these demands among the objectives for which it struggles.

The first problem to resolve, for the Turin communists, was how to modify the political stance and general ideology of the proletariat itself, as a national element which exists within the ensemble of state life and is unconsciously subjected to the influence of bourgeois education, the bourgeois press and bourgeois traditions. It is well known what kind of ideology has been disseminated in myriad ways among the masses in the North, by the propagandists of the bourgeoisie: the South is the ball and chain which prevents the social development of Italy from progressing more rapidly; the Southerners are biologically inferior beings, semi-barbarians or total barbarians, by natural destiny; if the South is backward, the fault does not lie with the capitalist system or with any other historical cause, but with Nature, which has made the Southerners lazy, incapable, criminal and barbaric – only tempering this harsh fate with the purely individual explosion of a few great geniuses, like isolated palm-trees in an arid and barren desert. The Socialist Party was to a great extent the vehicle for this bourgeois ideology within the Northern proletariat. The

Socialist Party gave its blessing to all the 'Southernist' literature of the clique of writers who made up the so-called positive school: Ferri, Sergi, Niceforo, Orano and their lesser followers, who in articles, tales, short stories, novels, impressions and memoirs, in a variety of forms, reiterated one single refrain. Once again, 'science' was used to crush the wretched and exploited; but this time it was dressed in socialist colours, and claimed to be the science of the proletariat.

[...]

The proletariat had itself to adopt [the approach of the Turin communists] for it to become politically effective: that goes without saying. No mass action is possible, if the masses in question are not convinced of the ends they wish to attain and the methods to be applied. The proletariat, in order to become capable as a class of governing, must strip itself of every residue of corporatism, every syndicalist prejudice and incrustation. What does this mean? that, in addition to the need to overcome the distinctions which exist between one trade and another, it is necessary – in order to win the trust and consent of the peasants and of some semi-proletarian urban categories – to overcome certain prejudices and conquer certain forms of egoism which can and do subsist within the working class as such, even when craft particularism has disappeared. The metalworker, the joiner, the building worker, etc., must not only think as proletarians, and no longer as metalworker, joiner, building worker, etc.; they must also take a further step. They must think as workers who are members of a class which aims to lead the peasants and intellectuals. Of a class which can win and build socialism only if it is aided and followed by the great majority of these social strata. If this is not achieved, the proletariat does not become the leading class; and these strata (which in Italy represent the majority of the population), remaining under bourgeois leadership, enable the state to resist the proletarian assault and wear it down.

Well, what has occurred on the terrain of the Southern question shows that the proletariat has understood these duties. Two events should be recalled: one took place in Turin; the other occurred at Reggio Emilia, i.e. in the very citadel of reformism, class corporatism and working-class protectionism which is cited as a prime example by the 'Southernists' in their propaganda among the peasants of the South.

After the occupation of the factories, the Fiat board proposed to the workers that they should run the firm as a co-operative. Naturally, the reformists were in favour. An industrial crisis was looming; the spectre of unemployment tormented the workers' families. If Fiat became a co-operative, a certain job security might be obtained by the skilled workers, and especially by the politically most active workers, who were convinced that they were marked out for dismissal. The Socialist Party section, led by the communists, intervened energetically on the question. The workers were told the following:

A great firm like Fiat can be taken over as a co-operative by the workers only if the latter have resolved to enter the system of bourgeois political forces which governs Italy today. The proposal of the Fiat board forms a part of Giolitti's political plan. In what does this plan consist? The bourgeoisie, even before the war, could not govern peacefully any longer. The rising of the Sicilian peasants in 1894 and the Milan insurrection of 1898 were the *experimentum crucis* of the Italian bourgeoisie.[9] After the bloody decade 1890-1900, the bourgeoisie was forced to renounce a dictatorship that was too exclusive, too violent, too direct. For there had risen against it *simultaneously*, even if not in a co-ordinated fashion, the Southern peasants and the Northern workers.

In the new century, the ruling class inaugurated a new policy of class alliances, class political blocs; i.e. bourgeois democracy. It had to choose: either a rural democracy, i.e. an alliance with the Southern peasants, a policy of free trade, universal suffrage, administrative decentralization and low prices for industrial products; or a capitalist/worker industrial bloc, without universal suffrage, with tariff barriers, with the maintenance of a highly centralized state (the expression of bourgeois dominion over the peasants, especially in the South and the Islands), and with a reformist policy on wages and trade-union freedoms. It chose, not by chance, the latter solution. Giolitti personified bourgeois rule; the Socialist Party became the instrument of Giolitti's policies.

If you look closely, it was in the decade 1900-1910 that the most radical crises occurred in the socialist and working-class movement. The masses reacted spontaneously against the policy of the reformist leaders. Syndicalism was born: the instinctive, elemental, primitive but healthy expression of working-class reaction against the bloc with the bourgeoisie and in favour of a bloc with the peasants – and *first and foremost with the Southern peasants*. Precisely that. Indeed, in a certain sense, syndicalism is a weak attempt on the part of the Southern peasants, represented by their most advanced intellectuals, to lead the proletariat. Who forms the leading nucleus of Italian syndicalism, and what is its ideological essence? The leading nucleus of syndicalism is made up almost exclusively of southerners: Labriola, Leone, Longobardi, Orano. The ideological essence of syndicalism is a new liberalism, more energetic, more aggressive, more pugnacious than the traditional variety. [...]

In the ten years in question, capitalism was strengthened and developed, and directed a part of its activity towards the agriculture of the Po Valley. The most characteristic feature of those ten years was the mass strikes of the agricultural workers of the Po Valley. A profound upheaval took place among the Northern peasants: there occurred a deep class differentiation (the number of *braccianti* [day labourers] increased by 50 per cent, according to the 1911 census figures), and to this there corresponded a recasting of political currents and spiritual attitudes. Christian democracy and Mussolinism were the two most outstanding products of the period. Romagna was the regional crucible of these two new activities; the *bracciante* seemed to have become the social protagonist of the political struggle. The left organs of social democracy (like *L'Azione* in Cesena) and Mussolinism too soon fell under the control of the 'Southernists'. *L'Azione* in Cesena was a regional edition of Gaetano Salvemini's *L'Unità*. *Avanti!*, under Mussolini's editorship, slowly but surely became transformed into a tribune for syndicalist and Southernist writers. [...] Everyone remembers that, in fact, when Mussolini left *Avanti!* and the Socialist Party, he was surrounded by this cohort of syndicalists and Southernists.

The most notable repercussion of this period in the revolutionary camp was the Red Week of June 1914: Romagna and the Marches were the epicentre of Red Week. In the field of bourgeois politics, the most notable repercussion was the Gentiloni pact.[10] Since the Socialist Party, as a consequence of the rural movements in the Po Valley, had returned after 1910 to an intransigent tactic, the industrial bloc supported and represented by Giolitti lost its effectiveness. Giolitti shifted his rifle to the other shoulder. He replaced the alliance between bourgeoisie and workers by an alliance between bourgeoisie and the Catholics, who represented the peasant masses of Northern and Central Italy. As a result of this alliance, Sonnino's conservative party was totally destroyed, preserving only a tiny cell in Southern Italy, around Antonio Salandra.[11]

[...]

Today, Giolitti is once more in power, and once more the big bourgeoisie is putting its trust in him, as a result of the panic which has filled it before the impetuous movement of the popular masses. Giolitti wants to tame the Turin workers. He has beaten them twice: in the strike of last April, and in the occupation of the factories – with the help of the CGL, i.e. of corporative reformism. He now thinks that he can tie them into the bourgeois state system. What in fact will happen if the skilled workforce of Fiat accepts the board's proposals? The present industrial shares will become debentures: in other words, the co-operative will have to pay to debenture-holders a fixed dividend, whatever the turnover may be. The Fiat company will be cut off in every way from the institutions of credit, which remains in the hands of the bourgeoisie, whose interest it is to get the workers at its mercy. The skilled workforce will perforce have to bind itself to the state, which will 'come to the assistance of the workers' through the activity of the working-class deputies: through the subordination of the working-class political party to government policies. That is Giolitti's plan as applied in full. The Turin proletariat will no longer exist as an independent class, but merely as an appendage of the bourgeois state. Class corporatism will have triumphed, but the proletariat will have lost its position and role as leader and guide. It will appear to the mass of poorer workers as privileged. It will appear to the peasants as an exploiter just like the bourgeoisie, because the bourgeoisie – as it has always done – will present the privileged nuclei of the working class to the peasant masses as the sole cause of their ills and their misery.

The skilled workers of Fiat accepted almost unanimously our point of view, and the board's proposals were rejected. But this experiment could not be sufficient. The Turin proletariat, in a whole series of actions, had shown that it had reached an extremely high level of political maturity and capability. The technicians and white-collar workers in the factories were able to improve their conditions in 1919 only because they were supported by the workers. To break the militancy of the technicians, the employers proposed to the workers that they should themselves nominate, through elections, new squad and shop foremen. The workers rejected the proposal, although they had many points of difference with the technicians, who had always been an instrument of repression and persecution for the bosses. Then the press waged a rabid campaign to isolate the technicians, highlighting their very high salaries, which reached as much as 7,000 lire a month. The skilled workers also gave support to the agitation of the hodmen, and it was only thus that the latter succeeded in winning their demands. Within the factories, all privileges and forms of exploitation of the less skilled by the more skilled categories were swept away. Through these actions, the proletarian vanguard won its position as a social vanguard. This was the basis upon which the Communist Party developed in Turin. But outside Turin? Well, we wanted expressly to take the problem outside Turin, and precisely to Reggio Emilia, where there existed the greatest concentration of reformism and class corporatism.

Reggio Emilia had always been the target of the 'Southernists'. A phrase of Camillo Prampolini: 'Italy is made up of Northerners and filthy Southerners' could be taken as the most characteristic expression of the violent hatred disseminated among Southerners against the workers of the North.[12] At Reggio Emilia, a problem arose similar to the one at Fiat: a big factory was to pass into the hands of the workers as a co-operative enterprise. The Reggio reformists were full of enthusiasm for the project and trumpeted its praises in their press and at meetings. A Turin communist went to Reggio, took the floor at a factory meeting, outlined the problem between North and South in its entirety, and the 'miracle' was achieved: the workers, by an overwhelming majority, rejected the reformist, corporate position. It was shown that the reformists did not represent the spirit of the Reggio workers; they represented merely their passivity, and other negative aspects. They had succeeded in establishing a political monopoly – thanks to the notable concentration in their ranks of organizers and propagandists with certain professional talents – and hence in preventing the development and organization of a revolutionary current. But the presence of a capable revolutionary was enough to thwart them and show that the Reggio workers are valiant fighters and not swine raised on government fodder.

In April 1921, 5,000 revolutionary workers were laid off by Fiat, the workers' councils were abolished, real wages were cut. At Reggio Emilia, something similar probably happened. In other words, the workers were defeated. But was the sacrifice that they had made useless? We do not believe so: indeed, we are certain that it was not useless – though it would certainly be difficult to adduce a whole series of great mass events which prove the immediate, lightning effectiveness of these actions. In any case, so far as the peasants are concerned, such proof is always difficult, indeed almost impossible: and it is yet more difficult in the case of the peasant masses in the South.

The South can be defined as a great social disintegration. The peasants, who make up the great majority of its population, have no cohesion among themselves (of course, some exceptions must be made: Apulia, Sardinia, Sicily, where there exist special characteristics within the great canvas of the South's structure). Southern society is a great agrarian bloc, made up of three social layers: the great amorphous, disintegrated mass of the peasantry;

the intellectuals of the petty and medium rural bourgeoisie; and the big landowners and great intellectuals. The Southern peasants are in perpetual ferment, but as a mass they are incapable of giving a centralized expression to their aspirations and needs. The middle layer of intellectuals receives the impulses for its political and ideological activity from the peasant base. The big landowners in the political field and the great intellectuals in the ideological field centralize and dominate, in the last analysis, this whole complex of phenomena. Naturally, it is in the ideological sphere that the centralization is most effective and precise. Giustino Fortunato and Benedetto Croce thus represent the keystones of the Southern system and, in a certain sense, are the two major figures of Italian reaction.[13]

The Southern intellectuals are one of the most interesting and important social strata in Italian national life. One only has to think of the fact that more than three fifths of the state bureaucracy is made up of Southerners to convince oneself of this. Now, to understand the particular psychology of the Southern intellectuals, it is necessary to keep in mind certain factual data.

1. In every country, the layer of intellectuals has been radically modified by the development of capitalism. The old type of intellectual was the organizing element in a society with a mainly peasant and artisanal basis. To organize the state, to organize commerce, the dominant class bred a particular type of intellectual organizer, the specialist in applied science. In the societies where the economic forces have developed in a capitalist direction to the point where they have absorbed the greater part of national activity, it is this second type of intellectual which has prevailed, with all his characteristics of order and intellectual discipline. In the countries, on the other hand, where agriculture still plays a considerable or even preponderant role, the old type has remained predominant. It provides the bulk of the state personnel; and locally too, in the villages and little country towns, it has the function of intermediary between the peasant and the administration in general. In Southern Italy this type predominates, with all its characteristic features. Democratic in its peasant face; reactionary in the face turned towards the big landowner and the government: politicking, corrupt and faithless. One could not understand the traditional cast of the Southern political parties, if one did not take the characteristics of this social stratum into account.

2. The Southern intellectual mainly comes from a layer which is still important in the South: the rural bourgeoisie. In other words, the small and medium landowner who is not a peasant, who does not work the land, who would be ashamed to be a farmer, but who wants to extract from the little land he has – leased out either for rent or on a simple share-cropping basis – the wherewithal to live fittingly; the wherewithal to send his sons to a university or seminary; and the wherewithal to provide dowries for his daughters, who must marry officers or civil functionaries of the state. From this social layer, the intellectuals derive a fierce antipathy to the working peasant – who is regarded as a machine for work to be bled dry, and one which can be replaced, given the excess working population. They also acquire an atavistic, instinctive feeling of crazy fear of the peasants with their destructive violence; hence, they practise a refined hypocrisy and a highly refined art of deceiving and taming the peasant masses.

3. Since the clergy belong to the social group of intellectuals, it is necessary to note the features which distinguish the Southern clergy as a whole from the Northern clergy. The Northern priest is generally the son of an artisan or a peasant, has democratic sympathies, is more tied to the mass of peasants. Morally, he is more correct than the southern priest, who often lives more or less openly with a woman. He therefore exercises a spiritual function that is more complete, from a social point of view, in that he guides a family's entire activities. In the North, the separation of Church from state and the expropriation of ecclesiastical goods was more radical than in the South, where the parishes and convents either have preserved or have reconstituted considerable assets, both fixed and movable. In the South, the priest appears to the peasant: 1. as a land administrator, with whom the peasant enters into conflict on the question of rents; 2. as a usurer, who asks for extremely high rates of interest and manipulates the religious element in order to make certain of collecting his rent or interest; 3. as a man subject to all the ordinary passions (women and money), and who therefore, from a spiritual point of view, inspires no confidence in his discretion and impartiality. Hence confession exercises only the most minimal role of guidance, and the Southern peasant, if often superstitious in a pagan sense, is not clerical. All this, taken together, explains why in the South the Popular Party (except in some parts of Sicily) does not have any

great position or possess any network of institutions and mass organizations. The attitude of the peasant towards the clergy is summed up in the popular saying: 'The priest is a priest at the altar; outside, he is a man like anyone else.'

The Southern peasant is bound to the big landowner through the mediation of the intellectual. The peasant movements, in so far as they do not take the form of autonomous, independent mass organizations, even in a formal sense (i.e. capable of selecting out peasant cadres, themselves of peasant origin, and of registering and accumulating the differentiation and progress achieved within the movement), always end up by finding themselves a place in the ordinary articulations of the state apparatus – communes, provinces, Chamber of Deputies. This process takes place through the composition and decomposition of local parties, whose personnel is made up of intellectuals, but which are controlled by the big landowners and their agents – like Salandra, Orlando, Di Cesarò.

The war appeared to introduce a new element into this type of organization, with the war veterans' movement. In this, the peasant-soldiers and the intellectual-officers formed a mutual bloc that was more closely united, and that was to some extent antagonistic to the big landowners. It did not last long, and its last residue is the National Union conceived of by Amendola, which has some phantom existence thanks to its anti-fascism. However, given the lack of any tradition of *explicit* organization of *democratic* intellectuals in the South, even this grouping must be stressed and taken into account, since it might be transformed from a tiny trickle of water into a swollen, muddy torrent, in changed general political conditions.

The only region where the war veterans' movement took on a more precise profile, and succeeded in creating a more solid social structure, was Sardinia. And this is understandable. Precisely because in Sardinia the big landowner class is very exiguous, carries out no function, and does not have the ancient cultural and governmental traditions of the mainland South. The pressure exerted from below, by the mass of peasants and herdsmen, finds no suffocating counterweight in the higher social stratum of the big landowners. The leading intellectuals feel the full weight of this pressure, and take steps forward which are more remarkable than the National Union.

The Sicilian situation has very specific features, which distinguish it both from Sardinia and from the South. The big landowners are far more compact and resolute there than in the mainland South. Moreover, there exists there a certain developed industry and commerce (Sicily is the richest region of the entire South and one of the richest in Italy). The upper classes feel very keenly their importance in national life and make its weight felt. Sicily and Piedmont are the two regions which have played a pre-eminent role since 1870. The popular masses of Sicily are more advanced than in the South, but their progress has taken on a typically Sicilian form. There exists a mass Sicilian Socialism, which has a whole tradition and development that is peculiar to it. In the 1922 Chamber, it had around 20 of the 52 deputies who had been elected from the island.

We have said that the Southern peasant is tied to the big landowner through the mediation of the intellectual. This type of organization is most widespread, throughout the mainland South and Sicily. It creates a monstrous agrarian bloc which, as a whole, functions as the intermediary and the overseer of Northern capitalism and the big banks. Its single aim is to preserve the *status quo*. Within it, there exists no intellectual light, no programme, no drive towards improvements or progress. If any ideas or programmes have been put forward, they have had their origins outside the South, in the conservative agrarian politicians (especially in Tuscany) who were associated in Parliament with the conservatives of the Southern agrarian bloc. [...]

Over and above the agrarian bloc, there functions in the South an intellectual bloc which in practice has so far served to prevent the cracks in the agrarian bloc becoming too dangerous and causing a landslide. Giustino Fortunato and Benedetto Croce are the exponents of this intellectual bloc, and they can thus be considered as the most active reactionaries of the whole peninsula.

We have already said that Southern Italy represents a great social disintegration. This formula can be applied not only to the peasants, but also to the intellectuals. It is a remarkable fact that in the South, side by side with huge property, there have existed and continue to exist great accumulations of culture and intelligence in single individuals, or small groups of great intellectuals, while there does not exist any organization of middle culture. There exist in the south the Laterza publishing house, and the review *La*

Critica. There exist academies and cultural bodies of the greatest erudition. But there do not exist small or medium-sized reviews, nor publishing houses around which medium groupings of Southern intellectuals might form. The Southerners who have sought to leave the agrarian bloc and pose the Southern question in a radical form have found hospitality in, and grouped themselves around, reviews printed outside the South. Indeed, one might say that all the cultural initiatives by medium intellectuals which have taken place in this century in Central and Northern Italy have been characterized by Southernism, because they have been strongly influenced by southern intellectuals [...].

Well, the supreme political and intellectual rulers of all these initiatives have been Giustino Fortunato and Benedetto Croce. In a broader sphere than the stifling agrarian bloc, they have seen to it that the problems of the South would be posed in a way which did not go beyond certain limits; did not become revolutionary. Men of the highest culture and intelligence, who arose on the traditional terrain of the South but were linked to European and hence to world culture, they had all the necessary gifts to satisfy the intellectual needs of the most sincere representatives of the cultured youth in the South; to comfort their restless impulses to revolt against existing conditions; to steer them along a middle way of classical serenity in thought and action. The so-called neo-Protestants or Calvinists have failed to understand that in Italy, since modern conditions of civilization rendered impossible any mass religious reform, the only historically possible reformation has taken place with Benedetto Croce's philosophy. The direction and method of thought have been changed and a new conception of the world has been constructed, transcending Catholicism and every other mythological religion. In this sense, Benedetto Croce has fulfilled an extremely important 'national' function. He has detached the radical intellectuals of the South from the peasant masses, forcing them to take part in national and European culture; and through this culture, he has secured their absorption by the national bourgeoisie and hence by the agrarian bloc.

L'Ordine Nuovo and the Turin communists – if in a certain sense they can be related to the intellectual formations to which we have alluded; and if, therefore, they too have felt the intellectual influence of Giustino Fortunato or of Benedetto Croce –

nevertheless represent at the same time a complete break with that tradition and the beginning of a new development, which has already borne fruit and which will continue to do so. As has already been said, they posed the urban proletariat as the modern protagonist of Italian history, and hence also of the Southern question. Having served as intermediaries between the proletariat and certain strata of left intellectuals, they succeeded in modifying – if not completely at least to a notable extent – their mental outlook.

This is the main factor in the figure of Piero Gobetti, if one reflects carefully.[14] Gobetti was not a Communist and would probably never have become one. But he had understood the social and historical position of the proletariat, and could no longer think in abstraction from this element. [...] The figure of Gobetti and the movement which he represented were spontaneous products of the new Italian historical climate. In this lies their significance and their importance. Comrades in the party sometimes reproved us for not having fought against the *Rivoluzione Liberale* current of ideas. Indeed, this absence of conflict seemed to prove the organic relationship, of a Machiavellian kind (as people used to say), between us and Gobetti. We could not fight against Gobetti, because he developed and represented a movement which should not be fought against, at least so far as its main principles are concerned.

Not to understand that, means not to understand the question of intellectuals and the function which they fulfil in the class struggle. Gobetti, in practice, served us as a link: 1. with those intellectuals born on the terrain of capitalist techniques who in 1919-20 had taken up a left position, favourable to the dictatorship of the proletariat; 2. with a series of Southern intellectuals who through more complex relationships, posed the Southern question on a terrain different from the traditional one, by introducing into it the proletariat of the North (of these intellectuals, Guido Dorso is the most substantial and interesting figure).[15] Why should we have fought against the *Rivoluzione Liberale* movement? Perhaps because it was not made up of pure communists who had accepted our programme and our ideas from A to Z? This could not be asked of them, because it would have been both politically and historically a paradox.

Intellectuals develop slowly, far more slowly than any other social group, by their very nature and historical function. They represent the entire cultural tradition of a people, seeking to resume and synthesize all of its history. This can be said especially of the old type of intellectual: the intellectual born on the peasant terrain. To think it possible that such intellectuals, *en masse*, can break with the entire past and situate themselves totally upon the terrain of a new ideology, is absurd. It is absurd for the mass of intellectuals, and perhaps it is also absurd for very many intellectuals taken individually as well – notwithstanding all the honourable efforts which they make and want to make.

Now, we are interested in the mass of intellectuals, and not just in individuals. It is certainly important and useful for the proletariat that one or more intellectuals, individually, should adopt its programme and ideas; should merge into the proletariat, becoming and feeling themselves to be an integral part of it. The proletariat, as a class, is poor in organizing elements. It does not have its own stratum of intellectuals, and can only create one very slowly, very painfully, after the winning of state power. But it is also important and useful for a break to occur in the mass of intellectuals: a break of an organic kind, historically characterized. For there to be formed, as a mass formation, a left tendency, in the modern sense of the word: i.e. one oriented towards the revolutionary proletariat.

The alliance between proletariat and peasant masses requires this formation. It is all the more required by the alliance between the proletariat and the peasant masses in the South. The proletariat will destroy the Southern agrarian bloc insofar as it succeeds, through its party, in organizing increasingly significant masses of poor peasants into autonomous and independent formations. But its greater or lesser success in this necessary task will also depend upon its ability to break up the intellectual bloc that is the flexible, but extremely resistant, armour of the agrarian bloc. The proletariat was helped towards the accomplishment of this task by Piero Gobetti, and we think that the dead man's friends will continue, even without his leadership, the work he undertook. This is gigantic and difficult, but precisely worthy of every sacrifice (even that of life, as in Gobetti's case) on the part of those intellectuals (and there are many of them, more than is believed) – from North and South – who have understood that only two social forces are essentially national and bearers of the future: the proletariat and the peasantry.

Drafted between September and November 1926.
SPWII, 441-62

PART TWO:
PRISON WRITINGS 1929-1935

VI HEGEMONY, RELATIONS OF FORCE, HISTORICAL BLOC

Introduction

The reality in which Gramsci found himself after 1926 was one in which socialist revolutions had either been defeated or had failed to take place in the West, where capitalism had managed to survive the post-war economic crisis and stabilize itself, where parliamentary regimes had stood firm or had been replaced with authoritarian ones. These conditions were very different from those of the phase of revolutionary offensive between 1917 and 1921. They demanded a new analysis of the political and ideological resources of capitalist societies, the sources of their extraordinary resilience. They also demanded a new strategy, one which would be different from that which had worked in Russia in 1917.

It is the basis of such an analysis and strategy that Gramsci sought to develop in the prison notebooks. One important strand of this work was theoretical. The Marxist tradition in which he had matured as a political militant was strong on general predictions about the course of capitalist development and about connections between economic crises and political transformation. But it was weak on detailed analyses of the forms of political power, the concrete relations between social classes and political representation and the cultural and ideological forms in which social antagonisms are fought out or regulated and dissipated. There was no adequate Marxist theory of the state or of what Gramsci called the 'sphere of the complex superstructures': political, legal, cultural. In order to conduct his analysis, therefore, Gramsci needed to make a theoretical critique of mechanistic forms of historical materialism, most notably 'economism' (see Glossary of Key Terms). He then needed to expand the space occupied by politics in the Marxist tradition.

To do this he went back not to the Marx of *Capital* or the Engels of *Anti-Dühring* but to the *Theses on Feuerbach* and to Marx and Engels's historical texts (*The Eighteenth Brumaire of Louis*

189

Bonaparte, The Civil War in France, Revolution and Counter-Revolution in Germany). He also drew on a non-Marxist source – the Italian idealist philosopher Benedetto Croce – for the latter's insights into the 'ethico-political' sphere, that is to say the ideological, moral and cultural cements which bond a society together. Significantly, too, he went back to the passage on structure (base) and superstructure in Marx's 1859 Preface to *A Contribution to the Critique of Political Economy* and read it in a strongly anti-economistic way. What the passage says, for Gramsci, is that changing socio-economic circumstances do not of themselves 'produce' political changes. They only set the conditions in which such changes become possible. What is crucial, in bringing about these changes, are the 'relations of force' obtaining at the political level, the degree of political organization and combativity of the opposing forces, the strength of the political alliances which they manage to bind together and their level of political consciousness, of preparation of the struggle on the ideological terrain. It is in the context of this discussion that two central concepts develop: 'hegemony' and 'historical bloc'.

1 Structure and Superstructure [i]

Economy and ideology. The claim (presented as an essential postulate of historical materialism) that every fluctuation of politics and ideology can be presented and expounded as an immediate expression of the structure, must be contested in theory as primitive infantilism, and combated in practice with the authentic testimony of Marx, the author of concrete political and historical works. Particularly important from this point of view are *The Eighteenth Brumaire* and the writings on the Eastern Question, but also other writings (*Revolution and Counter-Revolution in Germany, The Civil War in France* and lesser works). An analysis of these works allows one to establish better the Marxist historical methodology, integrating, illuminating and interpreting the theoretical affirmations scattered throughout his works.

One will be able to see from this the real precautions introduced by Marx into his concrete researches, precautions which could have no place in his general works. [...] Among these precautions the following examples can be enumerated:

1. The difficulty of identifying at any given time, statically (like an instantaneous photographic image) the structure. Politics in fact is at any given time the reflection of the tendencies of development in the structure, but it is not necessarily the case that these tendencies must be realized. A structural phase can be concretely studied and analysed only after it has gone through its whole process of development, and not during the process itself, except hypothetically and with the explicit proviso that one is dealing with hypotheses.

2. From this it can be deduced that a particular political act may have been an error of calculation on the part of the leaders of the dominant classes, an error which historical development, through the parliamentary and governmental 'crises' of the ruling classes, then corrects and goes beyond. Mechanical historical materialism does not allow for the possibility of error, but assumes that every political act is determined, immediately, by the structure, and therefore as a real and permanent (in the sense of achieved) modification of the structure. The principle of 'error' is a complex one: one may be dealing with an individual impulse based on mistaken calculations or equally it may be a manifestation of the attempts of specific groups or sects to take over hegemony within the directive grouping, attempts which may well be unsuccessful.

3. It is not sufficiently borne in mind that many political acts are due to internal necessities of an organizational character, that is they are tied to the need to give coherence to a party, a group, a society. This is made clear for example in the history of the Catholic Church. If, for every ideological struggle within the Church one wanted to find an immediate primary explanation in the structure one would really be caught napping: all sorts of politico-economic romances have been written for this reason. It is evident on the contrary that the majority of these discussions are connected with sectarian and organizational necessities. In the discussion between Rome and Byzantium on the Procession of the Holy Spirit,[1] it would be ridiculous to look in the structure of the European East for the claim that it proceeds only from the Father, and in that of the West for the claim that it proceeds from the Father and the Son. The two Churches, whose existence and

whose conflict is dependent on the structure and on the whole of history, posed questions which are principles of distinction and internal cohesion for each side, but it could have happened that either of the Churches could have argued what in fact was argued by the other. The principle of distinction and conflict would have been upheld all the same, and it is this problem of distinction and conflict that constitutes the historical problem, not the banner that happened to be hoisted by one side or the other. [...]

SPN, 407-9 (Q7§24)

2 [Structure and Superstructure ii]

The proposition contained in the Preface to *A Contribution to the Critique of Political Economy* to the effect that men acquire consciousness of structural conflicts on the level of ideologies should be considered as an affirmation of epistemological and not simply psychological and moral value.[2] From this, it follows that the theoretical-practical principle of hegemony has also epistemological significance, and it is here that Ilyich [Lenin]'s greatest theoretical contribution to the philosophy of praxis should be sought. In these terms one could say that Ilyich advanced philosophy as philosophy in so far as he advanced political doctrine and practice. The realization of a hegemonic apparatus, in so far as it creates a new ideological terrain, determines a reform of consciousness and of methods of knowledge: it is a fact of knowledge, a philosophical fact. In Crocean terms: when one succeeds in introducing a new morality in conformity with a new conception of the world, one finishes by introducing the conception as well; in other words, one determines a reform of the whole of philosophy.

SPN, 365-6 (Q10,II§12)

3 Structure and Superstructures [iii]

Structures and superstructures form a 'historical bloc'. That is to say the complex, contradictory and discordant ensemble of the superstructures is the reflection of the ensemble of the social relations of production. From this, one can conclude: that only a totalitarian system of ideologies gives a rational reflection of the contradiction of the structure and represents the existence of the objective conditions for the revolutionizing of praxis.[3] If a social group is formed which is one hundred per cent homogeneous on the level of ideology, this means that the premises exist one hundred per cent for this revolutionizing: that is that the 'rational' is actively and actually real. This reasoning is based on the necessary reciprocity between structure and superstructures, a reciprocity which is nothing other than the real dialectical process.

SPN, 366 (Q8§182)

4   [The Concept of 'Historical Bloc']

[...]

Croce's assertion that the philosophy of praxis 'detaches' the structure from the superstructures, thereby reviving theological dualism and positing a 'structure as hidden god', is not correct and it is not even a particularly profound invention. The accusation of theological dualism and of a breaking up of the process of reality is vacuous and superficial. It is strange that such an accusation should have come from Croce, who introduced the concept of the dialectic of distincts and for this is always being accused by the followers of Gentile of having himself broken up the process of reality.[4] But, leaving this aside, it is not true that the philosophy of praxis 'detaches' the structure from the superstructures when, rather, it conceives their development as intimately connected and necessarily interrelated and reciprocal. Nor can the structure be likened to a 'hidden god', even metaphorically. It is conceived in an ultra-realistic way, such that it can be studied with the methods of the natural and exact sciences. Indeed, it is precisely because of this objectively verifiable 'consistency' of the structure that the conception of history has been considered 'scientific'. Is it perhaps that the structure is thought of as something immobile and absolute and not rather as reality itself in movement? And does not the statement in the *Theses on Feuerbach* about the 'educator who must be educated' posit a necessary relation of active reaction by man upon the structure, affirming the unity of the process of reality? The concept of 'historical bloc' constructed by Sorel grasped precisely in full this unity upheld by the philosophy of praxis.[5] [...]

                                                        * (Q10,II§41.i)

5 [Ethico-Political History]

Definition of the concept of ethico-political history. Note that ethico-political history is an arbitrary and mechanical hypostasis of the moment of hegemony, of political leadership, of consent in the life and activities of the state and civil society. [...]

The most important problem to discuss in this paragraph is this: whether the philosophy of praxis excludes ethico-political history, whether it fails to recognize the reality of a moment of hegemony, treats moral and cultural leadership as unimportant and really judges superstructural facts as 'appearances'. One can say that not only does the philosophy of praxis not exclude ethico-political history but that, indeed, in its most recent stage of development, it consists precisely in asserting the moment of hegemony as essential to its conception of the state and to the 'accrediting' of the cultural fact, of cultural activity, of a cultural front as necessary alongside the merely economic and political ones. Croce commits the serious error of not applying to his criticism of the philosophy of praxis the methodological criteria that he applies to his study of much less important and significant philosophical currents. If he were to employ these criteria, he would be able to discover that the judgement contained in his attribution of the term 'appearance' to superstructures is none other than a judgement of their 'historicity' expressed in opposition to popular dogmatic conceptions and therefore couched in a 'metaphorical' language adapted to the public to whom it is destined. The philosophy of praxis thus judges the reduction of history to ethico-political history alone as improper and arbitrary, but does not exclude the latter. The opposition between Crocism and the philosophy of praxis is to be sought in the speculative character of Crocism.

                                        SCW, 104-7 (Q10,I§7)

6 [Ethico-Political History and Hegemony]

From everything that has been said previously it emerges that Croce's historiographical conception of history as ethico-political history must not be judged as futile, as something to be rejected out of hand. On the contrary, it needs to be forcefully established that Croce's historical thought, even in its most recent phase, must be studied and reflected upon with the greatest attention. Essentially it represents a reaction against 'economism' and fatalistic mechanism, even though it is put forward as the destructive supersession of the philosophy of praxis. The criterion that a philosophical current must be criticized and evaluated not for what it professes to be but for what it really is and shows itself to be in concrete historical works applies to Croce's thought too. For the philosophy of praxis the speculative method itself is not futile, but has generated 'instrumental' values of thought in the development of culture, instrumental values which the philosophy of praxis has incorporated (the dialectic, for example). Credit must therefore, at the very least, be given to Croce's thought as an instrumental value, and in this respect it may be said that it has forcefully drawn attention to the importance of facts of culture and thought in the development of history, to the function of great intellectuals in the organic life of civil society and the state, to the moment of hegemony and consent as the necessary form of the concrete historical bloc. That this is not futile is demonstrated by the fact that, in the same period as Croce, the greatest modern theorist of the philosophy of praxis [Lenin] has – on the terrain of political struggle and organization, and with political terminology – in opposition to the various tendencies of 'economism', revalued the front of cultural struggle and constructed the doctrine of hegemony as a complement to the theory of the state-as-force and as a contemporary form of the 1848 doctrine of 'permanent revolution'.[6] For the philosophy of praxis the conception of ethico-political history, in that it is independent of any realist conception, may be adopted as an 'empirical tool' of historical research, one which needs constantly to be borne in mind in examining and understanding historical development, if the aim is that of producing integral history and not partial and extrinsic history (history of economic forces as such etc.).

* (Q10,I§12)

7 [Political Ideologies]

One of the points which is most interesting to examine and analyse
in detail is Croce's doctrine of political ideologies. [...] For Croce
too, now, superstructures are merely apparent and illusory; but
has he thought through this change in his position and, in
particular, does it correspond to his activity as a philosopher?
Croce's doctrine on political ideologies is evidently derived from
the philosophy of praxis: they are practical constructions,
instruments of political leadership. In other words, one could say
that ideologies for the governed are mere illusions, a deception to
which they are subject, while for the governing they constitute a
willed and a knowing deception. For the philosophy of praxis,
ideologies are anything but arbitrary; they are real historical facts
which must be combatted and their nature as instruments of
domination revealed, not for reasons of morality etc., but for
reasons of political struggle: in order to make the governed
intellectually independent of the governing, in order to destroy
one hegemony and create another, as a necessary moment in the
revolutionizing of praxis. Croce would seem to be nearer than the
philosophy of praxis to the vulgar materialist interpretation. For
the philosophy of praxis the superstructures are an objective and
operative reality (or they become so, when they are not pure
products of the individual mind). It explicitly asserts that men
become conscious of their social position, and therefore of their
tasks, on the terrain of ideologies, which is no small affirmation of
reality. The philosophy of praxis itself is a superstructure, it is the
terrain on which determinate social groups become conscious of
their own social being, their own strength, their own tasks, their
own becoming. In this sense Croce himself is right when he asserts
that the philosophy of praxis 'is history already made or in the
process of becoming'.[7]
   There is however a basic difference between the philosophy of
praxis and other philosophies: other ideologies are non-organic
creations because they are contradictory, because they aim at
reconciling opposed and contradictory interests; their 'historicity'
will be brief because contradiction emerges after each event of
which they have been the instrument. The philosophy of praxis, on
the other hand, does not tend towards the peaceful resolution of
the contradictions existing within history. It is itself the theory of

those contradictions. It is not an instrument of government of dominant groups in order to gain the consent of and exercise hegemony over subaltern classes; it is the expression of these subaltern classes who want to educate themselves in the art of government and who have an interest in knowing all truths, even unpleasant ones, and in avoiding deceptions (impossible) by the ruling class and even more by themselves. The criticism of ideologies, in the philosophy of praxis, attacks the complex of superstructures and affirms their rapid transience in that they tend to hide reality – namely struggle and contradiction – even when they are 'formally' dialectical (like Crocism), that is to say they present a speculative and conceptual dialectic and do not see the dialectic in historical becoming itself. [...]

The concept of the concrete (historical) value of the superstructures in the philosophy of praxis must be enriched by juxtaposing it with Sorel's concept of the 'historical bloc'. If men become conscious of their social position and their tasks on the terrain of the superstructures, this means that between structure and superstructure a necessary and vital connection exists. One should find out what currents of historiography the philosophy of praxis was reacting against at the time of its foundation and what were the most widespread opinions at the time with respect to the other sciences too. The very images and metaphors on which the founders of the philosophy of praxis frequently draw give some clues in this direction: the argument that the economy is to society what anatomy is to biological sciences – one must remember the struggle that went on in the natural sciences to expel from the scientific terrain principles of classification that were based on external and transient elements. If animals were classified according to the colour of their skin, their hair or their plumage, everyone nowadays would protest. In the human body it certainly cannot be said that the skin (and also the historically prevalent type of physical beauty) are mere illusions and that the skeleton and anatomy are the only reality. However for a long time something similar to this was said. By highlighting the anatomy and the function of the skeleton nobody was trying to claim that man (still less woman) can live without the skin. Going on with the same metaphor one can say that it is not the skeleton (strictly speaking) which makes one fall in love with a woman, but that one nevertheless realizes how much the skeleton contributes to the grace of her movements etc.

Another element in the preface to *A Contribution to the Critique* is without doubt to be connected to the reform of legislation on trials and punishments. The preface says that just as one does not judge an individual by what he thinks of himself, so one cannot judge a society by its ideologies.[8] This affirmation is perhaps connected to the reform in penal judgements whereby material proofs and the oral evidence of witnesses have replaced the statements of the accused and the corresponding use of torture, etc.

Referring to so-called natural laws and the concept of nature (natural right, state of nature, etc.) 'which emerged in the philosophy of the seventeenth century and was dominant in the eighteenth', Croce mentions that 'This conception is in fact only obliquely attacked by Marx's critique which, analysing the concept of *nature*, showed how it was the ideological complement of the historical development of the bourgeoisie, an enormously powerful weapon which the bourgeoisie used against the privileges and oppressions it sought to destroy.' Croce uses this observation to make the following methodological statement: 'That concept may have arisen as an instrument for practical and occasional ends and yet it may still be intrinsically true. "Natural laws" are equivalent, in that case, to "rational laws"; and it is necessary to deny the rationality and excellence of those laws. Now, precisely because it is of metaphysical origin, that concept can be radically rejected, but one cannot refute it in its particularity. It wanes with the metaphysics to which it belonged; and it seems now to have waned for good. Peace be unto the "great goodness" of natural laws'.[9]

The passage as a whole is not very clear or lucid. One should reflect on the fact that in general (i.e. sometimes) a concept may arise as an instrument for a practical and occasional end and nonetheless be intrinsically true. But I do not believe there are many who would maintain that once a structure has altered, all the elements of the corresponding superstructure must necessarily collapse. What happens, rather, is that out of an ideology that arose to lead the popular masses and which therefore necessarily takes account of certain of their interests, several elements survive: the law of nature itself, which may have waned for the educated classes, is preserved by the Catholic religion and is more alive among the people than one thinks. Besides, in his critique of the concept the founder of the philosophy of praxis affirmed its historicity, its transience; he limited its intrinsic value to this historicity but did not deny it.

Note 1. The phenomena of the modern breakdown of parliamentarism can offer many examples of the function and concrete value of ideologies. The way in which this breakdown is presented so as to hide the reactionary tendencies of certain social groups is of the greatest interest. [...]

* (Q10,II§41.xii)

8 Ideologies

It seems to me that an element of error in assessing the value of ideologies is due to the fact (by no means casual) that the name ideology is given both to the necessary superstructure of a particular structure and to the arbitrary elucubrations of particular individuals. The bad sense of the word has become widespread, with the effect that the theoretical analysis of the concept of ideology has been modified and denatured. The process leading up to this error can be easily reconstructed:

1. ideology is identified as distinct from the structure, and it is asserted that it is not ideology that changes the structures but vice versa;

2. it is asserted that a given political solution is 'ideological', i.e. that it is insufficient for changing the structure, although it thinks that it can do so; it is asserted that it is useless, stupid, etc.;

3. one then passes to the assertion that every ideology is 'pure' appearance, useless, stupid, etc.

One must therefore distinguish between historically organic ideologies, those, that is, which are necessary to a given structure, and ideologies that are arbitrary, rationalistic, 'willed'. To the extent that ideologies are historically necessary they have a validity which is 'psychological'; they 'organize' human masses, they form the terrain on which men move, acquire consciousness of their position, struggle, etc. To the extent that they are 'arbitrary' they only create individual 'movements', polemics and so on (though even these are not completely useless, since they function like an error which by contrasting with truth, demonstrates it).

SPN, 376-7 (Q7§19)

9 Validity of Ideologies

Remember the frequent affirmation made by Marx on the 'solidity of popular beliefs' as a necessary element of a specific situation. What he says more or less is 'when this way of conceiving things has the force of popular beliefs', etc. (Find these statements and analyse them in the contexts in which they are expressed.)[10] Another affirmation of Marx's is that a popular conviction often has the same energy as a material force or something of the kind, which is extremely significant.[11] The analysis of these propositions tends, I think, to reinforce the conception of 'historical bloc' in which precisely material forces are the content and ideologies are the form, though this distinction between form and content has purely indicative value, since the material forces would be inconceivable historically without form and the ideologies would be individual fancies without the material forces.

SPN, 377 (Q7§21)

10 Analysis of Situations: Relations of Force

It is the problem of the relations between structure and superstructures which must be accurately posed and resolved if the forces which are active in the history of a particular period are to be correctly analysed and the relation between them determined. Two principles must orient the discussion: 1. that no society sets itself tasks for whose accomplishment the necessary and sufficient conditions do not either already exist or are not at least beginning to emerge and develop; 2. that no society breaks down and can be replaced until it has developed all the forms of life which are implicit in its internal relations [...].

'No social formation is ever destroyed before all the productive forces for which it is sufficient have been developed, and new superior relations of production never replace older ones before the material conditions for their existence have matured within the framework of the old society. Mankind thus inevitably sets itself only such tasks as it is able to solve since closer examination will always show that the problem itself arises only when the material conditions for its solution are already present or at least in the course of formation.' (Preface to *A Contribution to the Critique of Political Economy*)

From a reflection on these two principles, one can move on to develop a whole series of further principles of historical methodology. Meanwhile, in studying a structure, it is necessary to distinguish organic movements (relatively permanent) from movements which may be termed 'conjunctural' (and which appear as occasional, immediate, almost accidental). Conjunctural phenomena too depend on organic movements to be sure, but they do not have any very far-reaching historical significance; they give rise to political criticism of a minor, day-to-day character, which has as its subject small ruling groups and personalities with direct governmental responsibilities. Organic phenomena on the other hand give rise to socio-historical criticism, whose subject is wider social groupings – beyond the people with immediate responsibilities and beyond the ruling personnel. When a historical period comes to be studied, the great importance of this distinction becomes clear. A crisis occurs, sometimes lasting for decades. This exceptional duration means that incurable structural contradictions have revealed themselves (reached maturity), and that, despite this, the political forces which are struggling to conserve and defend the existing structure itself are making every effort to cure them, within certain limits, and to overcome them. These incessant and persistent efforts (since no social formation will ever admit that it has been superseded) form the terrain of the 'conjunctural', and it is upon this terrain that the forces of opposition organize. These forces seek to demonstrate that the necessary and sufficient conditions already exist to make possible, and hence imperative, the accomplishment of certain historical tasks (imperative, because any falling short before a historical duty increases the necessary disorder, and prepares more serious catastrophes). (The demonstration in the last analysis only succeeds and is 'true' if it becomes a new reality, if the forces of opposition triumph; in the immediate, it is developed in a series of ideological, religious, philosophical, political and juridical polemics, whose concreteness can be estimated by the extent to which they are convincing, and shift the previously existing disposition of social forces.)

A common error in historico-political analysis consists in an inability to find the correct relation between what is organic and what is conjunctural. This leads to presenting causes as immediately operative which in fact only operate indirectly, or to asserting that the immediate causes are the only effective ones. In the first case there is an excess of 'economism', or doctrinaire pedantry; in the second, an excess of 'ideologism'. In the first case there is an overestimation of mechanical causes, in the second an exaggeration of the voluntarist and individual element. (The distinction between organic 'movements' and facts and 'conjunctural' or occasional ones must be applied to all types of situation; not only to those in which a regressive development or an acute crisis takes place, but also to those in which there is a progressive development or one towards prosperity, or in which the productive forces are stagnant.) The dialectical nexus between the two categories of movement, and therefore of research, is hard to establish precisely. Moreover, if this error is serious in historiography, it becomes still more serious in the art of politics, when it is not the reconstruction of past history but the construction of present and future history which is at stake. One's own desires and one's baser and more immediate passions are the cause of error, in that they take the place of an objective and impartial analysis – and this happens not as a conscious 'means' to stimulate to action, but as self-deception. In this case too the snake bites the charlatan – in other words the demagogue is the first victim of his own demagogy.

The failure to consider the immediate moment of 'relations of force' is linked to residues of the vulgar liberal conception – of which syndicalism is a manifestation which thought itself more advanced when in reality it was taking a step backward. In fact the vulgar liberal conception, stressing relations between political forces organized in the various forms of party (newspaper readerships, parliamentary and local elections, the mass organizations of parties and trade unions in the strict sense), was more advanced than syndicalism, which gave primordial importance to the fundamental socio-economic relation and only to that. The vulgar liberal conception took implicit account of this socio-economic relation too (as many signs clearly indicate), but it put more emphasis on the relation of political forces – which was an expression of the former and in reality contained it. These residues of the vulgar liberal conception can be traced in a whole series of works purporting to be connected with the philosophy of praxis, and have given rise to infantile forms of optimism and folly.

These methodological criteria will acquire visibly and didactically their full significance if they are applied to the examination of concrete historical facts. This might usefully be done for the events which took place in France from 1789 to 1870. It seems to me that for greater clarity of exposition it is precisely necessary to take in the whole of this period. In fact, it was only in 1870-71, with the attempt of the Commune, that all the germs of 1789 were finally historically exhausted. It was then that the new bourgeois class struggling for power defeated not only the representatives of the old society unwilling to admit that it had been definitively superseded, but also the still newer groups who maintained that the new structure created by the 1789 revolution was itself already outdated; by this victory the bourgeoisie demonstrated its vitality *vis-à-vis* both the old and the very new.

Furthermore, it was in 1870-71 that the body of principles of political strategy and tactics engendered in practice in 1789, and developed ideologically around 1848, lost their efficacy. (I am referring to those which can be resumed in the formula of 'permanent revolution'; it would be interesting to study how much of this formula passed into Mazzini's strategy – for example, in the Milan insurrection of 1853 – and whether this happened consciously or not.) One piece of evidence for the correctness of this point of view is the fact that historians are by no means of one mind (and it is impossible that they should be) in fixing the limits of the group of events which constitute the French Revolution. For some (Salvemini, for instance) the Revolution was complete at Valmy: France had created its new state and had shown itself capable of organizing the politico-military force necessary to assert and to defend its territorial sovereignty. For others the Revolution continues until Thermidor – indeed they speak of various revolutions (10 August is a separate revolution, etc; see *La Révolution française* by A. Mathiez, in the A. Colin series.) The interpretation of Thermidor and of the work of Napoleon provokes the sharpest disagreements. Was it revolution or counter-revolution? For others the history of the Revolution continues until 1830, 1848, 1870 and even until the World War of 1914.

All these views are partially true. In reality the internal contradictions which develop after 1789 in the structure of French society are resolved to a relative degree only with the Third

Republic; and France has now enjoyed sixty years of stable political life only after eighty years of convulsions at ever longer intervals: 1789, 1794, 1799, 1804, 1815, 1830, 1848, 1870. It is precisely the study of these 'intervals' of varying frequency which enables one to reconstruct the relations on the one hand between structure and superstructure, and on the other between the development of the organic movement and that of the conjunctural movement in the structure. One might say that the dialectical mediation between the two methodological principles formulated at the beginning of this note is to be found in the historico-political formula of permanent revolution.

The question of so-called relations of force is an aspect of the same problem. One often reads in historical narratives the generic expression: 'relations of force favourable, or unfavourable, to this or that tendency'. In such abstract terms this formulation explains nothing, or almost nothing – since it merely repeats twice over the fact which needs to be explained, once as a fact and once as an abstract law and an explanation. The theoretical error consists therefore in making what is a principle of research and interpretation into an 'historical cause'.

Meanwhile, in the 'relation of forces' various moments or levels must be distinguished, and they are fundamentally the following:

1. A relation of social forces which is closely linked to the structure, objective, independent of human will, and which can be measured with the systems of the exact or physical sciences. The level of development of the material forces of production provides a basis for the emergence of the various social groupings, represents a function and has a specific position within production itself. This relation is what it is, a refractory reality: nobody can alter the number of firms or their employees, the number of cities or the given urban population, etc. This fundamental configuration allows one to study whether in a particular society there exist the necessary and sufficient conditions for its transformation – in other words, to check the degree of realism and practicability of the various ideologies which have been born on its own terrain, on the terrain of the contradictions which it has engendered during the course of its development.

2. A subsequent moment is the relation of political forces; in other words, an evaluation of the degree of homogeneity, self-awareness and organization attained by the various social

groups. This moment can in its turn be analysed and differentiated into various levels, corresponding to the various moments of collective political consciousness, as they have manifested themselves in history up till now. The first and most elementary of these is the economic-corporate level: a tradesman feels *obliged* to stand by another tradesman, a manufacturer by another manufacturer, etc., but the tradesman does not yet feel solidarity with the manufacturer; in other words, the members of the professional group are conscious of its unity and homogeneity, and of the need to organize it, but in the case of the wider social group this is not yet so. A second moment is that in which consciousness is reached of the solidarity of interests among all the members of the social group – but still in the purely economic field. Already in this moment the problem of the state is posed – but only in terms of winning politico-juridical equality with the ruling groups: the right is claimed to participate in legislation and administration, even to reform these – but within the existing fundamental structures. A third moment is that in which one becomes aware that one's own corporate interests, in their present and future development, transcend the corporate limits of the merely economic group, and can and must become the interests of other subordinate groups. This is the most purely political phase, and marks the decisive passage from the structure to the sphere of the complex superstructures; it is the phase in which previously germinated ideologies become 'party', come into confrontation and conflict, until only one of them, or at least a single combination of them, tends to prevail, to gain the upper hand, to propagate itself over the whole social area – bringing about not only a unison of economic and political aims, but also intellectual and moral unity, posing all the questions around which the struggle rages not on a corporate but on a 'universal' plane, and thus creating the hegemony of a fundamental social group over a series of subordinate groups. It is true that the state is seen as the organ of one particular group, destined to create favourable conditions for the latter's maximum expansion. But the development and expansion of the particular group are conceived of, and presented, as being the motor force of a universal expansion, of a development of all the 'national' energies. In other words, the dominant group is co-ordinated concretely with the general interests of the subordinate groups, and the life of the state is conceived of as a continuous process of formation and superseding of unstable equilibria (on the juridical plane) between the interests of the fundamental group and those of the subordinate groups – equilibria in which the interests of the dominant group prevail, but only up to a certain point, i.e. stopping short of narrowly economic-corporate interest.

In real history these moments imply each other reciprocally – horizontally and vertically, so to speak – i.e. according to socio-economic activity (horizontally) and to territories (vertically), combining and diverging in various ways. Each of these combinations may be represented by its own organized economic and political expression. It is also necessary to take into account the fact that international relations intertwine with these internal relations of nation-states, creating new, original and historically concrete combinations. A particular ideology, for instance, born in a highly developed country, is disseminated in less developed countries, impinging on the local interplay of combinations. (Religion, for example, has always been a source of such national and international ideological-political combinations, and so too have the other international organizations – Freemasonry, Rotarianism, the Jews, career diplomacy. These propose political solutions of diverse historical origin, and assist their victory in particular countries – functioning as international political parties which operate within each nation with the full concentration of the international forces. But religion, Freemasonry, Rotary, Jews, etc., can be subsumed into the social category of 'intellectuals', whose function, on an international scale, is that of mediating the extremes, of 'socializing' the technical discoveries which provide the impetus for all activities of leadership, of devising compromises between, and ways out of, extreme solutions.) This relation between international forces and national forces is further complicated by the existence within every state of several structurally diverse territorial sectors, with diverse relations of force at all levels (thus the Vendée was allied with the forces of international reaction, and represented them in the heart of French territorial unity; similarly Lyons in the French Revolution represented a particular knot of relations, etc.).

3. The third moment is that of the relation of military forces, which from time to time is directly decisive. (Historical development oscillates continually between the first and the third

moment, with the mediation of the second.) But this moment too
is not undifferentiated, nor is it susceptible to immediate
schematic definition. Here too, two levels can be distinguished:
the military level in the strict or technical military sense, and the
level which may be termed politico-military. In the course of
history these two levels have appeared in a great variety of
combinations. A typical example, which can serve as a
hypothetical demonstration, is the relation involved in a state's
military oppression of a nation seeking to attain its national
independence. The relation is not purely military, but politico-
military; indeed this type of oppression would be inexplicable if it
were not for the state of social disintegration of the oppressed
people, and the passivity of the majority among them;
consequently independence cannot be won with purely military
forces, it requires both military and politico-military ones. If the
oppressed nation, in fact, before embarking on its struggle for
independence, had to wait until the hegemonic state allowed it to
organize its own army in the strict and technical sense of the word,
it would have to wait quite a while. (It may happen that the claim
to have its own army is conceded by the hegemonic nation, but this
only means that a great part of the struggle has already been
fought and won on the politico-military terrain.) The oppressed
nation will therefore initially oppose the dominant military force
with a force which is only 'politico-military', that is to say a form of
political action which has the virtue of provoking repercussions of
a military character in the sense: 1. that it has the capacity to
destroy the war potential of the dominant nation from within;
2. that it compels the dominant military force to thin out and
disperse itself over a large territory, thus nullifying a great part of
its war potential. In the Italian Risorgimento the disastrous
absence of politico-military leadership may be noted, especially in
the Action Party (through congenital incapacity), but also in the
Piedmontese Moderate Party, both before and after 1848,[12] not to
be sure through incapacity but through 'politico-economic
Malthusianism' – in other words, because they were unwilling even
to hint at the possibility of an agrarian reform, and because they
had no desire to see a national constituent assembly convoked, but
merely waited for the Piedmont monarchy, free from any
conditions or limitations of popular origin, to extend its rule to the
whole of Italy – sanctioned only by regional plebiscites.

A further question connected with the foregoing is whether fundamental historical crises are directly determined by economic crises. The answer is contained implicitly in the foregoing paragraphs, where problems have been considered which are only another way of presenting the one now under consideration. Nevertheless it is still necessary, for didactic reasons, given the particular public which is being aimed at, to examine each of the ways in which a single question may present itself as if it were a new and independent problem. It may be ruled out that immediate economic crises of themselves produce fundamental historical events; they can simply create a terrain more favourable to the dissemination of certain modes of thought, and certains ways of posing and resolving questions involving the entire subsequent development of national life. Moreover, all assertions concerning periods of crisis or of prosperity may give rise to unilateral judgements. In his historical outline of the French Revolution [...] Mathiez, in opposition to the vulgar traditional history which aprioristically 'discovers' a crisis coinciding with every major rupture of social equilibrium, asserts that towards 1789 the economic situation was in an immediate sense rather good, so that it cannot be said that the downfall of the absolute state was due to a crisis of impoverishment. It should be observed that the state was in the throes of a mortal financial crisis and considering which of the privileged social orders would have to bear the sacrifices and burdens necessary for the state and royal finances to be put back in order. Furthermore, if the economic position of the bourgeoisie was flourishing, the situation of the popular classes was certainly not good either in the towns or, especially, on the land – where they suffered from endemic poverty. In any case, the rupture of the equilibrium of forces did not occur as the result of direct mechanical causes – i.e. the impoverishment of the social group which had an interest in breaking the equilibrium, and which did in fact break it. It occurred in the context of conflicts on a higher plane than the immediate world of the economy; conflicts related to class 'prestige' (future economic interests), and to an inflammation of sentiments of independence, autonomy and power. The specific question of economic hardship or well-being as a cause of new historical realities is a partial aspect of the question of the relations of force at their various levels. Changes can come about either because a situation of well being is threatened by the narrow self-interest of an opposing group, or because hardship has become intolerable and no force is visible in the old society capable of mitigating it and of re-establishing normality by legal means. Hence it may be said that all these elements are the concrete manifestation of the conjunctural fluctuations of the totality of social relations of force, on whose terrain the passage takes place from the latter to political relations of force, and finally to the military relation which is decisive.

If this process of development from one moment to the next is missing – and it is essentially a process which has as its actors men and their will and capability – the situation is not taken advantage of, and contradictory outcomes are possible: either the old society resists and ensures itself a breathing space, by physically exterminating the elite of the rival class and terrorizing its mass reserves; or a reciprocal destruction of the conflicting forces occurs, and a peace of the graveyard is established, perhaps even under the surveillance of a foreign guard.

But the most important observation to be made about any concrete analysis of the relations of force is the following: that such analyses cannot and must not be ends in themselves (unless the intention is merely to write a chapter of past history), but acquire significance only if they serve to justify a particularly practical activity, an initiative of will. They reveal the points of least resistance, at which the force of will can be most fruitfully applied; they suggest immediate tactical operations; they indicate how a campaign of political agitation may best be launched, what language will best be understood by the masses, etc. The decisive element in every situation is the permanently organized and long prepared force which can be put into the field when it is judged that a situation is favourable (and it can be favourable only in so far as such a force exists, and is full of fighting spirit). Therefore the essential task is that of systematically and patiently ensuring that this force is formed, developed and rendered ever more homogeneous, compact, and self-aware. This is clear from military history, and from the care with which in every period armies have been prepared in advance to be able to make war at any moment. The great states have been great precisely because they were at all times prepared to intervene effectively in favourable international conjunctures – which were precisely favourable because there was the concrete possibility of effectively intervening in them.

SPN, 177-85 (Q13§17)

11 Some Theoretical and Practical Aspects of 'Economism'

Economism – theoretical movement for free trade – theoretical syndicalism. It should be considered to what degree theoretical syndicalism derives originally from the philosophy of praxis, and to what degree from the economic doctrines of free trade – i.e. in the last analysis from liberalism. Hence it should be considered whether economism, in its most developed form, is not a direct descendant of liberalism, having very little connection with the philosophy of praxis even in its origins – and what connection it had only extrinsic and purely verbal.

The nexus between free-trade ideology and theoretical syndicalism is particularly evident in Italy, where the admiration of syndicalists like Lanzillo & Co. for Pareto is well known. The significance of the two tendencies, however, is very different. The former belongs to a dominant and directive social group; the latter to a group which is still subaltern, which has not yet gained consciousness of its strength, its possibilities, of how it is to develop, and which therefore does not know how to escape from the primitivist phase.

The approach of the free trade movement is based on a theoretical error whose practical origin is not hard to identify: namely the distinction between political society and civil society, which is made into and presented as an organic one, whereas in fact it is merely methodological. Thus it is asserted that economic activity belongs to civil society, and that the state must not intervene to regulate it. But since in actual reality civil society and state are one and the same, it must be made clear that *laissez-faire* too is a form of state 'regulation', introduced and maintained by legislative and coercive means. It is a deliberate policy, conscious of its own ends, and not the spontaneous, automatic expression of economic facts. Consequently, *laissez-faire* liberalism is a political programme, designed to change – in so far as it is victorious – a state's ruling personnel, and to change the economic programme of the state itself – in other words the distribution of the national income.

The case of theoretical syndicalism is different. Here we are dealing with a subaltern group, which is prevented by this theory from ever becoming dominant, or from developing beyond the economic-corporate stage and rising to the phase of ethico-political hegemony in civil society, and of domination in the state. In the case of *laissez-faire* liberalism, one is dealing with a fraction of the ruling class which wishes to modify not the structure of the state, but merely government policy; which wishes to reform the laws controlling commerce, but only indirectly those controlling industry (since it is undeniable that protection, especially in countries with a poor and restricted market, limits freedom of industrial enterprise and favours unhealthily the creation of monopolies). What is at stake is a rotation in governmental office of the ruling-class parties, not the foundation and organization of a new political society, and even less of a new type of civil society. In the case of the theoretical syndicalist movement the problem is more complex. It is undeniable that in it, the independence and autonomy of the subaltern group which it claims to represent are in fact sacrificed to the intellectual hegemony of the ruling class, since precisely theoretical syndicalism is merely an aspect of *laissez-faire* liberalism – justified with a few mutilated (and therefore banalized) theses from the philosophy of praxis. Why and how does this 'sacrifice' come about? The transformation of the subordinate group into a dominant one is excluded, either because the problem is not even considered (Fabianism, De Man,[13] an important part of the Labour Party), or because it is posed in an inappropriate and ineffective form (social-democratic tendencies in general), or because of a belief in the possibility of leaping from class society directly into a society of perfect equality with a syndical economy.

The attitude of economism towards expressions of political and intellectual will, action or initiative is to say the least strange – as if these did not emanate organically from economic necessity, and indeed were not the only effective expression of the economy. Thus it is incongruous that the concrete posing of the problem of hegemony should be interpreted as a fact subordinating the hegemonic group. Undoubtedly the fact of hegemony presupposes that account be taken of the interests and the tendencies of the groups over which hegemony is to be exercised, and that a certain compromise equilibrium should be formed – in other words, that the leading group should make sacrifices of an economic-corporate kind. But there is also no doubt that such sacrifices and such a compromise cannot touch the essential; for though hegemony is ethico-political, it must also be economic, must necessarily be based on the decisive function exercised by the leading group in the decisive nucleus of economic activity.

Economism appears in many other guises besides *laissez-faire* liberalism and theoretical syndicalism. All forms of electoral abstentionism belong to it (a typical example is the abstentionism of the Italian clericals after 1870, which became ever more attenuated after 1900 until 1919 and the formation of the Popular Party;[14] the organic distinction which the clericals made between the real Italy and the legal Italy was a reproduction of the distinction between economic world and politico-legal world); and there are many such forms, in the sense that there can be semi-abstentionism, 25 per cent abstentionism, etc. Linked with abstentionism is the formula 'the worse it gets, the better that will be', and also the formula of the so-called parliamentary 'intransigence' of certain groups of deputies. Economism is not always opposed to political action and to the political party, but the latter is seen merely as an educational organism similar in kind to a trade union. One point of reference for the study of economism, and for understanding the relations between structure and superstructure, is the passage in *The Poverty of Philosophy* where it says that an important phase in the development of a social group is that in which the individual components of a trade union no longer struggle solely for their own economic interests, but for the defence and the development of the organization itself (see the exact statement;[15] *The Poverty of Philosophy* is an essential moment in the formation of the philosophy of praxis; it can be considered as a development of the *Theses on Feuerbach*, while *The Holy Family* – an occasional work – is a vaguely intermediate stage, as is apparent from the passages devoted to Proudhon and especially to French materialism. The passage on French materialism is more than anything else a chapter of cultural history – not a theoretical passage as it is often interpreted as being – and as cultural history it is admirable. Recall the observation that the critique of Proudhon and of his interpretation of the Hegelian dialectic contained in *The Poverty of the Philosophy* may be extended to Gioberti and to the Hegelianism of the Italian moderate liberals in general. The parallel Proudhon-Gioberti, despite the fact that they represent non-homogeneous politico-historical phases, indeed precisely for that reason, can be interesting and productive.) In this connection Engels's statement too should be recalled, that the economy is only the mainspring of history 'in the last analysis' (to be found in his two letters on the philosophy of praxis also published in Italian),[16] this statement is to be related directly to the passage in the Preface to *A Contribution to the Critique of Political Economy* which says that it is on the terrain of ideologies that men become conscious of conflicts in the world of the economy.

At various points in these notes it is stated that the philosophy of praxis is far more widely diffused than is generally conceded. The assertion is correct if what is meant is that historical economism – as Professor Loria[17] now calls his more or less incoherent theories – is widely diffused, and that consequently the cultural environment has completely changed from the time in which the philosophy of praxis began its struggles. One might say, in Crocean terminology, that the greatest heresy which has grown in the womb of the 'religion of freedom' has itself too like orthodox religion degenerated, and has become disseminated as 'super-stition' – in other words, has combined with *laissez-faire* liberalism and produced economism. However, it remains to be seen whether – in contrast to orthodox religion, which has by now quite shrivelled up – this heretical superstition has not in fact always maintained a ferment which will cause it to be reborn as a higher form of religion; in other words, if the dross of superstition is not in fact easily got rid of.

A few characteristics of historical economism: 1. in the search for historical connections it makes no distinction between what is 'relatively permanent' and what is a passing fluctuation, and by an economic fact it means the self-interest of an individual or small group, in an immediate and 'dirty-Jewish' sense. In other words, it does not take economic class formations into account, with all their inherent relations, but assumes motives of mean and usurious self-interest, especially when it takes forms which the law defines as criminal; 2. the doctrine according to which economic development is reduced to the course of technical change in the instruments of work. Professor Loria has produced a splendid demonstration of this doctrine in application, in his article on the social influence of the aeroplane published in *Rassegna Contemporanea* in 1912; 3. the doctrine according to which economic and historical development are made to depend directly on the changes in some important element of production – the discovery of a new raw material or fuel, etc. – which necessitate the application of new methods in the construction and design of machines. In recent times there has been an entire literature on the subject of petroleum: Antonio Laviosa's article in *Nuova Antologia* of 16 May 1929 can be read as a typical example. The discovery of new fuels and new forms of energy, just as of new raw materials to be transformed, is certainly of great importance, since it can alter the position of individual states; but it does not determine historical movement, etc.

It often happens that people combat historical economism in the belief that they are attacking historical materialism. This is the case, for instance, with an article in the Paris *Avenir* of 10 October 1930 (reproduced in *Rassegna Settimanale della Stampa Estera* [Weekly Review of the Foreign Press] of 21 October 1930, pp. 2303-4), which can be quoted as typical: 'We have been hearing for some time, especially since the war, that it is self-interest which governs nations and drives the world forward. It was the Marxists who invented this thesis, to which they give the somewhat doctrinaire title of "historical materialism". In pure Marxism, men taken as a mass obey economic necessity and not their own passions. Politics is passion; patriotism is passion; these two demanding ideas merely act as a façade in history. In reality, the history of peoples throughout the centuries is to be explained by a changing, constantly renewed interplay of material causes. Everything is economics. Many "bourgeois" philosophers and economists have taken up this refrain. They pretend to be able to explain high international politics to us by the current price of grain, oil or rubber. They use all their ingenuity to prove that diplomacy is entirely governed by questions of custom tariffs and cost prices. These explanations enjoy a high esteem. They have a modicum of scientific appearance, and proceed from a sort of superior scepticism which would like to pass for the last word in elegance. Emotions in foreign policy? Feelings in home affairs? Enough of that! That stuff is all right for the common people. The great minds, the initiates, know that everything is governed by debits and credits.

Now this is an absolute pseudo-truth. It is utterly false that peoples only allow themselves to be moved by considerations of self-interest, and it is entirely true that they are above all motivated by desire for, and ardent belief in, prestige. Anyone who does not understand this, does not understand anything.' The article (entitled 'The Desire for Prestige') goes on to cite the examples of German and Italian politics, which it claims are governed by considerations of prestige, and not dictated by material interests. In short, it includes most of the more banal polemical gibes that are directed against the philosophy of praxis; but the real target of the polemic is crude economism of Loria's kind. However, the author is not very strong in argument in other respects either. He does not understand that 'passions' may be simply a synonym for economic interests, and that it is difficult to maintain that political activity is a permanent state of raw emotion and of spasm. Indeed he himself presents French politics as systematic and coherent 'rationality', i.e. purged of all elements of passion, etc.

In its most widespread form as economistic superstition, the philosophy of praxis loses a great part of its capacity for cultural expansion among the top layer of intellectuals, however much it may gain among the popular masses and the second-rate intellectuals, who do not intend to overtax their brains but still wish to appear to know everything, etc. As Engels wrote, many people find it very convenient to think that they can have the whole of history and all political and philosophical wisdom in their pockets at little cost and no trouble, concentrated into a few short formulas. They forget that the thesis which asserts that men become conscious of fundamental conflicts on the terrain of ideologies is not psychological or moralistic in character, but structural and epistemological; and they form the habit of considering politics, and hence history, as a continuous *marché de dupes*, a competition in conjuring and sleight of hand. 'Critical' activity is reduced to the exposure of swindles, to creating scandals, and to prying into the pockets of public figures.

It is thus forgotten that since 'economism' too is, or is presumed to be, an objective principle of interpretation (objective-scientific), the search for direct self-interest should apply to all aspects of history, to those who represent the 'thesis' as well as to those who represent the 'antithesis'. Furthermore, another proposition of the philosophy of praxis is also forgotten: that 'popular beliefs' and similar ideas are themselves material forces. The search for 'dirty-Jewish' interests has sometimes led to monstrous and comical errors of interpretation, which have consequently reacted negatively on the prestige of the original body of ideas. It is therefore necessary to combat economism not only in the theory of historiography, but also and especially in the theory and practice of politics. In this field, the struggle can and must be carried on by developing the concept of hegemony – as has been done in practice in the development of the theory of the political party, and in the actual history of certain political parties (the struggle against the theory of the so-called permanent revolution – to which was counterposed the concept of revolutionary-democratic dictatorship; the extent of the support given to constituentist ideologies, etc.)[18] A study could be made of how certain political movements were judged during the course of their development. One could take as a model the Boulangist movement (from 1886 to 1890 approximately) or the Dreyfus trial or even the coup d'état of 2 December (one would analyse the classic work on the subject[19] and consider how much relative importance is given on the one hand to immediate economic factors, and on the other to the concrete study of 'ideologies'). Confronted with these events, economism asks the question: 'who profits directly from the initiative under consideration?', and replies with a line of reasoning which is as simplistic as it is fallacious: the ones who profit directly are a certain fraction of the ruling class. Furthermore, so that no mistake shall be made, the choice falls on that fraction which manifestly has a progressive function, controlling the totality of economic forces. One can be certain of not going wrong, since necessarily, if the movement under consideration comes to power, sooner or later the progressive fraction of the ruling group will end up by controlling the new government, and by making it its instrument for turning the state apparatus to its own benefit. This sort of infallibility, therefore, comes very cheap. It not only has no theoretical significance – it has only minimal political implications or practical efficacy. In general, it produces nothing but moralistic sermons, and interminable questions of personality.

When a movement of the Boulangist type occurs, the analysis realistically should be developed along the following lines: 1. social content of the mass following of the movement; 2. what function did this mass have in the balance of forces – which is in process of transformation, as the new movement demonstrates by its very coming into existence? 3. what is the political and social significance of those of the demands presented by the movement's leaders which find general assent? To what effective needs do they correspond? 4. examination of the conformity of the means to the proposed end; 5. only in the last analysis, and formulated in political not moralistic terms, is the *hypothesis* considered that such a movement will necessarily be perverted, and serve quite different ends from those which the mass of its followers expect. But economism puts forward this hypothesis in advance, when no concrete fact (that is to say, none which appears as such to the evidence of common sense – rather than as a result of some esoteric 'scientific' analysis) yet exists to support it. It thus appears as a moralistic accusation of duplicity and bad faith, or (in the case of the movement's followers) of naïvety and stupidity. Thus the political struggle is reduced to a series of personal affairs between on the one hand those with the genie in the lamp who know everything and on the other those who are fooled by their own leaders but are so incurably thick that they refuse to believe it.

Moreover, until such movements have gained power, it is always possible to think that they are going to fail – and some indeed have failed (Boulangism itself, which failed as such and then was definitively crushed with the rise of the Dreyfusard movement; the movement of Georges Valois; that of General Gajda).[20] Research must therefore be directed towards identifying their strengths and weaknesses. The 'economist' hypothesis asserts the existence of an immediate element of strength – i.e. the availability of a certain direct or indirect financial backing (a large newspaper supporting the movement is also a form of indirect financial backing) – and is satisfied with that. But it is not enough.

In this case too, an analysis of the balance of forces – at all levels – can only culminate in the sphere of hegemony and ethico-political relations.

SPN, 158-67 (Q13§18)

12   Observations on Certain Aspects of the Structure of Political Parties in Periods of Organic Crisis

(To be connected to the notes on situations and relations of force.) At a certain point in their historical lives, social groups become detached from their traditional parties. In other words, the traditional parties in that particular organizational form, with the particular men who constitute, represent, and lead them, are no longer recognized by their class (or fraction of a class) as its expression. When such crises occur, the immediate situation becomes delicate and dangerous, because the field is open for violent solutions, for the activities of unknown forces, represented by charismatic 'men of destiny'.

These situations of conflict between 'represented and representatives' reverberate out from the terrain of the parties (the party organizations properly speaking, the parliamentary-electoral field, newspaper organization) throughout the state organism, reinforcing the relative power of the bureaucracy (civil and military), of high finance, of the Church, and generally of all bodies relatively independent of the fluctuations of public opinion. How are they created in the first place? In every country the process is different, although the content is the same. And the content is the crisis of the ruling class's hegemony, which occurs either because the ruling class has failed in some major political undertaking for which it has requested, or forcibly extracted, the consent of the broad masses (war, for example), or because huge masses (especially of peasants and petty-bourgeois intellectuals) have passed suddenly from a state of political passivity to a certain activity, and put forward demands which taken together, albeit not organically formulated, add up to a revolution. A 'crisis of authority' is spoken of: this is precisely the crisis of hegemony, or crisis of the state as a whole.

The crisis creates situations which are dangerous in the short run, since the various strata of the population are not all capable of orienting themselves equally swiftly, or of reorganizing with the same rhythm. The traditional ruling class, which has numerous trained cadres, changes men and programmes and, with greater speed than is achieved by the subordinate classes, reabsorbs the control that was slipping from its grasp. Perhaps it may make sacrifices, and expose itself to an uncertain future by demagogic promises; but it retains power, reinforces it for the time being, and uses it to crush its adversary and disperse his leading cadres, who cannot be very numerous or highly trained. The passage of the troops of many different parties under the banner of a single party, which better represents and resumes the needs of the entire class, is an organic and normal phenomenon, even if its rhythm is very swift – indeed almost like lightning in comparison with periods of calm. It represents the fusion of an entire social class under a single leadership, which alone is held to be capable of solving an overriding problem of its existence and of fending off a mortal danger. When the crisis does not find this organic solution, but that of the charismatic leader, it means that a static equilibrium exists (whose factors may be disparate, but in which the decisive one is the immaturity of the progressive forces); it means that no group, neither the conservatives nor the progressives, has the strength for victory, and that even the conservative group needs a master (see *The Eighteenth Brumaire of Louis Bonaparte*).

This order of phenomena is connected to one of the most important questions concerning the political party – namely the party's capacity to react against force of habit, against the tendency to become mummified and anachronistic. Parties come into existence, and constitute themselves as organizations, in order to influence the situation at moments which are historically vital for their class; but they are not always capable of adapting themselves to new tasks and to new epochs, nor of evolving *pari passu* with the overall relations of force (and hence the relative position of their class) in the country in question, or in the international field. In analysing the development of parties, it is necessary to distinguish: their social group; their mass membership; their bureaucracy and general staff. The bureaucracy is the most dangerously hidebound and conservative force; if it ends up by constituting a compact body, which stands on it own and feels itself independent of the mass of members, the party ends up by becoming anachronistic and at moments of acute crisis it is voided of its social content and left as though suspended in mid-air. One can see what has happened to a number of German parties as a result of the expansion of Hitlerism. French parties are a rich field for such research: they are all mummified and anachronistic – historico-political documents of the various phases of past French history, whose outdated terminology they continue to repeat; their crisis could become even more catastrophic than that of the German parties.

[...]

One point which should be added to the note on economism, as an example of the so-called intransigence theories, is the rigid aversion on principle to what are termed compromises – and the derivative of this, which can be termed 'fears of dangers'. It is clear that this aversion on principle to compromise is closely linked to economism. For the conception upon which the aversion is based can only be the iron conviction that there exist objective laws of historical development similar in kind to natural laws, together with a belief in a predetermined teleology like that of a religion: since favourable conditions are inevitably going to appear, and since these, in a rather mysterious way, will bring about palingenetic events, it is evident that any deliberate initiative tending to predispose and plan these conditions is not only useless but even harmful. Side by side with these fatalistic beliefs however, there exists the tendency 'thereafter' to rely blindly and indiscriminately on the regulatory properties of armed conflict. Yet this too is not entirely without its logic and its consistency, since it goes with a belief that the intervention of will is useful for destruction but not for reconstruction (already under way in the very moment of destruction). Destruction is conceived of mechanically, not as destruction/reconstruction. In such modes of thinking, no account is taken of the 'time' factor, nor in the last analysis even of 'economics'. For there is no understanding of the fact that mass ideological factors always lag behind mass economic phenomena, and that therefore, at certain moments, the automatic thrust due to the economic factor is slowed down, obstructed or even momentarily broken by traditional ideological elements – hence that there must be a conscious, planned struggle to ensure that the exigencies of the economic position of the masses, which may conflict with the traditional leadership's policies, are understood. An appropriate political initiative is always necessary to liberate the economic thrust from the dead weight of traditional policies – i.e. to change the political direction of certain forces which have to be absorbed if a new, homogeneous politico-economic historical bloc, without internal contradictions, is to be successfully formed. And, since two 'similar' forces can only be welded into a new organism either through a series of compromises or by force of arms, either by binding them to each other as allies or by forcibly subordinating one to the other, the question is whether one has the necessary force, and whether it is 'productive' to use it. If the union of two forces is necessary in order to defeat a third, a recourse to arms and coercion (even supposing that these are available) can be nothing more than a methodological hypothesis; the only concrete possibility is compromise. Force can be employed against enemies, but not against a part of one's own side which one wishes rapidly to assimilate, and whose 'good will' and enthusiasm one needs.

[…]

SPN, 210-11; 167-8 (Q13§23)

VII THE ART AND SCIENCE OF POLITICS

Introduction

These notes on the state and civil society and on the political party can be thought of as continuous with those in the preceding section. Gramsci's critique there of economism at the theoretical level is complemented by his critique here of its practical consequences. Rosa Luxemburg's conception of the mass strike and Trotsky's theory of the permanent revolution are, for Gramsci, forms of economistic political thinking. Trotsky's theory is also criticized as an abstract form of internationalism, insufficiently attentive to national conditions. Using military analogies, Gramsci says these approaches assume that on the level of political tactics an economic crisis opens a breach in the enemy's ranks through which a successful political offensive can take place. What they both underestimate, Gramsci says, is the capacity of resistance to these 'frontal attacks' in advanced industrial states and the need for a work of preparation among the 'troops', in other words the formation of a collective will among the people. In Russia in 1917 a frontal assault on the state was able to succeed because there 'the state was everything, civil society was primordial and gelatinous'. In the West the state is 'only an outer ditch' behind which is a sturdy civil society. Hence in the West there must be a transition from the war of movement to a 'war of position'.

These remarks of Gramsci's develop positions he had taken before his arrest. In August 1926 he had told a Central Committee meeting: 'in the advanced capitalist countries, the ruling class possesses organizational reserves which it did not possess, for instance, in Russia ... The state apparatus is far more resistant than is often possible to believe, and it succeeds, in moments of crisis, in organizing greater forces loyal to the regime than the depth of the crisis might lead one to suppose.' (SPW II, pp. 408-9). At the same time, his remarks in the prison notebooks had a precise contemporary reference. They were first drafted in late

222

1930, at the height of the Comintern's so-called Third Period (1929-34) which had launched the analysis of a terminal world crisis of capitalism and a tactic of frontal attack ('class against class'). In 1930 the surviving PCdI leadership, after a long deliberation, accepted this analysis and proceeded to expel three Political Bureau members who opposed it. Gramsci in prison came to know of these developments and was highly critical of them. In Italy Fascism was ever more entrenched and the Communist Party was reduced to a membership of about 4,000. Moreover, his own diagnosis of Italian capitalism after the 1929 world crisis was one not of terminal decay but of restructuring; an intensification of exploitation achieved through new forms of management and new corporatist strategies, an expansion of state intervention in the economy and society. In this context, a frontal attack or war of movement was simply suicidal for the left.

Gramsci's East/West contrast in this respect is very significant. But it should not be taken as indicating that Gramsci thought conditions were uniform throughout the 'East' or 'West': nothing could be further from the spirit of his work. At most he identifies certain minimum shared features of advanced capitalist societies. The Italian society in which he operated politically, with its large areas of semi-feudal peasant agriculture, its immature parliamentary traditions and its powerful priesthood, possessed characteristics of both 'East' and 'West' which made it very different from Britain or the United States in his own time, let alone today. The 'Americanism and Fordism' notes (see Section IX) show how closely he attended to these differences *within* the West. It should also be observed that, contrary to what is sometimes asserted, his advocacy of a war of position does not entail a renunciation of revolution, only a change in its strategy and form. His argument that the advanced capitalist societies possess political and ideological resources which make necessary a transition from war of manoeuvre to a long war of position must be grasped for what it is: as an argument that the specific conditions which made possible a successful revolution in Russia in 1917 cannot and will not present themselves in the West. The strategy therefore must be different. It must involve the building of hegemony between the working class and its allies. It must involve ideological struggle. It must involve the construction of a mass democratic movement. But this does not add up to an

A Gramsci Reader

abandonment of the revolutionary goal of socialism and its replacement by a strategy of piecemeal reforms.

The contrast war of movement/war of position is paralleled by the contrast between state and civil society (on Gramsci's somewhat unstable usage of the word 'state' see the Glossary of Key Terms). War of movement is a frontal assault on the state whereas war of position is conducted mainly on the terrain of civil society. Civil society is a site of consent, hegemony, direction, in conceptual opposition to the state (political society) which is a site of coercion, dictatorship, domination. Civil society is therefore, in Gramsci, at once the political terrain on which the dominant class organizes its hegemony and the terrain on which opposition parties and movements organize, win allies and build their social power.

Gramsci says that his distinction between state (political society) and civil society is not 'organic' but 'methodological' (*metodica*) (see above p.210). By this he means that, although the two levels must be analytically distinguished from one another, they must also be seen as being intertwined in practice. One might illustrate this by saying that a state education system is at one level clearly part of political society, just as trade unions are when they take part in tripartite planning with employers and government. But this does not mean that everything which takes place in schools or trade unions is subservient to the state or reflects ruling-class interests. By making such a 'methodological' distinction between the two spheres, Gramsci avoids on the one hand a liberal reductionism, which sees civil society as a realm of free individuality entirely apart from the state, and on the other a statist and functionalist reductionism, which sees everything in society as belonging to the state and serving its interests. In Gramsci's own time the first kind of reductionism was exemplified by the liberal Croce, the second by the Fascist Giovanni Gentile. The latter reductionism, however, has been frequent enough on the left as well: one might cite Althusser's notion of 'ideological state apparatus'.

The last two notes included here deal with that key element in the political process: the party. Gramsci treats it, by analogy with the prince in Machiavelli's sixteenth-century treatise, as an organism which helps to form and galvanize a 'national-popular collective will'. The party must help to perform the 'Jacobin' task (see also Section VIII) of setting in motion a hegemonic alliance between the proletariat and other social strata, and it must help

precipitate a process of 'intellectual and moral reformation' (see
also Section XI). In order to function in this way, the party cannot
be an organization of closed cadres and it must not degenerate into
a bureaucratic apparatus (see 'Fetishism'). It must be democratic
in its structure and practices if it is to widen out to a whole class
which will tend to 'unify the whole of humanity' (p.382).

1   [War of Position and War of Manoeuvre]

On the subject of parallels betwen the concepts of war of
manoeuvre and war of position in military science and the
corresponding concepts in political science, Rosa [Luxemburg]'s
pamphlet [*Mass Strike, Party and Trade Unions*], translated (from
French) into Italian in 1919 by C. Alessandri, should be recalled.

In this pamphlet, Rosa – a little hastily, and rather superficially
too – theorized the historical experiences of 1905. She in fact
disregarded the 'voluntary' and organizational elements which
were far more extensive and important in those events than –
thanks to a certain 'economistic' and spontaneist prejudice – she
tended to believe. All the same, this pamphlet (with others of the
same author's essays) is one of the most significant documents
theorizing the war of manoeuvre applied to political science. The
immediate economic element (crises, etc.) is seen as the field
artillery which in war opens a breach in the enemy's defences – a
breach sufficient for one's own troops to rush in and obtain a
definitive (strategic) victory, or at least an important victory in the
context of the strategic line. Naturally the effects of immediate
economic factors in historical science are held to be far more
complex than the effects of heavy artillery in a war of manoeuvre,
since they are conceived of as having a double effect: 1. they
breach the enemy's defences, after throwing him into disarray and
causing him to lose faith in himself, his forces, and his future; 2. in
a flash they organize one's own troops and create the necessary
cadres – or at least in a flash they put the existing cadres (formed,
until that moment, by the general historical process) in positions
which enable them to encadre one's scattered forces; 3. in a flash
they bring about the necessary ideological concentration on the

A Gramsci Reader

common objective to be achieved. This view was a form of iron economic determinism, with the aggravating factor that it was conceived of as operating with lightning speed in time and in space. It was thus out and out historical mysticism, the awaiting of a sort of miraculous illumination.

General Krasnov asserted (in his novel)[1] that the Entente did not wish for the victory of Imperial Russia (for fear that the Eastern Question would be definitively resolved in favour of Tsarism), and therefore obliged the Russian General Staff to adopt trench warfare (absurd, in view of the enormous length of the Front from the Baltic to the Black Sea, with vast marshy and forest zones), whereas the only possible strategy was a war of manoeuvre. This assertion is merely silly. In actual fact, the Russian Army did attempt a war of manoeuvre and sudden incursion, especially in the Austrian sector (but also in East Prussia), and won successes which were as brilliant as they were ephemeral. The truth is that one cannot choose the form of war one wants, unless from the start one has a crushing superiority over the enemy. It is well known what losses were caused by the stubborn refusal of the General Staffs to recognise that a war of position was 'imposed' by the overall relation of the forces in conflict. A war of position is not, in reality, constituted simply by the actual trenches, but by the whole organizational and industrial system of the territory which lies to the rear of the army in the field. It is imposed notably by the rapid fire-power of cannons, machine-guns and rifles, by the armed strength which can be concentrated at a particular spot, as well as by the abundance of supplies which make possible the swift replacement of material lost after an enemy breakthrough or a retreat. A further factor is the great mass of men under arms; they are of very unequal calibre, and are precisely only able to operate as a mass force. It can be seen how on the Eastern Front it was one thing to make an incursion in the Austrian Sector, and quite another in the German Sector; and how even in the Austrian Sector, reinforced by picked German troops and commanded by Germans, incursion tactics ended in disaster. The same thing occurred in the Polish campaign of 1920; the seemingly irresistible advance was halted before Warsaw by General Weygand, on the line commanded by French officers. Even those military experts whose minds are now fixed on the war of position, just as they were previously on that of manoeuvre, naturally do not maintain that the latter should be considered as expunged from military science. They merely maintain that, in wars among the more industrially and socially advanced states, the war of manoeuvre must be considered as reduced to more of a tactical than a strategic function; that it must be considered as occupying the same position as siege warfare used to occupy previously in relation to it.

The same reduction must take place in the art and science of politics, at least in the case of the most advanced states, where 'civil society' has become a very complex structure and one which is resistant to the catastrophic 'incursions' of the immediate economic element (crises, depressions, etc.). The superstructures of civil society are like the trench-systems of modern warfare. In war it would sometimes happen that a fierce artillery attack seemed to have destroyed the enemy's entire defensive system, whereas in fact it had only destroyed the outer perimeter; and at the moment of their advance and attack the assailants would find themselves confronted by a line of defence which was still effective. The same thing happens in politics, during great economic crises. A crisis cannot give the attacking forces the ability to organize with lightning speed in time and in space; still less can it endow them with fighting spirit. Similarly, the defenders are not demoralized, nor do they abandon their positions, even among the ruins, nor do they lose faith in their own strength or their own future. Of course, things do not remain exactly as they were; but it is certain that one will not find the element of speed, of accelerated time, of the definitive forward march expected by the strategists of political Cadornism.[2]

The last occurrence of the kind in the history of politics was the events of 1917. They marked a decisive turning-point in the history of the art and science of politics. Hence it is a question of studying 'in depth' which elements of civil society correspond to the defensive systems in a war of position. The use of the phrase 'in depth' is intentional, because 1917 has been studied – but only either from superficial and banal viewpoints, as when certain social historians study the vagaries of women's fashions, or from a 'rationalistic' viewpoint – in other words, with the conviction that certain phenomena are destroyed as soon as they are 'realistically' explained, as if they were popular superstitions (which anyway are not destroyed either merely by being explained).

The question of the meagre success achieved by new tendencies in the trade-union movement should be related to this series of problems.[3]

One attempt to begin a revision of the current tactical methods was perhaps that outlined by L. Dav. Br. [Trotsky] at the fourth meeting, when he made a comparison between the Eastern and Western fronts. The former had fallen at once, but unprecedented struggles had then ensued; in the case of the latter, the struggles would take place 'beforehand'.[4] The question, therefore, was whether civil society resists before or after the attempt to seize power; where the latter takes place, etc. However, the question was outlined only in a brilliant, literary form, without directives of a practical character.

SPN, 233-6 (Q13§24)

2   War of Position and War of Manoeuvre or Frontal War

It should be seen whether Bronstein [Trotsky]'s famous theory about the *permanent* character of the movement[5] is not the political reflection of the theory of war of manoeuvre (recall the observation of the cossack general Krasnov) – i.e. in the last analysis, a reflection of the general-economic-cultural-social conditions in a country in which the structures of national life are embryonic and loose, and incapable of becoming 'trench or fortress'. In this case one might say that Bronstein, apparently 'Western', was in fact a cosmopolitan – i.e. superficially national and superficially Western or European. Ilyich [Lenin] on the other hand was profoundly national and profoundly European.

Bronstein in his memoirs recalls being told that his theory had been proved true ... fifteen years later, and replying to the epigram with another epigram.[6] In reality his theory, as such, was good neither fifteen years earlier nor fifteen years later. As happens to the obstinate, of whom Guicciardini speaks, he guessed more or less correctly; that is to say, he was right in his more general practical prediction. It is as if one was to prophesy that a little four-year-old girl would become a mother, and when at twenty she did so one said: 'I guessed that she would' – overlooking the fact, however, that when she was four years old one had tried to rape the girl, in the belief that she would become a mother even then. It seems to me that Ilyich understood that a change was necessary from the war of manoeuvre applied victoriously in the East in 1917, to a war of position which was the only form possible in the West – where, as Krasnov observes, armies could rapidly accumulate endless quantities of munitions, and where the social structures were of themselves still capable of becoming heavily armed fortifications. This is what the formula of the 'united front'[7] seems to me to mean, and it corresponds to the conception of a single front for the Entente under the sole command of Foch.

Ilyich, however, did not have time to expand his formula – though it should be borne in mind that he could only have expanded it theoretically, whereas the fundamental task was a national one; that is to say it required a reconnaisance of the terrain and identification of the elements of trench and fortress represented by the elements of civil society, etc. In the East the state was everything, civil society was primordial and gelatinous; in the West, there was a proper relation between state and civil society, and when the state trembled a sturdy structure of civil society was at once revealed. The state was only an outer ditch, behind which there stood a powerful system of fortresses and earthworks: more or less numerous from one state to the next, it goes without saying – but this precisely necessitated an accurate reconnaissance of each individual country.

Bronstein's theory can be compared to that of certain French syndicalists on the general strike, and to Rosa's theory in the work translated by Alessandri. Rosa's pamphlet and theories anyway influenced the French syndicalists, as is clear from some of Rosmer's articles on Germany in *Vie Ouvrière* (first series in pamphlet form). It partly depends too on the theory of spontaneity.

SPN, 236-8 (Q7§16)

3 Transition from the War of Manoeuvre (and from Frontal Attack) to the War of Position in the Political Field as Well

This seems to me to be the most important question of political theory that the post-war period has posed, and the most difficult to solve correctly. It is related to the problems raised by Bronstein who in one way or another can be considered the political theorist of frontal attack in a period in which it only leads to defeats. This transition in political science is only indirectly (mediately) related to that which took place in the military field, although certainly a relation exists and an essential one. The war of position demands enormous sacrifices by infinite masses of people. So an unprecedented concentration of hegemony is necessary, and hence a more 'interventionist' government, which will take the offensive more openly against the oppositionists and organize permanently the 'impossibility' of internal disintegration – with controls of every kind, political, administrative, etc., reinforcement of the hegemonic 'positions' of the dominant group, etc. All this indicates that we have entered a culminating phase in the political-historical situation, since in politics the 'war of position', once won, is decisive definitively. In politics, in other words, the war of manoeuvre subsists so long as it is a question of winning positions which are not decisive, so that all the resources of the state's hegemony cannot be mobilized. But when, for one reason or another, these positions have lost their value and only the decisive positions are at stake, then one passes over to siege warfare; this is concentrated, difficult, and requires exceptional qualities of patience and inventiveness. In politics, the siege is a reciprocal one, despite all appearances, and the mere fact that the ruler has to muster all his resources demonstrates how seriously he takes his adversary.

SPN, 238-9 (Q6§138)

4 [Internationalism and National Policy]

A work (in the form of questions and answers) by Joseph Bessarion [Stalin] dating from September 1927: it deals with certain key problems of the science and art of politics.[8] The problem which seems to me to need further elaboration is the following: how, according to the philosophy of praxis (as it manifests itself politically) – whether as formulated by its founder [Marx] or particularly as restated by its most recent great theoretician [Lenin] – the international situation should be considered in its national aspect. In reality, the internal relations of any nation are the result of a combination which is 'original' and (in a certain sense) unique: these relations must be understood and conceived in their originality and uniqueness if one wishes to dominate them and direct them. To be sure, the line of development is towards internationalism, but the point of departure is 'national' – and it is from this point of departure that one must begin. Yet the perspective is international and cannot be otherwise. Consequently, it is necessary to study accurately the combination of national forces which the international class [the proletariat] will have to lead and develop, in accordance with the international perspective and directives [i.e. those of the Comintern]. The leading class is in fact only such if it accurately interprets this combination – of which it is itself a component and precisely as such is able to give the movement a certain direction, within certain perspectives. It is on this point, in my opinion, that the fundamental disagreement between Leo Davidovici [Trotsky] and Bessarion as interpreter of the majority movement [Bolshevism] really hinges. The accusations of nationalism are inept if they refer to the nucleus of the question. If one studies the majoritarians' struggle from 1902 up to 1917, one can see that its originality consisted in purging internationalism of every vague and purely ideological (in a pejorative sense) element, to give it a real-istic political content. It is in the concept of hegemony that those exigencies which are national in character are knotted together; one can well understand how certain tendencies either do not mention such a concept, or merely skim over it. A class that is international in character has – in as much as it guides social strata which are narrowly national (intellectuals), and indeed frequently even less than national: particularistic and municipalistic (the peasants) – to 'nationalize' itself in a certain sense. Moreover, this sense is not a very narrow one either, since before the conditions can be created for an economy that follows a world plan, it is necessary to pass through multiple phases in which the regional combinations (of groups of nations) may be of various kinds. Furthermore, it must never be forgotten that historical development follows the laws of necessity until the initiative has decisively passed over to those forces which tend towards construction in accordance with a plan of peaceful and solidary division of labour. That non-national concepts (i.e. ones that cannot be referred to each individual country) are erroneous can be seen *ab absurdo*: they have led to passivity and inertia in two quite distinct phases: 1. in the first phase, nobody believed that they ought to make a start – that is to say, they believed that by making a start they would find themselves isolated; they waited for everybody to move together, and nobody in the meantime moved or organized the movement; 2. the second phase is perhaps worse, because what is being awaited is an anachronistic and anti-natural form of 'Napoleonism' (since not all historical phases repeat themselves in the same form).[9] The theoretical weaknesses of this modern form of the old mechanicism are masked by the general theory of permanent revolution, which is nothing but a generic forecast presented as a dogma, and which demolishes itself by not in fact coming true.

SPN, 240-1 (Q14§68)

5 Question of The 'Collective Man' or 'Social Conformism'

Educative and formative role of the state, whose aim is always that of creating new and higher types of civilization; of adapting the 'civilization' and the morality of the broadest popular masses to the necessities of the continuous development of the economic apparatus of production; hence of evolving even physically new types of humanity. But how will each single individual succeed in incorporating himself into the collective man, and how will educative pressure be applied to single individuals so as to obtain their consent and their collaboration, turning necessity and coercion into 'freedom'? Question of 'right': this concept will have to be extended to include those activities which are at present classified as 'juridically indifferent', and which belong to the domain of civil society; the latter operates without 'sanctions' or compulsory 'obligations', but nevertheless exerts a collective pressure and obtains objective results in the form of an evolution of customs, ways of thinking and acting, morality, etc.

Political concept of the so-called 'permanent revolution', which emerged before 1848 as a scientifically evolved expression of the Jacobin experience from 1789 to Thermidor.[10] The formula belongs to a historical period in which the great mass political parties and the great economic trade unions did not yet exist, and society was still, so to speak, in a state of fluidity from many points of view: greater backwardness of the countryside, and almost complete monopoly of political and state power by a few cities or even by a single one (Paris in the case of France); a relatively rudimentary state apparatus, and greater autonomy of civil society from state activity; a specific system of military forces and of national armed services; greater autonomy of the national economies from the economic relations of the world market, etc. In the period after 1870, with the colonial expansion of Europe, all these elements change: the internal and international organizational relations of the state become more complex and massive, and the 1848 formula of the 'permanent revolution' is expanded and transcended in political science by the formula of 'civil hegemony'. The same thing happens in the art of politics as happens in military art: war of movement increasingly becomes war of position and it can be said that a state will win a war in so far as it prepares for it minutely and technically in peacetime. The massive structures of the modern democracies, both as state organizations, and as complexes of associations in civil society, constitute for the art of politics as it were the 'trenches' and the permanent fortifications of the front in the war of position: they render merely 'partial' the element of manoeuvre which before used to be 'the whole' of war, etc.

This question is posed for the modern states, but not for backward countries or for colonies, where forms which elsewhere have been superseded and have become anachronistic are still in force. [...]

SPN, 242-3 (Q13§7)

6 Concept of State

That the everyday concept of state is one-sided and leads to grotesque errors can be demonstrated with reference to Daniel Halévy's recent book *Décadence de la liberté*, of which I have read a review in *Les Nouvelles Littéraires*. For Halévy, 'state' is the representative apparatus; and he discovers that the most important events of French history from 1870 until the present day have not been due to initiatives by political organisms deriving from universal suffrage, but to those either of private organisms (capitalist firms, general staffs, etc.) or of great civil servants unknown to the country at large, etc. But what does that signify if not that by 'state' should be understood not only the apparatus of government, but also the 'private' apparatus of 'hegemony' or civil society? It should be noted how from this critique of the state which does not intervene, which trails behind events, etc., there is born the dictatorial ideological current of the Right, with its reinforcement of the executive, etc. However, Halévy's book should be read to see whether he too has taken this path: it is not unlikely in principle, given his antecedents (sympathies for Sorel, for Maurras, etc.).[11]

SPN, 260-1 (Q6§137)

7 Ethical or Cultural State

In my opinion, the most reasonable and concrete thing that can be said about the ethical and cultural state is this: every state is ethical in as much as one of its most important functions is to raise the great mass of the population to a particular cultural and moral level, a level (or type) which corresponds to the needs of the productive forces of development, and hence to the interests of the ruling classes. The school as a positive educative function, and the courts as a repressive and negative educative function, are the most important state activities in this sense: but, in reality, a multitude of other so-called private initiatives and activities tend to the same end – initiatives and activities which form the apparatus of the political and cultural hegemony of the ruling classes. Hegel's conception belongs to a period in which the spreading development of the bourgeoisie could seem limitless, so that its ethicity or universality could be asserted: all mankind will be bourgeois. But, in reality, only the social group that poses the end of the state and its own end as the target to be achieved can create an ethical state, one which tends to put an end to the internal divisions of the ruled, etc., and to create a technically and morally unitary social organism.

SPN, 258-9 (Q8§179)

8 State as Gendarme – Nightwatchman, etc.

The following argument is worth reflecting upon: is the conception of the *gendarme*-nightwatchman state (leaving aside the polemical designation: *gendarme*, nightwatchman, etc.) not in fact the only conception of the state to transcend the purely 'economic-corporate' stages?

We are still on the terrain of the identification of state and government – an identification which is precisely a representation of the economic-corporate form, in other words of the confusion between civil society and political society. For it should be remarked that the general notion of state includes elements which need to be referred back to the notion of civil society (in the sense that one might say that state = political society + civil society, in other words hegemony protected by the armour of coercion). In a doctrine of the state which conceives the latter as tendentially capable of withering away and of being subsumed into regulated society, the argument is a fundamental one. It is possible to imagine the coercive element of the state withering away by degrees, as ever-more conspicuous elements of regulated society (or ethical state or civil society) make their appearance.

The expressions 'ethical state' or 'civil society' would thus mean that this 'image' of a state without a state was present to the greatest political and legal thinkers, in so far as they placed themselves on the terrain of pure science (pure utopia, since based on the premise that all men are really equal and hence equally rational and moral, i.e. capable of accepting the law spontaneously, freely, and not through coercion, as imposed by another class, as something external to consciousness).

It must be remembered that the expression 'nightwatchman' for the liberal state comes from Lassalle, i.e. from a dogmatic and undialectical statist (look closely at Lassalle's doctrines on this point and on the state in general, in contrast with Marxism).[12] In the doctrine of the state → regulated society, one will have to pass from a phase in which 'state' will equal 'government', and 'state' will be identified with 'civil society', to a phase of the state as nightwatchman – i.e. of a coercive organization which will safeguard the development of the continually proliferating elements of regulated society, and which will therefore progressively reduce its own authoritarian and forcible interventions. Nor can this conjure up the idea of a new 'liberalism', even though the beginning of an era of organic liberty be imminent.

SPN, 262-3 (Q6§88)

9 The State as *Veilleur de Nuit*

In the (anyway superficial) polemic over the functions of the state
(which here means the state as a politico-juridical organization in
the narrow sense), the expression 'the state as *veilleur de nuit*'
[nightwatchman] corresponds to the Italian expression '*Stato
carabiniere*' and means a state whose functions are limited to the
safeguarding of public order and of respect for the laws. The fact is
glossed over that in this form of regime (which has never existed
except, at the very most, on paper) historical development is led
by private forces, by civil society, which is 'state' too, indeed it is
the state itself.

It seems that the expression *veilleur de nuit*, which should have a
more sarcastic ring than '*Stato carabiniere*' or 'policeman state',
comes from Lassalle. Its opposite should be 'ethical state' or
'interventionist state' in general, but there are differences between
the two expressions. The concept of ethical state is of
philosophical and intellectual origin (belonging to the intellectuals: Hegel), and in fact could be brought into conjunction with
the concept of state-*veilleur de nuit*; for it refers rather to the
autonomous, educative and moral activity of the secular state, by
contrast with the cosmopolitanism and the interference of the
religious-ecclesiastical organization as a medieval residue. The
concept of interventionist state is of economic origin, and is
connected on the one hand with tendencies supporting protection
and economic nationalism, and on the other with the attempt to
force a particular state personnel, of landowning and feudal origin,
to take on the 'protection' of the working classes against the
excesses of capitalism (policy of Bismarck and of Disraeli).

These diverse tendencies may combine in various way, and in
fact have so combined. Naturally liberals ('economists') are for the
'state as *veilleur de nuit*', and would like the historical initiative to
be left to civil society and to the various forces which spring up
there – with the 'state' as guardian of 'fair play' and of the rules of
the game. Intellectuals draw very significant distinctions when they
are liberals and when they are interventionists (they may be
liberals in the economic field and interventionists in the cultural
field, etc.).

The Catholics would like the state to be interventionist one
hundred per cent in their favour; failing that, or where they are in

a minority, they call for a 'neutral' state, so that it should not support their adversaries.

SPN, 261-2 (Q26§6)

10 Economic-Corporate Phase of the State

If it is true that no type of state can avoid passing through a phase of economic-corporate primitivism, it may be deduced that the content of the political hegemony of the new social group which has founded the new type of state must be predominantly of an economic order: what is involved is the reorganization of the structure and the real relations between men and the world of the economy or of production. The superstructural elements will inevitably be few in number, and have a character of foresight and of struggle, but as yet few 'planned' elements. Cultural policy will above all be negative, a critique of the past; it will be aimed at erasing from the memory and at destroying. The lines of construction will as yet be 'broad lines', sketches, which might (and should) be changed at all times, so as to be consistent with the new structure as it is formed. This precisely did not happen in the period of the medieval communes; for culture, which remained a function of the Church, was precisely anti-economic in character (i.e. against the nascent capitalist economy); it was not directed towards giving hegemony to the new class, but rather to preventing the latter from acquiring it. Hence Humanism and the Renaissance were reactionary, because they signalled the defeat of the new class, the negation of the economic world which was proper to it, etc.

SPN, 263-4 (Q8§185)

11 Statolatry

Attitude of each particular social group towards its own state. The analysis would not be accurate if no account were taken of the two forms in which the state presents itself in the language and culture of specific epochs, i.e. as civil society and as political society. The term 'statolatry' [literally, 'state worship'] is applied to a particular attitude towards the 'government by functionaries' or political society, which in everyday language is the form of state life to which the term of 'state' is applied and which is commonly understood as the entire state. The assertion that the state can be identified with individuals (the individuals of a social group), as an element of active culture (i.e. as a movement to create a new civilization, a new type of man and of citizen), must serve to determine the will to construct within the husk of political society a complex and well-articulated civil society, in which the individual can govern himself without his self-government thereby entering into conflict with political society – but rather becoming its normal continuation, its organic complement. For some social groups, which before their ascent to autonomous state life have not had a long independent period of cultural and moral development on their own (as was made possible in medieval society and under the absolute regimes by the juridical existence of the privileged estates or orders), a period of statolatry is necessary and indeed opportune. This 'statolatry' is nothing other than the normal form of 'state life', or at least of initiation to autonomous state life and to the creation of a 'civil society' which it was not historically possible to create before the ascent to independent state life. However, this kind of 'statolatry' must not be abandoned to itself, must not, especially, become theoretical fanaticism or be conceived of as 'perpetual'. It must be criticized, precisely in order to develop and produce new forms of state life, in which the initiative of individuals and groups will have a 'state' character, even if it is not due to the 'government of the functionaries' (make state life become 'spontaneous').

SPN, 268-9 (Q8§130)

12 [The Political Party as Modern 'Prince']

The basic thing about *The Prince* is that it is not a systematic treatment, but a 'live' work, in which political ideology and political science are fused in the dramatic form of a 'myth'. Before Machiavelli, political science had taken the form either of the utopia or of the scholarly treatise. Machiavelli, combining the two, gave imaginative and artistic form to his conception by embodying the doctrinal, rational element in the person of a *condottiere*, who represents plastically and 'anthropomorphically' the symbol of the 'collective will'. In order to represent the process whereby a given collective will, directed towards a given political objective, is formed, Machiavelli did not have recourse to long-winded arguments or pedantic classifications of principles and criteria for a method of action. Instead he represented this process in terms of the qualities, characteristics, duties and requirements of a concrete individual. Such a procedure stimulates the artistic imagination of those who have to be convinced, and gives political passions a more concrete form. [...]

Machiavelli's *Prince* could be studied as a historical exemplification of the Sorelian 'myth' – i.e. of a political ideology expressed neither in the form of a cold utopia nor as learned theorizing, but rather as a creation of concrete fantasy which acts on a dispersed and shattered people to arouse and organize its collective will.[13] [...]

A study might be made of how it came about that Sorel never advanced from his conception of ideology-myth to an understanding of the political party, but stopped short at the idea of the trade union. It is true that for Sorel the 'myth' found its fullest expression not in the trade union as organization of a collective will, but in its practical action – sign of a collective will already operative. The highest achievement of this practical action was to have been the general strike – i.e. a 'passive activity', so to speak, of a negative and preliminary kind (it could only be given a positive character by the realization of a common accord between the various wills involved), an activity which does not envisage an 'active and constructive' phase of its own. Hence in Sorel there was a conflict of two necessities: that of myth, and that of the critique of myth – in that 'every pre-established plan is utopian and reactionary'. The outcome was left to the intervention of the irrational, to chance (in the Bergsonian sense of '*élan vital*') or to 'spontaneity'. [...] Can a myth, however, be 'non-constructive'? How could an instrument conceivably be effective if, as in Sorel's vision of things, it leaves the collective will in the primitive and elementary phase of its mere formation, by differentiation ('*scission*') – even when this differentiation is violent, that is to say destroys existing moral and juridical relations? Will not that collective will, with so rudimentary a formation, at once cease to exist, scattering into an infinity of individual wills which in the positive phase then follow separate and conflicting paths? Quite apart from the fact that destruction and negation cannot exist without an implicit construction and affirmation – this not in a 'metaphysical' sense but in practice, i.e. politically, as party programme. In Sorel's case it is clear that behind the spontaneity there lies a purely mechanistic assumption, behind the liberty (will – life-force) a maximum of determinism, behind the idealism an absolute materialism.

The modern prince, the myth-prince, cannot be a real person, a concrete individual. It can only be an organism, a complex element of society in which a collective will, which has already been recognized and has to some extent asserted itself in action, begins to take concrete form. History has already provided this organism, and it is the political party – the first cell in which there come together germs of a collective will tending to become universal and total. In the modern world, only those historico-political actions which are immediate and imminent, characterized by the necessity for lightning speed, can be incarnated mythically by a concrete individual. Such speed can only be made necessary by a great and imminent danger, a great danger which precisely fans passion and fanaticism suddenly to a white heat, and annihilates the critical sense and the corrosive irony which are able to destroy the 'charismatic' character of the *condottiere* (as happened in the Boulanger adventure).[14] But an improvised action of such a kind, by its very nature, cannot have a long-term and organic character. It will in almost all cases be appropriate to restoration and reorganization, but not to the founding of new states or new national and social structures (as was at issue in Machiavelli's *Prince*, in which the theme of restoration was merely a rhetorical element, linked to the literary concept of an Italy descended from Rome and destined to restore the order and the power of Rome). It will be defensive rather than capable of original creation. Its underlying assumption will be that a collective will, already in existence, has become nerveless and dispersed, has suffered a collapse which is dangerous and threatening but not definitive and catastrophic, and that it is necessary to reconcentrate and reinforce it – rather than that a new collective will must be created from scratch, to be directed towards goals which are concrete and rational, but whose concreteness and rationality have not yet been put to the critical test by a real and universally known historical experience.

The abstract character of Sorel's conception of the myth is manifest in its aversion (which takes the emotional form of an ethical repugnance) for the *Jacobins*, who were certainly a 'categorical embodiment' of Machiavelli's Prince. The modern *Prince* must have a part devoted to *Jacobinism* (in the integral sense which this notion has had historically, and must have conceptually), as an exemplification of the concrete formation and operation of a collective will which at least in some aspects was an original, *ex novo* creation. And a definition must be given of collective will, and of political will in general, in the modern sense: will as operative awareness of historical necessity, as protagonist of a real and effective historical drama.

One of the first sections must precisely be devoted to the 'collective will', posing the question in the following terms: 'When can the conditions for awakening and developing a national-popular collective will be said to exist?' Hence a historical (economic) analysis of the social structure of the given country and a 'dramatic' representation of the attempts made in the course of the centuries to awaken this will, together with the reasons for the successive failures. Why was there no absolute monarchy in Italy in Machiavelli's time? One has to go back to the Roman Empire (the language question, problem of the intellectuals, etc.), and understand the function of the medieval Communes, the significance of Catholicism etc. In short, one has to make an outline of the whole history of Italy – in synthesis, but accurate.

The reason for the failures of the successive attempts to create a national-popular collective will is to be sought in the existence of certain specific social groups which were formed at the dissolution of the Communal bourgeoisie; in the particular character of other groups which reflect the international function of Italy as seat of the Church and depositary of the Holy Roman Empire; and so on. This function and the position which results from it brought about an internal situation which may be called 'economic-corporate' – politically, the worst of all forms of feudal society, the least progressive and the most stagnant. An effective *Jacobin* force was always missing, and could not be constituted; and it was precisely such a Jacobin force which in other nations awakened and organized the national-popular collective will, and founded the modern states. Do the necessary conditions for this will finally exist, or rather what is the present relation between these conditions and the forces opposed to them? Traditionally the forces of opposition have been the landed aristocracy and, more generally, landed property as a whole with its characteristic Italian feature which is a special 'rural bourgeoisie', a legacy of parasitism bequeathed to modern times by the disintegration as a class of the Communal bourgeoisie (the hundred cities, the cities of silence). The positive conditions are to be sought in the existence of urban social groups which have attained an adequate development in the field of industrial production and a certain level of historico-political culture. Any formation of a national-popular collective will is impossible unless the great mass of peasant farmers bursts *simultaneously* into political life. That was Machiavelli's intention through the reform of the militia, and it was achieved by the Jacobins in the French Revolution. That Machiavelli understood it reveals a precocious Jacobinism that is the (more or less fertile) germ of his conception of national revolution. All history from 1815 onwards shows the efforts of the traditional classes to prevent the formation of a collective will of this kind, and to maintain 'economic-corporate' power in an international system of passive equilibrium.

An important part of the modern *Prince* will have to be devoted to the question of intellectual and moral reformation, that is to the question of religion or world-view. In this field too we find in the existing tradition an absence of Jacobinism and fear of Jacobinism. [...] The modern Prince must be and cannot but be the proclaimer and organizer of an intellectual and moral reformation, which also means creating the terrain for a subsequent development of the national-popular collective will towards the realization of a superior, total form of modern civilization.

These two basic points – the formation of a national-popular collective will, of which the modern Prince is at one and the same time the organizer and the active, operative expression; and intellectual and moral reformation should structure the entire work. The concrete, programmatic points must be incorporated in the first part, that is they should result from the line of discussion 'dramatically', and not be a cold and pedantic exposition of arguments.

Can there be cultural reform, and can the position of the depressed strata of society be improved culturally, without a previous economic reform and a change in their position in the social and economic fields? Intellectual and moral reformation has to be linked with a programme of economic reform – indeed the programme of economic reform is precisely the concrete form in which every intellectual and moral reformation presents itself. The modern Prince, as it develops, revolutionizes the whole system of intellectual and moral relations, in that its development means precisely that any given act is seen as useful or harmful, as virtuous or as wicked, only in so far as it has as its point of reference the modern Prince itself, and helps to strengthen or to oppose it. The Prince takes the place, in people's consciousness, of the divinity or the categorical imperative, and becomes the basis for a modern laicism and for a complete laicization of all aspects of life and of all customary relationships.

SPN, 125-33 (Q13§1)

13   Fetishism

How fetishism can be described. A collective organism is made up of single individuals, who form the organism in that they have given themselves a hierarchy and a determinate leadership which they actively accept. If each of the single components thinks of the collective organism as an entity extraneous to himself, it is evident that this organism no longer exists in reality, but becomes a phantasm of the intellect, a fetish. It should be seen whether this way of thinking, which is very widespread, is not a residue of Catholic transcendentalism and of the old paternalistic regimes. It is common to a series of organisms, from the state to the nation to political parties, etc. It is natural that it should occur in the Church because, at least in Italy, the age-old effort by the Vatican leadership to obliterate all traces of inner democracy and involvement by the faithful in religious activity has been wholly successful and has become second nature to the faithful, although it has produced that special form of Catholicism which is distinctive to the Italian people. What is surprising, and it is characteristic, is that this kind of fetishism should also be found in 'voluntary' organisms, in other words those not of a 'public' or state type, such as parties and trade unions. The relations between the individual and the organism come to be seen as a dualism, and a critical outward attitude arises on the individual's part towards the organism (when the attitude is not one of uncritical enthusiastic admiration). At any event a fetishistic relation. The individual expects the organism to act, even though he himself does not act and does not consider that, precisely because his attitude is shared by many others, the organism is necessarily inactive.

Moreover it needs to be recognized that since a deterministic and mechanical conception of history is very widespread (a common sense conception which is connected to the passivity of the great masses of the people) each individual, when he sees that despite his lack of intervention something happens all the same, is led to think that precisely above individuals there exists a phantasmagorical entity, the abstraction of the collective organism, a sort of autonomous divinity, which does not think with a specific head but which thinks all the same, which does not move with the legs of specific men but which moves all the same, etc.

It might seem that certain ideologies, such as that of contemporary idealism (Ugo Spirito) in which the individual and the state are identified with one another, should re-educate the consciousness of individuals. But in practice this does not seem to occur because this identification is merely verbal and verbalistic. The same must be said of every form of so-called 'organic centralism',[15] which is founded upon the presupposition – true only at exceptional moments, when the passions of the people reach fever pitch – that the relation between governors and governed is given by the fact that the governors carry out the interests of the governed and therefore 'must' enjoy the latters' consent, in other words there must be an identification between the individual and the whole, the whole (whatever organism it is) being represented by the leaders. For organisms such as the Catholic Church a conception of this kind must be seen as not only useful but necessary and indispensable: every form of intervention from below would in fact break up the Church (one sees this in the Protestant churches). But for other organisms it is vital that there should be not passive and indirect consent but active and direct consent, the participation of individual members, even if this provokes an appearance of break up and tumult. A collective consciousness, in other words a living organism, is not formed except after multiplicity has been unified through the friction of the individual members. Nor can it be said that 'silence' is not multiplicity. An orchestra in rehearsal, each instrument playing for itself, gives the impression of the most dreadful cacophony. And yet these rehearsals are necessary for the orchestra to live as a single 'instrument'.

                                                          * (Q15§13)

VIII PASSIVE REVOLUTION, CAESARISM, FASCISM

Introduction

This section contains some of Gramsci's most important notes on bourgeois hegemony from the French Revolution to Fascism. They constitute an essential historical complement to his reflections on the contemporary situation. Gramsci viewed the French Revolution, through the lenses of Marx, Lenin and the historian Albert Mathiez, as an abrupt displacement of aristocratic rule by that of the bourgeoisie whose radical peak had come with the revolutionary dictatorship of the Jacobins in 1792-94. For Gramsci the radicalism of the Jacobins consisted in their broadening of what had been a narrowly bourgeois revolution into a national and popular revolution under bourgeois hegemony. Gramsci associated this acceleration of the revolutionary momentum with Marx's later slogan (used after 1848) of 'permanent revolution'. This association of 'Jacobinism' with hegemony and permanent revolution was probably influenced by Lenin's identification of the Communists as modern 'Jacobins' who ally with the poor peasantry to bring about socialism.

In Gramsci's analysis the initial demands of the moderate revolutionary leaders of 1789 had been of a limited economic-corporate character – the articulation merely of bourgeois self-interest behind the mask of a universalizing rhetoric. By contrast, those of the Jacobins were properly universal because they involved economic sacrifices by the bourgeoisie and an alliance with the urban workers and peasant masses: notably through the breaking up of the great estates into peasant smallholdings. Jacobin rule collapsed, however, because this hegemony was imperfect: the Jacobins ultimately 'remained on bourgeois ground'. At a certain point their policies came into contradiction with the interests of the urban workers, whose rights of assembly they curtailed (Le Chapelier Law) and whose wages they held down in an effort to curb inflation (Law of the Maximum). This provoked a popular reaction which, allied with the moderate-bourgeois reaction, brought about their downfall (Thermidor). Nevertheless, a diluted moderate form of 'Jacobinism' was consolidated under Napoleon and subsequently by the parliamentary regimes of the nineteenth century, in the sense that these secured 'the permanent hegemony of the bourgeoisie over the rest of the population', of city over countryside.

Gramsci saw the Risorgimento – the movement for Italian national liberation which culminated in the unification of 1860-61 – in essentially negative terms as a missed opportunity to make a revolution of such a Jacobin type. Of the two main 'parties' – the Moderates around Cavour and the Action Party around Mazzini and Garibaldi – the latter failed to achieve their aim of the democratic republic because they did not put themselves at the head of the peasant masses, making the latters' demands their own. The Moderates, on the other hand, had a more organic base in the northern bourgeoisie and succeeded in imposing their liberal solution: the annexation of the rest of Italy by the Piedmontese monarchy, the institution of a centralized government and administration based upon limited suffrage. Instead of the 'expansive' hegemony exemplified by the Jacobins, the Moderates exercised a restrictive form of hegemony which rested on a class alliance with the big landowners and an 'absorption' of the democratic opposition in parliament through a practice known as 'transformism'.

The Moderates exemplified what Gramsci calls a *passive revolution* (also a 'revolution without a revolution' or 'revolution-restoration'), in other words a process whereby a social group comes to power without rupturing the social fabric (as in France) but rather by adapting to it and gradually modifying it. Gramsci subsequently extends the term 'passive revolution' first to nineteenth-century liberal-constitutional movements as a whole, and then – by a historical analogy between the post-Napoleonic restoration (1815-48) and the 'restoration' after the social upheavals around the First World War – to fascism. 'Is not fascism', he writes, 'precisely the form of "passive revolution" proper to the twentieth century as liberalism was to the nineteenth?' (p.265). Gramsci, in other words, sees fascism not as a purely defensive reaction by the bourgeoisie, nor as corresponding to capitalist stagnation and crisis (the dominant interpretations then current in the Third International), but as a 'revolution-restoration' whereby a partial transition from a competitive market to a planned economy is effected without a violent social upheaval. Fascism modernizes the economy repressively by liquidating the free organizations of the working class and forcibly conscripting them into the 'corporate' economy and state (Gramsci's analysis of fascism in these terms is developed in the next section, 'Americanism and Fordism'). It can be noted in passing that Gramsci applies his term 'war of position' here to the nineteenth-century passive revolutions and their modern counterpart, fascism. In other words its meaning – like that of hegemony – is not restricted to a strategy for the left but extends also to the dominant classes.

Gramsci's concept of 'Caesarism' is related to that of passive revolution. It is developed through a similar kind of historical analogy – though he insists it is 'a polemical-ideological formula, not a canon of historical interpretation'. His discussion is clearly influenced by Marx's *Eighteenth Brumaire* and is in line with his other analyses of political situations as dynamic and shifting equilibria of social forces. In Gramsci's analysis of Italian history, Caesarism is the logical consequence of the limited or 'passive' form of hegemony achieved by the Moderates at unification. Unlike in France or Britain, where the bourgeoisie had managed to construct a hegemonic alliance with the people which centred upon parliament, the liberal-democratic structures in Italy (parliament, parties) remained limited, unrepresentative and weak. This resulted in an autonomization of the bureaucracy, in 'transformism' – in which the opposition was simply 'co-opted' into the majority – and in a succession of Caesarist 'parliamentary dictators' (Depretis, Crispi, Giolitti). When, after the First World War, the conflict between the fundamental classes became so acute that these parliamentary dictatorships could no longer contain it, another form of Caesarism emerged, that of Fascism.

In treating Fascism as a form of Caesarism and of 'revolution-restoration', Gramsci illuminates its *novel* and dynamic character. It is not simply reaction. It is a mass movement which constructs a new equilibrium by shattering the political power of the old bourgeois liberal forces, as well as that of the left, and by involving and permanently organizing from the right the middle-class and subaltern masses. It is one of those 'modern politico-historical movements ... which are certainly not revolutions, but which are not entirely reactions either – at least in the sense that they shatter stifling and ossified state structures in the dominant [bourgeois] camp as well, and introduce into national life and social activity a different and more numerous personnel'. (p.273)

1 The Problem of Political Leadership in the Formation and Development of the Modern State in Italy

The whole problem of the connection between the various political currents of the Risorgimento – of their relations with each other, and of their relations with the homogeneous or subordinate social groups existing in the various historical sections (or sectors) of the national territory – can be reduced to the following basic factual datum. The Moderates represented a relatively homogeneous social group, and hence their leadership underwent relatively limited oscillations (in any case, subject to an organically progressive line of development); whereas the so-called Action Party did not base itself specifically on any historical class, and the oscillations which its leading organs underwent were resolved, in the last analysis, according to the interests of the Moderates. In other words, the Action Party was led historically by the Moderates. The assertion attributed to Victor Emmanuel II that he 'had the Action Party in his pocket', or something of the kind, was in practice accurate – not only because of the King's personal contacts with Garibaldi, but because the Action Party was in fact 'indirectly' led by Cavour and the King.[1]

The methodological criterion on which our own study must be based is the following: that the supremacy of a social group manifests itself in two ways, as 'domination' (*dominio*) and as 'intellectual and moral leadership' (*direzione*). A social group dominates antagonistic groups, which it tends to 'liquidate', or to subjugate perhaps even by armed force; it leads kindred and allied groups. A social group can, and indeed must, already exercise 'leadership' before winning governmental power (this indeed is one of the principal conditions for the winning of such power); it subsequently becomes dominant when it exercises power, but even if it holds it firmly in its grasp, it must continue to 'lead' as well.

The Moderates continued to lead the Action Party even after 1870 and 1876, and so-called 'transformism' was only the parliamentary expression of this action of intellectual, moral and political hegemony.[2] Indeed one might say that the entire state life of Italy from 1848 onwards has been characterized by transformism – in other words by the formation of an ever more extensive ruling class, within the framework established by the Moderates after 1848 and the collapse of the neo-Guelph and federalist utopias.[3] The formation of this class involved the gradual but continuous absorption, achieved by methods which varied in their effectiveness, of the active elements produced by allied groups – and even of those which came from antagonistic groups and seemed irreconcilably hostile. In this sense political leadership became merely an aspect of the function of domination – in as much as the absorption of the enemies' elites means their decapitation, and annihilation often for a very long time. It seems clear from the policies of the Moderates that there can, and indeed must, be hegemonic activity even before the rise to power, and that one should not count only on the material force which power gives in order to exercise an effective leadership. It was precisely the brilliant solution of these problems which made the Risorgimento possible, in the form in which it was achieved (and with its limitations) – as 'revolution' without a 'revolution', or as 'passive revolution' to use an expression of Cuoco's in a slightly different sense from that which Cuoco intended.[4]

In what forms, and by what means, did the Moderates succeed in establishing the apparatus (mechanism) of their intellectual, moral and political hegemony? In forms, and by means, which may be called 'liberal' – in other words through individual, 'molecular', 'private' initiative (i.e. not through a party programme worked out and constituted according to a plan, in advance of the practical and organizational action). However, that was 'normal' given the structure and the function of the social groups of which the Moderates were the representatives, the leading stratum, the organic intellectuals.

For the Action Party, the problem presented itself deliberately, and different systems of organization should have been adopted. The Moderates were intellectuals already naturally 'condensed' by the organic nature of their relation to the social groups whose expression they were. (As far as a whole series of them were concerned, there was realized the identity of the represented and the representative; in other words, the Moderates were a real, organic vanguard of the upper classes, to which economically they belonged. They were intellectuals and political organizers, and at the same time company bosses, rich farmers or estate managers, commercial and industrial entrepreneurs, etc.) Given this organic condensation or concentration, the Moderates exercised a powerful attraction 'spontaneously', on the whole mass of intellectuals of every degree who existed in the peninsula, in a 'diffused', 'molecular' state, to provide for the requirements, however rudimentarily satisfied, of education and administration. One may detect here the methodological consistency of a criterion of historico-political research: there does not exist any independent class of intellectuals, but every social group has its own stratum of intellectuals, or tends to form one; however, the intellectuals of the historically (and concretely) progressive class, in the given conditions, exercise such a power of attraction that, in the last analysis, they end up by subjugating the intellectuals of the other social groups; they thereby create a system of solidarity between all the intellectuals, with bonds of a psychological nature (vanity, etc.) and often of a caste character (technico-juridical, corporate, etc.).

This phenomenon manifests itself 'spontaneously' in the historical periods in which the given social group is really progressive – i.e. really causes the whole society to move forward, not merely satisfying its own existential requirements, but continuously augmenting its cadres for the conquest of ever new spheres of economic and productive activity. As soon as the dominant social group has exhausted its function, the ideological bloc tends to crumble away; then 'spontaneity' may be replaced by 'constraint' in ever less disguised and indirect forms, culminating in outright police measures and coups d'état.

The Action Party not only could not have – given its character – a similar power of attraction, but was itself attracted and influenced: on the one hand, as a result of the atmosphere of intimidation (panic fear of a terror like that of 1793, reinforced by the events in France of 1848-49) which made it hesitate to include in its programme certain popular demands (for instance, agrarian reform); and, on the other, because certain of its leading personalities (Garibaldi) had, even if only desultorily (they wavered), a relationship of personal subordination to the Moderate leaders. For the Action Party to have become an autonomous force and, in the last analysis, for it to have succeeded at the very least in stamping the movement of the Risorgimento with a more markedly popular and democratic character (more than that perhaps it could not have achieved, given the fundamental premisses of the movement itself), it would have had to counterpose to the 'empirical' activity of the Moderates (which was empirical only in a manner of speaking, since it corresponded perfectly to the objective) an organic programme of government which would reflect the essential demands of the popular masses, and in the first place of the peasantry. To the 'spontaneous' attraction of the Moderates it would have had to counterpose a resistance and a counter-offensive 'organized' according to a plan.

[...] The Action Party was steeped in the traditional rhetoric of Italian literature. It confused the cultural unity which existed in the peninsula – confined, however, to a very thin stratum of the population, and polluted by the Vatican's cosmopolitanism – with the political and territorial unity of the great popular masses, who were foreign to that cultural tradition and who, even supposing that they knew of its existence, couldn't have cared less about it. A comparison may be made between the Jacobins and the Action Party. The Jacobins strove with determination to ensure a bond between town and country, and they succeeded triumphantly. Their defeat as a specific party was due to the fact that at a certain point they came up against the demands of the Paris workers; but in reality they were perpetuated in another form by Napoleon, and today, very wretchedly, by the radical-socialists of Herriot and Daladier.

[...]

If one goes deeper into the question, it appears that from many aspects the difference between many members of the Action Party and the Moderates was more one of 'temperament' than of an organically political character. The term 'Jacobin' has ended up by taking on two meanings: there is the literal meaning, characterized historically, of a particular party in the French Revolution, which conceived of the development of French life in a particular way, with a particular programme, on the basis of particular social forces; and there are also the particular methods of party and government activity which they displayed, characterized by extreme energy, decisiveness and resolution, dependent on a fanatical belief in the virtue of that programme and those methods. In political language the two aspects of Jacobinism were split, and the term 'Jacobin' came to be used for a politician who was energetic, resolute and fanatical, because fanatically convinced of the thaumaturgical virtues of his ideas, whatever they might be. This definition stressed the destructive elements derived from hatred of rivals and enemies, more than the constructive one derived from having made the demands of the popular masses one's own; the sectarian elements of the clique, of the small group, of unrestrained individualism, more than the national political element. [...] It is obvious that, in order to counterpose itself effectively to the Moderates, the Action Party ought to have allied itself with the rural masses, especially those in the South, and ought to have been 'Jacobin' not only in external 'form', in temperament, but most particularly in socio-economic content. The binding together of the various rural classes, which was accomplished in a reactionary bloc by means of the various legitimist-clerical intellectual strata, could be dissolved, so as to arrive at a new liberal-national formation, only if support was won from two directions: from the peasant masses, by accepting their elementary demands and making these an integral part of the new programme of government; and from the intellectuals of the middle and lower strata, by concentrating them and stressing the themes most capable of interesting them (and the prospect of a new apparatus of government being formed, with the possibilities of employment which it offered, would already have been a formidable element of attraction for them – if that prospect had appeared concrete, because based on the aspirations of the peasantry).

The relation between these two actions was dialectical and reciprocal: the experience of many countries, first and foremost that of France in the period of the great Revolution, has shown that, if the peasants move through 'spontaneous' impulses, the intellectuals start to waver; and, reciprocally, if a group of intellectuals situates itself on a new basis of concrete pro-peasant policies, it ends up by drawing with it ever more important elements of the masses. However, one may say that, given the dispersal and the isolation of the rural population and hence the difficulty of welding it into solid organizations, it is best to start the movement from the intellectual groups; however, in general, it is the dialectical relation between the two actions which has to be kept in mind. It may also be said that peasant parties in the strict sense of the word are almost impossible to create. The peasant party generally is achieved only as a strong current of opinion, and not in schematic forms of bureaucratic organization. However, the existence even of only a skeleton organization is of immense usefulness, both as a selective mechanism, and for controlling the intellectual groups and preventing caste interests from transporting them imperceptibly onto different ground.

[...]

On the subject of Jacobinism and the Action Party, an element to be highlighted is the following: that the Jacobins won their function of 'leading' [*dirigente*] party by a struggle to the death; they literally 'imposed' themselves on the French bourgeoisie, leading it into a far more advanced position than the originally strongest bourgeois nuclei would have spontaneously wished to take up, and even far more advanced than that which the historical premisses should have permitted – hence the various forms of backlash and the function of Napoleon I. This feature, characteristic of Jacobinism (but before that, also of Cromwell and the Roundheads) and hence of the entire French Revolution, which consists in (apparently) forcing the situation, in creating irreversible *faits accomplis*, and in a group of extremely energetic and determined men driving the bourgeois forward with kicks in the backside, may be schematized in the following way. The Third Estate was the least homogeneous of the estates; it had a very disparate intellectual elite, and a group which was very advanced economically but politically moderate. Events developed along highly interesting lines. The representatives of the Third Estate initially only posed those questions which interested the actual physical members of the social group, their immediate 'corporate' interests (corporate in the traditional sense, of the immediate and narrowly selfish interests of a particular category). The precursors of the Revolution were in fact moderate reformers, who shouted very loud but actually demanded very little. Gradually a new elite was selected out which did not concern itself solely with 'corporate' reforms, but tended to conceive of the bourgeoisie as the hegemonic group of all the popular forces. This selection occurred through the action of two factors: the resistance of the old social forces, and the international threat. The old forces did not wish to concede anything, and if they did concede anything they did it with the intention of gaining time and preparing a counter-offensive. The Third Estate would have fallen into these successive 'pitfalls' without the energetic action of the Jacobins, who opposed every 'intermediate' halt in the revolutionary process, and sent to the guillotine not only the elements of the old society which was hard a-dying, but also the revolutionaries of yesterday – today become reactionaries. The Jacobins, consequently, were the only party of the revolution in progress, in as much as they not only represented the immediate needs and aspirations of the actual physical individuals who constituted the French bourgeoisie, but they also represented the revolutionary movement as a whole, as an integral historical development. For they represented future needs as well, and, once again, not only the needs of those particular physical individuals, but also of all the national groups which had to be assimilated to the existing fundamental group. It is necessary to insist, against a tendentious and fundamentally anti-historical school of thought, that the Jacobins were realists of the Machiavelli stamp and not abstract dreamers. They were convinced of the absolute truth of their slogans about equality, fraternity and liberty, and, what is more important, the great popular masses whom the Jacobins stirred up and drew into the struggle were also convinced of their truth.

The Jacobins' language, their ideology, their methods of action reflected perfectly the exigencies of the epoch, even if 'today', in a different situation and after more than a century of cultural evolution, they may appear 'abstract' and 'frenetic'. Naturally they reflected those exigencies according to the French cultural tradition. One proof of this is the analysis of Jacobin language which is to be found in *The Holy Family*.[5] Another is Hegel's admission, when he places as parallel and reciprocally translatable the juridico-political language of the Jacobins and the concepts of classical German philosophy – which is recognized today to have the maximum of concreteness and which was the source of modern historicism.[6] The first necessity was to annihilate the enemy forces, or at least to reduce them to impotence in order to make a counter-revolution impossible. The second was to enlarge the cadres of the bourgeoisie as such, and to place the latter at the head of all the national forces; this meant identifying the interests and the requirements common to all the national forces, in order to set these forces in motion and lead them into the struggle, obtaining two results: (*a*) that of opposing a wider target to the blows of the enemy, i.e. of creating a politico-military relation favourable to the revolution; (*b*) that of depriving the enemy of every zone of passivity in which it would be possible to enrol Vendée-type armies.[7] Without the agrarian policy of the Jacobins, Paris would have had the Vendée at its very doors.

The resistance of the Vendée properly speaking is linked to the national question, which had become envenomed among the peoples of Brittany and in general among those alien to the slogan of the 'single and indivisible republic' and to the policy of bureaucratic-military centralization – a slogan and a policy which the Jacobins could not renounce without committing suicide. The Girondins tried to exploit federalism in order to crush Jacobin Paris, but the provincial troops brought to Paris went over to the revolutionaries. Except for certain marginal areas, where the national (and linguistic) differentiation was very great, the agrarian question proved stronger than aspirations to local autonomy. Rural France accepted the hegemony of Paris; in other words, it understood that in order definitively to destroy the old regime it had to make a bloc with the most advanced elements of the Third Estate, and not with the Girondin moderates. If it is true that the Jacobins 'forced' its hand, it is also true that this always occurred in the direction of real historical development. For not only did they organize a bourgeois government, i.e. make the bourgeois the dominant class – they did more. They created the bourgeois state, made the bourgeoisie into the leading, hegemonic class of the nation, in other words gave the new state a permanent basis and created the compact modern French nation.

That the Jacobins, despite everything, always remained on bourgeois ground is demonstrated by the events which marked their end, as a party cast in too specific and inflexible a mould, and by the death of Robespierre. Maintaining the Le Chapelier law, they were not willing to concede to the workers the right of combination; as a consequence they had to pass the law of the *maximum*.[8] They thus broke the Paris urban bloc: their assault forces, assembled in the Commune, dispersed in disappointment, and Thermidor gained the upper hand. The Revolution had found its widest class limits. The policy of alliances and of permanent revolution had finished by posing new questions which at that time could not be resolved; it had unleashed elemental forces which only a military dictatorship was to succeed in containing.

In the Action Party there was nothing to be found which resembled this Jacobin approach, this inflexible will to become the 'leading' [*dirigente*] party. Naturally one has to allow for the differences: in Italy the struggle manifested itself as a struggle against old treaties and the existing international order, and against a foreign power – Austria – which represented these and upheld them in Italy, occupying a part of the peninsula and controlling the rest. This problem arose in France too, in a certain sense at least, since at a certain point the internal struggle became a national struggle fought at the frontiers. But this only happened after the whole territory had been won for the revolution, and the Jacobins were able to utilize the external threat as a spur to greater energy internally: they well understood that in order to defeat the external foe they had to crush his allies internally, and they did not hesitate to carry out the September massacres.[9] In Italy, although a similar connection, both explicit and implicit, did exist between Austria and at least a segment of the intellectuals, the nobles and the landowners, it was not denounced by the Action Party; or at least it was not denounced with the proper energy and in the most practically effective manner, and it did not become a real political issue. It became transformed 'curiously' into a question of greater or lesser patriotic dignity, and subsequently gave rise to a trail of acrimonious and sterile polemics which continued even after 1898. [...]

If in Italy a Jacobin party was not formed, the reasons are to be sought in the economic field, that is to say in the relative weakness of the Italian bourgeoisie and in the different historical climate in Europe after 1815. The limit reached by the Jacobins, in their policy of forced reawakening of French popular energies to be allied with the bourgeoisie, with the Le Chapelier law and that of the *maximum*, appeared in 1848 as a 'spectre' which was already threatening – and this was skilfully exploited by Austria, by the old governments and even by Cavour (quite apart from the Pope). The bourgeoisie could not (perhaps) extend its hegemony further over the great popular strata – which it did succeed in embracing in France – (could not for subjective rather than objective reasons); but action directed at the peasantry was certainly always possible.

Differences between France, Germany and Italy in the process by which the bourgeoisie took power (and England). It was in France that the process was richest in developments, and in active and positive political elements. In Germany, it evolved in ways which in certain aspects resembled what happened in Italy, and in others what happened in England. In Germany, the movement of 1848 failed as a result of the scanty bourgeois concentration (the Jacobin-type slogan was furnished by the democratic extreme left: 'permanent revolution'[10]), and because the question of renewal of the state was intertwined with the national question. The wars of 1864, 1866 and 1870 resolved both the national question and, in an intermediate form, the class question: the bourgeoisie obtained economic-industrial power, but the old feudal classes remained as the government stratum of the political state, with wide corporate privileges in the army, the administration and on the land. Yet at least, if these old classes kept so much importance in Germany and enjoyed so many privileges, they exercised a national function, became the 'intellectuals' of the bourgeoisie, with a particular temperament conferred by their caste origin and by tradition.

In England, where the bourgeois revolution took place before that in France, we have a similar phenomenon to the German one of fusion between the old and the new – this notwithstanding the extreme energy of the English 'Jacobins', i.e. Cromwell's Roundheads. The old aristocracy remained as a governing stratum, with certain privileges, and it too became the intellectual stratum of the English bourgeoisie (it should be added that the English aristocracy has an open structure, and continually renews itself with elements coming from the intellectuals and the bourgeoisie). [...]

The explanation given by Antonio Labriola of the fact that the Junkers and Kaiserism continued in power in Germany, despite the great capitalist development, adumbrates the correct explanation: the class relations created by industrial development, with the limits of bourgeois hegemony reached and the position of the progressive classes reversed, have induced the bourgeoisie not to struggle with all its strength against the old regime, but to allow a part of the latter's façade to subsist, behind which it can disguise its own real domination.

These variations in the process whereby the same historical development manifests itself in different countries have to be

related not only to the differing combinations of internal relations
within the different nations, but also to the differing international
relations (international relations are usually underestimated in this
kind of research). The Jacobin spirit, audacious, dauntless, is
certainly related to the hegemony exercised for so long by France
in Europe, as well as to the existence of an urban centre like Paris
and to the centralization attained in France thanks to the absolute
monarchy. The Napoleonic wars on the other hand, intellectually
so fertile for the renovation of Europe, nonetheless through their
enormous destruction of manpower – and these were men taken
from among the boldest and most enterprising – weakened not
only the militant political energy of France but that of other
nations as well.

International relations were certainly very important in
determining the line of development of the Italian Risorgimento,
but they were exaggerated by the Moderate Party, and by Cavour
for party reasons. Cavour's case is noteworthy in this connection.
Before the Quarto expedition and the crossing of the Straits, he
feared Garibaldi's initiative like the devil, because of the
international complications which it might create. He was then
himself impelled by the enthusiasm created by the Thousand in
European opinion to the point where he saw as feasible an
immediate new war against Austria.[11] There existed in Cavour a
certain professional diplomat's distortion, which led him to see
'too many' difficulties, and induced him into 'conspiratorial'
exaggerations, and into prodigies (which to a considerable extent
were simply tightrope-walking) of subtlety and intrigue. In any
case Cavour acted eminently as a party man. Whether in fact his
party represented the deepest and most durable national interests,
even if only in the sense of the widest extension which could be
given to the community of interests between the bourgeoisie and
the popular masses, is another question.

With respect to the 'Jacobin' slogan formulated in 1846-49, its
complex fortunes are worth studying.[12] Taken up again,
systematized, developed, intellectualized by the Parvus-Bronstein
group, it proved inert and ineffective in 1905, and subsequently. It
had become an abstract thing, belonging in the scientist's cabinet.
The tendency which opposed it in this literary form, and indeed
did not use it 'on purpose', applied it in fact in a form which
adhered to actual, concrete, living history, adapted to the time and

the place; as something that sprang from all the pores of the particular society which had to be transformed; as the alliance of two social groups with the hegemony of the urban group.

In one case, you had the Jacobin temperament without an adequate political content; in the second, a Jacobin temperament and content derived from the new historical relations, and not from a literary and intellectualistic label.

SPN, 55-85 (Q19§24)

2 Notes on French National Life

[...]

The development of Jacobinism (of content), and of the formula of the permanent revolution put into practice in the active phase of the French Revolution, was 'perfected' in juridico-constitutional terms in the parlimentary regime. This regime achieved – in the period richest in 'private' energies within society – the permanent hegemony of the urban class over the whole population, in the Hegelian form of a government with permanently organized consent (the organization of consent was, however, left to private initiative; it therefore had a moral or ethical character, because it was consent which one way or another was given 'voluntarily'). The 'limit' which the Jacobins met in the Le Chapelier law and the law of the *maximum* was overcome and progressively pushed further back through a complete process, in which the activity of propaganda alternated with practical (economic, politico-juridical) activity. Industrial and commercial development continually enlarged and deepened the economic base. The social elements that possessed the greatest energy and entrepreneurial spirit raised themselves up from the lower classes to the ruling classes. The whole society was in a continuous process of formation and dissolution followed by more complex formations replete with possibilities. This lasted, overall, until the age of imperialism and culminated in the world war.

In this process there was an alternation of insurrectionary attempts and ruthless repressions, widenings and narrowings of the suffrage, freedom of association and limitations or annulments of this freedom, trade-union freedoms but not political ones, voting by lists or by single-member electoral colleges, the proportional system and the individual one, together with the various combinations that derived from these – two chamber or single-chamber elective system, with various kinds of election for each (chambers with life members and hereditary members, fixed-term Senate, but with different system of election of Senators from that of deputies, etc.). The equilibrium of powers varied, so that the magistrature could be an independent power or merely an order, controlled and led by ministerial circulars. Different functions were attributed to the prime minister and the state. There was a different internal equilibrium between the various territorial levels (centralism, or decentralization, greater or lesser powers given to prefects, provincial councils, local councils, etc.). There was also a different equilibrium between the conscripted and the professional armed forces (police, gendarmerie), with each of these professional bodies being dependent on one or the other organs of the state (magistrature, ministry of the interior, high command). [...]

The 'normal' exercise of hegemony in what became the classic terrain of the parliamentary regime is characterized by the combination of force and consent variously balancing one another, without force exceeding consent too much. Indeed one tries to make it appear that force is supported by the consent of the majority, expressed by the so-called organs of public opinion – newspapers and associations – which are therefore, in certain situations, artificially increased in number. Between consent and force there is corruption-fraud (which is characteristic of certain situations in which the exercise of the hegemonic function is difficult because the use of force is too dangerous) in other words tl.e weakening and paralysing of one's opponent or opponents by the taking over of their leaders, whether covertly or – in cases of emergent danger – overtly, in order to create confusion and disorder in the opposing ranks.

In the post-war period, the hegemonic apparatus cracks and the exercise of hegemony becomes permanently difficult and uncertain. The phenomenon is presented and discussed under various names and in its secondary and derived aspects. The most trivial labels are 'crisis of the authority principle' and 'dissolution of the parliamentary regime'. Naturally what is being described are only the 'theatrical' manifestations of the problem on the terrain of parliament and political government. These are explained precisely by the failure of certain 'principles' (the parliamentary, the democratic principle, etc.) and by the 'crisis' of the authority principle (others, no less superficial and superstitious, will speak of the failure of this principle). In practice the crisis takes the form of an ever increasing difficulty in forming governments and an ever increasing instability of the governments themselves. It has its immediate origin in the multiplication of parliamentary parties and in the permanent internal crises of each of these parties (one finds in each party what one finds in parliament as a whole: difficulty in governing and unstable leadership). The forms of this phenomenon are also, to a certain extent, corruption and moral dissolution: every party fraction believes it has the infallible recipe for arresting the weakening of the party as a whole, and it uses every means to take over the leadership, or at least take part in it, just as in parliament the party believes it is the only one that can form the government which will save the country, or at least it asserts that in order to support the government it must have extensive representation within it. [...]

The endemic crisis of French parliamentarism indicates that there is a widespread unease in the country. But this unease has not yet had a radical character, it has not brought intangible questions into play. There has been a widening of the industrial base and therefore increased urbanization. Rural masses have poured into the cities, but not because there was unemployment or unsatisfied land hunger; because people in the cities are better off, there are more satisfactions, etc. (land is extremely cheap and much good land is abandoned to the Italians). The parliamentary crisis reflects (so far) more a normal movement of masses (not due to an acute economic crisis), with an arduous search for new equilibria of representation and of parties and a vague malaise which is only the premonition of the possibility of a great political crisis. The very sensitivity of the political organism makes it exaggerate the symptoms of the malaise. So far it has been more than anything else a case of a series of struggles for the division of state responsibilities and benefits. Thus the crisis has been within the middle parties – primarily the Radicals – who represent the middle and small cities and the most advanced peasants. The political forces are getting ready for the great struggles to come and are looking for a better settlement. The forces outside the state are making themselves felt more noticeably and are pushing their men forward in a more brutal manner.

[...]

* (but partially in SPN, 80, footnote 49) (Q13§37)

3 The Concept of 'Passive Revolution' [i]

Can the concept of 'passive revolution', in the sense attributed by Vincenzo Cuoco to the first period of the Italian Risorgimento, be related to the concept of 'war of position' in contrast to war of manoeuvre? In other words, did these concepts have a meaning after the French Revolution, and can the twin figures of Proudhon and Gioberti be explained in terms of the panic created by the Terror of 1793, as Sorelism can be in terms of the panic following the Paris massacres of 1871?[13] In other words, does there exist an absolute identity between war of position and passive revolution? Or at least does there exist, or can there be conceived, an entire historical period in which the two concepts must be considered identical – until the point at which the war of position once again becomes a war of manoeuvre? [...]

SPN, 108 (Q15§11)

4 [The Concept of Passive Revolution ii]

The concept of 'passive revolution' must be rigorously derived from the two fundamental principles of political science; 1. that no social formation disappears as long as the productive forces which have developed within it still find room for further forward movement; 2. that a society does not set itself tasks for whose solution the necessary conditions have not already been incubated, etc.[14] It goes without saying that these principles must first be developed critically in all their implications, and purged of every residue of mechanicism and fatalism. They must therefore be referred back to the description of the three fundamental moments into which a 'situation' or an equilibrium of forces can be distinguished, with the greatest possible stress on the second moment (equilibrium of political forces), and especially on the third moment (politico-military equilibrium).[15] [...]

SPN, 106-7 (Q15§17)

5 [The Concept of Passive Revolution iii]

The thesis of the 'passive revolution' as an interpretation of the Risorgimento period, and of every epoch characterized by complex historical upheavals. Utility and dangers of this thesis. Danger of historical defeatism, i.e. of indifferentism, since the whole way of posing the question may induce a belief in some kind of fatalism, etc. Yet the conception remains a dialectical one – in other words, presupposes, indeed postulates as necessary, a vigorous antithesis which can present intransigently all its potentialities for development. Hence theory of the 'passive revolution' not as a programme, as it was for the Italian liberals of the Risorgimento, but as a criterion of interpretation, in the absence of other active elements to a dominant extent. (Hence struggle against the political morphinism which exudes from Croce and from his historicism.) (It would seem that the theory of the passive revolution is a necessary critical corollary to the preface to *A Contribution to the Critique of Political Economy*.) Revision of certain sectarian ideas on the theory of the party, theories which precisely represent a form of fatalism of a 'divine right' type. Development of the concepts of mass party and small elite party, and mediation between the two. (Theoretical and practical mediation: is it theoretically possible for there to exist a group, relatively small but still of significant size, let us say several thousand strong, that is socially and ideologically homogeneous, without its very existence demonstrating a widespread state of affairs and corresponding state of mind which only mechanical, external and hence transitory causes prevent from being expressed?)

SPN, 114 (Q15§62)

6 [Fascism as Passive Revolution: First Version]

Given that Croce's *History of Europe in the Nineteenth Century* is a kind of paradigm of ethico-political history for world culture, criticism of the book is necessary. It can be noted that Croce's basic 'trick' consists in this: that he starts his history after the fall of Napoleon. But does 'the nineteenth century' exist without the French Revolution and the Napoleonic Wars? Can the events Croce deals with be organically conceived without these precedents? Croce's book is a treatise of passive revolutions, to use Cuoco's expression, which cannot be justified and understood without the French Revolution, which was a European and world event, not just a French one. (Can this treatment be given a contemporary reference? In modern conditions, is not 'fascism' precisely a new 'liberalism'? Is not fascism precisely the form of 'passive revolution' proper to the twentieth century as liberalism was to the nineteenth? I have touched on this in another note, and the whole argument needs to be gone into further.) (One could suggest the following: the passive revolution here consists in the fact that the economic structure is transformed in a 'reformist' way from an individualistic to a planned economy (command economy). The advent of an 'intermediate economy' between the purely individualistic one and the integrally planned one allows the transition to more developed political and cultural forms without radical and destructive cataclysms of an exterminating kind. 'Corporativism' could be or could become, as it develops, this intermediate economic form of a 'passive' character.) This conception could be compared with what in politics can be called 'war of position' in opposition to the war of manoeuvre. According to this, the historical cycle up to the French Revolution was a 'war of manoeuvre' and the liberal era of the nineteenth century a long war of position.

* (Q8§236)

7 [Fascism as Passive Revolution: Second Version]

Paradigms of ethico-political history. The *History of Europe in the Nineteenth Century* seems to be the work of ethico-political history destined to become the paradigm of Crocean historiography offered to European culture. However, his other studies must be taken into account too: *History of the Kingdom of Naples*; *History of Italy from 1871 to 1915*; *The Neapolitan Revolution of 1799*; and *History of the Baroque Era in Italy*. The most tendentious and revealing, however, are the *History of Europe* and the *History of Italy*. With respect to these two works, the questions at once arise: is it possible to write (conceive of) a history of Europe in the nineteenth century without an organic treatment of the French Revolution and the Napoleonic Wars? And is it possible to write a history of Italy in modern times without a treatment of the struggles of the Risorgimento? In other words: is it fortuitous, or is it for a tendentious motive, that Croce begins his narratives from 1815 and 1871? i.e. that he excludes the moment of struggle; the moment in which the conflicting forces are formed, are assembled and take up their positions; the moment in which one ethico-political system dissolves and another is formed by fire and by steel; the moment in which one system of social relations disintegrates and falls and another arises and asserts itself? Is it fortuitous or not that he placidly takes as history the moment of cultural or ethico-political expansion? One can say, therefore, that the book on the *History of Europe* is nothing but a fragment of history, the 'passive' aspect of the great revolution which started in France in 1789 and which spilled over into the rest of Europe with the republican and Napoleonic armies – giving the old regimes a powerful shove, and resulting not in their immediate collapse as in France but in the 'reformist' corrosion of them which lasted up to 1870.

The problem arises of whether this Crocean construction, in its tendentious nature, does not have a contemporary and immediate reference. Whether it does not aim to create an ideological movement corresponding to that of the period with which Croce is dealing, i.e. the period of restoration-revolution, in which the demands which in France found a Jacobin-Napoleonic expression were satisfied by small doses, legally, in a reformist manner – in such a way that it was possible to preserve the political and economic position of the old feudal classes, to avoid agrarian reform, and, especially, to avoid the popular masses going through a period of political experience such as occurred in France in the years of Jacobinism, in 1831, and in 1848. But, in present conditions, is it not precisely the fascist movement which in fact corresponds to the movement of moderate and conservative liberalism in the last century?

Perhaps it is not without significance that, in the first years of its development, Fascism claimed a continuity with the tradition of the old 'historic' Right. It might be one of the numerous paradoxical aspects of history (a ruse of nature, to put it in Vico's language) that Croce, with his own particular preoccupations, should in effect have contributed to a reinforcement of Fascism – furnishing it indirectly with an intellectual justification, after having contributed to purging it of various secondary characteristics, of a superficially romantic type but nevertheless irritating to his classical serenity modelled on Goethe. The ideological hypotheses could be presented in the following terms: that there is a passive revolution involved in the fact that – through the legislative intervention of the state, and by means of the corporative organization – relatively far-reaching modifications are being introduced into the country's economic structure in order to accentuate the 'plan of production' element; in other words, that socialization and co-operation in the sphere of production are being increased, without however touching (or at least not going beyond the regulation and control of) individual and group appropriation of profit. In the concrete framework of Italian social relations, this could be the only solution whereby to develop the productive forces of industry under the direction of the traditional ruling classes, in competition with the more advanced industrial formations of countries which monopolize raw materials and have accumulated massive capital sums.

Whether or not such a schema could be put into practice, and to what extent, is only of relative importance. What is important from the political and ideological point of view is that it is capable of creating – and indeed does create – a period of expectation and hope, especially in certain Italian social groups such as the great mass of urban and rural petty bourgeois. It thus reinforces the hegemonic system and the forces of military and civil coercion at the disposal of the traditional ruling classes.

This ideology thus serves as an element of a 'war of position' in the international economic field (free competition and free exchange here corresponding to the war of movement), just as 'passive revolution' does in the political field. In Europe from 1789 to 1870 there was a (political) war of movement in the French Revolution and a long war of position from 1815 to 1870. In the present epoch, the war of movement took place politically from March 1917 to March 1921; this was followed by a war of position whose representative – both practical (for Italy) and ideological (for Europe) – is fascism.

SPN, 118-20 (Q10,I§9)

8 Agitation and Propaganda

The weakness of the Italian political parties (excepting to some extent the Nationalist party)[16] throughout their period of activity, from the Risorgimento onwards, has consisted in what one might call an imbalance between agitation and propaganda – though it can also be termed lack of principle, opportunism, absence of

organic continuity, imbalance between tactics and strategy, etc.
The principal reason why the parties are like this is to be sought in
the deliquescence of the economic classes, in the gelatinous
economic and social structure of the country – but this explanation
is somewhat fatalistic. In fact, if it is true that parties are only the
nomenclature for classes, it is also true that parties are not simply a
mechanical and passive expression of those classes, but react
energetically upon them in order to develop, solidify and
universalize them. This precisely did not occur in Italy, and the
result of this 'omission' is precisely the imbalance between
agitation and propaganda – or however else one wishes to term it.

The state/government has a certain responsibility in this state of
affairs: one can call it a responsibility, in so far as it prevented the
strengthening of the state itself, i.e. demonstrated that the
state/government was not a national factor. The government in
fact operated as a 'party'. It set itself over and above the parties,
not so as to harmonize their interests and activities within the
permanent framework of the life and interests of the nation and
state, but so as to disintegrate them, to detach them from the
broad masses and obtain 'a force of non-party men linked to the
government by paternalistic ties of a Bonapartist-Caesarist type'.
This is the way in which the so-called *dictatorships* of Depretis,
Crispi and Giolitti, and the parliamentary phenomenon of
transformism, should be analysed.[17] Classes produce parties, and
parties form the personnel of state and government, the leaders of
civil and political society. There must be a useful and fruitful
relation in these manifestations and functions. There cannot be
any formation of leaders without the theoretical, doctrinal activity
of parties, without a systematic attempt to discover and study the
causes which govern the nature of the class represented and the
way in which it has developed. Hence, scarcity of state and
government personnel; squalor of parliamentary life; ease with
which the parties can be disintegrated, by corruption and
absorption of the few individuals who are indispensable. Hence,
squalor of cultural life and wretched inadequacy of high culture.
Instead of political history, bloodless erudition; instead of religion,
superstition; instead of books and great reviews, daily papers and
broadsheets; instead of serious politics, ephemeral quarrels and
personal clashes. The universities, and all the institutions which
develop intellectual and technical abilities, since they were not

permeated by the life of the parties, by the living realities of national life, produced apolitical national cadres, with a purely rhetorical and non-national mental formation. Thus the bureaucracy became estranged from the country, and via its administrative positions became a true political party, the worst of all, because the bureaucratic hierarchy replaced the intellectual and political hierarchy. The bureaucracy became precisely the state/Bonapartist party.

See the books which after 1919 criticized a 'similar' state of affairs (but far richer in terms of the life of 'civil society') in the Kaiser's Germany, for example Max Weber's book *Parliament and Government in the German New Order: a Political Critique of Bureaucracy and Party Life*. [...]

SPN, 227-8 (Q3§119)

9 Caesarism

Caesar, Napoleon I, Napoleon III, Cromwell, etc. Compile a catalogue of the historical events which have culminated in a great 'heroic' personality.

Caesarism can be said to express a situation in which the forces in conflict balance each other in a catastrophic manner; that is to say, they balance each other in such a way that a continuation of the conflict can only terminate in their reciprocal destruction. When the progressive force A struggles with the regressive force B, not only may A defeat B or B defeat A, but it may happen that neither A nor B defeats the other – that they bleed each other mutually and than a third force C intervenes from outside subjugating what is left of both A and B. In Italy, after the death of Lorenzo il Magnifico, this is precisely what occurred.

But Caesarism – although it always expresses the particular solution in which a great personality is entrusted with the task of 'arbitration' over a historico-political situation characterised by an equilibrium of forces heading towards catastrophe – does not in all cases have the same historical significance. There can be both a progressive and a regressive form of Caesarism; the exact significance of each form can, in the last analysis, be reconstructed only through concrete history, and not by means of any sociological schema. Caesarism is progressive when its intervention helps the progressive force to triumph, albeit with its victory tempered by certain compromises and limitations. It is regressive when its intervention helps the regressive force to triumph – in this case too with certain compromises and limitations, which have, however, a different value, extent, and significance than in the former. Caesar and Napoleon I are examples of progressive Caesarism. Napoleon III and Bismarck of regressive Caesarism. The problem is to see whether in the dialectic 'revolution/restoration' it is revolution or restoration which predominates; for it is certain that in the movement of history there is never any turning back, and that restorations *in toto* do not exist. Besides, Caesarism is a polemical-ideological formula, and not a canon of historical interpretation. A Caesarist solution can exist even without a Caesar, without any great 'heroic' and representative personality. The parliamentary system has also provided a mechanism for such compromise solutions. The 'Labour' governments of MacDonald were to a certain degree solutions of this kind; and the degree of Caesarism increased when the government was formed which had MacDonald as its head and a Conservative majority.[18] Similarly in Italy from October 1922 until the defection of the 'Popolari', and then by stages until 3 January 1925, and then until 8 November 1926, there was a politico-historical movement in which various gradations of Caesarism succeeded each other, culminating in a more pure and permanent form – though even this was not static or immobile.[19] Every coalition government is a first stage of Caesarism, which either may or may not develop to more significant stages (the common opinion of course is that coalition governments, on the contrary, are the most 'solid bulwark' against Caesarism).

In the modern world, with its great economic-trade-union and party-political coalitions, the mechanism of the Caesarist phenomenon is very different from what it was up to the time of Napoleon III. In the period up to Napoleon III, the regular military forces or soldiers of the line were a decisive element in the advent of Caesarism, and this came about through quite precise coups d'état, through military actions, etc. In the modern world trade-union and political forces, with the limitless financial means which may be at the disposal of small groups of citizens, complicate the problem. The functionaries of the parties and economic unions can be corrupted or terrorized, without any need for military action in the grand style – of the Caesar or 18

Brumaire type. The same situation recurs in this field as was examined in connection with the Jacobin/1848 formula of the so-called 'permanent revolution'. Modern political technique became totally transformed after 1848; after the expansion of parliamentarism and of the associative systems of union and party, and the growth in the formation of vast state and 'private' bureaucracies (i.e. politico-private, belonging to parties and trade unions); and after the transformations which took place in the organization of the forces of order in the wide sense – i.e. not only the public service designed for the repression of crime, but the totality of forces organized by the state and by private individuals to safeguard the political and economic domination of the ruling classes. In this sense, entire 'political' parties and other organizations – economic or otherwise – must be considered as organs of political order, of an investigational and preventive character.

The generic schema of forces A and B in conflict with catastrophic prospects – i.e. with the prospect that neither A nor B will be victorious, in the struggle to constitute (or reconstitute) an organic equilibrium, from which Caesarism is born (can be born) – is precisely a generic hypothesis, a sociological schema (convenient for the art of politics). It is possible to render the hypothesis ever more concrete, to carry it to an ever greater degree of approximation to concrete historical reality, and this can be achieved by defining certain fundamental elements.

Thus, in speaking of A and B, it has merely been asserted that they are respectively a generically progressive, and a generically regressive, force. But one might specify the type of progressive and regressive force involved, and so obtain closer approximations. In the case of Caesar and of Napoleon I, it can be said that A and B, though distinct and in conflict, were nevertheless not such as to be 'absolutely' incapable of arriving, after a molecular process, at a reciprocal fusion and assimilation. And this was what in fact happened, at least to a certain degree (sufficient, however, for the historico-political objectives in question – i.e. the halting of the fundamental organic struggle, and hence the transcendence of the catastrophic phase). This is one element of closer approximation. Another such element is the following: the catastrophic phase may be brought about by a 'momentary' political deficiency of the traditional dominant force, and not by any necessarily insuperable organic deficiency. This was true in the case of Napoleon III. The dominant force in France from 1815 up to 1848 had split politically (factiously) into four camps: legitimists, Orleanists, Bonapartists, Jacobin-republicans. The internal faction struggle was such as to make possible the advance of the rival force B (progressive) in a precocious form; however, the existing social form had not yet exhausted its possibilities for development, as subsequent history abundantly demonstrated. Napoleon III represented (in his own manner, as fitted the stature of the man, which was not great) these latent and immanent possibilities: his Caesarism therefore has a particular coloration. The Caesarism of Caesar and Napoleon I was, so to speak, of a quantitative/qualitative character; in other words it represented the historical phase of passage from one type of state to another type – a passage in which the innovations were so numerous, and of such a nature, that they represented a complete revolution. The Caesarism of Napoleon III was merely, and in a limited fashion, quantitative; there was no passage from one type of state to another, but only 'evolution' of the same type along unbroken lines.

In the modern world, Caesarist phenomena are quite different, both from those of the progressive Caesar/Napoleon I type, and from those of the Napoleon III type – although they tend towards the latter. In the modern world, the equilibrium with catastrophic prospects occurs not between forces which could in the last analysis fuse and unite – albeit after a wearying and bloody process – but between forces whose opposition is historically incurable and indeed becomes especially acute with the advent of Caesarist forms. However, in the modern world Caesarism also has a certain margin – larger or smaller, depending on the country and its relative weight in the global context, for a social form 'always' has marginal possibilities for further development and organizational improvement, and in particular can count on the relative weakness of the rival progressive force as a result of its specific character and way of life. It is necessary for the dominant social form to preserve this weakness: this is why it has been asserted that modern Caesarism is more a police than a military system.

SPN, 219-22 (Q13§27)

10 Caesarism and 'Catastrophic' Equilibrium of Politico-Social Forces

It would be an error of method (an aspect of sociological mechanicism) to believe that in Caesarism – whether progressive, regressive, or of an intermediate and episodic character – the entire new historical phenomenon is due to the equilibrium of the 'fundamental' forces. It is also necessary to see the interplay of relations between the principal groups (of various kinds, socio-economic and technical-economic) of the fundamental classes and the auxiliary forces directed by, or subjected to, their hegemonic influence. Thus it would be impossible to understand the coup d'état of 2 December [1852] without studying the function of the French military groups and peasantry.

A very important historical episode from this point of view is the so-called Dreyfus affair in France. This too belongs to the present series of observations, not because it led to 'Caesarism', indeed precisely for the opposite reason: because it prevented the advent of a Caesarism in gestation, of a clearly reactionary nature. Nevertheless, the Dreyfus movement is characteristic, since it was a case in which elements of the dominant social bloc itself thwarted the Caesarism of the most reactionary part of that same bloc. And they did so by relying for support not on the peasantry and the countryside, but on the subordinate strata in the towns under the leadership of reformist socialists (though they did in fact draw support from the most advanced part of the peasantry as well). There are other modern historico-political movements of the Dreyfus type to be found, which are certainly not revolutions, but which are not entirely reactions either – at least in the sense that they shatter stifling and ossified state structures in the dominant camp as well, and introduce into national life and social activity a different and more numerous personnel. These movements too can have a relatively 'progressive' content, in so far as they indicate that there were effective forces latent in the old society which the older leaders did not know how to exploit – perhaps even 'marginal forces'. However, such forces cannot be absolutely progressive, in that they are not 'epochal'. They are rendered historically effective by their adversary's inability to construct, not by an inherent force of their own. Hence they are linked to a particular situation of equilibrium between the conflicting forces –

both incapable in their respective camps of giving autonomous expression to a will for reconstruction.

SPN, 222-3 (Q14§23)

IX AMERICANISM AND FORDISM

Introduction

The notes on 'Americanism and Fordism' deal with new forms of
interpenetration in the 1920s and 30s between the economy and
the political and cultural spheres. Gramsci treats the sphere of
production not as a mechanically determining economic 'base' but
as part of a complex 'historical bloc'. In other words he sees a
given form of production as reciprocally conditioning and
conditioned by a particular political framework, a particular
culture, ideology, morality and behaviour. He is interested in the
forms of 'social conformism' which accompany Americanism as
well as its literary and intellectual manifestations.

The analysis centres on the organization of production and the
labour process associated with the Ford Motor Company in
Detroit, namely mass production, or production in series.
'Fordism' involved the production of large quantities of goods to a
standardized design, the concentration of the whole production
cycle in a single plant, the mechanization of assembly (parts
moving on belts or chains), a high degree of division of labour and
the reduction of the worker's movements and tasks to a simple
routine. Gramsci is interested in the framework of coercion and
consent in which Fordism operates: the exclusion of free labour
unions, 'high wage' incentives, the hiring of workers of 'good
moral standing', the surveillance of workers' lives outside working
hours. He is also interested in the techniques of 'scientific
management' ('Taylorism', after their pioneer Frederick Taylor)
and in the political and social context of 'Americanism' which
makes the Taylor-Ford system possible and successful. North
America, Gramsci argues, has a more 'rationalized' social
structure than 'Old Europe' (particularly Southern Europe) which
is characterized by residues of feudalism and vast 'parasitic' middle
strata. It also has a liberal state which encourages and protects
untrammelled private enterprise, it has the corporatist ideologies
and practices of Roosevelt's New Deal, prohibition and an
officially encouraged conservative sexual morality and family life.

'Hegemony here', as Gramsci puts it in a striking sentence 'is born in the factory and requires for its exercise only a minute quantity of professional political and ideological intermediaries.' (pp.278-9)

Gramsci's interest in these questions is twofold. Firstly, he shares with many other Marxists in the inter-war period, both in the Soviet Union and elsewhere, an interest in the way industrial production and productivity were being increased in the United States by these new techniques and methods of management. He wants to understand how far Fordist and Taylorist methods are dictated by specifically *capitalist* requirements of intensified exploitation and the 'policing' of the factory and the workforce and how far, on the other hand, they correspond to 'rational' modernizing tendencies which *socialists* might be able to learn from and develop. It needs to be noted here that several of Gramsci's observations in this area have been seen as problematic, particularly those which appear to reflect a 'productivist' cast of thought (i.e. one in which the forces of production appear as neutral and their development unequivocally beneficial), an ends-means and value-free conception of 'rationality' (i.e. one in which the rationality of a particular form of production is measured only by its suitability to obtaining a given end) and, related to this, some staid views on sexual morality, women and the family.

Secondly, Gramsci is concerned to assess what might be called Americanist tendencies in Italian capitalism under Fascism. In the inter-war period, key sectors of Italian big industry – automobiles, chemicals and steel – underwent a process of concentration and modernization within the 'corporatist' framework provided by the Fascist state, that is to say the replacement of free trade unions by Fascist syndicates and corporations with no right to strike, participation in planning agreements, the provision by management of welfare and other benefits (health care, training, etc.) for the workforce and their families. However, as Gramsci points out here, these tendencies entered into contradiction with other tendencies in Fascist Italy, since the Fascists simultaneously promoted their policy of 'ruralism' by entrenching peasant smallholdings and also swelled the parasitic tertiary sector by creating hundreds of new jobs for state employees and Fascist Party functionaries.

1 Rationalization of the Demographic Composition of Europe

In Europe the various attempts which have been made to introduce certain aspects of Americanism and Fordism have been due to the old plutocratic stratum which would like to reconcile what, until proved to the contrary, appear to be irreconcilables: on the one hand the old, anachronistic, demographic social structure of Europe, and on the other hand an ultra-modern form of production and of working methods – such as is offered by the most advanced American variety, the industry of Henry Ford.

For this reason, the introduction of Fordism encounters so much 'intellectual' and 'moral' resistance, and takes place in particularly brutal and insidious forms, and by means of the most extreme coercion. Europe wants to have its cake and eat it, to have all the benefits which Fordism brings to its competitive power while retaining its army of parasites who, by consuming vast sums of surplus value, aggravate initial costs and reduce competitive power on the international market. The reaction of Europe to Americanism merits, therefore, close examination. From its analysis can be derived more than one element necessary for the understanding of the present situation of a number of states in the old world and the political events of the post-war period.

Americanism, in its most developed form, requires a preliminary condition which has not attracted the attention of the American writers who have treated the problems arising from it, since in America it exists quite 'naturally'. This condition could be called 'a rational demographic composition' and consists in the fact that there do not exist numerous classes with no essential function in the world of production, in other words classes which are purely parasitic. European 'tradition', European 'civilization', is, conversely, characterized precisely by the existence of such classes, created by the 'richness' and 'complexity' of past history. This past history has left behind a heap of passive sedimentations produced by the phenomenon of the saturation and fossilization of civil service personnel and intellectuals, of clergy and landowners, piratical commerce and the professional (and later conscript, but for the officers always professional) army. One could even say that the more historic a nation the more numerous and burdensome are these sedimentations of idle and useless masses living on 'their ancestral patrimony', pensioners of economic history. [...]

This situation is not unique to Italy; to a greater or lesser extent it exists also in all countries of Old Europe and it exists in an even worse form in India and China, which explains the historical stagnation of those countries and their politico-military impotence. (In the examination of this problem, what is immediately in question is not the form of economico-social organization, but the rationality of the proportional relationships between the various sectors of the population in the existing social system. Every system has its own law of fixed proportions in its demographic composition, its own 'optimum' equilibrium and forms of disequilibrium which, if not redressed, by appropriate legislation, can be catastrophic in themselves in that, apart from any other disintegrative element, they dry up the sources of economic life.)

America does not have 'great historical and cultural traditions'; but neither does it have this leaden burden to support. This is one of the main reasons (and certainly more important than its so-called natural wealth) for its formidable accumulation of capital which has taken place in spite of the superior living standard enjoyed by the popular classes compared with Europe. The non-existence of viscous parasitic sedimentations left behind by past phases of history has allowed industry, and commerce in particular, to develop on a sound basis. It also allows a continual reduction of the economic function of transport and trade to the level of a genuinely subaltern activity of production. Indeed, it has led to the attempt to absorb these activities into productive activity itself. Recall here the experiments conducted by Ford and the economies made by his firm through direct management of transport and distribution of the product. These economies affected production costs and permitted higher wages and lower selling prices. Since these preliminary conditions existed, already rendered rational by historical evolution, it was relatively easy to rationalize production and labour by a skilful combination of force (destruction of working-class trade unionism on a territorial basis) and persuasion (high wages, various social benefits, extremely subtle ideological and political propaganda) and thus succeed in making the whole life of the nation revolve around production. Hegemony here is born in the factory and requires for its exercise only a minute quantity of professional political and ideological intermediaries. The phenomenon of the 'masses' which so struck [Lucien] Romier is nothing but the form taken by this 'rationalized' society in which the 'structure' dominates the superstructures more immediately and in which the latter are also 'rationalized' (simplified and reduced in number).

[...]

In America rationalization has determined the need to elaborate a new type of man suited to the new type of work and productive process. This elaboration is still only in its initial phase and therefore (apparently) still idyllic. It is still at the stage of psycho-physical adaptation to the new industrial structure, aimed for through high wages. Up to the present (until the 1929 crash) there has not been, except perhaps sporadically, any flowering of the 'superstructure'. In other words, the fundamental question of hegemony has not yet been posed. The struggle is conducted with arms taken from the old European arsenal, bastardized and therefore anachronistic compared with the development of 'things.' The struggle taking place in America, as described by [André] Philip, is still in defence of craft rights against 'industrial liberty'. In other words, it is similar to the struggle that took place in Europe in the eighteenth century, although in different conditions. American workers' unions are, more than anything else, the corporate expression of the rights of qualified crafts and therefore the industrialists' attempts to curb them have a certain 'progressive' aspect. The absence of the European historical phase, marked also in the economic field by the French Revolution, has left the American popular masses in a backward state. To this should be added the absence of national homogeneity, the mixture of race-cultures, the negro question.

In Italy there have been the beginnings of a Fordist fanfare: exaltation of big cities, overall planning for the Milan conurbation, etc.; the affirmation that capitalism is only at its beginnings and that it is necessary to prepare for it grandiose patterns of development (on this see some articles by [Alessandro] Schiavi in *La Riforma Sociale*). But afterwards came a conversion to ruralism, the disparagement of the cities typical of the Enlightenment, exaltation of the artisan and of idyllic patriarchalism, reference to craft rights and a struggle against industrial liberty. All the same, even though the development is

slow and full of understandable caution, one cannot say that the
conservative side, the side that represents old European culture
with all its train of parasites, has not encountered opposition.

[...]

SPN, 280-7 (Q22§2)

2 Some Aspects of the Sexual Question

[...] Sexual instincts are those that have undergone the greatest
degree of repression from society in the course of its development.
'Regulation' of sexual instincts, because of the contradictions it
creates and the perversions that are attributed to it, seems
particularly 'unnatural'. Hence the frequency of appeals to
'nature' in this area. 'Psychoanalytical' literature is also a kind of
criticism of the regulation of sexual instincts in a form which often
recalls the Enlightenment, as in its creation of a new myth of the
'savage' on a sexual basis (including relations between parents and
children).[1]

There is a split, in this field, between city and country, but with
no idyllic bias in favour of the country, where the most frequent
and the most monstrous sexual crimes take place and where
bestiality and sodomy are widespread. In the parliamentary
enquiry on the South in 1911 it is stated that in Abruzzo and the
Basilicata, which are the regions where there is most religious
fanaticism and patriarchalism and the least influence of urban
ideas (to such an extent that, according to Serpieri, in the years
1919-20 there was not even any peasant unrest in those areas)
there is incest in 30 per cent of families. And it does not appear
that the situation has changed since then.

Sexuality as reproductive function and as sport: the 'aesthetic'
ideal of woman oscillates between the conceptions of 'brood mare'
and of 'dolly'. But it is not only in the cities that sexuality has
become a 'sport'. The popular proverbs, 'man is a hunter, woman
a temptress', 'the man who has no choice goes to bed with his
wife', etc., show how widespread the conception of sex as sport is
even in the countryside and in sexual relations between members
of the same class.

The economic function of reproduction. This is not only a
general fact which concerns the whole of society in its totality,

because society demands a certain proportion between age-groups for purposes of production and of supporting the section of the population that for normal reasons (age, illness, etc.) is passive. It is also a 'molecular' fact which operates within the smallest economic units, such as the family. The expression about the 'staff of old age' demonstrates an instinctive consciousness of the economic need for there to be a certain ratio of young to old over the entire area of society. The sight of the maltreatment meted out in country villages to old people without a family encourages couples to want to have children. (The proverb to the effect that 'a mother may raise a hundred sons, but a hundred sons do not support a mother', shows another side to this question.) Among the people old men without children are treated in the same way as bastards. Medical advance, which has raised the average expectancy of human life, is making the sexual question increasingly important as a fundamental and autonomous aspect of the economic, and this sexual aspect raises, in its turn, complex problems of a 'superstructural' order. The increase of life-expectancy in France, where the birth-rate is low and where there is a rich and complex productive apparatus to be kept going, has already given rise to a number of problems connected with the national question. The older generations are finding themselves in an increasingly abnormal relationship with the younger generations of the same national culture, and the working masses are being swollen by immigrant elements from abroad which modify the base. The same phenomenon is happening there as in America, that of a certain division of labour, with the native population occupying the qualified trades and, of course, the functions of direction and organization, and the immigrants the unskilled work.

In a number of states a similar relationship, with important negative economic consequences, exists between industrial cities with a low birth-rate and a prolific countryside. Life in industry demands a general apprenticeship, a process of psycho-physical adaptation to specific conditions of work, nutrition, housing, customs, etc. This is not something 'natural' or innate, but has to be acquired, and the urban characteristics thus acquired are passed on by heredity or rather are absorbed in the development of childhood and adolescence. As a result the low birth-rate in the cities imposes the need for continual massive expenditure on the training of a continual flow of new arrivals in the city and brings with it a continual change in the socio-political composition of the city, thus continually changing the terrain on which the problem of hegemony is to be posed.

The formation of a new feminine personality is the most important question of an ethical and civil order connected with the sexual question. Until women can attain not only a genuine independence in relation to men but also a new way of conceiving themselves and their role in sexual relations, the sexual question will remain full of unhealthy characteristics and caution must be exercised in proposals for new legislation. Every crisis brought about by unilateral coercion in the sexual field unleashes a 'romantic' reaction which could be aggravated by the abolition of organized legal prostitution. All these factors make any form of regulation of sex and any attempt to create a new sexual ethic suited to the new methods of production and work extremely complicated and difficult. However, it is still necessary to attempt this regulation and to attempt to create a new ethic. It is worth drawing attention to the way in which industrialists (Ford in particular) have been concerned with the sexual affairs of their employees and with their family arrangements in general. One should not be misled, any more than in the case of prohibition, by the 'puritanical' appearance assumed by this concern. The truth is that the new type of man demanded by the rationalization of production and work cannot be developed until the sexual instinct has been suitably regulated and until it too has been rationalized.

SPN, 294-7 (Q22§3)

3 Financial Autarky of Industry

A noteworthy article by Carlo Pagni, 'A proposito di un tentativo di teoria pura del corporativismo' (*La Riforma Sociale*, September/October 1929) examines Massimo Fovel's book *Economia e corporativismo* (Ferrara, S.A.T.E., 1929) and refers to another work by the same author *Rendita e salario nello Stato Sindacale* (Rome, 1928). But he does not realize, or does not point out explicitly, that Fovel in his writings conceives of 'corporatism' as the premiss for the introduction into Italy of the most advanced American systems of production and labour. It would be interesting to know whether Fovel is writing 'out of his head' or whether he has behind him specific social forces (practically speaking and not just in general) which back him and urge him on. Fovel has never been a 'pure scientist', since all intellectuals, however 'pure', are always expressive of certain tendencies. [...]

What would appear significant in Fovel's thesis, as summarized by Pagni, is his conception of the corporation as an autonomous industrial productive bloc destined to resolve in a modern and increasingly capitalist direction the problem of further development of the Italian economic apparatus. This is opposed to the semi-feudal and parasitic elements of society which appropriate an excessive amount of surplus value and to the so-called 'producers of savings'. The production of savings should become an internal (more economical) function of the productive bloc itself, with the help of a development of production at diminishing costs which would allow, in addition to an increase of surplus value, higher wages as well. The result of this would be a larger internal market, a certain level of working-class saving and higher profits. In this way one should get a more rapid rhythm of capital accumulation within the enterprise rather than through the intermediary of the 'producers of savings' who are really nothing other than predators of surplus value. Within the industrial-productive bloc, the technical element, management and workers, should be more important than the 'capitalistic' element in the petty sense of the word. The alliance of captains of industry and petty-bourgeois savers should be replaced by a bloc consisting of all the elements which are directly operative in production and which are the only ones capable of combining in a union and thus constituting the productive corporation. [...] Fovel's greatest weaknesses consist in his having neglected the economic function which the state has always had in Italy because of the diffident attitude of small savers towards the industrialists, and in having neglected the fact that the corporative trend did not originate from the need for changes in the technical conditions of industry, or even from that of a new economic policy, but rather from the need for economic policing, a need which was aggravated by the 1929 crisis which is still going on.

In reality skilled workers in Italy have never, as individuals or through union organizations, actively or passively opposed innovations leading towards lowering of costs, rationalization of work or the introduction of more perfect forms of automation and more perfect technical organization of the complex of the enterprise. On the contrary. However, this has happened in America and has resulted in the semi-liquidation of the free trade unions and their replacement by a system of mutually isolated factory-based workers' organizations. In Italy on the other hand even the slightest and most cautious attempt to make the factory the centre of the trade union organization (recall the question of the 'shop stewards') has been bitterly contested and resolutely crushed. A careful analysis of Italian history before 1922, or even up to 1926, which does not allow itself to be distracted by external trappings but manages to seize on the essential moments of the working-class struggle, must objectively come to the conclusion that it was precisely the workers who brought into being newer and more modern industrial requirements and in their own way upheld these strenuously. It could also be said that some industrialists understood this movement and tried to appropriate it to themselves. This explains Agnelli's attempt to absorb the *Ordine Nuovo* and its school into the Fiat complex and thus to institute a school of workers and technicians qualified for industrial change and for work with 'rationalized' systems. The YMCA tried to open courses of abstract 'Americanism', but despite all the money spent they were not a success.

These considerations apart, a further series of questions is raised. The corporative movement exists. It is also true that in some ways the juridical changes which have already taken place have created the formal conditions within which major technical-economic change can happen on a large scale, because the workers are not in a position either to oppose it or to struggle to become themselves the standard-bearers of the movement. Corporative organization could become the form of the new change, but one asks oneself: shall we experience one of Vico's 'ruses of providence' in which men, without either proposing or willing it, are forced to obey the imperatives of history? For the moment one is more inclined to be dubious. The negative element of 'economic policing' has so far had the upper hand over the positive element represented by the requirements of a new economic policy which can renovate, by modernizing it, the socio-economic structure of the nation while remaining within the framework of the old industrialism.

The juridical form possible is one of the conditions required, but not the only one or even the most important: it is only the most important of the immediate conditions. Americanization requires a particular environment, a particular social structure (or at least a determined intention to create it) and a certain type of state. This state is the liberal state, not in the sense of free-trade liberalism or of effective political liberty, but in the more fundamental sense of free initiative and of economic individualism which, with its own means, on the level of 'civil society', through historical development, itself arrives at a regime of industrial concentration and monopoly. The disappearance of the semi-feudal type of *rentier* is in Italy one of the major conditions of an industrial revolution (and, in part, the revolution itself) and not a consequence. The economic and financial policy of the state is the instrument of their disappearance through the amortization of the national debt, compulsory registration of shares, and by giving a greater weight to direct rather than indirect taxation in the governmental budget. But it does not seem that this has been or is going to become the trend of financial policy. Indeed, the state is creating new *rentiers*, that is to say it is promoting the old forms of parasitic accumulation of savings and tending to create closed social formations. In reality the corporative trend has operated to shore up crumbling positions of the middle classes and not to eliminate them, and is becoming, because of the vested interests that arise from the old foundations, more and more a machinery to preserve the existing order just as it is rather than a propulsive force. Why is this? Because the corporative trend is also dependent on unemployment. It defends for the employed a certain minimum standard which, if there were free competition, would likewise collapse and thus provoke serious social disturbances; and it creates new forms of employment, organizational and not productive, for the unemployed of the middle classes. But there still remains a way out: the corporative trend, born in strict dependence on such a delicate situation whose essential equilibrium must at all costs be maintained if monstrous catastrophe is to be averted, could yet manage to proceed by very slow and almost imperceptible stages to modify the social structure without violent shocks: even the most tightly swathed baby manages nevertheless to develop and grow. This is why it would be interesting to know whether Fovel is speaking just for himself or whether he is the representative of economic forces which are looking for a way forward at all costs. In any case, the process would be so long and encounter so many difficulties that new interests could grow up in the meanwhile and once again oppose its development so tenaciously as to crush it entirely.

SPN, 289-94 (Q22§6)

4 'Animality' and Industrialism

The history of industrialism has always been a continuing struggle (which today takes an even more marked and vigorous form) against the element of 'animality' in man. It has been an uninterrupted, often painful and bloody process of subjugating natural (i.e. animal and primitive) instincts to new, more complex and rigid norms and habits of order, exactitude and precision which can make possible the increasingly complex forms of collective life which are the necessary consequence of industrial development. This struggle is imposed from outside, and the results to date, though they have great immediate practical value, are to a large extent purely mechanical: the new habits have not yet become 'second nature'. But has not every new way of life, in the period in which it was forced to struggle against the old, always been for a certain time a result of mechanical repression? Even the instincts which have to be overcome today because they are too 'animal' are really a considerable advance on earlier, even more primitive instincts. Who could describe the 'cost' in human lives and in the grievous subjugation of instinct involved in the passage from nomadism to a settled agricultural existence? The process includes the first forms of rural serfdom and trade bondage, etc. Up to now all changes in modes of existence and modes of life have taken place through brute coercion, that is to say through the dominion of one social group over all the productive forces of society. The selection or 'education' of men adapted to the new forms of civilization and to the new forms of production and work has taken place by means of incredible acts of brutality which have cast the weak and the non-conforming into the limbo of the underclasses or have eliminated them entirely.

With the appearance of new types of civilization, or in the course of their development, there have always been crises. But who has been involved in these crises? Not so much the working masses as the middle classes and a part even of the ruling class which had undergone the process of coercion which was necessarily being exercised over the whole area of society. Crises of *libertinism* have been many, and there has been one in every historical epoch.

When the pressure of coercion is exercised over the whole complex of society (and this has taken place in particular since the fall of slavery and the coming of Christianity) puritan ideologies develop which give an external form of persuasion and consent to the intrinsic use of force. But once the result has been achieved, if only to a degree, the pressure is fragmented. Historically this fragmentation has assumed many different forms, which is to be expected, since the pressure itself has always taken original and often personal forms – it has been identified with a religious movement, it has created an apparatus of its own incarnated in particular strata or castes, it has taken the name of a Cromwell or a Louis XV as the case may be. It is at this point that the crisis of libertinism ensues. The French crisis following the death of Louis XV, for example, cannot be compared with the crisis in America following the appearance of Roosevelt, nor does prohibition, with its consequent gangsterism, etc., have any parallel in preceding epochs. But the crisis does not affect the working masses except in a superficial manner, or it can affect them indirectly, in that it depraves their women folk. These masses have either acquired the habits and customs necessary for the new systems of living and working, or else they continue to be subject to coercive pressure through the elementary necessities of their existence. Opposition to prohibition was not wanted by the workers, and the corruption brought about by bootlegging and gangsterism was widespread amongst the upper classes.

In the post-war period there has been a crisis of morals of unique proportions, but it took place in opposition to a form of coercion which had not been imposed in order to create habits suited to forms of work but arose from the necessities, admitted as transitory, of wartime life and life in the trenches. This pressure involved a particular repression of sexual instincts, even the most normal, among great masses of young people, and the crisis which broke out with the return to normal life was made even more violent by the disappearance of so many young men and by a permanent disequilibrium in the numerical proportions of individuals of the two sexes. The institutions connected with sexual life were profoundly shaken and new forms of enlightened utopias developed around the sexual question. The crisis was made even more violent, and still is, by the fact that it affected all strata of the population and came into conflict with the necessities of the new methods of work which were meanwhile beginning to impose themselves (Taylorism and rationalization in general). These new methods demand a rigorous discipline of the sexual instincts (at the level of the nervous system) and with it a strengthening of the 'family' in the wide sense (rather than a particular form of the familial system) and of the regulation and stability of sexual relations.

It is worth insisting on the fact that in the sexual field the most depraving and 'regressive' ideological factor is the enlightened and libertarian conception proper to those classes which are not tightly bound to productive work and spread by them among the working classes. This element becomes particularly serious in a state where the working masses are no longer subject to coercive pressure from a superior class and where the new methods of production and work have to be acquired by means of reciprocal persuasion and by convictions proposed and accepted by each individual. A two-fold situation can then create itself in which there is an inherent conflict between the 'verbal' ideology which recognizes the new necessities and the real 'animal' practice which prevents physical bodies from effectively acquiring the new attitudes. In this case one gets the formation of what can be called a situation of totalitarian social hypocrisy. Why totalitarian? In other situations the popular strata are compelled to practise 'virtue'. Those who preach it do not practise it, although they pay it verbal homage. The hypocrisy is therefore a question of strata: it is not total. This is a situation which cannot last, and is certain to lead to a crisis of libertinism, but only when the masses have already assimilated 'virtue' in the form of more or less permanent habits, that is with ever-decreasing oscillations. On the other hand, in the case where no coercive pressure is exercised by a superior class, 'virtue' is affirmed in generic terms but is not practised either through conviction or through coercion, with the result that the psycho-physical attitudes necessary for the new methods of work are not acquired. The crisis can become 'permanent' – that is, potentially catastrophic – since it can be resolved only by coercion. This coercion is a new type, in that it is exercised by the elite of a class over the rest of that same class. It can also only be self-coercion and therefore self-discipline (like Alfieri tying himself to the chair).[2] In any case in the sphere of sexual relations what can be opposed to this function of the elites is the enlightened and libertarian mentality. The struggle against the libertarian conception means therefore precisely creating the elites necessary for the historical task, or at least developing them so that their function is extended to cover all spheres of human activity.

SPN, 298-301 (Q22§10)

5 Rationalization of Production and Work

The tendency represented by Leo Davidov [Trotsky] was closely connected to this series of problems, a fact which does not seem to me to have been fully brought out. Its essential content, from this point of view, consisted in an 'over'-resolute (and therefore not rationalized) will to give supremacy in national life to industry and industrial methods, to accelerate, through coercion imposed from the outside, the growth of discipline and order in production, and to adapt customs to the necessities of work. Given the general way in which all the problems connected with this tendency were conceived, it was destined necessarily to end up in a form of Bonapartism. Hence the inexorable necessity of crushing it. The preoccupations were correct, but the practical solutions were profoundly mistaken, and in this imbalance between theory and practice there was an inherent danger – the same danger, incidentally, which had manifested itself earlier, in 1921. The principle of coercion, direct or indirect, in the ordering of production and work, is correct: but the form which it assumed was mistaken. The military model had become a pernicious prejudice and the militarization of labour was a failure.[3] Interest of Leo Davidov in Americanism. He wrote articles, researched into the 'byt' [mode of living] and into literature.[4] These activities were less disconnected than might appear, since the new methods of work are inseparable from a specific mode of living and of thinking and feeling life. One cannot have success in one field without tangible results in the other.

In America rationalization of work and prohibition are undoubtedly connected. The enquiries conducted by the industrialists into the workers' private lives and the inspection services created by some firms to control the 'morality' of their workers are necessities of the new methods of work. People who laugh at these initiatives (failures though they were) and see in them only a hypocritical manifestation of 'puritanism' thereby deny themselves any possibility of understanding the importance, significance and objective import of the American phenomenon, which is *also* the biggest collective effort to date to create, with unprecedented speed, and with a consciousness of purpose unmatched in history, a new type of worker and of man. The expression 'consciousness of purpose' might appear humorous to say the least to anyone who recalls Taylor's phrase about the 'trained gorilla!'.[5] Taylor is in fact expressing with brutal cynicism the purpose of American society – developing in the worker to the highest degree automatic and mechanical attitudes, breaking up the old psycho-physical nexus of qualified professional work, which demands a certain active participation of intelligence, fantasy and initiative on the part of the worker, and reducing productive operations exclusively to the mechanical, physical aspect. But these things, in reality, are not original or novel: they represent simply the most recent phase of a long process which began with industrialism itself. This phase is more intense than preceding phases, and manifests itself in more brutal forms, but it is a phase which will itself be superseded by the creation of a psycho-physical nexus of a new type, both different from its predecessors and undoubtedly *superior*. A forced selection will ineluctably take place; a part of the old working class will be pitilessly eliminated from the world of labour, and perhaps from the world *tout court*.

It is from this point of view that one should study the 'puritanical' initiative of American industrialists like Ford. It is certain that they are not concerned with the 'humanity' or the 'spirituality' of the worker, which are immediately smashed. This 'humanity and spirituality' cannot be realized except in the world of production and work and in productive 'creation'. They exist most in the artisan, in the 'demiurge', when the worker's personality was reflected whole in the object created and when the link between art and labour was still very strong. But it is precisely against this 'humanism' that the new industrialism is fighting. 'Puritanical' initiatives simply have the purpose of preserving, outside of work, a certain psycho-physical equilibrium which prevents physiological collapse of the worker, exhausted by the new method of production. This equilibrium can only be something purely external and mechanical, but it can become internalized if it is proposed by the worker himself, and not imposed from the outside, if it is proposed by a new form of society, with appropriate and original methods. American industrialists are concerned to maintain the continuity of the physical and muscular-nervous efficiency of the worker. It is in their interests to have a stable, skilled labour force, a permanently well adjusted complex, because the human complex (the collective worker) of an enterprise is also a machine which cannot, without considerable loss, be taken to pieces too often and renewed with single new parts.

The element of so-called high wages also depends on this necessity. It is the instrument used to select and maintain in stability a skilled labour force suited to the system of production and work. But high wages are a double-edged weapon. It is necessary for the worker to spend his extra money 'rationally' to maintain, renew and, if possible, increase his muscular-nervous efficiency and not to corrode or destroy it. Thus the struggle against alcohol, the most dangerous agent of destruction of labouring power, becomes a function of the state. It is possible for other 'puritanical' struggles as well to become functions of the state if the private initiative of the industrialists proves insufficient or if a moral crisis breaks out among the working masses which is too profound and too widespread, as might happen as a result of a long and widespread crisis of unemployment.

The sexual question is again connected with that of alcohol. Abuse and irregularity of sexual functions is, after alcoholism, the most dangerous enemy of nervous energies, and it is commonly observed that 'obsessional' work provokes alcoholic and sexual depravation. The attempts made by Ford, with the aid of a body of inspectors, to intervene in the private lives of his employees and to control how they spent their wages and how they lived is an indication of these tendencies. Though these tendencies are still only 'private' or only latent, they could become, at a certain point, state ideology, inserting themselves into traditional puritanism and presenting themselves as a renaissance of the pioneer morality, of the 'true' Americanism, etc. The most noteworthy fact in the

292 A Gramsci Reader

American phenomenon in relation to these manifestations is the gap which has been formed and is likely to be increasingly accentuated, between the morality and way of life of the workers and those of other strata of the population.

Prohibition has already given an example of this gap. Who drank the alcohol brought into the United States by the bootleggers? Alcohol became a luxury product and even the highest wages were not enough to enable it to be consumed by large strata of the working masses. Someone who works for a wage, with fixed hours, does not have time to dedicate himself to the pursuit of drink or to sport or evading the law. The same observation can be made about sexuality. 'Womanizing' demands too much leisure. The new type of worker will be a repetition, in a different form, of peasants in the villages. The relative stability of sexual unions among the peasants is closely linked to the system of work in the country. The peasant who returns home in the evening after a long and hard day's work wants the '*venerem facilem parabilemque* [easy and accessible love] of Horace.[6] It is not his style to spoon over casual women. He loves his own woman, sure and unfailing, who is free from affectation and doesn't play little games about being seduced or raped in order to be possessed. It might seem that in this way the sexual function has been mechanized, but in reality we are dealing with the growth of a new form of sexual union shorn of the bright and dazzling colour of the romantic tinsel typical of the petty bourgeois and the Bohemian layabout. It seems clear that the new industrialism wants monogamy: it wants the man as worker not to squander his nervous energies in the disorderly and stimulating pursuit of occasional sexual satisfaction. The employee who goes to work after a night of 'excess' is no good for his work. The exaltation of passion cannot be reconciled with the timed movements of productive motions connected with the most perfected automatism. This complex of direct and indirect repression and coercion exercised on the masses will undoubtedly produce results and a new form of sexual union will emerge whose fundamental characteristic would apparently have to be monogamy and relative stability.

It would be interesting to know the statistical occurrence of deviation from the sexual behaviour officially propagandized in the United States, broken down according to social group.

It will show that in general divorce is particularly frequent among the upper classes. This demonstrates the moral gap in the United States between the working masses and the ever more numerous elements of the ruling classes. This moral gap seems to me one of the most interesting phenomena and one which is most rich in consequences. Until recently the American people was a working people. The 'vocation of work' was not a trait inherent only in the working class but it was a specific quality of the ruling classes as well. The fact that a millionaire continued to be practically active until forced to retire by age or illness and that his activity occupied a very considerable part of his day, is a typically American phenomenon. This, for the average European, is the weirdest American extravagance. We have noted above that this difference between Americans and Europeans is determined by the absence of 'tradition' in the United States, in so far as tradition also means passive residues of all the social forms eclipsed by past history. In the United States, on the other hand, there is a recent 'tradition' of the pioneers, the tradition of strong individual personalities in whom the vocation of work had reached its greatest intensity and strength, men who entered directly, not by means of some army of servants and slaves, into energetic contact with the forces of nature in order to dominate them and exploit them victoriously. In Europe it is the passive residues that resist Americanism (they 'represent quality', etc.) because they have the instinctive feeling that the new forms of production and work would sweep them away implacably. But if it is true that in Europe the old but still unburied residues are due to be definitively destroyed; what is beginning to happen in America itself? The moral gap mentioned above shows that ever wider margins of social passivity are in the process of being created. It would appear that women have a particularly important role here. The male industrialist continues to work even if he is a millionaire, but his wife and daughters are turning, more and more, into 'luxury mammals'. Beauty competitions, competitions for new film actresses (recall the 30,000 Italian girls who sent photographs of themselves in bathing costumes to Fox in 1926), the theatre, etc., all of which select the feminine beauty of the world and put it up for auction, stimulate the mental attitudes of prostitution, and 'white slaving' is practised quite legally among the upper classes. The women, with nothing to do, travel; they are continually crossing the ocean to come to Europe, escaping prohibition in

A Gramsci Reader

their own country and contracting 'marriages' for a season. (It is worth recalling that ships' captains in the United States have been deprived of their right to celebrate marriages on board ship, since so many couples get married on leaving Europe and divorced again before disembarking in America.) Prostitution in a real sense is spreading, in a form barely disguised by fragile legal formulae.

These phenomena proper to the upper classes will make more difficult any coercion on the working masses to make them conform to the needs of the new industry. In any case they are determining a psychological split and accelerating the crystallization and saturation of the various social groups, thereby making evident the way that these groups are being transformed into castes just as they have been in Europe.

SPN, 301-6 (Q22§11)

6 Taylorism and the Mechanization of the Worker

Taylorism supposedly produces a gap between manual labour and the 'human content' of work. On this subject some useful observations can be made on the basis of past history and specifically of those professions thought of as amongst the most intellectual, that is to say the professions connected with the reproduction of texts for publication or other forms of diffusion and transmission: the scribes of the days before the invention of printing, compositors on hand presses, linotype operators, stenographers and typists. If one thinks about it, it is clear that in these trades the process of adaptation to mechanization is more difficult than elsewhere. Why? Because it is so hard to reach the height of professional qualification when this requires of the worker that he should 'forget' or not think about the intellectual content of the text he is reproducing: this in order to be able, if he is a scribe, to fix his attention exclusively on the calligraphic form of the single letters; or to be able to break down phrases into 'abstract' words and then words into characters, and rapidly select the pieces of lead in the cases; or to be able to break down not single words but groups of words, in the context of discourse, and group them mechanically into shorthand notation; or to acquire speed in typing, etc. The worker's interest in the intellectual content of the text can be measured from his mistakes. In other words, it is a professional failing. Conversely his qualification is commensurate with his lack of intellectual interest, i.e. the extent to which he has become 'mechanized'. The medieval copyist who was interested in the text changed the spelling, the morphology and the syntax of the text he was copying; he missed out entire passages which because of his meagure culture he could not understand; the train of thoughts aroused in his mind by his interest in the text led him to interpolate glosses and observations; if his language or dialect was different from that of the text he would introduce nuances deriving from his own speech: he was a bad scribe because in reality he was 'remaking' the text. The slow speed of the art of writing in the Middle Ages explains many of these weaknesses: there was too much time in which to reflect, and consequently 'mechanization' was more difficult. The compositor has to be much quicker; he has to keep his hands and eyes constantly in movement, and this makes his mechanization easier. But if one really thinks about it, the effort that these workers have to make in order to isolate from the often fascinating intellectual content of a text (and the more fascinating it is the less work is done and the less well) its written symbolization, this perhaps is the greatest effort that can be required in any trade. However it is done, and it is not the spiritual death of man. Once the process of adaptation has been completed, what really happens is that the brain of the worker, far from being mummified, reaches a state of complete freedom. The only thing that is completely mechanized is the physical gesture; the memory of the trade, reduced to simple gestures repeated at an intense rhythm, 'nestles' in the muscular and nervous centres and leaves the brain free and unencumbered for other occupations. One can walk without having to think about all the movements needed in order to move, in perfect synchronization, all the parts of the body, in the specific way that is necessary for walking. The same thing happens and will go on happening in industry with the basic gestures of the trade. One walks automatically, and at the same time thinks about whatever one chooses. American industrialists have understood all too well this dialectic inherent in the new industrial methods. They have understood that 'trained gorilla' is just a phrase, that 'unfortunately' the worker remains a man and even that during his work he thinks more, or at least has greater opportunities for thinking, once he has overcome the crisis of adaptation without being eliminated: and not only does the worker think, but the fact that he gets no immediate satisfaction from his work and realises that they are trying to reduce him to a trained gorilla, can lead him into a train of thought that is far from conformist. That the industrialists are concerned about such things is made clear from a whole series of cautionary measures and 'educative' initiatives which are well brought out in Ford's books and the work of Philip.[7]

SPN, 308-10 (Q22§12)

7 [Babbitt]

See Carlo Linati's article 'Babbitt compra il mondo' [Babbitt buys the world] in *Nuova Antologia*, 16 October 1929. A mediocre article, but for that very reason significant as an expression of an average opinion. It can serve to establish what the more intelligent of the petty bourgeoisie think of Americanism. The article is a variation on Edgard Ansel Mowrer's book *This American World*, which Linati judges 'truly acute, rich with ideas and written with a pleasing concision between the classical and the brutal, by a writer who clearly lacks neither a spirit of observation nor a sense of historical nuances nor variety of culture'. Mowrer reconstructs the cultural history of the United States up to the breaking of the umbilical cord with Europe and the advent of Americanism.

It would be interesting to analyse the reasons why *Babbitt* was such a great success in Europe.[8] It is not a great book: it is constructed schematically and its mechanism is also too apparent. It is of cultural more than artistic importance: the criticism of manners prevails over art. That there exists in America a realistic literary current that starts out as a criticism of manners is a very important cultural fact. It means that there is an increase in self-criticism, that a new American civilization is being born that is aware of its strengths and its weaknesses. The intellectuals are breaking loose from the dominant class in order to unite themselves to it more intimately, to be a real superstructure and not only an inorganic and indistinct element of the structure-corporation.

European intellectuals have already partially lost this function. They no longer represent the cultural self-consciousness, the self-criticism of the dominant class. Once again they have become the immediate agents of the dominant class, or else they have completely broken loose from it by making up a caste in themselves, without roots in national-popular life. They laugh at Babbitt and are amused at his mediocrity, his naïve stupidity, his automatic way of thinking and his standardized mentality. They do not even ask the question: are there Babbitts in Europe? The point is that in Europe the standardized petty bourgeois exists but his standardization, instead of being national (and of a great nation like the United States), is regional and local. The European Babbitts belong to a historical gradation inferior to that of the American Babbitt: they are a national weakness, whereas the American one is a national strength. They are more picturesque, but also more stupid and ridiculous. Their conformism is based on a rotten and debilitating superstition, whereas Babbitt's is naïve and spontaneous and based on an energetic and progressive superstition.

For Linati, Babbitt is 'the prototype of the modern American industrialist'. In fact, Babbitt is a petty bourgeois and his most typical mania is that of being friends with 'modern industrialists', being their equal, and showing off their moral and social 'superiority'. The modern industrialist is a model to be emulated, the social type to which one must conform, while for the European Babbitt the model and type are given by the canon of the cathedral, the petty nobleman from the provinces and the section head at the ministry. This uncritical attitude of European intellectuals is worth noting: in the preface to his book on the United States [*Les États-Unis d'aujourd hui*, Paris 1928], [André] Siegfried compares the artisan of a Parisian luxury goods industry to the Taylorized American worker, as if the former were a common type of worker. In general, European intellectuals think that Babbitt is a purely American type and are delighted with old Europe. This anti-Americanism is comical before it is stupid.

SCW, 278-9 (Q5§105)

8 Babbitt Again

The European petty bourgeois laughs at Babbitt and therefore laughs at America which is supposedly populated by 120 million Babbitts. The petty bourgeois cannot get outside of himself or understand himself, just as the imbecile is incapable of understanding that he is an imbecile (without demonstrating thereby that he is intelligent). The real imbecile is the one who doesn't know he is one, and the philistine who doesn't know he is one is the real petty bourgeois. The European petty bourgeois laughs at the philistinism of Americans but is not aware of his own. He does not know that he is the European Babbitt, inferior to the Babbitt of Lewis's novel in that he tries to escape and not to be Babbitt. The European Babbitt does not struggle with his philistinism but basks in it, believing that the croaking he makes like a frog stuck in the quagmire is a nightingale's song. In spite of everything, Babbitt is the philistine of a country in motion; the European petty bourgeois is the philistine of conservative countries that are rotting in the stagnant swamp of commonplaces about the great tradition and great culture. The European philistine believes that he discovered America with Christopher Columbus and that Babbitt is a puppet intended for the amusement of those like him, weighed down with millennia of history. Meanwhile, no European writer has been able to depict the European Babbitt for us and show that he is capable of self-criticism: in fact, the only imbecile and philistine is precisely the one who isn't aware of it.

SCW, 279-80 (Q6§49)

9 Notes on American Culture

In 'Strange Interlude' (*Corriere della Sera*, 15 March 1932), G.A. Borgese divides the population of the United States into four strata: the financial class, the political class, the Intelligentsia, the Common Man. Compared to the first two, the Intelligentsia is extremely small: a few tens of thousands, concentrated especially in the East, among which are a few thousand writers. 'One should not judge by numbers alone. It is intellectually among the best equipped in the world. Someone who belongs to this class compares it to what the Encyclopaedists were in eighteenth-century France. For the moment, to one who likes to stick to the facts, it appears to be a brain without limbs, a soul without locomotive power; its influence over the public realm is almost nil.' He notes that after the crisis, the financial class which at first controlled the political class has in recent months 'undergone' the latter's assistance and virtual control. 'Congress is supporting the banks and the stock market; the Capitol in Washington is propping up Wall Street. This is undermining the old equilibrium of the American state, but without the rise of a new order.' Since in reality the financial class and the political class are the same in America, or two aspects of the same thing, this can only mean that a real differentiation has taken place, that the economic-corporate phase of American history is in crisis and America is about to enter a new phase. This will be evident only if the traditional parties (Republican and Democratic) enter into crisis and a major new party is created that can organize the Common Man on a permanent basis. The seeds of such a development were already there (the Progressive Party), but the economic-corporate structure has so far always reacted effectively against them.

The observation that the American Intelligentsia has a historical position like that of the French Encyclopaedists of the eighteenth century is very acute and can be developed.

SCW, 280-1 (Q8§89)

X INTELLECTUALS AND EDUCATION

Introduction

'I greatly extend the notion of intellectuals', Gramsci wrote to his sister-in-law Tatiana Schucht in 1931, 'and I do not restrict myself to the current notion which refers to great intellectuals' (*Lettere dal carcere*, ed. S. Caprioglio and E. Fubini, Turin 1965, p. 481). As he redefines the word it comes to designate anyone whose function in society is primarily that of organizing, administering, directing, educating or leading others. Gramsci is concerned both with the analysis of those intellectuals who function directly or indirectly on behalf of a dominant social group to organize coercion and consent and with the problem of how to form intellectuals of the subaltern social groups who will be capable of opposing and transforming the existing social order.

Gramsci's interest in the intellectuals can be seen as developing out of his early writings on education (see Section II above) and from his non-economistic conception of the functioning of a historical bloc. If social classes do not exercise power directly but through political and cultural intermediaries, then the role of these intermediaries – the intellectuals – in maintaining and reproducing a given economic and social order (in the exercise of hegemony), is of decisive importance. In order for the working class to challenge that existing order, and become hegemonic in its turn without becoming dependent on intellectuals from another class, it must create 'organic' intellectuals of its own.

Here however it faces a historic obstacle. The division of labour in class society separates manual from mental (intellectual) workers and largely reserves intellectual functions – which are functions of power – to specific social groups who reproduce themselves through the education system. For Gramsci this obstacle can be surmounted in two complementary ways: through the mass political party, which itself functions as a 'collective intellectual' and trains its cadres in deliberative and organizational skills, and through the school, which must be reformed so as to overcome the streaming into manual and mental skills and to enable a 'new equilibrium' between them to emerge. These two developments would also be part of a wider movement towards human liberation and self-government, since they would break down that historic separation between leaders and led, intellectuals and 'non-intellectuals', which for Gramsci lay at the root of the formation of 'bureaucratic centralism'.

1 [Intellectuals]

Are intellectuals an autonomous and independent social group, or does every social group have its own particular specialized category of intellectuals? The problem is a complex one, because of the variety of forms assumed to date by the real historical process of formation of the different categories of intellectuals. The most important of these forms are two:

1. Every social group, coming into existence on the original terrain of an essential function in the world of economic production, creates together with itself, organically, one or more strata of intellectuals which give it homogeneity and an awareness of its own function not only in the economic but also in the social and political fields. The capitalist entrepreneur creates alongside himself the industrial technician, the specialist in political economy, the organizer of a new culture, of a new legal system, etc. It should be noted that the entrepreneur himself represents a higher level of social elaboration, already characterized by a certain directive [*dirigente*] and technical (i.e. intellectual) capacity: he must have a certain technical capacity, not only in the limited sphere of his activity and initiative but in other spheres as well, at least in those which are closest to economic production. He must be an organizer of masses of men; he must be an organizer of the 'confidence' of investors in his business, of the customers for his product, etc.

If not all entrepreneurs, at least an elite amongst them must have the capacity to be an organizer of society in general, including all its complex organism of services, right up to the state organism, because of the need to create the conditions most favourable to the expansion of their own class; or at the least they must possess the capacity to choose the deputies (specialized employees) to whom to entrust this activity of organizing the general system of relationships external to the business itself. It can be observed that the 'organic' intellectuals which every new class creates alongside itself and elaborates in the course of its development, are for the most part 'specializations' of partial aspects of the primitive activity of the new social type which the new class has brought into prominence. Even feudal lords were possessors of a particular technical capacity – military capacity – and it is precisely from the moment at which the aristocracy loses its monopoly of technico-military capacity that the crisis of feudalism begins. But the formation of intellectuals in the feudal world and in the preceding classical world is a question to be examined separately: this formation and elaboration follows ways and means which must be studied concretely. Thus it is to be noted that the mass of the peasantry, although it performs an essential function in the world of production, does not elaborate its own 'organic' intellectuals, nor does it 'assimilate' any stratum of 'traditional' intellectuals, although it is from the peasantry that other social groups draw many of their intellectuals and a high proportion of traditional intellectuals are of peasant origin.)

2. However, every 'essential' social group which emerges into history out of the preceding economic structure, and as an expression of a development of this structure, has found (at least in all of history up to the present) categories of intellectuals already in existence and which seemed indeed to represent a historical continuity uninterrupted even by the most complicated and radical changes in political and social forms.

The most typical of these categories of intellectuals is that of the ecclesiastics, who for a long time (for a whole phase of history, which is partly characterized by this very monopoly) held a monopoly of a number of important services: religious ideology, that is the philosophy and science of the age, together with schools, education, morality, justice, charity, good works, etc. The category of ecclesiastics can be considered the category of intellectuals organically bound to the landed aristocracy. It had equal status juridically with the aristocracy, with which it shared the exercise of feudal ownership of land, and the use of state privileges connected with property. But the monopoly held by the ecclesiastics in the superstructural field (from this monopoly derived the general meaning of 'intellectual' or 'specialist' of the word *cleric* in many Romance languages, or those influenced through Church Latin by the Romance languages, together with its correlative *layman* in the sense of 'profane', 'non-specialist') was not exercised without a struggle or without limitations, and hence there took place the birth, in various forms (to be gone into and studied concretely), of other categories, favoured and enabled to expand by the growing strength of the central power of the monarch, right up to absolutism. Thus we find the formation of the *noblesse de robe*, with its own privileges, a stratum of administrators, etc., scholars and scientists, theorists, non-ecclesiastical philosophers, etc.

Since these various categories of traditional intellectuals experience through an '*esprit de corps*' their uninterrupted historical continuity and their special qualification, they thus put themselves forward as autonomous and independent of the dominant social group. This self-assessment is not without consequences in the ideological and political field, consequences of wide-ranging import. The whole of idealist philosophy can easily be connected with this position assumed by the social complex of intellectuals and can be defined as the expression of that social utopia by which the intellectuals think of themselves as 'independent', autonomous, endowed with a character of their own, etc.

One should note however that if the Pope and the leading hierarchy of the Church consider themselves more linked to Christ and to the apostles than they are to senators Agnelli and Benni,[1] the same does not hold for Gentile and Croce, for example: Croce in particular feels himself closely linked to Aristotle and Plato, but he does not conceal, on the other hand, his links with senators Agnelli and Benni, and it is precisely here that one can discern the most significant character of Croce's philosophy.

<(This research into the history of the intellectuals will not be of a 'sociological' character but will lead to a series of essays of 'cultural history' (*Kulturgeschichte*) and history of political science. All the same, it will be difficult to avoid certain schematic and abstract forms that will be reminiscent of those of 'sociology': it will therefore be necessary to find the most suitable form of writing for making this exposition 'non-sociological'. The first part

of the research could be a methodical critique of existing works on intellectuals, which are nearly all of a sociological type. It is therefore indispensable to collect a bibliography on the subject.)>

What are the 'maximum' limits of acceptance of the term 'intellectual'? Can one find a unitary criterion to characterize equally all the diverse and disparate activities of intellectuals and to distinguish these at the same time and in an essential way from the activities of other social groupings? The most widespread error of method seems to me that of having looked for this criterion of distinction in the intrinsic nature of intellectual activities, rather than in the ensemble of the system of relations in which these activities (and therefore the intellectual groups who personify them) have their place within the general complex of social relations. Indeed the worker or proletarian, for example, is not specifically characterized by his manual or instrumental work, but by performing this work in specific conditions and in specific social relations (apart from the consideration that purely physical labour does not exist and that even Taylor's phrase of 'trained gorilla' is a metaphor to indicate a limit in a certain direction: in any physical work, even the most degraded and mechanical, there exists a minimum of technical qualification, that is, a minimum of creative intellectual activity). And we have already observed that the entrepreneur, by virtue of his very function, must have to some degree a certain number of qualifications of an intellectual nature although his part in society is determined not by these, but by the general social relations which specifically characterize the position of the entrepreneur within industry.

All men are intellectuals, one could therefore say; but not all men have in society the function of intellectuals (thus, because it can happen that everyone at some time fries a couple of eggs or sews up a tear in a jacket, we do not necessarily say that everyone is a cook or a tailor). Thus there are historically formed specialized categories for the exercise of the intellectual function. They are formed in connection with all social groups, but especially in connection with the most important social groups, and they undergo more extensive and complex elaboration in connection with the dominant social group. One of the most important characteristics of any group that is developing towards dominance is its struggle to assimilate and to conquer 'ideologically' the traditional intellectuals, but this assimilation and conquest is made quicker and more efficacious the more the group in question succeeds in simultaneously elaborating its own organic intellectuals.

The enormous development of activity and organization of education in the broad sense in the societies that emerged from the medieval world is an index of the importance assumed in the modern world by intellectual functions and categories. Parallel with the attempt to deepen and to broaden the 'intellectuality' of each individual, there has also been an attempt to multiply and narrow the various specializations. This can be seen from educational institutions at all levels, up to and including the organisms that exist to promote so-called 'high culture' in all fields of science and technology.

(The education system is the instrument through which intellectuals of various levels are elaborated. The complexity of the intellectual function in different states can be measured objectively by the number and gradation of specialized schools: the more extensive the 'area' covered by education and the more numerous the 'vertical' 'levels' of schooling, the more complex is the cultural world, the civilization, of a particular state. A point of comparison can be found in the sphere of industrial technology: the industrialization of a country can be measured by how well equipped it is in the production of machines with which to produce machines, and in the manufacture of ever more accurate instruments for making both machines and further instruments for making machines, etc. The country which is best equipped in the construction of instruments for experimental scientific laboratories and in the construction of instruments with which to test the first instruments, can be regarded as the most complex in the technical-industrial field, with the highest level of civilization, etc. The same applies to the preparation: schools and institutes of high culture can be assimiliated to each other.) (In this field also, quantity cannot be separated from quality. To the most refined technical-cultural specialization there cannot but correspond the maximum possible diffusion of primary education and the maximum care taken to expand the middle grades numerically as much as possible. Naturally this need to provide the widest base possible for the selection and elaboration of the top intellectual qualifications – i.e. to give a democratic structure to high culture and top-level technology – is not without its disadvantages: it creates the possibility of vast crises of unemployment for the middle intellectual strata, and in all modern societies this actually takes place.)

It is worth noting that the elaboration of intellectual strata in concrete reality does not take place on the terrain of abstract democracy but in accordance with very concrete traditional historical processes. Strata have grown up which traditionally 'produce' intellectuals and these strata coincide with those which have specialized in 'saving', i.e. the petty and middle landed bourgeoisie and certain strata of the petty and middle urban bourgeoisie. The varying distribution of different types of school (classical and professional) over the 'economic' territory and the varying aspirations of different categories within these strata determine, or give form to, the production of various branches of intellectual specialization. Thus in Italy the rural bourgeoisie produces in particular state functionaries and professional people, whereas the urban bourgeoisie produces technicians for industry. Consequently it is largely northern Italy which produces technicians and the South which produces functionaries and professional men.

The relationship between the intellectuals and the world of production is not as direct as it is with the fundamental social groups but is, in varying degrees, 'mediated' by the whole fabric of society and by the complex of superstructures, of which the intellectuals are, precisely, the 'functionaries'. It should be possible both to measure the degree of 'organicism' of the various intellectual strata and their degree of connection with a fundamental social group, and to establish a gradation of their functions and of the superstructures from the bottom to the top (from the structural base upwards). What we can do, for the moment, is to fix two major superstructural 'levels': the one that can be called 'civil society', that is the ensemble of organisms commonly called 'private', and that of 'political society' or 'the state'. These two levels correspond on the one hand to the function of 'hegemony' which the dominant group exercises throughout society and on the other hand to that of 'direct domination' or command exercised through the state and 'juridical' government. The functions in question are precisely organizational and connective. The intellectuals are the dominant group's 'deputies' exercising the subaltern functions of social hegemony and political government. These comprise:

1. The 'spontaneous' consent given by the great masses of the

population to the general direction imposed on social life by the dominant fundamental group; this consent is 'historically' caused by the prestige (and consequent confidence) which the dominant group enjoys because of its position and function in the world of production.

2. The apparatus of state coercive power which 'legally' enforces discipline on those groups who do not 'consent' either actively or passively. This apparatus is, however, constituted for the whole of society in anticipation of moments of crisis of command and direction when spontaneous consent has failed.

This way of posing the problem has as a result a considerable extension of the concept of intellectual, but it is the only way which enables one to reach a concrete approximation of reality. It also clashes with preconceptions of caste. The function of organizing social hegemony and state domination certainly gives rise to a particular division of labour and therefore to a whole hierarchy of qualifications in some of which there is no apparent attribution of directive or organizational functions. For example, in the apparatus of social and state direction there exists a whole series of jobs of a manual and instrumental character (non-executive work, agents rather than officials or functionaries). It is obvious that such a distinction has to be made just as it is obvious that other distinctions have to be made as well. Indeed, intellectual activity must also be distinguished in terms of its intrinsic characteristics, according to levels which in moments of extreme opposition represent a real qualitative difference – at the highest level would be the creators of the various sciences, philosophy, art, etc., at the lowest the most humble 'administrators' and divulgators of pre-existing, traditional, accumulated intellectual wealth. Here again military organization offers a model of complex gradations between subaltern officers, senior officers and general staff, not to mention the NCOs, whose importance is greater than is generally admitted. It is worth observing that all these parts feel a solidarity and indeed that it is the lower strata that display the most blatant *esprit de corps*, from which they derive a certain 'conceit' which is apt to lay them open to jokes and witticisms.

In the modern world the category of intellectuals, understood in this sense, has undergone an unprecedented expansion. The democratic-bureaucratic system has given rise to a great mass of functions which are not all justified by the social necessities of production, though they are justified by the political necessities of the dominant fundamental group. Hence Loria's conception of the unproductive 'worker'[2] (but unproductive in relation to whom and to what mode of production?), a conception which could in part be justified if one takes account of the fact that these masses exploit their position to take for themselves a large cut out of the national income. Mass training has standardized individuals both psychologically and in terms of individual qualification and has produced the same phenomena as with other standardized masses: competition which creates the need for professional associations and leads to unemployment, over-production of qualified people by the education system, emigration, etc.

Different position of intellectuals of the urban type and the rural type. Intellectuals of the urban type have grown up along with industry and are linked to its fortunes. Their function can be compared to that of subaltern officers in the army. They have no autonomous initiative in elaborating plans for construction. Their job is to articulate the relationship between the entrepreneur and the instrumental mass and to carry out the immediate execution of the production plan decided by the industrial general staff, controlling the elementary stages of work. On the whole the average urban intellectuals are very standardized, while the top urban intellectuals are more and more identified with the industrial general staff itself.

Intellectuals of the rural type are for the most part 'traditional', that is they are linked to the social mass of country people and the town (particularly small-town) petty bourgeoisie, not as yet elaborated and set in motion by the capitalist system. This type of intellectual brings into contact the peasant masses with the local and state administration (lawyers, notaries, etc.). Because of this activity they have an important politico-social function, since professional mediation is difficult to separate from political. Furthermore: in the countryside the intellectual (priest, lawyer, notary, teacher, doctor, etc.), has on the whole a higher or at least a different living standard from that of the average peasant and consequently represents a social model for the peasant to look to in his aspiration to escape from or improve his condition. The peasant always thinks that at least one of his sons could become an intellectual (especially a priest), thus becoming a gentleman and raising the social level of the family by facilitating its economic life through the connections which he is bound to acquire with the rest of the gentry. The peasant's attitude towards the intellectual is double and appears contradictory. He respects the social position of the intellectuals and in general that of state employees, but sometimes affects contempt for it, which means that his admiration is mingled with instinctive elements of envy and impassioned anger. One can understand nothing of the collective life of the peasantry and of the germs and ferments of development which exist within it, if one does not take into consideration and examine concretely and in depth this effective subordination to the intellectuals. Every organic development of the peasant masses, up to a certain point, is linked to and depends on movements among the intellectuals.

With the urban intellectuals it is another matter. Factory technicians do not exercise any political function over the instrumental masses, or at least this is a phase that has been superseded. Sometimes, rather, the contrary takes place, and the instrumental masses, at least in the person of their own organic intellectuals, exercise a political influence on the technicians.

The central point of the question remains the distinction between intellectuals as an organic category of every fundamental social group and intellectuals as a traditional category. From this distinction there flows a whole series of problems and possible questions for historical research.

The most interesting problem is that which, when studied from this point of view, relates to the modern political party, its real origins, its developments and the forms which it takes. What is the character of the political party in relation to the problem of the intellectuals? Some distinctions must be made:

1. The political party for some social groups is nothing other than their specific way of elaborating their own category of organic intellectuals directly in the political and philosophical field rather than in the field of productive technique. These intellectuals are formed in this way and cannot indeed be formed in any other way, given the general character and the conditions of formation, life and development of the social group within productive technique those strata are formed which can be said to correspond to NCOs in the army, that is to say, for the town, skilled and specialized workers and, for the country (in a more complex fashion)

share-croppers and tenant farmers – since in general terms these types of farmer correspond more or less to the type of the artisan, who is the skilled worker of a medieval economy.

2. The political party, for all groups, is precisely the mechanism which carries out in civil society the same function as the state carries out, more synthetically and over a larger scale, in political society. In other words it is responsible for welding together the organic intellectuals of a given group – the dominant one – and the traditional intellectuals. The party carries out this function in strict dependence on its basic function, which is that of elaborating its own component parts – those elements of a social group which has been born and developed as an 'economic' group – and of turning them into qualified political intellectuals, leaders and organizers of all the activities and functions inherent in the organic development of an integral society, both civil and political. Indeed it can be said that within its field the political party accomplishes its function more completely and organically than the state does within its admittedly far larger field. An intellectual who joins the political party of a particular social group is merged with the organic intellectuals of the group itself, and is linked tightly with the group. This takes place through participation in the life of the state only to a limited degree and often not at all. Indeed it happens that many intellectuals think that they *are* the state, a belief which, given the magnitude of the category, occasionally has important consequences and leads to unpleasant complications for the fundamental economic group which *really* is the state.

That all members of a political party should be regarded as intellectuals is an affirmation that can easily lend itself to mockery and caricature. But if one thinks about it nothing could be more exact. There are of course distinctions of level to be made. A party might have a greater or lesser proportion of members in the higher grades or in the lower, but this is not the point. What matters is the function, which is directive and organizational, i.e. educative, i.e. intellectual. A tradesman does not join a political party in order to do business, nor an industrialist in order to produce more at lower cost, nor a peasant to learn new methods of cultivation, even if some aspects of these demands of the tradesman, the industrialist or the peasant can find satisfaction in the party (common opinion tends to oppose this, maintaining that the tradesman, industrialist or peasant who engages in 'politicking' loses rather than gains, and is the worst type of all – which is debatable. For these purposes, within limits, there exists the professional asociation, in which the economic-corporate activity of the tradesman, industrialist or peasant is most suitably promoted. In the political party the elements of an economic social group get beyond that moment of their historical development and become agents of more general activities of a national and international character.

[...]

SPN, 5-16 (Q12§1)

2 Observations on the School: In Search of the Educational Principle

<The rift created by the Gentile reform between primary and middle school on the one hand and high school on the other. Before the reform the only marked rift of this kind had been between professional schools on the one hand and middle and high schools on the other: primary school was placed in a sort of limbo, because of certain characteristics specific to it.>

In the primary school, there were two elements in the educational formation of the children. They were taught the rudiments of natural science, and the idea of civic rights and duties. Scientific ideas were intended to insert the child into the *societas rerum*, the world of things, while lessons in rights and duties were intended to insert him into the state and into civil society. The scientific ideas the children learned conflicted with the magical conception of the world and nature which they absorbed from an environment steeped in folklore; while the idea of civic rights and duties conflicted with tendencies towards individualistic and localistic barbarism – another dimension of folklore. The school combated folklore, indeed every residue of traditional conceptions of the world. It taught a more modern outlook based essentially on an awareness of the simple and fundamental fact that there exist objective, intractable natural laws to which man must adapt himself if he is to master them in his turn – and that there exist social and state laws which are the product of human activity, which are established by men and can be altered by men in the interests of their collective development. These laws of the state and of society create that human order which historically best enables men to dominate the laws of nature, that is to say which most facilitates their *work*. For work is the specific mode by which man actively participates in natural life in order to transform and socialize it more and more deeply and extensively.

Thus one can say that the educational principle which was the basis of the primary school was the idea of work. Human work cannot be realized in all its power of expansion and productivity without an exact and realistic knowledge of natural laws and without a legal order which organically regulates men's life in common. Men must respect this legal order through spontaneous assent, and not merely as an external imposition – it must be a necessity recognized and proposed to themselves as freedom, and not simply the result of coercion. The idea and the fact of work (of theoretical and practical activity) was the educational principle latent in the primary school, since it is by means of work that the social and state order (rights and duties) is introduced and identified within the natural order. The discovery that the relations between the social and natural orders are mediated by work, by man's theoretical and practical activity, creates the first elements of an intuition of the world free from all magic and superstition. It provides a basis for the subsequent development of a historical, dialectical conception of the world, which understands movements and change, which appreciates the sum of effort and sacrifice which the present has cost the past and which the future is costing the present, and which conceives the contemporary world as a synthesis of the past, of all past generations, which projects itself into the future. This is the real basis of the primary school. Whether it yielded all its fruits, and whether the actual teachers were aware of the nature and philosophical content of their task, is another question. This requires an analysis of the degree of civic consciousness of the entire nation, of which the teaching body was merely an expression, and rather a poor expression – certainly not a vanguard.

It is not entirely true that 'instruction' is something quite different from 'education'.[3] An excessive emphasis on this distinction has been a serious error of idealist educationalists and its effects can already be seen in the school system as they have reorganized it. For instruction to be wholly distinct from education, the pupil would have to be pure passivity, a 'mechanical receiver' of abstract notions – which is absurd and is anyway 'abstractly' denied by the supporters of pure educativity precisely in their opposition to mere mechanistic instruction. The 'certain' becomes 'true' in the child's consciousness. But the child's consciousness is not something 'individual' (still less individuated), it reflects the sector of civil society in which the child participates, and the social relations which are formed within his family, his neighbourhood, his village, etc. The individual consciousness of the overwhelming majority of children reflects social and cultural relations which are different from and antagonistic to those which are represented in the school curricula: thus the 'certain' of an advanced culture becomes 'true' in the framework of a fossilized and anachronistic culture. There is no unity between school and life, and so there is no automatic unity between instruction and education. In the school, the nexus between instruction and education can only be realized by the living work of the teacher. For this he must be aware of the contrast between the type of culture and society which he represents and the type of culture and society represented by his pupils, and conscious of his obligation to accelerate and regulate the child's formation in conformity with the former and in conflict with the latter. If the teaching body is not adequate and the nexus between instruction and education is dissolved, while the problem of teaching is conjured away by cardboard schemata exalting educativity, the teacher's work will as a result become yet more inadequate. We will have rhetorical schools, quite unserious, because the material solidity of what is 'certain' will be missing, and what is 'true' will be a truth only of words: that is to say, precisely, rhetoric.

This degeneration is even clearer in the secondary school, in the literature and philosophy syllabus. Previously, the pupils at least acquired a certain 'baggage' or 'equipment' (according to taste) of concrete facts. Now that the teacher must be specifically a philosopher and aesthete, the pupil does not bother with concrete facts and fills his head with formulae and words which usually mean nothing to him, and which are forgotten at once. It was right to struggle against the old school, but reforming it was not so simple as it seemed. The problem was not one of model curricula but of men, and not just of the men who are actually teachers themselves but of the entire social complex which they express. In reality a mediocre teacher may manage to see to it that his pupils become more *informed*, although he will not succeed in making them better educated; he can devote a scrupulous and bureaucratic conscientiousness to the mechanical part of teaching – and the pupil, if he has an active intelligence, will give an order of his own, with the aid of his social background, to the 'baggage' he accumulates. With the new curricula, which coincide with a general lowering of the level of the teaching profession, there will no longer be any 'baggage' to put in order. The new curricula should have abolished examinations entirely; for to take an examination now must be fearfully more chancy than before. A date is always a date, whoever the examiner is, and a definition is always a definition. But an aesthetic judgement or a philosophical analysis?

The educational efficacy of the old Italian secondary school, as organized by the Casati Act,[4] was not to be sought (or rejected) in its explicit aim as an 'educative' system, but in the fact that its structure and its curriculum were the expression of a traditional mode of intellectual and moral life, of a cultural climate diffused throughout Italian society by ancient tradition. It was the fact that this climate and way of life were in their death-throes, and that the school had become cut off from life, which brought about the crisis in education. A criticism of the curricula and disciplinary structure of the old system means less than nothing if one does not keep this situation in mind. Thus we come back to the truly active participation of the pupil in the school, which can only exist if the school is related to life. The more the new curricula nominally affirm and theorize the pupil's activity and working collaboration with the teacher, the more they are actually designed as if the pupil were purely passive.

In the old school the grammatical study of Latin and Greek, together with the study of their respective literatures and political histories, was an educational principle – for the humanistic ideal, symbolized by Athens and Rome, was diffused throughout society, and was an essential element of national life and culture. Even the mechanical character of the study of grammar was enlivened by this cultural perspective. Individual facts were not learnt for an immediate practical or professional end. The end seemed disinterested, because the real interest was the interior development of personality, the formation of character by means of the absorption and assimilation of the whole cultural past of modern European civilization. Pupils did not learn Latin and

Greek in order to speak them, to become waiters, interpreters or commercial letter-writers. They learnt them in order to know at first hand the civilization of Greece and of Rome – a civilization that was a necessary precondition of our modern civilization: in other words, they learnt them in order to be themselves and know themselves consciously. Latin and Greek were learnt through their grammar, mechanically; but the accusation of formalism and aridity is very unjust and inappropriate. In education one is dealing with children in whom one has to inculcate certain habits of diligence, precision, poise (even physical poise), ability to concentrate on specific subjects, which cannot be acquired without the mechanical repetition of disciplined and methodical acts. Would a scholar at the age of forty be able to sit for sixteen hours on end at his work-table if he had not, as a child, compulsorily, through mechanical coercion, acquired the appropriate psychophysical habits? If one wishes to produce great scholars, one still has to start at this point and apply pressure throughout the educational system in order to succeed in creating those thousands or hundreds or even only dozens of scholars of the highest quality which are necessary to every civilization. (Of course, one can improve a great deal in this field by the provision of adequate funds for research, without going back to the educational methods of the Jesuits.)

Latin is learned (or rather studied) by analysing it down to its smallest parts – analysing it like a dead thing, it is true, but all analyses made by children can only be of dead things. Besides, one must not forget that the life of the Romans is a myth which to some extent has already interested the child and continues to interest him, so that in the dead object there is always present a greater living being. Thus, the language is dead, it is analysed as an inert object, as a corpse on the dissecting table, but it continually comes to life again in examples and in stories. Could one study Italian in the same way? Impossible. No living language could be studied like Latin: it would be and *would seem* absurd. No child knows Latin when he starts to study it by these analytical methods. But a living language can be known and it would be enough for a single child to know it, and the spell would be broken: everybody would be off to the Berlitz school at once. Latin (like Greek) appears to the imagination as a myth, even for the teacher. One does not study Latin in order to learn the language. For a long time, as a

result of a cultural and scholarly tradition whose origin and
development one might investigate, Latin has been studied as an
element in an ideal curriculum, an element which combines and
satisfies a whole series of pedagogic and psychological
requirements. It has been studied in order to accustom children to
studying in a specific manner, and to analysing a historical body
which can be treated as a corpse which returns continually to life;
in order to accustom them to reason, to think abstractly and
schematically while remaining able to plunge back from
abstraction into real and immediate life, to see in each fact or
datum what is general and what is particular, to distinguish the
concept from the specific instance.

For what after all is the educational significance of the constant
comparison between Latin and the language one speaks? It
involves the distinction and the identification of words and
concepts; suggests the whole of formal logic, from the
contradiction between opposites to the analysis of distincts;
reveals the historical movement of the entire language, modified
through time, developing and not static. In the eight years of
ginnasio and *liceo* the entire history of the real language is studied,
after it has first been photographed in one abstract moment in the
form of grammar. It is studied from Ennius (or rather from the
words of the fragments of the twelve tablets) right up to Phaedrus
and the Christian writers in Latin: a historical process is analysed
from its sources until its death in time – or seeming death, since we
know that Italian, with which Latin is continually contrasted in
school, is modern Latin. Not only the grammar of a certain epoch
(which is an abstraction) or its vocabulary are studied, but also, for
comparison, the grammar and the vocabulary of each individual
author and the meaning of each term in each particular stylistic
'period'. Thus the child discovers that the grammar and the
vocabulary of Phaedrus are not those of Cicero, nor those of
Plautus, nor of Lactantius or Tertullian, and that the same nexus
of sounds does not have the same meaning in different periods and
for different authors. Latin and Italian are continually compared;
but each word is a concept, a symbol, which takes on different
shades of meaning according to the period and the writer in each
of the two languages under comparison. The child studies the
literary history of the books written in that language, the political
history, the achievements of the men who spoke that language.

His education is determined by the whole of this organic complex, by the fact that he has followed that itinerary, if only in a purely literal sense, he has passed through those various stages, etc. He has plunged into history and acquired a historicizing understanding of the world and of life, which becomes a second – nearly spontaneous – nature, since it is not inculcated pedantically with an openly educational intention. These studies educated without an explicitly declared aim of doing so, with a minimal 'educative' intervention on the part of the teacher: they educated because they gave instruction. Logical, artistic, psychological experience was gained unawares, without a continual self-consciousness. Above all a profound 'synthetic', philosophical experience was gained, of an actual historical development. This does not mean – it would be stupid to think so – that Latin and Greek, as such, have intrinsically thaumaturgical qualities in the educational field. It is the whole cultural tradition, which also and particularly lives outside the school, which in a given ambience produces such results. In any case one can see today, with the changes in the traditional idea of culture, the way in which the school is in crisis and with it the study of Latin and Greek.

It will be necessary to replace Latin and Greek as the fulcrum of the formative school, and they will be replaced. But it will not be easy to deploy the new subject or subjects in a didactic form which gives equivalent results in terms of education and general personality-formation, from early childhood to the threshold of the adult choice of career. For in this period what is learnt, or the greater part of it, must be – or appear to the pupils to be – disinterested, i.e. not have immediate or too immediate practical purposes. It must be formative, while being 'instructive' – in other words rich in concrete facts. In the present school, the profound crisis in the traditional culture and its conception of life and of man has resulted in a progressive degeneration. Schools of the vocational type, i.e. those designed to satisfy immediate, practical interests, are beginning to predominate over the formative school, which is not immediately 'interested'. The most paradoxical aspect of it all is that this new type of school appears and is advocated as being democratic, while in fact it is destined not merely to perpetuate social differences but to crystallize them in Chinese complexities.

The traditional school was oligarchic because it was intended for the new generation of the ruling class, destined to rule in its turn: but it was not oligarchic in its mode of teaching. It is not the fact that the pupils learn how to rule there, nor the fact that it tends to produce gifted men, which gives a particular type of school its social character. This social character is determined by the fact that each social group has its own type of school, intended to perpetuate a specific traditional function, ruling or subordinate. If one wishes to break this pattern one needs, instead of multiplying and grading different types of vocational school, to create a single type of formative school (primary-secondary) which would take the child up to the threshold of his choice of job, forming him during this time as a person capable of thinking, studying, and ruling – or controlling those who rule.

The multiplication of types of vocational school thus tends to perpetuate traditional social differences; but since, within these differences, it tends to encourage internal diversification, it gives the impression of being democratic in tendency. The labourer can become a skilled worker, for instance, the peasant a surveyor or petty agronomist. But democracy, by definition, cannot mean merely that an unskilled worker can become skilled. It must mean that every 'citizen' can 'govern' and that society places him, even if only abstractly, in a general condition to achieve this. Political democracy tends towards a coincidence of the rulers and the ruled (in the sense of government with the consent of the governed), ensuring for each non-ruler a free training in the skills and general technical preparation necessary to that end. But the type of school which is now developing as the school for the people does not tend even to keep up this illusion. For it is organized ever more fully in such a way as to restrict recruitment to the technically qualified government stratum, in a social and political context which makes it increasingly difficult for 'personal initiative' to acquire such skills and technical-political preparation. Thus we are really going back to a division into juridically fixed and crystallized estates rather than moving towards the transcendence of class divisions. The multiplication of vocational schools which specialize increasingly from the very beginning of the child's educational career is one of the most notable manifestations of this tendency. It is noticeable that the new pedagogy has concentrated its fire on 'dogmatism' in the field of instruction and the learning of concrete facts – i.e. precisely in the field in which a certain dogmatism is practically indispensable and can be reabsorbed and dissolved only in the whole cycle of the educational process (historical grammar could not be taught in *liceo* classes). On the other hand, it has been forced to accept the introduction of dogmatism *par excellence* in the field of religious thought, with the result that the whole history of philosophy is now implicitly seen as a succession of ravings and delusions.[5] In the philosophy course, the new curriculum impoverishes the teaching and in practice lowers its level (at least for the overwhelming majority of pupils who do not receive intellectual help outside the school from their family or home environment, and who have to form themselves solely by means of the knowledge they receive in the classroom) – in spite of seeming very rational and fine, fine as any utopia. The traditional descriptive philosophy, backed by a course in the history of philosophy and by the reading of a certain number of philosophers, in practice seems the best thing. Descriptive, definitional philosophy may be a dogmatic abstraction, just as grammar and mathematics are, but it is an educational necessity. 'One equals one' is an abstraction, but it leads nobody to think that one fly equals one elephant. The rules of formal logic are abstractions of the same kind, they are like the grammar of normal thought; but they still need to be studied, since they are not something innate, but have to be acquired through work and reflection. The new curriculum presupposes that formal logic is something you already possess when you think, but does not explain how it is to be acquired, so that in practice it is assumed to be innate. Formal logic is like grammar: it is assimilated in a 'living' way even if the actual learning process has been necessarily schematic and abstract. For the learner is not a passive and mechanical recipient, a gramophone record – even if the liturgical conformity of examinations sometimes makes him appear so. The relation between these educational forms and the child's psychology is always active and creative, just as the relation of the worker to his tools is active and creative. A calibre is likewise a complex of abstractions, but without calibration it is not possible to produce real objects – real objects which are social relations, and which implicitly embody ideas.

The child who sweats at *Barbara, Baralipton*[6] is certainly performing a tiring task, and it is important that he does only what is absolutely necessary and no more. But it is also true that it will always be an effort to learn physical self-discipline and self-control; the pupil has, in effect, to undergo a psycho-physical training. Many people have to be persuaded that studying too is a job, and a very tiring one, with its own particular apprenticeship – involving muscles and nerves as well as intellect. It is a process of adaptation, a habit acquired with effort, tedium and even suffering. Wider participation in secondary education brings with it a tendency to ease off the discipline of studies, and to ask for 'relaxations'. Many even think that the difficulties of learning are artificial, since they are accustomed to think only of manual work as sweat and toil. The question is a complex one. Undoubtedly the child of a traditionally intellectual family acquires this psycho-physical adaptation more easily. Before he ever enters the classroom he has numerous advantages over his comrades, and is already in possession of attitudes learnt from his family environment: he concentrates more easily, since he is used to 'sitting still', etc. Similarly, the son of a city worker suffers less when he goes to work in a factory than does a peasant's child or a young peasant already formed by country life. (Even diet has its importance, etc.) This is why many people think that the difficulty of study conceals some 'trick' which handicaps them – that is, when they do not simply believe that they are stupid by nature. They see the 'gentleman' – and for many, especially in the country, 'gentleman' means intellectual – complete, speedily and with apparent ease, work which costs their sons tears and blood, and they think there is a 'trick'. In the future, these questions will become extremely acute and it will be necessary to resist the tendency to render easy that which cannot become easy without being distorted. If our aim is to produce a new stratum of intellectuals, including those capable of the highest degree of specialization, from a social group which has not traditionally developed the appropriate attitudes, then we have unprecedented difficulties to overcome.

SPN 33-43 (Q12§2)

3 [Intellectuals and Non-Intellectuals]

When one distinguishes between intellectuals and non-intellectuals, one is referring in reality only to the immediate social function of the professional category of the intellectuals, that is, one has in mind the direction in which their specific professional activity is weighted, whether towards intellectual elaboration or towards muscular-nervous effort. This means that, although one can speak of intellectuals, one cannot speak of non-intellectuals, because non-intellectuals do not exist. But even the relationship between efforts of intellectual-cerebral elaboration and muscular-nervous effort is not always the same, so that there are varying degrees of specific intellectual activity. There is no human activity from which every form of intellectual participation can be excluded: *homo faber* cannot be separated from *homo sapiens*. Each man, finally, outside his professional activity, carries on some form of intellectual activity, that is, he is a 'philosopher', an artist, a man of taste, he participates in a particular conception of the world, has a conscious line of moral conduct, and therefore contributes to sustain a conception of the world or to modify it, that is, to bring into being new modes of thought.

The problem of creating a new stratum of intellectuals consists therefore in the critical elaboration of the intellectual activity that exists in everyone at a certain degree of development, modifying its relationship with the muscular-nervous effort itself, in so far as it is an element of a general practical activity, which is perpetually innovating the physical and social world, becomes the foundation of a new and integral conception of the world. The traditional and vulgarized type of the intellectual is given by the man of letters, the philosopher, the artist. Therefore journalists, who claim to be men of letters, philosophers, artists, also regard themselves as the 'true' intellectuals. In the modern world, technical education, closely bound to industrial labour even at the most primitive and unqualified level, must form the basis of the new type of intellectual.

On this basis the weekly *Ordine Nuovo* worked to develop certain forms of new intellectualism and to determine the new concepts, and this was not the least of the reasons for its success, since such a conception corresponded to latent aspirations and conformed to the development of the real forms of life. The mode of being of the new intellectual can no longer consist in eloquence, which is an exterior and momentary mover of feelings and passions, but in active participation in practical life, as constructor, organizer, 'permanent persuader' and not just a simple orator (but superior at the same time to the abstract mathematical spirit);

from technique-as-work one proceeds to technique-as-science and to the historical humanistic conception without which one remains a 'specialist' and does not become a 'leader' [*dirigente*] (specialist + politician).

SPN, 9-10 (Q12§3)

XI PHILOSOPHY, COMMON SENSE, LANGUAGE AND FOLKLORE

Introduction

The problem which preoccupies Gramsci in the notes in this section is that of how to overcome the separation between Marxism as a philosophy (the 'philosophy of praxis') and people's actual consciousness. His approach to this problem is, in a double movement, firstly to break down the notion of philosophy, and consequently of Marxism, as something specialized and remote by seeing it as like other 'conceptions of the world' (religion, folklore, everyday language) and secondly to restore to philosophy a specificity as more coherent and critical than these other conceptions of the world. Ultimately, for Gramsci, the philosophy of praxis will in turn found, in conjunction with material changes, a new common sense, bringing about an 'intellectual and moral reformation', a wholesale transformation of people's conceptions of the world and norms of conduct analogous in function and scale to the Protestant Reformation in the sixteenth century.

It is important to see that Gramsci does not think of Marxism in this process as imposing itself mechanically from the outside, but rather as drawing out and elaborating elements of critical awareness and 'good sense' which are already present within people's 'common sense' (on the latter concept, see Glossary of Key Terms). The passage (p.333) where he discusses 'contradictory consciousness' is particularly important in clarifying this conception (for a good discussion see Femia 1981:45-6 and *passim*). The philosophy of praxis can exert a leverage on people's consciousness because a part of that consciousness is already aware of its truth. It thus draws out and elaborates that which people already 'feel' but do not 'know', in other words that which is present in nascent or inchoate form in their consciousness but which is contradicted and immobilized by other conceptions. In order for them to break out of the state of 'moral and intellectual passivity' which these contradictions produce, an ideological struggle must take place, a 'struggle of political "hegemonies" '.

323

In order to shift people's common sense, Marxism must engage
with what they actually think. Gramsci sees it as a major limitation
of Bukharin's *The Theory of Historical Materialism. A Manual of
Popular Sociology* (1921) not to have started from such a critique
of common sense.

Gramsci's writings on language and folklore are closely related
to this discussion. For Gramsci 'every language contains the
elements of a conception of the world'. He sees the process by
which a given conception of the world exerts an influence over
others in terms of the influence of one form of a language upon
another, as well as in relation to the educational process. It has
been argued (by Franco Lo Piparo, *Lingua intellettuali egemonia
in Gramsci*, Rome-Bari 1979), that Gramsci's conception of
hegemony was influenced by the concepts of 'prestige' and
'radiation of innovations' in historical linguistics – the subject of
his unfinished degree thesis. These terms designated the process
by which the speakers of one form of a language exert an influence
over others, changing the way the latter speak, either by simple
everyday contact or through the mediation of the education system
and other channels of cultural communication. Gramsci extends
this process from language to other relations of political and
cultural influence of an 'active', 'expansive' and consensual rather
than a passive, mechanical or merely coercive kind. In the case of
'folklore', he is extremely critical, indeed dismissive of much of the
content of traditional popular culture. His point, however, is that
one needs to understand popular conceptions of the world in order
to bring about a situation in which 'the separation between
modern culture or popular culture of folklore will disappear'. All
this is part of the process of 'intellectual and moral reformation'.

1 Notes for an Introduction and an Approach to the Study of Philosophy and the History of Culture

i Some preliminary reference points

It is essential to destroy the widespread prejudice that philosophy
is a strange and difficult thing just because it is the specific
intellectual activity of a particular category of specialists or of

professional and systematic philosophers. It must first be shown
that all men are 'philosophers', by defining the limits and
characteristics of the 'spontaneous philosophy' which is proper to
everybody. This philosophy is contained in: 1. language itself,
which is a totality of determined notions and concepts and not just
of words grammatically devoid of content; 2. 'common sense' and
'good sense', 3. popular religion and, therefore, also in the entire
system of beliefs, superstitions, opinions, ways of seeing things
and of acting, which are collectively bundled together under the
name of 'folklore'.

Having first shown that everyone is a philosopher, though in his
own way and unconsciously, since even in the slightest
manifestation of any intellectual activity whatever, in 'language',
there is contained a specific conception of the world, one then
moves on to the second level, which is that of awareness and
criticism. That is to say, one proceeds to the question: is it better
to 'think', without having a critical awareness, in a disjointed and
episodic way, to take part in a conception of the world
mechanically imposed by the external environment, i.e. by one of
the many social groups in which everyone is automatically
involved from the moment of entry into the conscious world (and
this can be one's village or province; it can have its origins in the
parish and the 'intellectual activity' of the local priest or ageing
patriarch whose wisdom is law, or in the little old woman who has
inherited the lore of the witches or the minor intellectual soured by
his own stupidity and inability to act) or is it better to work out
consciously and critically one's own conception of the world and
thus, in connection with the labours of one's own brain, choose
one's sphere of activity, take an active part in the creation of the
history of the world, be one's own guide, refusing to accept
passively and supinely from outside the moulding of one's
personality?

Note I. In acquiring one's conception of the world one always
belongs to a particular grouping which is that of all the social
elements which share the same mode of thinking and acting. We
are all conformists of some conformism or other, always
man-in-the-mass or collective man. The question is this: of what
historical type is the conformism, the mass humanity to which one
belongs? When one's conception of the world is not critical and
coherent but disjointed and episodic, one belongs simultaneously

to a multiplicity of mass human groups. The personality is strangely composite: it contains Stone Age elements and principles of a more advanced science, prejudices from all past phases of history at the local level and intuitions of a future philosophy which will be that of a human race united the world over. To criticize one's own conception of the world means therefore to make it a coherent unity and to raise it to the level reached by the most advanced thought in the world. It therefore also means criticism of all previous philosophy, in so far as this has left stratified deposits in popular philosophy. The starting-point of critical elaboration is the consciousness of what one really is, and is 'knowing thyself'[1] as a product of the historical process to date which has deposited in you an infinity of traces, without leaving an inventory. Such an inventory must therefore be made at the outset.

Note II. Philosophy cannot be separated from the history of philosophy, nor can culture from the history of culture. In the most immediate and relevant sense, one cannot be a philosopher, by which I mean have a critical and coherent conception of the world, without having a consciousness of its historicity, of the phase of development which it represents and of the fact that it contradicts other conceptions or elements of other conceptions. One's conception of the world is a response to certain specific problems posed by reality, which are quite specific and 'original' in their immediate relevance. How is it possible to consider the present, and quite specific present, with a mode of thought elaborated for a past which is often remote and superseded? When someone does this, it means that he is a walking anachronism, a fossil, and not living in the modern world, or at the least that he is strangely composite. And it is in fact the case that social groups which in some ways express the most developed modernity, lag behind in other respects, given their social position, and are therefore incapable of complete historical autonomy.

Note III. If it is true that every language contains the elements of a conception of the world and of a culture, it could also be true that from anyone's language one can assess the greater or lesser complexity of his conception of the world. Someone who only speaks dialect, or understands the standard language incompletely, necessarily has an intuition of the world which is more or less limited and provincial, which is fossilized and anachronistic in relation to the major currents of thought which dominate world history. His interests will be limited, more or less corporate or economistic, not universal. While it is not always possible to learn a number of foreign languages in order to put oneself in contact with other cultural lives, it is at the least necessary to learn the national language properly. A great culture can be translated into the language of another great culture, that is to say a great national language with historic richness and complexity, and it can translate any other great culture and can be a world-wide means of expression. But a dialect cannot do this.

Note IV. Creating a new culture does not only mean one's own individual 'original' discoveries. It also, and most particularly, means the diffusion in a critical form of truths already discovered, their 'socialization' as it were, and even making them the basis of vital action, an element of co-ordination and intellectual and moral order. For a mass of people to be led to think coherently and in the same coherent fashion about the real present world, is a 'philosophical' event far more important and 'original' than the discovery by some philosophical 'genius' of a truth which remains the property of small groups of intellectuals.

Connection between 'common sense', religion and philosophy. Philosophy is an intellectual order, which neither religion nor common sense can be. It is to be observed that religion and common sense do not coincide either, but that religion is an element of fragmented common sense. Moreover common sense is a collective noun, like religion: there is not just one common sense, for that too is a product of history and a part of the historical process. Philosophy is criticism and the superseding of religion and 'common sense'. In this sense it coincides with 'good' as opposed to 'common' sense. Relations between science – religion – common sense. Religion and common sense cannot constitute an intellectual order, because they cannot be reduced to unity and coherence even within an individual consciousness, let alone collective consciousness. Or rather they cannot be so reduced 'freely' – for this may be done by 'authoritarian' means, and indeed within limits this has been done in the past.

Note the problem of religion taken not in the confessional sense but in the secular sense of a unity of faith between a conception of the world and a corresponding norm of conduct. But why call this unity of faith 'religion' and not 'ideology', or even 'politics'?

Philosophy in general does not in fact exist. Various philosophies or conceptions of the world exist, and one always makes a choice between them. How is this choice made? Is it merely an intellectual event, or is it something more complex? And is it not frequently the case that there is a contradiction between one's intellectual choice and one's mode of conduct? Which therefore would be the real conception of the world: that logically affirmed as an intellectual choice? or that which emerges from the real activity of each man, which is implicit in his mode of action? And since all action is political, can one not say that the real philosophy of each man is contained in its entirety in his political action?

This contrast between thought and action, i.e the co-existence of two conceptions of the world, one affirmed in words and the other displayed in effective action, is not simply a product of self-deception [*malafede*]. Self-deception can be an adequate explanation for a few individuals taken separately, or even for groups of a certain size, but it is not adequate when the contrast occurs in the life of great masses. In these cases the contrast between thought and action cannot but be the expression of profounder contrasts of a social historical order. It signifies that the social group in question may indeed have its own conception of the world, even if only embryonic; a conception which manifests itself in action, but occasionally and in flashes – when, that is, the group is acting as an organic totality. But this same group has, for reasons of submission and intellectual subordination, adopted a conception which is not its own but is borrowed from another group; and it affirms this conception verbally and believes itself to be following it, because this is the conception which it follows in 'normal times' – that is when its conduct is not independent and autonomous, but submissive and subordinate. Hence the reason why philosophy cannot be divorced from politics. And one can show furthermore that the choice and the criticism of a conception of the world is also a political matter.

What must next be explained is how it happens that in all periods there co-exist many systems and currents of philosophical thought, how these currents are born, how they are diffused, and why in the process of diffusion they fracture along certain lines and in certain directions. The fact of this process goes to show how necessary it is to order in a systematic, coherent and critical fashion one's own intuitions of life and the world, and to determine exactly what is to be understood by the word 'systematic', so that it is not taken in the pedantic and academic sense. But this elaboration must be, and can only be, performed in the context of the history of philosophy, for it is this history which shows how thought has been elaborated over the centuries and what a collective effort has gone into the creation of our present method of thought which has subsumed and absorbed all this past history, including all its follies and mistakes. Nor should these mistakes themselves be neglected, for, although made in the past and since corrected, one cannot be sure that they will not be reproduced in the present and once again require correcting.

What is the popular image of philosophy? It can be reconstructed by looking at expressions in common usage. One of the most usual is 'being philosophical about it', which, if you consider it, is not to be entirely rejected as a phrase. It is true that it contains an implicit invitation to resignation and patience, but it seems to me that the most important point is rather the invitation to people to reflect and to realize fully that whatever happens is basically rational and must be confronted as such, and that one should apply one's power of rational concentration and not let oneself be carried away by instinctive and violent impulses. These popular turns of phrase could be compared with similar expressions used by writers of a popular stamp – examples being drawn from a large dictionary – which contain the terms 'philosophy' or 'philosophically'. One can see from these examples that the terms have a quite precise meaning: that of overcoming bestial and elemental passions through a conception of necessity which gives a conscious direction to one's activity. This is the healthy nucleus that exists in 'common sense', the part of it which can be called 'good sense' and which deserves to be made more unitary and coherent. So it appears that here again it is not possible to separate what is known as 'scientific' philosophy from the common and popular philosophy which is only a fragmentary collection of ideas and opinions.

But at this point we reach the fundamental problem facing any conception of the world, any philosophy which has become a cultural movement, a 'religion', a 'faith', any that has produced a form of practical activity or will in which the philosophy is contained as an implicit theoretical 'premiss'. One might say 'ideology' here, but on condition that the word is used in its highest sense of a conception of the world that is implicitly manifest in art, in law, in economic activity and in all manifestations of individual and collective life. This problem is that of preserving the ideological unity of the entire social bloc which that ideology serves to cement and to unify. The strength of religions, and of the Catholic Church in particular, has lain, and still lies, in the fact that they feel very strongly the need for the doctrinal unity of the whole mass of the faithful and strive to ensure that the higher intellectual stratum does not get separated from the lower. The Roman Church has always been the most vigorous in the struggle to prevent the 'official' formation of two religions, one for the 'intellectuals' and the other for the 'simple souls'. This struggle has not been without serious disadvantages for the Church itself, but these disadvantages are connected with the historical process which is transforming the whole of civil society and which contains overall a corrosive critique of all religion, and they only serve to emphasize the organizational capacity of the clergy in the cultural sphere and the abstractly rational and just relationship which the Church has been able to establish in its own sphere between the intellectuals and the simple. The Jesuits have undoubtedly been the major architects of this equilibrium, and in order to preserve it they have given the Church a progressive forward movement which has tended to allow the demands of science and philosophy to be to a certain extent satisfied. But the rhythm of the movement has been so slow and methodical that the changes have passed unobserved by the mass of the simple, although they appear 'revolutionary' and demagogic to the 'integralists'.

One of the greatest weaknesses of immanentist philosophies in general consists precisely in the fact that they have not been able to create an ideological unity between the bottom and the top, between the 'simple' and the intellectuals. In the history of Western civilization the fact is exemplified on a European scale, with the rapid collapse of the Renaissance and to a certain extent also the Reformation faced with the Roman Church. Their weakness is demonstrated in the educational field, in that the immanentist philosophies have not even attempted to construct a conception which could take the place of religion in the education of children. Hence the pseudo-historicist sophism whereby non-religious, non-confessional, and in reality atheist, educationalists justify allowing the teaching of religion on the grounds that religion is the philosophy of the infancy of mankind renewed in every non-metaphorical infancy.[2] Idealism has also shown itself opposed to cultural movements which 'go out to the people', as happened with the so-called 'Popular Universities' and similar institutions.[3] Nor was the objection solely to the worst aspects of the institutions, because in that case they could simply have tried to improve them. And yet these movements were worthy of attention, and deserved study. They enjoyed a certain success, in the sense that they demonstrated on the part of the 'simple' a genuine enthusiasm and a strong determination to attain a higher cultural level and a higher conception of the world. What was lacking, however, was any organic quality either of philosophical thought or of organizational stability and central cultural direction. One got the impression that it was all rather like the first contacts of English merchants and the negroes of Africa: trashy baubles were handed out in exchange for nuggets of gold. In any case one could only have had cultural stability and an organic quality of thought if there had existed the same unity between the intellectuals and the simple as there should be between theory and practice. That is, if the intellectuals had been organically the intellectuals of those masses, and if they had worked out and made coherent the principles and the problems raised by the masses in their practical activity, thus constituting a cultural and social bloc. The question posed here was the one we have already referred to, namely this: is a philosophical movement properly so called when it is devoted to creating a specialized culture among restricted intellectual groups, or rather when, and only when, in the process of elaborating a form of thought superior to 'common sense' and coherent on a scientific plane, it never forgets to remain in contact with the 'simple' and indeed finds in this contact the source of the problems it sets out to study and to resolve? Only by this contact does a philosophy become 'historical', purify itself of intellectualistic elements of an individual character and become 'life'.

(Perhaps it is useful to make a 'practical' distinction between philosophy and common sense in order to indicate more clearly the passage from one moment to the other. In philosophy the features of individual elaboration of thought are the most salient: in common sense on the other hand it is the diffuse, unco-ordinated features of a generic form of thought common to a particular period and a particular popular environment. But every philosophy has a tendency to become the common sense of a fairly limited environment (that of all the intellectuals). It is a matter therefore of starting with a philosophy which already enjoys, or could enjoy, a certain diffusion, because it is connected to and implicit in practical life, and elaborating it so that it becomes a renewed common sense possessing the coherence and the sinew of individual philosophies. But this can only happen if the demands of cultural contact with the 'simple' are continually felt.)

A philosophy of praxis cannot but present itself at the outset in a polemical and critical guise, as superseding the existing mode of thinking and existing concrete thought (the existing cultural world). First of all, therefore, it must be a criticism of 'common sense', basing itself initially, however, on common sense in order to demonstrate that 'everyone' is a philosopher and that it is not a question of introducing from scratch a scientific form of thought into everyone's individual life, but of renovating and making 'critical' an already existing activity. It must then be a criticism of the philosophy of the intellectuals out of which the history of philosophy developed and which, in so far as it is a phenomenon of individuals (in fact it develops essentially in the activity of single particularly gifted individuals) can be considered as marking the 'high points' of the progress made by common sense, or at least the common sense of the more educated strata of society but through them also of the people. Thus an introduction to the study of philosophy must expound in synthetic form the problems that have grown up in the process of the development of culture as a whole and which are only partially reflected in the history of philosophy. (Nevertheless it is the history of philosophy which, in the absence of a history of common sense, impossible to reconstruct for lack of documentary material, must remain the main source of reference.) The purpose of the synthesis must be to criticize the problems, to demonstrate their real value, if any, and the significance they have had as superseded links of an intellectual chain, and to determine what the new contemporary problems are and how the old problems should now be analysed.

The relation between common sense and the upper level of philosophy is assured by 'politics', just as it is politics that assures the relationship between the Catholicism of the intellectuals and that of the simple. There are, however, fundamental differences between the two cases. That the Church has to face up to a problem of the 'simple' means precisely that there has been a split in the community of the faithful. This split cannot be healed by raising the simple to the level of the intellectuals (the Church does not even envisage such a task, which is both ideologically and economically beyond its present capacities), but only by imposing an iron discipline on the intellectuals so that they do not exceed certain limits of differentiation and so render the split catastrophic and irreparable. In the past such divisions in the community of the faithful were healed by strong mass movements which led to, or were absorbed in, the creation of new religious orders centred on strong personalities (St Dominic, St Francis). [...]

The position of the philosophy of praxis is the antithesis of this Catholic one. The philosophy of praxis does not tend to leave the 'simple' in their primitive philosophy of common sense, but rather to lead them to a higher conception of life. If it affirms the need for contact between intellectuals and simple it is not in order to restrict scientific activity and preserve unity at the low level of the masses, but precisely in order to construct an intellectual-moral bloc which can make politically possible the intellectual progress of the mass and not only of small intellectual groups.

The active man-in-the-mass has a practical activity, but has no clear theoretical consciousness of his practical activity, which nonetheless is an understanding of the world in so far as it transforms it. His theoretical consciousness can indeed be historically in opposition to his activity. One might almost say that he has two theoretical consciousnesses (or one contradictory consciousness): one which is implicit in his activity and which in reality unites him with all his fellow-workers in the practical transformation of the real world; and one, superficially explicit or verbal, which he has inherited from the past and uncritically absorbed. But this 'verbal' conception is not without consequences. It attaches one to a specific social group, it influences moral conduct and the direction of will, with varying efficacy but often powerfully enough to produce a situation in which the contradictory state of consciousness does not permit of any action, any decision or any choice, and produces a condition of moral and political passivity. Critical understanding of self takes place therefore through a struggle of political 'hegemonies', from opposing directions, first in the ethical field and then in that of politics, in order to arrive at the working out at a higher level of one's own conception of reality. Consciousness of being part of a particular hegemonic force (that is to say, political consciousness) is the first stage towards a further progressive self-consciousness in which theory and practice will finally be one. Even the unity of theory and practice is not therefore a matter of mechanical fact, but a part of the historical process, whose elementary and primitive phase is to be found in the sense of being 'different' and 'apart', in a barely instinctive feeling of independence, and which progresses to the level of real and complete possession of a single and coherent conception of the world. This is why it must be stressed that the political development of the concept of hegemony represents a great philosophical advance as well as a politico-practical one. For it necessarily involves and supposes an intellectual unity and an ethic in conformity with a conception of reality that has gone beyond common sense and has become, if only within as yet narrow limits, a critical conception.

However, in the most recent developments of the philosophy of praxis the exploration and refinement of the concept of the unity of theory and practice is still only at an early stage. There still remain residues of mechanism, since people speak about theory as a 'complement' or an 'accessory' of practice, or as the handmaid of practice. It would seem right for this question too to be considered historically, as an aspect of the political question of the intellectuals. Critical self-consciousness means, historically and politically, the creation of an elite of intellectuals. A human mass does not 'distinguish' itself, does not become independent in its own right without, in the widest sense, organizing itself; and there is no organization without intellectuals, that is without organizers and leaders, in other words, without the theoretical aspect of the theory-practice nexus being distinguished concretely by the existence of a group of people 'specialized' in conceptual and philosophical elaboration of ideas. But the process of creating intellectuals is long, difficult, full of contradictions, advances and retreats, dispersals and regroupings, in which the loyalty of the masses is often sorely tried. (And one must not forget that at this early stage loyalty and discipline are the ways in which the masses participate and collaborate in the development of the cultural movement as a whole.)

The process of development is tied to a dialectic between the intellectuals and the masses. The intellectual stratum develops both quantitatively and qualitatively, but every leap forward towards a new breadth and complexity of the intellectual stratum is tied to an analogous movement on the part of the mass of the 'simple', who raise themselves to higher levels of culture and at the same time extend their circle of influence towards the stratum of specialized intellectuals, producing outstanding individuals and groups of greater or less importance. In the process, however, there continually recur moments in which a gap develops between the mass and the intellectuals (at any rate between some of them, or a group of them), a loss of contact, and thus the impression that theory is an 'accessory', a 'complement' and something subordinate. Insistence on the practical element of the theory-practice nexus, after having not only distinguished but separated and split the two elements (an operation which in itself is merely mechanical and conventional) means that one is going through a relatively primitive historical phase, one which is still economic-corporate, in which the general framework of the 'base' is being quantitatively transformed and the appropriate quality-superstructure is in the process of emerging, but is not yet organically formed. One should stress the importance and significance which, in the modern world, political parties have in the elaboration and diffusion of conceptions of the world, because essentially what they do is to work out the ethics and the politics corresponding to these conceptions and act as it were as their historical 'laboratory'. The parties recruit individuals out of the working mass, and the selection is made on practical and theoretical criteria at the same time. The relation between theory and practice becomes even closer the more the conception is vitally and radically innovatory and opposed to old ways of thinking. For this reason one can say that the parties are the elaborators of new integral and totalitarian intelligentsias and the crucibles where the unification of theory and practice, understood as a real historical process, takes place. It is clear from this that the parties should be formed by individual memberships and not on the pattern of the British Labour Party, because, if it is a question of providing an organic leadership for the entire economically active mass, this leadership should not follow old schemas but should innovate. But innovation cannot come from the mass, at least at the beginning, except through the mediation of an elite for whom the conception implicit in human activity has already become to a certain degree a coherent and systematic ever-present awareness and a precise and decisive will.

One of these phases can be studied by looking at the recent discussion in which the latest developments of the philosophy of praxis are brought out, and which has been summarized in an article by D.S. Mirsky, a collaborator on *La Cultura*.[4] One can see from this that a change has taken place from a mechanistic and purely external conception to one which is activist and, as has been pointed out, closer to a correct understanding of the unity of theory and practice, although it has not yet attained the full synthetic meaning of the concept. It should be noted how the deterministic, fatalistic and mechanistic element has been a direct ideological 'aroma' emanating from the philosophy of praxis, rather like religion or drugs (in their stupefying effect). It has been made necessary and justified historically by the 'subaltern' character of certain social strata.

When you don't have the initiative in the struggle and the struggle itself comes eventually to be identified with a series of defeats, mechanical determinism becomes a tremendous force of moral resistance, of cohesion and of patient and obstinate perseverance. 'I have been defeated for the moment, but the tide of history is working for me in the long term.' Real will takes on the garments of an act of faith in a certain rationality of history and in a primitive and empirical form of impassioned finalism which appears in the role of a substitute for the predestination or Providence of confessional religions. It should be emphasised, though, that a strong activity of the will is present even here, directly intervening in the 'force of circumstance', but only implicitly, and in a veiled and, as it were, shamefaced manner. Consciousness here, therefore, is contradictory and lacking critical unity, etc. But when the 'subaltern' becomes directive and responsible for the economic activity of the masses, mechanicism at a certain point becomes an imminent danger and a revision must take place in modes of thinking because a change has taken place in the social mode of existence. The boundaries and the dominion of the 'force of circumstance' become restricted. But why? Because, basically, if yesterday the subaltern element was a thing, today it is no longer a thing but a historical person, a protagonist; if yesterday it was not responsible, because 'resisting' a will external to itself, now it feels itself to be responsible because it is no longer resisting but an agent, necessarily active and taking the initiative.

But even yesterday was it ever mere 'resistance', a mere 'thing', mere 'non-responsibility'? Certainly not. Indeed one should emphasize how fatalism is nothing other than the clothing worn by real and active will when in a weak position. This is why it is essential at all times to demonstrate the futility of mechanical determinism: for, although it is explicable as a naïve philosophy of the mass and as such, but only as such, can be an intrinsic element of strength, nevertheless when it is adopted as a thought-out and coherent philosophy on the part of the intellectuals, it becomes a cause of passivity, of idiotic self-sufficiency. This happens when they don't even expect that the subaltern will become directive and responsible. In fact, however, some part of even a subaltern mass is always directive and responsible, and the philosophy of the part always precedes the philosophy of the whole, not only as its theoretical anticipation but as a necessity of real life.

That the mechanicist conception has been a religion of the subaltern is shown by an analysis of the development of the Christian religion. Over a certain period of history in certain specific historical conditions religion has been and continues to be a 'necessity', a necessary form taken by the will of the popular masses and a specific way of rationalizing the world and real life, which provided the general framework for real practical activity. This quotation from an article in *La Civiltà Cattolica* ('Individualismo pagano e individualismo cristiano': issue of 5 March 1932) seems to me to express very well this function of Christianity:

> Faith in a secure future, in the immortality of the soul destined to beatitude, in the certainty of arriving at eternal joy, was the force behind the labour for intense inner perfection and spiritual elevation. True Christian individualism found here the impulse that led it to victory. All the strength of the Christian was gathered around this noble end. Free from the flux of speculation which weakens the soul with doubt, and illuminated by immortal principles, man felt his hopes reborn; sure that a superior force was supporting him in the struggle against Evil, he did violence to himself and conquered the world.

But here again it is naïve Christianity that is being referred to: not Jesuitized Christianity, which has become a pure narcotic for the popular masses.

The position of Calvinism, however, with its iron conception of predestination and grace, which produces a vast expansion of the spirit of initiative (or becomes the form of this movement) is even more revealing and significant. (On this question see: Max Weber, *L'etica protestante e lo spirito del capitalismo*; published in *Nuovi Studi*, volume for 1931 *et seq.* and Groethuysen's book on the religious origins of the bourgeoisie in France [*Origines de l'esprit bourgeois en France*, Vol. I. *L'Eglise et la bourgeoisie*, Paris, 1927].)

What are the influential factors in the process of diffusion (which is also one of a substitution of the old conception, and, very often, of combining old and new), how do they act, and to what extent? Is it the rational form in which the new conception is expounded and presented? Or is it the authority (in so far as this is recognized and appreciated, if only generically) of the expositor and the thinkers and experts whom the expositor calls in in his support? Or the fact of belonging to the same organization as the man who upholds the new conception (assuming, that is, that one has entered the organization for other reasons than that of already sharing the new conception)?

In reality these elements will vary according to social groups and the cultural level of the groups in question. But the enquiry has a particular interest in relation to the popular masses, who are slower to change their conceptions, or who never change them in the sense of accepting them in their 'pure' form, but always and only as a more or less heterogeneous and bizarre combination. The rational and logically coherent form, the exhaustive reasoning which neglects no argument, positive or negative, of any significance, has a certain importance, but is far from being decisive. It can be decisive, but in a secondary way, when the person in question is already in a state of intellectual crisis, wavering between the old and the new, when he has lost his faith in the old and has not yet come down in favour of the new, etc.

One could say this about the authority of thinkers and experts: it is very important among the people, but the fact remains that every conception has its thinkers and experts to put forward, and authority does not belong to one side; further, with every thinker it is possible to make distinctions, to cast doubt on whether he really said such and such a thing, etc.

One can conclude that the process of diffusion of new conceptions takes place for political (that is, in the last analysis, social) reasons; but that the formal element, that of logical coherence, the element of authority and the organizational elements have a very important function in this process immediately after the general orientation has been reached, whether by single individuals or groups of a certain size. From this we must conclude, however, that in the masses *as such*, philosophy can only be experienced as a faith.

Imagine the intellectual position of the man of the people: he has formed his own opinions, convictions, criteria of discrimination, standards of conduct. Anyone with a superior intellectual formation with a point of view opposed to his can put forward arguments better than he and really tear him to pieces logically and so on. But should the man of the people change his opinions just because of this? Just because he cannot impose himself in a bout of argument? In that case he might find himself having to change every day, or every time he meets an ideological adversary who is his intellectual superior. On what elements, therefore, can his philosophy be founded? and in particular his philosophy in the form which has the greatest importance for his standards of conduct?

The most important element is undoubtedly one whose character is determined not by reason but by faith. But faith in whom, or in what? In particular in the social group to which he belongs, in so far as in a diffuse way it thinks as he does. The man of the people thinks that so many like-thinking people can't be wrong, not so radically, as the man he is arguing against would like him to believe; he thinks that, while he himself, admittedly, is not able to uphold and develop his arguments as well as the opponent, in his group there is someone who could do this and could certainly argue better than the particular man he has against him; and he remembers, indeed, hearing expounded, discursively, coherently, in a way that left him convinced, the reasons behind his faith. He has no concrete memory of the reasons and could not repeat them, but he knows that reasons exist, because he has heard them expounded, and was convinced by them. The fact of having once suddenly seen the light and been convinced is the permanent reason for his reasons persisting, even if the arguments in its favour cannot be readily produced.

These considerations lead, however, to the conclusion that new conceptions have an extremely unstable position among the popular masses; particularly when they are in contrast with orthodox convictions (which can themselves be new) comforming socially to the general interests of the ruling classes. This can be seen if one considers the fortunes of religions and churches. Religion, or a particular church, maintains its community of faithful (within the limits imposed by the necessities of general historical development) in so far as it nourishes its faith permanently and in an organized fashion, indefatigably repeating its apologetics, struggling at all times and always with the same kind of arguments, and maintaining a hierarchy of intellectuals who give to the faith, in appearance at least, the dignity of thought. Whenever the continuity of relations between the Church and the faithful has been violently interrupted, for political reasons, as happened during the French Revolution, the losses suffered by the Church have been incalculable. If the conditions had persisted for a long time in which it was difficult to carry on practising one's own religion, it is quite possible that these losses would have been definitive, and a new religion would have emerged, as indeed one did emerge in France in combination with the old Catholicism. Specific necessities can be deduced from this for any cultural movement which aimed to replace common sense and old conceptions of the world in general:

1. Never to tire of repeating its own arguments (though offering literary variation of form): repetition is the best didactic means for working on the popular mentality.

2. To work incessantly to raise the intellectual level of ever-growing strata of the populace, in other words, to give a personality to the amorphous mass element. This means working to produce elites of intellectuals of a new type which arise directly out of the masses, but remain in contact with them to become, as it were, the whalebone in the corset.

This second necessity, if satisfied, is what really modifies the 'ideological panorama' of the age. But these elites cannot be formed or developed without a hierarchy of authority and intellectual competence growing up within them. The culmination of this process can be a great individual philosopher. But he must be capable of re-living concretely the demands of the massive ideological community and of understanding that this cannot have the flexibility of movement proper to an individual brain, and must succeed in giving formal elaboration to the collective doctrine in the most relevant fashion, and the one most suited to the modes of thought of a collective thinker.

It is evident that this kind of mass construction cannot just happen 'arbitrarily', around any ideology, simply because of the formally constructive will of a personality or a group which puts it forward solely on the basis of its own fanatical philosophical or religious convictions. Mass adhesion or non-adhesion to an ideology is the real critical test of the rationality and historicity of modes of thinking. Any arbitrary constructions are pretty rapidly eliminated by historical competition, even if sometimes, through a combination of immediately favourable circumstances, they manage to enjoy popularity of a kind; whereas constructions which respond to the demands of a complex organic period of history always impose themselves and prevail in the end, even though they may pass through several intermediary phases during which they manage to affirm themselves only in more or less bizarre and heterogeneous combinations.

These developments pose many problems, the most important of which can be subsumed in the form and the quality of the relations between the various intellectually qualified strata; that is, the importance and the function which the creative contribution of superior groups must and can have in connection with the organic capacity of the intellectually subordinate strata to discuss and develop new critical concepts. It is a question, in other words, of fixing the limits of freedom of discussion and propaganda, a freedom which should not be conceived of in the administrative and police sense, but in the sense of a self-limitation which the leaders impose on their own activity, or, more strictly, in the sense of fixing the direction of cultural policy. In other words – who is to fix the 'rights of knowledge' and the limits of the pursuit of knowledge? And can these rights and limits indeed be fixed? It seems necessary to leave the task of researching after new truths and better, more coherent, clearer formulations of the truths themselves to the free initiative of individual specialists, even though they may continually question the very principles that seem most essential. And it will in any case not be difficult to expose the fact whenever such proposals for discussion arise because of interested and not scientific motives. Nor is it inconceivable that individual initiatives should be disciplined and subject to an ordered procedure, so that they have to pass through the sieve of academies or cultural institutes of various kinds and only become public after undergoing a process of selection.

It would be interesting to study concretely the forms of cultural organization which keep the ideological world in movement within a given country, and to examine how they function in practice. A study of the numerical relationship between the section of the population professionally engaged in active cultural work in the country in question and the population as a whole, would also be useful, together with an approximate calculation of the unattached forces. The education system, at all levels, and the Church, are the two biggest cultural organizations in every country, in terms of the number of people they employ. Then there are newspapers, magazines and the book trade and private educational institutions, either those which are complementary to the state system, or cultural institutions like the Popular Universities. Other professions include among their specialized activities a fair proportion of cultural activity. For example, doctors, army officers, the legal profession. But it should be noted that in all countries, though in differing degrees, there is a great gap between the popular masses and the intellectual groups, even the largest ones, and those nearest to the peripheries of national life, like priests and school teachers. The reason for this is that, however much the ruling class may affirm to the contrary, the state, as such, does not have a unitary, coherent and homogeneous conception, with the result that intellectual groups are scattered between one stratum and the next, or even within a single stratum. The universities, except in a few countries, do not exercise any unifying influence: often an independent thinker has more influence than the whole university institution, etc.

Note 1. With regard to the historical role played by the fatalistic conception of the philosophy of praxis one might perhaps prepare its funeral oration, emphasizing its usefulness for a certain period of history, but precisely for this reason underlining the need to bury it with all due honours. Its role could really be compared with that of the theory of predestination and grace for the beginnings of the modern world, a theory which found its culmination in classical German philosophy and in its conception of freedom as the consciousness of necessity. It has been a replacement in the popular consciousness for the cry of ''tis God's will', although even on this primitive, elementary plane it was the beginnings of a more modern and fertile conception than that contained in the expression "'tis God's will' or in the theory of grace. Is it possible that 'formally' a new conception can present itself in a guise other than the crude, unsophisticated version of the populace? And yet the historian, with the benefit of all necessary perspective, manages to establish and to understand the fact that the beginnings of a new world, rough and jagged though they always are, are better than the passing away of the world in its death-throes and the swan-song that it produces. [...]

SPN, 323-43 (Q11§12)

ii Observations and critical notes on an attempt at a 'Popular Manual of Sociology'

A work like the *Popular Manual* [Bukharin's *The Theory of Historical Materialism. A Manual of Popular Sociology*], which is essentially destined for a community of readers who are not professional intellectuals, should have taken as its starting point a critical analysis of the philosophy of common sense, which is the 'philosophy of non-philosophers', or in other words the conception of the world which is uncritically absorbed by the various social and cultural environments in which the moral individuality of the average man is developed. Common sense is not a single unique conception, identical in time and space. It is the 'folklore' of philosophy, and, like folklore, it takes countless different forms. Its most fundamental characteristic is that it is a conception which, even in the brain of one individual, is fragmentary, incoherent and inconsequential, in conformity with the social and cultural position of those masses whose philosophy it is. At those times in history when a homogeneous social group is brought into being, there comes into being also, in opposition to common sense, a homogeneous – in other words coherent and systematic – philosophy. The *Popular Manual* makes the mistake of starting (implicitly) from the assumption that the great systems of traditional philosophy and the religion of the upper clergy – i.e. the conception of the world of the intellectuals and high culture – are in opposition to this elaboration of an original philosophy of the popular masses. In reality these systems are unknown to the multitude and have no direct influence on its way of thinking and

acting. This does not mean of course that they are altogether
without influence but it is influence of a different kind. These
systems influence the popular masses as an external political force,
an element of cohesive force exercised by the ruling classes and
therefore an element of subordination to an external hegemony.
This limits the original thought of the popular masses in a negative
direction, without having the positive effect of a vital ferment of
transformation of what the masses think in an embryonic and
chaotic form about the world and life. The principal elements of
common sense are provided by religions, and consequently the
relationship between common sense and religion is much more
intimate than that between common sense and the philosophical
systems of the intellectuals. But even within religion some critical
distinctions should be made. Every religion, even Catholicism
(indeed Catholicism more than any, precisely because of its efforts
to retain a 'surface' unity and avoid splintering into national
churches and social stratifications), is in reality a multiplicity of
distinct and often contradictory religions: there is one Catholicism
for the peasants, one for the petty bourgeoisie and the urban
workers, one for women, and one for intellectuals which is itself
variegated and disconnected. But common sense is influenced not
only by the crudest and least elaborated forms of these sundry
Catholicisms as they exist today. Previous religions have also had
an influence and remain components of common sense to this day,
and the same is true of previous forms of present Catholicism –
popular heretical movements, scientific superstitions connected
with past cults, etc.

   In common sense it is the 'realistic', materialistic elements which
are predominant, the immediate product of crude sensation. This
is by no means in contradiction with the religious element, far
from it. But here these elements are 'superstitious' and acritical.
This, then, is a danger of the *Popular Manual*, which often
reinforces, instead of scientifically criticising, these acritical
elements which have caused common sense to remain Ptolemaic,
anthropomorphic and anthropocentric. The above remarks about
the way in which the *Popular Manual* criticizes systematic
philosophies instead of starting from a critique of common sense,
should be understood as a methodological point and within certain
limits. Certainly they do not mean that the critique of the
systematic philosophies of the intellectuals is to be neglected.

When an individual from the masses succeeds in criticizing and going beyond common sense, he by this very fact accepts a new philosophy. Hence the necessity, in an exposition of the philosophy of praxis, of a polemic with traditional philosophies. Indeed, because by its nature it tends towards being a mass philosophy, the philosophy of praxis can only be conceived in a polemical form and in the form of a perpetual struggle. None the less the starting point must always be that common sense which is the spontaneous philosophy of the multitude who must be made ideologically homogenous.

More than in any other national literature there exist in French philosophical literature treatments of 'common sense': this is due to the more strictly 'popular-national' character of French culture, in other words to the fact that the intellectuals, because of certain specific traditional conditions, tend more than elsewhere to approach the people in order to guide it ideologically and keep it linked with the leading group. One will be able to find in French literature a lot of material on common sense that can be used and elaborated. The attitude of French philosophical culture towards common sense can indeed offer a model of hegemonic ideological construction. American and English culture can also offer some suggestions, but not in such an organic and complete way as the French. 'Common sense' has been considered in various ways. Sometimes it has even been criticized from the point of view of another philosophy. In reality, in either case, the result was to transcend a particular form of common sense and to create another which was closer to the conception of the world of the leading group. [...]

Croce's attitude towards 'common sense' seems unclear. In Croce, the proposition that all men are philosophers has an excessive influence on his judgment about common sense. It seems that Croce often likes to feel that certain philosophical propositions are shared by common sense. But what can this mean concretely? Common sense is a chaotic aggregate of disparate conceptions, and one can find there anything that one likes. Furthermore, this attitude of Croce's towards common sense has not led to a conception of culture which is productive from the national-popular point of view, that is to a more concretely historicist conception of philosophy – but that in any case could happen only with the philosophy of praxis.

[...]

What has been said so far does not mean that there are no truths in common sense. It means rather that common sense is an ambiguous, contradictory and multiform concept, and that to refer to common sense as a confirmation of truth is a nonsense. It is possible to state correctly that a certain truth has become part of common sense in order to indicate that it has spread beyond the confines of intellectual groups, but all one is doing in that case is making a historical observation and an assertion of the rationality of history. In this sense, and used with restraint, the argument has a certain validity, precisely because common sense is crudely conservative and opposed to novelty so that to have succeeded in forcing the introduction of a new truth is a proof that the truth in question is exceptionally evident and capable of great expansion. Recall Giusti's epigram:

Good sense, which once ruled far and wide,
Now in our schools to rest is laid.
Science, its once beloved child,
Killed it to see how it was made.[5]

This quotation can serve to indicate how the terms good sense and common sense are used ambiguously: as 'philosophy', as a specific mode of thought with a certain content of beliefs and opinions, and as an attitude of amiable indulgence, though at the same time contemptuous, towards anything abstruse and ingenious. It was therefore necessary for science to kill a particular form of traditional good sense, in order to create a 'new' good sense.

References to common sense and to the solidity of its beliefs are frequent in Marx.[6] But Marx is referring not to the validity of the content of these beliefs but rather to their formal solidity and to the consequent imperative character they have when they produce norms of conduct. There is, further, implicit in these references an assertion of the necessity for new popular beliefs, that is to say a new common sense and with it a new culture and a new philosophy which will be rooted in the popular consciousness with the same solidity and imperative quality as traditional beliefs.

[...]

In the teaching of philosophy which is aimed not at giving the student historical information about the development of past philosophy, but at giving him a cultural formation and helping him to elaborate his own thought critically so as to be able to participate in an ideological and cultural community, it is necessary to take as one's starting point what the student already knows and his philosophical experience (having first demonstrated to him precisely that he has such an experience, that he is a 'philosopher' without knowing it). And since one presupposes a certain average cultural and intellectual level among the students, who in all probability have hitherto only acquired scattered and fragmentary bits of information and have no methodological and critical preparation, one cannot but start in the first place from common sense, then secondly from religion, and only at a third stage move on to the philosophical systems elaborated by traditional intellectual groups.

SPN, 419-25 (Q11§13)

2 Language, Languages, Common Sense

We have established that philosophy is a conception of the world and that philosophical activity is not to be conceived solely as the 'individual' elaboration of systematically coherent concepts, but also and above all as a cultural battle to transform the popular 'mentality' and to diffuse the philosophical innovations which will demonstrate themselves to be 'historically true' to the extent that they become concretely – i.e. historically and socially – universal. Given all this, the questions of languages in general and of languages in the technical sense must be put in the forefront of our enquiry. [...] It seems that one can say that 'language' is essentially a collective term which does not presuppose any single thing existing in time and space. Language also means culture and philosophy (if only at the level of common sense) and therefore the fact of 'language' is in reality a multiplicity of facts more or less organically coherent and co-ordinated. At the limit it could be said that every speaking being has a personal language of his own, that is his own particular way of thinking and feeling. Culture, at its various levels, unifies in a series of strata, to the extent that they come into contact with each other, a greater or lesser number of individuals who understand each other's mode of expression in differing degrees, etc. It is these historico-social distinctions and differences which are reflected in common language and produce those 'obstacles' and 'sources of error' which the pragmatists have talked about.

From this one can deduce the importance of the 'cultural aspect' also in practical (collective) activity. An historical act can only be performed by 'collective man', and this presupposes the attainment of a 'cultural-social' unity through which a multiplicity of dispersed wills, with heterogeneous aims, are welded together with a single aim, on the basis of an equal and common conception of the world, both general and particular, operating in transitory bursts (in emotional ways) or permanently (where the intellectual base is so well rooted, assimilated and experienced that it becomes passion.) Since this is the way things happen, great importance is assumed by the general question of language, that is, the question of collectively attaining a single cultural 'climate'.

This problem can and must be related to the modern way of considering educational doctrine and practice, according to which the relationship between teacher and pupil is active and reciprocal so that every teacher is always a pupil and every pupil a teacher. But the educational relationship should not be restricted to the strictly 'classroom' relationships by means of which the new generation comes into contact with the old and absorbs its experiences and its historically necessary values and 'matures' and develops a personality of its own which is historically and culturally superior. This form of the relationship exists throughout society as a whole and for every individual relative to other individuals. It exists between intellectual and non-intellectual sections of the population, between the rulers and the ruled, elites and their followers, leaders [*dirigenti*] and led, the vanguard and the body of the army. Every relationship of 'hegemony' is necessarily an educational relationship and occurs not only within a nation, between the various forces of which the nation is composed, but in the international and world-wide field, between complexes of national and continental civilizations.

One could say therefore that the historical personality of an individual philosopher is also given by the active relationship which exists between him and the cultural environment he is proposing to modify. The environment reacts back on the philosopher and imposes on him a continual process of self-criticism. It is his 'teacher'. This is why one of the most important demands that the modern intelligentsias have made in the political field has been that of the so-called 'freedom of thought and of the expression of thought' ('freedom of the press', 'freedom of association'). For the relationship between master and disciple in the general sense referred to above is only realized where this political condition exists, and only then do we get the 'historical' realization of a new type of philosopher, whom we could call a 'democratic philosopher' in the sense that he is a philosopher convinced that his personality is not limited to himself as a physical individual but is an active social relationship of modification of the cultural environment. When the 'thinker' is content with his own thought, 'subjectively' free, that is abstractly free, he nowadays becomes a joke. The unity of science and life is precisely an active unity, in which alone liberty of thought can be realized; it is a master-pupil relationship, one between the philosopher and the cultural environment in which he has to work and from which he can draw the necessary problems for formulation and resolution. In other words, it is the relationship between philosophy and history.

SPN, 348-51 (Q10,II§44)

3 ['Knowledge' and 'Feeling']

Passage from knowing to understanding and to feeling and vice versa from feeling to understanding and to knowing. The popular element 'feels' but does not always know or understand; the intellectual element 'knows' but does not always understand and in particular does not always feel. The two extremes are therefore pedantry and philistinism on the one hand and blind passion and sectarianism on the other. Not that the pedant cannot be impassioned; far from it. Impassioned pedantry is every bit as ridiculous and dangerous as the wildest sectarianism and demagogy. The intellectual's error consists in believing that one can know without understanding and even more without feeling and being impassioned (not only for knowledge in itself but also for the object of knowledge): in other words that the intellectual can be an intellectual (and not a pure pedant) if distinct and separate from the people-nation, that is, without feeling the elementary passions of the people, understanding them and therefore explaining and justifying them in the particular historical situation and connecting them dialectically to the laws of history and to a superior conception of the world, scientifically and coherently elaborated – i.e. knowledge. One cannot make politics-history without this passion, without this connection of feeling between intellectuals and people-nation. In the absence of such a nexus the relations between the intellectual and the people-nation are, or are reduced to, relationships of a purely bureaucratic and formal order; the intellectuals become a caste, or a priesthood (so-called organic centralism).[7]

If the relationship between intellectuals and people-nation, between the leaders and the led, the rulers and the ruled, is provided by an organic cohesion in which feeling-passion becomes understanding and thence knowledge (not mechanically but in a way that is alive), then and only then is the relationship one of representation. Only then does there take place the exchange of individual elements between governed and governing, between led and leaders, and one achieves the life of the whole which alone is the social force, one creates the 'historical bloc'. [...]

SPN, 418 (Q11§67)

4 [The Philosophy of Praxis and 'Intellectual and Moral Reformation']

[...]
A conception of the philosophy of praxis as a modern popular reformation (since those people who expect a religious reformation in Italy, a new Italian edition of Calvinism, like [Mario] Missiroli and Co., are living in cloud-cuckooland) was perhaps hinted at by Georges Sorel, but his vision was fragmentary and intellectualistic, because of his kind of Jansenist fury against the squalor of parliamentarism and political parties. Sorel took from Renan the concept of the necessity of an intellectual and moral reformation; he affirmed (in a letter to Missiroli) that often great historical movements are [not] represented by a modern culture, etc.[8] It seems to me, though, that a conception of this kind is implicit in Sorel when he uses primitive Christianity as a touchstone, in a rather literary way it is true, but nevertheless with more than a grain of truth; with mechanical and often contrived references, but nevertheless with occasional flashes of profound intuition.

The philosophy of praxis presupposes all this cultural past: Renaissance and Reformation, German philosophy and the French Revolution, Calvinism and English classical economics, secular liberalism and this historicism which is at the root of the whole modern conception of life. The philosophy of praxis is the crowning point of this entire movement of intellectual and moral reformation, made dialectical in the contrast between popular culture and high culture. It corresponds to the nexus Protestant Reformation + French Revolution: it is a philosophy which is also politics, and a politics which is also philosophy. It is still going through its populist phase: creating a group of independent intellectuals is not an easy thing; it requires a long process, with actions and reactions, coming together and drifting apart and the growth of very numerous and complex new formations. It is the conception of a subaltern social group, deprived of historical initiative, in continuous but disorganic expansion, unable to go beyond a certain qualitative level, which still remains below the level of the possession of the state and of the real exercise of hegemony over the whole of society which alone permits a certain organic equilibrium in the development of the intellectual group. The philosophy of praxis has itself become 'prejudice' and 'superstition'. As it stands, it is the popular aspect of modern historicism, but it contains in itself the principle through which this historicism can be superseded. In the history of culture, which is much broader than the history of philosophy, every time that there has been a flowering of popular culture because a revolutionary phase was being passed through and because the metal of a new class was being forged from the ore of the people, there has been a flowering of 'materialism': conversely, at the same time the traditional classes clung to philosophies of the spirit. Hegel, half-way between the French Revolution and the Restoration, gave dialectical form to the two moments of the life of thought, materialism and spiritualism, but his synthesis was 'a man walking on his head'.[9] Hegel's successors destroyed this unity and there was a return to materialist systems on the one side and spiritualist ones on the other. The philosophy of praxis, through its founder, relived all this experience of Hegelianism, Feuerbachianism and French materialism, in order to reconstruct the synthesis of dialectical unity, 'the man walking on his feet'. The laceration which happened to Hegelianism has been repeated with the

352 A Gramsci Reader

philosophy of praxis. That is to say, from dialectical unity there has been a regress to philosophical materialism on the one hand, while on the other hand modern idealist high culture has tried to incorporate that part of the philosophy of praxis which was needed in order for it to find a new elixir.

'Politically' the materialist conception is close to the people, to 'common sense'. It is closely linked to many beliefs and prejudices, to almost all popular superstitions (witchcraft, spirits, etc.). This can be seen in popular Catholicism, and, even more so, in Byzantine orthodoxy. Popular religion is crassly materialistic, and yet the official religion of the intellectuals attempts to impede the formation of two distinct religions, two separate strata, so as not to become officially, as well as in reality, an ideology of restricted groups. But from this point of view it is important not to confuse the attitude of the philosophy of praxis with that of Catholicism. Whereas the former maintains a dynamic contact and tends continually to raise new strata of the population to a higher cultural life, the latter tends to maintain a purely mechanical contact, an external unity based in particular on the liturgy and on a cult visually imposing to the crowd. Many heretical movements were manifestations of popular forces aiming to reform the Church and bring it closer to the people by exalting them. The reaction of the Church was often very violent: it has created the Society of Jesus; it has clothed itself in the protective armour of the Council of Trent; although it has organized a marvellous mechanism of 'democratic' selection of its intellectuals, they have been selected as single individuals and not as the representative expression of popular groups.

In the history of cultural developments, it is important to pay special attention to the organization of culture and the personnel through whom this organization takes concrete form. G. De Ruggiero's volume on Renaissance and Reformation [*Rinascimento, Riforma, Controriforma*, Bari 1930] brings out the attitude of very many intellectuals, with Erasmus at their head: they gave way in the face of persecution and the stake. The bearer of the Reformation was therefore the German people itself in its totality, as undifferentiated mass, not the intellectuals. It is precisely this desertion of the intellectuals in the face of the enemy which explains the 'sterility' of the Reformation in the immediate sphere of high culture, until, by a process of selection, the people, which remained faithful to the cause, produced a new group of intellectuals culminating in classical philosophy.

Something similar has happened up to now with the philosophy of praxis. The great intellectuals formed on the terrain of this philosophy, besides being few in number, were not linked with the people, they did not emerge from the people, but were the expression of traditional intermediary classes, to which they returned at the great 'turning points' of history. Some remained, but rather to subject the new conception to a systematic revision than to advance its autonomous development. The affirmation that the philosophy is a new, independent and original conception, even though it is also a moment of world historical development, is an affirmation of the independence and originality of a new culture in incubation, which will develop with the development of social relations. What exists at any given time is a variable combination of old and new, a momentary equilibrium of cultural relations corresponding to the equilibrium of social relations. Only after the creation of the new state does the cultural problem impose itself in all its complexity and tend towards a coherent solution. In any case the attitude to be taken up before the formation of the new state can only be critico-polemical, never dogmatic; it must be a romantic attitude, but of a romanticism which is consciously aspiring to its classical composure.

[...]

SPN, 395-8 (Q16§9)

5 How Many Forms of Grammar Can There Be?

Several, certainly. There is the grammar 'immanent' in language itself, by which one speaks 'according to grammar' without knowing it, as Molière's character produced prose without knowing it.[10] Nor does this point seem useless because Panzini (*Guida alla Grammatica italiana* [...]) seems not to distinguish between this 'grammar' and the 'normative', written one which he intends to speak about and which seems to be for him the only possible grammar there can be. The preface to the first edition is full of inanities, which are however significant in someone who writes (and is considered a specialist) on grammatical matters, like the statement 'we can write and speak even without grammar'.

Besides the 'immanent grammar' in every language, there is also in reality (i.e., even if not written) a 'normative' grammar (or more than one). This is made up of the reciprocal monitoring, reciprocal teaching and reciprocal 'censorship' expressed in such questions as 'What did you mean to say?', 'What do you mean?', 'Make yourself clearer', etc., and in mimicry and teasing. This whole complex of actions and reactions come together to create a grammatical conformism, to establish 'norms' or judgements of correctness or incorrectness. But this 'spontaneous' expression of grammatical conformity is necessarily disconnected, discontinuous and limited to local social strata or local centres. (A peasant who moves to the city ends up conforming to urban speech through the pressure of the city environment. In the country, people try to imitate urban speech; the subaltern classes try to speak like the dominant classes and the intellectuals, etc.)

One could sketch a picture of the 'normative grammar' that operates spontaneously in every given society, in that this society tends to become unified both territorially and culturally, in other words it has a governing class whose function is recognized and followed. The number of 'immanent or spontaneous grammars' is incalculable and, theoretically, one can say that each person has a grammar of his own. Alongside this actual 'fragmentation', however, one should also point out the movements of unification, with varying degrees of amplitude both in terms of territory and 'linguistic volume'. Written 'normative grammars' tend to embrace the entire territory of a nation and its total 'linguistic volume', to create a unitary national linguistic conformism. This, moreover, places expressive 'individualism' at a higher level because it creates a more robust and homogeneous skeleton for the national linguistic body, of which every individual is the reflection and interpreter. (Taylor system and self-education.)

Historical as well as normative grammars. But it is obvious that someone who writes a normative grammar cannot ignore the history of the language of which he wishes to propose an 'exemplary phase' as the 'only' one worthy to become, in an 'organic' and 'totalitarian' way, the 'common' language of a nation in competition and conflict with other 'phases' and types or schemes that already exist (connected to traditional developments or to the inorganic and incoherent attempts of forces which, as we have seen, act continuously on the spontaneous 'grammars' immanent in the language). Historical grammar cannot but be 'comparative': an expression that, analysed thoroughly, indicates the deep-seated awareness that the linguistic fact, like any other historical fact, cannot have strictly defined national boundaries, but that history is always 'world history' and that particular histories exist only within the frame of world history. Normative grammar has other ends, even though the national language cannot be imagined outside the frame of other languages that exert an influence on it through innumerable channels which are often difficult to control. (Who can control the linguistic innovations introduced by returning emigrants, travellers, readers of foreign newspapers and languages, translators, etc.?)

Written normative grammar, then, always presupposes a 'choice', a cultural tendency, and is thus always an act of national-cultural politics. One might discuss the best way to present the 'choice' and the 'tendency' in order to get them accepted willingly, that is, one might discuss the most suitable means to obtain the goal; but there can be no doubt that there is a goal to be reached, that adequate and suitable means are needed, in other words that we are dealing with a political act.

Questions: what is the nature of this political act, and is it going to raise oppositions of 'principle', a *de facto* collaboration, opposition to the details, etc.? If one starts from the assumption of centralizing what already exists in a diffused, scattered but inorganic and incoherent state, it seems obvious that an opposition on principle is not rational. On the contrary, it is rational to collaborate practically and willingly to welcome everything that may serve to create a common national language, the non-existence of which creates friction particularly in the popular masses among whom local particularisms and phenomena of a narrow and provincial mentality are more tenacious than is believed. In other words, it is a question of stepping up the struggle against illiteracy. There is already *de facto* opposition in the resistance of the masses to shedding their particularistic habits and ways of thinking, a stupid resistance caused by the fanatical advocates of international languages. It is clear that with this set of problems the question of the national struggle of a hegemonic culture against other nationalities or residues of nationalities cannot be discussed.

Panzini does not even remotely consider these problems and, as a result, his publications on grammar are ambiguous, contradictory and wavering. For example, he does not ask what is the centre from which linguistic innovations are presently diffused from below; yet this is a problem of no small practical importance. Florence, Rome, Milan. On the other hand he does not even ask if (and where) there is a spontaneous centre of diffusion from above, i.e. in a relatively organic, continuous and efficient form, and whether it can be regulated and intensified.

SCW, 180-2 (Q29§2)

6 Sources of Diffusion of Linguistic Innovations in the Tradition and of a National Linguistic Conformism in the Broad National Masses

1) The education system; 2) newspapers; 3) artistic writers and popular writers; 4) the theatre and sound films; 5) radio; 6) public meetings of all kinds, including religious ones; 7) the relations of 'conversation' between the more educated and less educated strata of the population (a question which is perhaps not given all the attention it deserves is that of the 'words' in verse learnt by heart in the form of songs, snatches of operas, etc. It should be noted that the people do not bother really to memorize these words, which are often strange, antiquated and baroque, but reduce them to kinds of nursery rhymes that are only helpful for remembering the tune); 8) the local dialects, understood in various senses (from the more localized dialects to those which embrace more or less broad regional complexes: thus Neapolitan for southern Italy, the dialects of Palermo and Catania for Sicily).

Since the process of formation, spread and development of a unified national language occurs through a whole complex of molecular processes, it helps to be aware of the entire process as a whole in order to be able to intervene actively in it with the best possible results. One need not consider this intervention as 'decisive' and imagine that the ends proposed will all be reached in detail, i.e. that one will obtain a *specific* unified language. One will obtain a *unified language*, if it is a necessity, and the organized intervention will speed up the already existing process. What this language will be, one cannot foresee or establish: in any case, if the intervention is 'rational', it will be organically tied to tradition, and this is of no small importance in the economy of culture.

Manzonians and 'classicists'. They had a type of language which they wanted to make prevail. It is not correct to say that these discussions were useless and have not left traces in modern culture, even if the traces are modest. Over the last century a unified culture has in fact been extended, and therefore also a common unified language. But the entire historical formation of the Italian nation moved at too slow a pace. Every time the question of the language surfaces, in one way or another, it means that a series of other problems are coming to the fore: the formation and enlargement of the governing class, the need to establish more intimate and secure relationships between the governing groups and the national-popular mass, in other words to reorganize the cultural hegemony. Today, we have witnessed various phenomena which indicate a rebirth of these questions: the publications of Panzini, Trabalza-Allodoli, Monelli, columns in the newspapers, intervention by union leaderships, etc.

SCW, 183-4 (Q29§3)

7 Historical and Normative Grammars

Taking normative grammar to be a political act and taking this starting-point as the only one from which one can 'scientifically' justify its existence and the enormous amount of patience needed to learn it (all the effort required to form hundreds of thousands of recruits, of the most disparate origins and mental preparation, into a homogeneous army capable of moving and acting in a disciplined and united manner, all the 'practical and theoretical lessons' on the regulations, etc.), one needs to posit its relationship to historical grammar. The failure to define this relationship explains many inconsistencies of normative grammars, including that of Trabalza-Allodoli. We are dealing with two distinct and in part different things, like history and politics, but they cannot be considered independently, any more than politics and history. Besides, since the study of languages as a cultural phenomenon grew out of political needs (more or less conscious and consciously expressed), the needs of normative grammar have exerted an influence on historical grammar and on its 'legislative conceptions' (or at least this traditional element has reinforced, during the last century, the application of the positivist-naturalist method to the study of the history of languages conceived as the 'science of language'). It appears from Trabalza's grammar and from Schiaffini's damning review of it (*Nuova Antologia*, 16 September 1934), that not even the so-called 'idealists' have understood the innovation which the doctrines of Bartoli have brought to the science of language.[11] The 'idealist' current has found its most complete expression in Bertoni: it involves a return to old rhetorical conceptions, to words which are 'beautiful' and 'ugly' in and by themselves, conceptions which have been glossed over with a new pseudo-scientific language. What these people are really looking for is an extrinsic justification of normative grammar, after having 'demonstrated', in an equally extrinsic fashion, its theoretical and also practical 'uselessness'.

Trabalza's essay on 'The History of Grammar' could be a useful source on the interferences between historical grammar (or better, the history of language) and normative grammar, on the history of the problem, etc.

SCW, 184-5 (Q29§5)

8 Grammar and Technique

Does grammar involve the same question as 'technique' in general? Is grammar only the technical aspect of language? At all events, are the idealists (especially the Gentilians) justified in their arguments about the uselessness of grammar and its exclusion from the schools?[12] If one speaks (expresses oneself with words) in a manner which is historically determined by nations and linguistic areas, can one dispense with teaching this 'historically determined manner'? Granted that traditional normative grammar was inadequate, is this a good reason for teaching no grammar at all, for not being in the least concerned with speeding up the process of learning the particular way of speaking of a certain linguistic area, and rather leaving 'the language to be learnt through living it', or some other expression of this sort used by Gentile or his followers? All in all, this is a 'liberalism' of the most bizarre and eccentric stripe. Differences between Croce and Gentile. As usual, Gentile bases himself on Croce, exaggerating some of the latter's theoretical tenets to the point of absurdity. Croce maintains that grammar does not pertain to any of the theoretical activities of the spirit elaborated by him, but ends up justifying in the 'practical' sphere many activities denied at the theoretical level. At first, Gentile also excludes from practice what he denies theoretically, only to find a theoretical justification for the most outdated and technically unjustified practical manifestations.

Does a technique have to be learnt 'systematically'? In practice, the technique of the village artisan has been set against that of Ford. Think of the variety of ways in which 'industrial technique' is learnt: artisanally, during factory work itself, watching how others work (and hence wasting more time and energy and learning only partially); in professional schools (where the whole trade is systematically learnt, even though some of the notions one learns will be applied very rarely in one's lifetime, if ever); by combining various methods, with the Taylor-Ford system which created a new kind of qualification and a skill limited to certain factories, or even to specific machines and stages of the production process.

Normative grammar, which only by abstraction can be considered as divorced from the living language, tends to make one learn the entire organism of the language in question and to create a spiritual attitude that enables one always to find one's way around the linguistic environment (see note on the study of Latin in the classical curriculum).[13] If grammar is excluded from education and is not 'written', it cannot thereby be excluded from 'real life', as I have already pointed out elsewhere. The only thing excluded is the unitarily organized intervention in the process of learning the language. In practice the national-popular mass is excluded from learning the educated language, since the highest level of the ruling class, which traditionally speaks standard Italian, passes it on from generation to generation, through a slow process that begins with the first stutterings of the child under the guidance of its parents, and continues through conversation (with its 'this is how one says it', 'it must be said like this', etc.) for the rest of one's life. In reality, one is 'always' studying grammar (by imitating the model one admires, etc.). In Gentile's attitude there is much more politics than one thinks and a great deal of unconscious reactionary thought, as has in any case already been noted at other times and on other occasions. There is all the reactionary thought of the old liberal view, a '*laissez faire, laissez passer*' which is not justified, as it was in Rousseau (and Gentile is

more like Rousseau than he thinks) by opposition to the paralysis
of Jesuit education,[14] but which has become an abstract,
'ahistorical' ideology.

SCW, 185-7 (Q29§6)

9 Observations on Folklore

[...] One can say that until now folklore has been studied primarily
as a 'picturesque' element. (Actually, until now only scholarly
material has been collected. The science of folklore mostly consists
of methodological studies on how to collect, select and classify
such material, i.e. of the investigation of the practical precautions
and empirical principles necessary for profitably carrying out a
particular aspect of scholarship. To say this is not to disregard the
importance and historical significance of some of the major
scholars of folklore.) Folklore should instead be studied as a
'conception of the world and life' implicit to a large extent in
determinate (in time and space) strata of society and in opposition
(also for the most part implicit, mechanical and objective) to
'official' conceptions of the world (or in a broader sense, the
conceptions of the cultured parts of historically determinate
societies) that have succeeded one another in the historical
process. (Hence the strict relationship between folklore and
'common sense', which is philosophical folklore.) This conception
of the world is not elaborated and systematic because, by
definition, the people (the sum total of the instrumental and
subaltern classes of every form of society that has so far existed)
cannot possess conceptions which are elaborated, systematic and
politically organized and centralized in their albeit contradictory
development. It is, rather, many-sided – not only because it
includes different and juxatposed elements, but also because it is
stratified, from the more crude to the less crude – if, indeed, one
should not speak of a confused agglomerate of fragments of all the
conceptions of the world and of life that have succeeded one
another in history. In fact, it is only in folklore that one finds
surviving evidence, adulterated and mutilated, of the majority of
these conceptions.

Philosophy and modern science are also constantly contributing new elements to 'modern folklore' in that certain opinions and scientific notions, removed from their context and more or less distorted, constantly fall within the popular domain and are 'inserted' into the mosaic of tradition. (*La scoperta de l'America* by C. Pascarella shows how notions about Christopher Columbus and about a whole set of scientific opinions, put about by school textbooks and the 'Popular Universities', can be strangely assimilated.[15]) Folklore can be understood only as a reflection of the conditions of cultural life of the people, although certain conceptions specific to folklore remain even after these conditions have been (or seem to be) modified or have given way to bizarre combinations.

Certainly, there is a 'religion of the people', especially in Catholic and Orthodox countries, which is very different from that of the intellectuals (the religious ones) and particularly from that organically set up by the ecclesiastical hierarchy. One could claim, though, that all religions, even the most refined and sophisticated, are 'folklore' in relation to modern thought. But there is the essential difference that religions, in the first place Catholicism, are 'elaborated and set up' by the intellectuals (as above) and the ecclesiastical hierarchy. Therefore, they present special problems. (One should see if such an elaboration and set-up may not be necessary to keep folklore scattered and many-sided: the conditions of the Church before and after the Reformation and the Council of Trent and the different historico-cultural development of the Reformed and Orthodox countries after the Reformation and Trent are highly significant elements.) Thus it is true that there is a 'morality of the people', understood as a determinate (in space and time) set of principles for practical conduct and of customs that derive from them or have produced them. Like superstition, this morality is closely tied to real religious beliefs. Imperatives exist that are much stronger, more tenacious and more effective than those of official 'morality'. In this sphere, too, one must distinguish various strata: the fossilized ones which reflect conditions of past life and are therefore conservative and reactionary, and those which consist of a series of innovations, often creative and progressive, determined spontaneously by forms and conditions of life which are in the process of developing and which are in contradiction to or simply different from the morality of the governing strata.

[...]

It is clear that, in order to achieve the desired end, the spirit of folklore studies should be changed, as well as deepened and extended. Folklore must not be considered an eccentricity, an oddity or a picturesque element, but as something which is very serious and is to be taken seriously. Only in this way will the teaching of folklore be more efficient and really bring about the birth of a new culture among the broad popular masses, so that the separation between modern culture and popular culture of folklore will disappear. An activity of this kind, thoroughly carried out, would correspond on the intellectual plane to what the Reformation was in Protestant countries.

SCW, 188-91 (Q27§1)

XII POPULAR CULTURE

Introduction

Gramsci's interest in popular culture was bound up with his conception of revolutionary change as a process in which popular mentalities and behaviour are transformed (see Section XI). In Italy, there had been historically – with the partial exception of opera – no 'national-popular' culture, that is to say no form of culture in which there was an organic relationship between Italian intellectuals and the broad national masses. This, Gramsci argues, is because of the age-old detachment of Italian intellectuals from the people, their tendency to make up a 'caste' remote from popular life. The intellectuals' failure to forge a national-popular alliance had contributed to the perpetuation of a gap in Italy between elite culture and popular culture, of which the most manifest signs were the lack of a unified national language or of popular cultural traditions at a higher level than the local region or village. Gramsci's observations on the non-national character of Italian culture parallel those on the passive, non-Jacobin character of bourgeois revolution in Italy, the failure of the bourgeoisie to become an expansively hegemonic class (see Section VIII). In Italy, the 'lay [i.e. non-Catholic] forces ... have not known how to elaborate a modern "humanism" able to reach right to the simplest and most uneducated classes' (p.369). Instead popular culture has become permeated with foreign products (such as French crime stories) and with a bombastic and insincere 'operatic' style.

The cultural situation in which Gramsci was writing was one of transition to modernity, and this needs to be taken into account when reading these notes. At the time of his imprisonment a large market for books had not developed in Italy, mainly because of a still high illiteracy rate, though illustrated magazines and comics were taking off. Cinema and sound-recording had been around since the turn of the century, but radio broadcasting was still in its infancy and television would not be introduced until the 1950s.

Gramsci was interested, in this situation, in drawing up a 'map' of popular taste in order to establish the 'terrain' upon which cultural transformation might take place. His aim was not to produce a static, descriptive picture but to explore the relations between dominant and subaltern cultural forms in dynamic terms, as they act upon each other historically. He has a form of 'seepage theory' of popular culture. He sees popular culture and folklore as containing the 'sediments' or residues of earlier dominant cultural forms which have remained from the past and have entered into combination with other forms. For example, he sees the popular literature of rural areas as containing residues of medieval and Renaissance romances of chivalry and of earlier, superseded scientific conceptions. By a converse process, he sees popular cultural forms as being 'raised' into the dominant artistic literature. Dostoyevsky for instance 'passes through' popular serial fiction in order to draw materials for writing artistic fiction (see Section XIV below, p.397). This latter process interests Gramsci in particular because of its bearing on how a dominated class can become hegemonic in its turn.

In his notes on popular culture Gramsci tends explicitly to privilege written over spoken or visual cultural forms like radio and film, even though the latter were becoming increasingly important in the 1930s. This may be attributable in part to a widespread tendency in Italy at that period to identify culture largely with the written word. But more particularly it seems to be bound up with Gramsci's own conception of hegemony and intellectual and moral reformation as a process of acquisition of a critical outlook, of logical capacities, of 'coherent and systematic thought', all of which he tends to identify with writing and the print media.

1 Concept of 'National-Popular'

A note in *Critica Fascista* of 1 August 1930 complains that two major daily newspapers, one in Rome and the other in Naples, have begun serial publication of these novels: *The Count of Monte-Cristo* and *Joseph Balsamo* by Alexandre Dumas and *A Mother's Calvary* by Paul Fontenay. *Critica* writes:

The nineteenth century in France was undoubtedly a golden period for the serial novel; but those newspapers which reprint novels of a century ago (as if taste, interest and literary experience had not changed at all from then until now) must have a very poor idea of their readers. Furthermore, why not take account of the fact that, despite opinions to the contrary, a modern Italian novel exists? And to think that these people are ready to shed tears of ink over the sad fate of our national literature.

Critica is confusing different categories of problems: that of the non-circulation of so-called artistic literature among the people; and that of the non-existence in Italy of a 'popular' literature, which means that the newspapers are 'forced' to take in supplies abroad. Of course, in theory nothing prevents the possible existence of an artistic popular literature. The most obvious example is the 'popular' success, even today, of the great Russian novelists. But in fact neither a popular artistic literature nor a local production of 'popular' literature exists because 'writers' and 'people' do not have the same conception of the world. In other words the feelings of the people are not lived by the writers as their own, nor do the writers have a 'national educative' function: they have not and do not set themselves the problem of elaborating popular feelings after having relived them and made them their own. Nor does *Critica* set itself these problems and it is unable to draw the 'realistic' conclusions from the fact that if people like the novels of a hundred years ago, it means that their taste and ideology are precisely those of a hundred years ago. Newspapers are politico-financial bodies, and they do not propose to put out *belles-lettres* in their own columns if these *belles-lettres* increase the return of unsold issues. The serial novel is a way of circulating newspapers among the popular classes – remember the example of *Il Lavoro* of Genoa, under the editorship of Giovanni Ansaldo, which reprinted all the French serial literature, while at the same time trying to give the most refined cultural tone to the other parts of the newspaper – and this means political and financial success. Hence the newspaper looks for that novel, that type of novel, which the people are 'certain' to enjoy and which will assure a permanent and 'continuous' clientele. The man of the people buys only one newspaper, when he buys one. The choice is not even personal, but is often that of the family as a group. The women have a large say in the choice and insist on the 'nice interesting novel'. (This does not mean that the men do not read the novel too, but it is the women who are particular interested in it and in items of local news.) This always meant that purely political papers or papers of pure opinion never had a large circulation (except in periods of intense political struggle). They were bought by young people, men and women, without too many family worries, who were keenly interested in the fortunes of their political opinions, and by a small number of families highly compact in their ideas. In general, those who read the newspapers do not share the opinion of the newspaper they buy or are minimally influenced by it. From the point of view of journalistic technique, then, one should study the case of *Il Secolo* and *Il Lavoro* which used to publish up to three serial novels in order to gain a large and steady circulation. (One does not consider that for many readers the 'serial novel' has the same importance as quality 'literature' has for educated people. It used to be a kind of 'social obligation' for the porters, the courtyard and the people upstairs to know the 'novel' that *La Stampa* was publishing. Every instalment led to 'conversations' sparkling with the logical and psychological intuitions of the 'most distinguished' presences. It can be claimed that the readers of serial novels enthuse about their authors with far more sincerity and a much livelier human interest than was shown in so-called cultured drawing rooms for the novels of D'Annunzio or is shown there now for the works of Pirandello.)

But the most interesting problem is this: if the Italian newspapers of 1930 want to increase (or maintain) their circulation, why must they publish serial novels of a hundred years ago (or modern ones of the same kind)? Why is there no 'national' literature of this type in Italy, even though it must be profitable? One should note that in many languages, 'national' and 'popular' are either synonymous or nearly so (they are in Russian, in German, where *völkisch* has an even more intimate meaning of race, and in the Slavonic languages in general; in France the meaning of 'national' already includes a more politically elaborated notion of 'popular' because it is related to the concept of 'sovereignty': national sovereignty and popular sovereignty have, or had, the same value).[1] In Italy the term 'national' has an ideologically very restricted meaning, and does not in any case coincide with 'popular' because in Italy the intellectuals are distant

from the people, i.e. from the 'nation'. They are tied instead to a
caste tradition that has never been broken by a strong popular or
national political movements from below. This tradition is abstract
and 'bookish', and the typical modern intellectual feels closer to
Annibal Caro or Ippolito Pindemonte than to an Apulian or Sicilian
peasant.[2] The current term 'national' is connected in Italy to this
intellectual and bookish tradition. Hence the foolish and ultimately
dangerous facility of calling 'anti-national' whoever does not have
this archaeological and moth-eaten conception of the country's
interests.

One should also see Umberto Fracchia's articles in the June 1930
issues of *L'Italia Letteraria* and Ugo Ojetti's 'Letter to Umberto
Fracchia on Criticism' in the August 1930 number of *Pégaso*.
Fracchia's complaints are very similar to those of *Critica Fascista*.
The so-called 'artistic' 'national' literature is not popular in Italy.
Whose fault is it? That of the public, which does not read? That of
the critics, who are not able to present and extol literary 'values' to
the public? That of the newspapers, which publish the old *Count of
Monte-Cristo* instead of serializing the 'modern Italian novel'? But
why does the public not read in Italy, when in other countries it
does? Besides, is it true that in Italy nobody reads? Would it not be
more accurate to state the problem in this way: why does the Italian
public read foreign literature, popular and non-popular, instead of
reading its own? Has not Fracchia himself published ultimatums to
the editors who publish (and thus must sell, relatively speaking)
foreign works, threatening them with governmental measures?
And has the government not tried to intervene, at least partly, in the
person of Michele Bianchi, Undersecretary of Internal Affairs?

What is the meaning of the fact that the Italian people prefer to
read foreign writers? It means that they *undergo* the moral and
intellectual hegemony of foreign intellectuals, that they feel more
closely related to foreign intellectuals than to 'domestic' ones, that
there is no national intellectual and moral bloc, either hierarchical
or, still less, egalitarian. The intellectuals do not come from the
people, even if by accident some of them have origins among the
people. They do not feel tied to them (rhetoric apart), they do not
know and sense their needs, aspirations and feelings. In relation to
the people, they are something detached, without foundation, a
caste and not an articulation with organic functions of the people
themselves.

The question must be extended to the entire national-popular culture and not restricted just to narrative fiction. The same things must be said about the theatre, about scientific literature in general (the sciences of nature, history, etc.). Why do no writers like Flammarion emerge in Italy?[3] Why has no popularized scientific literature arisen as in France and other countries? These foreign books are read and sought after in translation and are often very successful. All this means that the entire 'educated class', with its intellectual activity, is detached from the people-nation, not because the latter has not shown and does not show itself to be interested in this activity at all levels, from the lowest (dreadful serial novels) to the highest – indeed it seeks out foreign books for this purpose – but because in relation to the people-nation the indigenous intellectual element is more foreign than the foreigners. The question has not just arisen now. It has been posed since the foundation of the Italian state, and its previous existence is a document for explaining the delay in forming the peninsula into a national political unit: see Ruggero Bonghi's book on the unpopularity of Italian literature. The question of the language posed by Manzoni also reflects this problem, that of the moral and intellectual unity of the nation and the state, sought in the unity of the language.[4] The unity of the language, though, is one of the external means, and not an exclusively necessary one, of national unity. Anyway, it is an effect and not a cause. See F. Martini's writings on the theatre: there is an entire literature on the theatre which is still developing.

A national-popular literature, narrative and other kinds, has always been lacking in Italy and still is. (In poetry there have been no figures like Béranger or the French *chansonnier* in general.) Still, there have been individual popular writers who have been successful. Guerrazzi, for instance, was successful and his books are still published and circulated. People once read Carolina Invernizio and perhaps still do, even though she is inferior to the Ponsons and the Montépins. People also read Francesco Mastriani. (G. Papini wrote an article on Invernizio in *Il Resto del Carlino*, during the war, in 1916 or so: check if the article is included in a collection. He had something interesting to say on this old trooper of popular literature, observing precisely that she got herself read by ordinary people. [...])

In the absence of their own 'modern' literature, certain strata of the *menu peuple* have satisfied their intellectual and artistic needs (which do exist, albeit in a plain and elementary form) in a variety of ways: the circulation of medieval romances of chivalry – the *Reali di Francia, Guerino detto il Meschino*, etc. – especially in southern Italy and the mountains; the *Maggi* in Tuscany (the subjects represented by the *Maggi* are taken from books, tales and especially popular legends like Pia dei Tolomei; there are various publications on the *Maggi* and their repertoire).[5]

The lay forces have failed in their historical task as educators and elaborators of the intellect and the moral awareness of the people-nation. They have been incapable of satisfying the intellectual needs of the people precisely because they have failed to represent a lay culture, because they have not known how to elaborate a modern 'humanism' able to reach right to the simplest and most uneducated classes, as was necessary from the national point of view, and because they have been tied to an antiquated world, narrow, abstract, too individualistic or caste-like. French popular literature, on the other hand, which is the most widespread in Italy, does represent this modern humanism, this in its own way modern secularism, to a greater or lesser degree, and in a more or less attractive way. Guerrazzi, Mastriani and our few other popular writers were also representations of it. Yet if the lay forces have failed, the Catholics have not had any more success. One should not be deceived by the moderately high circulation of certain Catholic books. This is due to the vast powerful organization of the Church, not to an inner force of expansion. The books are given away at the innumerable ceremonies and are read for chastisement, on command or out of desperation.

It is a striking fact that in the field of adventure literature the Catholics have only managed to produce mediocrities: and yet they possess an excellent source in the travels of the missionaries and their eventful and often risky lives. Yet even when the geographical adventure novel was in its heyday, the Catholic version of this literature was mediocre and in no way comparable to its French, English and German secular counterparts. The most remarkable book is the story of Cardinal Massaja's life in Abyssinia. This apart there has been an invasion of books by Ugo Mioni (formerly a Jesuit priest) which are utterly sub-standard. In scientific popular literature, too, the Catholics offer very little, despite their great astronomers, like Father Secchi (a Jesuit), and the fact that astronomy is the science which interests the people most. This Catholic literature oozes with Jesuitic apologetics, like a goat with musk, and is nauseating in its mean narrow-mindedness. The inadequacy of Catholic intellectuals and the limited success of their literature are one of the most eloquent indications of the profound split that exists between religion and the people. The people are reduced to an extreme state of indifference and lack of a lively spiritual life. Religion has remained at the level of superstition, but it has not been replaced by a new humanistic and secular morality, because of the impotence of the lay intellectuals. (Religion has neither been replaced, nor internally transformed and nationalized as it has in other countries – like Jesuitism itself in America. Popular Italy is still in the conditions created immediately after the Counter-Reformation. At best, religion has been combined with pagan folklore and has remained at this stage.)

SCW, 206-12 (Q21§5)

2 Various Types of Popular Novel

A certain variety of types of popular novel exists and it should be noted that, although all of them simultaneously enjoy some degree of success and popularity, one of them nevertheless predominates by far. From this predominance one can identify a change in fundamental tastes, just as from the simultaneous success of the various types one can prove that there exist among the people various cultural levels, different 'masses of feelings' prevalent in one or the other level, various popular 'hero-models'. It is thus important for the present essay to draw up a catalogue of these types and to establish historically their greater or lesser degree of success: 1) The Victor Hugo – Eugène Sue (*Les Misérables, The Mysteries of Paris*) type: overtly ideologico-political in character and with democratic tendencies linked to the ideologies of 1848; 2) The sentimental type, not strictly political, but which expresses what could be defined as a 'sentimental democracy' (Richebourg – Decourcelle, etc.); 3) The type presented as pure intrigue, but which has a conservative-reactionary ideological content (Montépin); 4) The historical novel of A. Dumas and Ponson du Terrail which, besides its historical aspect, has a politico-ideological character, but less marked: Ponson du Terrail, is, however, a conservative-reactionary and his exaltation of the aristocrats and their faithful servants is quite different from the historical representations of Alexandre Dumas, even though Dumas has no overt democratic-political tendency but is pervaded by 'passive' and generic democratic feelings and often comes close to the 'sentimental' type; 5) The detective novel in its double aspect (Lecoq, Rocambole, Sherlock Holmes, Arsène Lupin); 6) The gothic novel (ghosts, mysterious castles, etc.: Ann Radcliffe, etc.); 7) The geographical, scientific adventure novel which can be tendentious or consist simply of intrigue (Jules Verne – Boussenard).

Each of these types also has different national characteristics (in America the adventure novel is the epic of the pioneers). One can observe how in the overall production of each country there is an implicit nationalism, not rhetorically expressed, but skilfully insinuated into the story. In Verne and the French there is a very deep anti-English feeling, related to the loss of the colonies and the humiliating naval defeats. In the geographical adventure novel the French do not clash with the Germans but with the English. But there is also an anti-English feeling in the historical novel and even in the sentimental novel (e.g. George Sand). (Reaction due to the Hundred Years War and the killing of Joan of Arc, and to the defeat of Napoleon.)

In Italy none of these types has had many writers of stature (not literary stature, but 'commercial' value, in the sense of inventiveness and ingeniously constructed plots which, although complicated, are worked out with a certain rationality). Not even the detective novel, which has been so successful internationally (and, for authors and publishers, financially), has found writers in Italy. Yet many novels, especially historical ones, have chosen for their subject Italy and the historical events of its cities, regions, institutions and men. Thus Venetian history, with its political, judicial and police organizations, has provided and continues to provide subject matter for popular novelists of every country, except Italy. Popular literature on the life of brigands has had a certain success in Italy but its quality is extremely poor.

The latest type of popular book is the novelized biography, which at any rate represents an unconscious attempt to satisfy the cultural needs of some of the popular strata who are more smart culturally and are not satisfied with the Dumas type of story. This literature, too, has few representatives in Italy (Mazzucchelli, Cesare Giardini, etc.). Not only do Italian writers not compare with the French, the Germans and the English in terms of numbers, significantly, they choose their subjects outside Italy (Mazzucchelli and Giardini in France, Eucardio Momigliano in England) in order to adapt to the Italian popular taste formed on historical novels, especially French ones. The Italian man of letters would not write a novelized biography of Masaniello, Michele di Lando or Cola di Rienzo without feeling obliged to cram it with tiresome, rhetorical 'padding', for fear people might think ... might wonder ... etc. It is true that the success of novelized biographies has induced many publishers to start running series of biographies, but these books are to the novelized biography what *The Nun of Monza* is to *The Count of Monte-Cristo*.[6] They consist of the familiar, often philologically correct, biographical scheme which can at most find a few thousand readers but cannot become popular.

One should note that some of the types of popular novel listed above have parallels in the theatre and now in cinema. In the theatre the considerable success of Dario Niccodemi is doubtless due to his ability to dramatize ideas and motifs eminently related to popular ideology. This is true of *Scampolo*, *L'Aigrette* and *La Volata*, etc. There is also something similar in G. Forzano's work, but on the model of Ponson du Terrail, with conservative tendencies. The theatrical work – of an Italian character – that has had the greatest popular success in Italy is Giacometti's *La morte civile*, but it has not had imitators of any merit (still speaking in a non-literary sense). In this section on the theatre, we might note how a whole series of playwrights of great literary value can be enormously liked by the people as well. The people in the cities greatly enjoy Ibsen's *A Doll's House* because the feelings depicted and the author's moral tendency find a profound resonance in the popular psyche. And what should the so-called *theatre of ideas* be if not this, the representation of passions related to social behaviour, with dramatic solutions which can depict a 'progressive' catharsis,[7] which can depict the drama of the most intellectually and morally advanced part of a society, that which expresses the historical growth immanent in present social behaviour itself? This drama and these passions, though, must be represented and not expounded like a thesis or a propaganda speech. In other words, the author must live in the real world with all its contradictory needs and not express feelings absorbed merely from books.

SCW, 185-7 (Q21§6)

3 The Operatic Conception of Life

It is not true that a bookish and non-innate sense of life is only to be found in certain inferior strata of the intelligentsia. Among the popular classes, too, there is a 'bookish' degeneration of life which comes not only from books but also from other instruments of diffusion of culture and ideas. Verdi's music, or rather the libretti and plots of the plays set to music by Verdi, are responsible for a whole range of 'artificial' poses in the life of people, for ways of thinking, for a 'style'. 'Artificial' is perhaps not the right word because among the popular classes this artificiality assumes naïve and moving forms. To many common people the baroque and the operatic appear as an extraordinarily fascinating way of feeling and acting, a means of escaping what they consider low, mean and contemptible in their lives and education in order to enter a more select sphere of great feelings and noble passions. Serial novels and below-stairs reading (all that literature which is mawkish, mellifluous and whimpery) provide the heroes and heroines. But opera is the most pestiferous because words set to music are more easily recalled, and they become matrices in which thought takes shape out of flux. Look at the writing-style of many common people: it is modelled on a repertory of clichés.

However, sarcasm is too corrosive. Remember that we are not dealing with superficial snobs, but with something deeply felt and experienced.

SCW, 377-8 (Q8§46)

4 Popular Literature. Operatic Taste

How can one combat in Italy the operatic taste of the man of the people when he comes into contact with literature, especially poetry? He thinks that poetry is characterized by certain external traits, largely rhyme and the hammering of metrical accents, but above all bombastic solemnity, oratory and operatic sentimentalism, a theatrical rendering coupled with a baroque vocabulary. One of the causes of this taste is to be sought in the fact that it has been formed not through private and individual meditations on poetry and art but through the collective expressions of oratory and theatre. 'Oratory' does not just refer to the notorious popular assemblies of the past but to a whole series of urban and rural instances. In the country, for example, funeral oratory and that of the local magistrate's court and law-courts is closely followed. All of these manifestations have a popular audience of 'fans' and, for the law-courts, an audience made up those waiting their turn, witnesses, etc. In certain district magistrate's courts, the hall is always full of these people who memorize the turns of phrase and the solemn words, feed on them and remember them. It is the same for the funerals of important people which always draw large crowds, often just to hear the speeches. Lectures in the cities have the same function and likewise the law-courts. Popular theatres, with what are called arena performances (and today perhaps sound films, but also the subtitles of old silent films, all done in an operatic style) are of the utmost importance for the creation of this taste and its corresponding language.

This taste can be combated in two principal ways: by ruthlessly criticizing it, and by circulating books of poetry written or translated in non-'elevated' language, where the feelings expressed are not rhetorical or operatic.

See the anthology compiled by Schiavi; Gori's poems. Perhaps translations of Marcel Martinet and other writers who are more numerous now than before: sober translations, like Togliatti's versions of Whitman and Martinet.[8]

SCW, 379-80 (Q14§19)

5 Oratory, Conversation, Culture

In his essay 'On the Athenian orators' (check the source), Macaulay attributes the facility with which even the most educated Greeks let themselves be dazzled by almost puerile sophisms to the predominance of live and spoken discourse in Greek life and education.[9] The habit of conversation in oratory generates a certain ability to find very quickly arguments that are apparently brilliant and that momentarily silence one's adversary and leave the listener dazed. This observation can also be applied to certain phenomena of modern life and to the ephemeral cultural preparation of some social groups like the urban workers. This partly explains why the peasants are distrustful of intellectuals speaking at political meetings. The peasants spend a long time chewing over the statements they have heard and whose sparkle has temporarily struck them. But, after the emotion stirred up by the words has cooled and their good sense has regained the upper hand, they see the deficiencies and the superficiality and become distrustful as a matter of course.

There is another important observation by Macaulay that is worth recalling. He reports a remark by Eugene of Savoy, who said that those who ended up being the greatest generals were those who were suddenly put in charge of the army and thus had to concern themselves with large-scale operations and manoeuvres. In other words, he who by profession has become a slave of trivial details is the victim of bureaucracy. He sees the tree, but loses sight of the wood; he sees the regulation and not the strategic plan. Yet the great captains could take care of both: the soldiers' rations as well as large-scale manoeuvres, etc.

One might add that the newspaper comes very close to oratory and conversation. Newspaper articles are usually written in a hurry, improvised, and are almost always like speeches made at public meetings because of the rapidity with which they are conceived and constructed. Few newspapers have specialist editors; when they do, their work is largely improvised. Specialization helps one to improvise better and more rapidly. Especially in the Italian newspapers there are no pondered and detailed periodical reviews for such sectors as the theatre and the economy. The contributors only partially make up for this and, lacking a unified approach, do not leave much of a mark. The solidity of a culture can thus be measured in three principal degrees: a) the culture of those who only read the newspapers, b) of those who also read magazines (not the variety ones), c) of those who read books – not to mention all those people (the majority) who do not even read the newspapers and who form their handful of opinions by attending occasional public meetings, such as those held in election periods, where they hear speakers of widely differing levels. Observations made in prison in Milan, where *Il Sole* was available: most of the prisoners, including politicals, read *La Gazzetta dello Sport*. Among about 2,500 prisoners, eighty copies at the most of *Il Sole* were sold. After the *Gazzetta dello Sport* the most read publications were the *Domenica del Corriere* and *Il Corriere dei Piccoli*.

It is evident that for a very long time the process of intellectual civilizing has especially taken an oratorical and rhetorical form, in other words one with no or too few written aids. The recollection of notions expounded by word of mouth was the basis of any education (and still is in some countries, for example Abyssinia). A new tradition began in the Humanist period when the 'written exercise' was introduced into schools and teaching. But already in the Middle Ages, with scholasticism, there was an implicit criticism of the tradition of teaching based on oratory and an effort to supply the memory with a firmer and more permanent skeleton. It can be seen, on reflection, that the importance given by the schools to the study of formal logic is in fact a reaction against the old loose style of exposition in teaching. Errors of formal logic are especially common in spoken arguments.

The art of printing then revolutionized the entire cultural world, giving to memory an aid of inestimable value and allowing an unprecedented extension of educational activity. Another kind of extension is thus implicit in this research, that of the qualitative as well as quantitative modifications (mass extension) brought about in ways of thinking by the technical and mechanical development of cultural organization.

Even today, spoken communication is a means of ideological diffusion which has a rapidity, a field of action, and an emotional simultaneity far greater than written communication (theatre, cinema and radio, with its loudspeakers in public squares, beat all forms of written communication, including books, magazines, newspapers and newspapers posted on walls) – but superficially, not in depth.

The academies and universities as organizations of culture and means for its diffusion. In the universities: oral lectures, seminars and workshops, the role of the great professor and the assistant. The role of the professional assistant and that of the 'elders of Santa Zita' in the school of Basilio Puoti, mentioned by De Sanctis,[10] namely the formation in the class itself of 'voluntary' assistants, spontaneously selected from among the students themselves, who help the teacher and give follow-up lectures, teaching others by practical example how to study.

Some of the preceding observations have been suggested by reading the *Popular Manual of Sociology*, which is imbued with all the deficiencies of conversation, the superficial argumentation of oratory, and the weak structure of formal logic. It would be interesting to use this book as an example of all the logical errors indicated by the schoolmen, recalling the very true observation that even ways of thinking are acquired and not innate and that, once acquired, their correct use corresponds to a professional qualification. Not to possess them, not to be aware of not possessing them, not to raise the problem of acquiring them through 'apprenticeship' is like claiming to be able to build an automobile while knowing that one must rely on the workshop and the tools of a village blacksmith. The study of the 'old formal logic' has now fallen into disrepute, and to an extent with good reason. But the problem of putting people through an apprenticeship in formal logic to act as a check upon the loose expository manner of oratory reappears as soon as one raises the fundamental problem of creating a new culture on a new social base, which does not have traditions in the way the old class of intellectuals does. A 'traditional intellectual bloc', with its complex and capillary articulations, is able to assimilate the 'apprenticeship in logic' element into the organic development of each of its individual components without even needing a distinct and specialized apprenticeship (just as the children of educated parents learn to speak 'grammatically', in other words they learn the language of educated people, without even having to go through specific and tiring grammatical exercises, unlike the children of parents who speak a dialect or Italian mixed with a dialect). But not even this occurs without difficulty, friction and loss of energy.

The development of the technical-professional schools in all the post-elementary grades has posed this problem anew in other forms. According to Professor G. Peano, even in the Polytechnic and the higher institutes of mathematics the students from grammar schools are better trained than those from the technical institutes. This better training is due to the overall 'humanist' instruction (history, literature, philosophy) as is more amply demonstrated in other notes (those dealing with the 'intellectuals' and the problem of education). Why cannot mathematics (the study of mathematics) give the same results, if it is so close to formal logic that it can be confused with it? As occurs in matters of teaching, if there is a similarity there is also an enormous difference. Mathematics is essentially based on the numerical series, on an infinite series of equivalences $(1 = 1)$ that can be combined in infinite ways. Formal logic tends to do the same, but only up to a point: its abstractness is maintained only at the beginning of the learning process, in the immediate and basic formulation of its principles, but it becomes concretely operative in the very discourse in which the abstract formulation is made. The language exercises that one does in the grammar school make it apparent after a time that in Latin-Italian and Greek-Italian translations there is never identity between the terms of the languages placed side by side, or at least that what identity there seemed to be at the beginning of the exercise (Italian 'rosa' = Latin 'rosa') becomes increasingly complicated as the 'apprenticeship' progresses, moves increasingly away from the mathematical scheme and arrives at a historical judgement or a judgement of taste, in which nuances, 'unique and individualized' expressiveness, prevail. And this occurs not only when one compares two languages, but also when one studies the history of a single 'language', where it emerges how a single sound/word varies semantically through time and how its function in a clause (morphological, syntactic and semantic as well as phonetic changes) varies too.

Note. An experiment made to demonstrate the evanescent impact of the 'oratorical' method of instruction: twelve well-educated persons repeat one to another a complex fact and then each person writes down what he has heard. Often, the twelve versions are amazingly different from the original account (which is written down as a control). Repeated, this experiment can be used to show that the memory which is not trained with appropriate methods should not be trusted.

SCW, 380-5 (Q16§21)

XIII JOURNALISM

Introduction

The notes on journalism included here are mainly of a prescriptive and 'ideal' kind. They deal, that is, with the kind of press Gramsci would like to see the Communist Party organize if it were not prevented from doing so by the conditions of Fascist repression and censorship at the time he was writing. His discussion is consequently drawn largely from his experience of pre-fascist journalism and is 'projected' onto the future as a model of an ideal party press, subdivided into publications of various types and levels suitable for different functions and different readerships. This forward projection gives the notes a rather generic and abstract character, yet it is this very character which is one of the reasons for their rich suggestiveness.

For in fact the notes dealing with the party press provide, beyond their immediate reference to problems of journalism, valuable indications of the way Gramsci conceived of the relations between party, class and class allies. This is because the relations between a party press and its readers are at the same time the relations between the party centre and its rank and file and allied groups: the press is a crucial means by which information is relayed to supporters and new members are won over. It is clear from these notes that Gramsci conceives of these relations in a dynamic, expansive way. He defines what he calls 'integral journalism' as one which is able to 'create and develop' its readers' needs and 'progressively enlarge' its readership (p.383). This expansive process will be paralysed if the press/party become bureaucratized. It is essential, rather that the press should stimulate the needs of its readers and develop their potential. In this way, 'the association [the party] does not set itself up as something fixed and definitive, but as tending to widen itself out towards a whole social grouping, which in turn is conceived as tending to unify the whole of humanity.' (p.382).

Similarly, Gramsci's discussion of types of periodical that can be imitated or adapted by the left is of great interest for what it indicates about his conception of social transformation in a situation where there are many different cultural strata. He touches here on the 'vanguardist' risks implicit in the conception according to which a mass movement can be created in a uniform way from a single political centre: what he calls 'organic diffusion from a homogeneous centre of a homogeneous way of thinking and acting'. Different people, he insists, are at different cultural and educational levels. If one wants to reach them all, one needs to make adjustments to these levels: he uses here the analogy of a single ray of light being refracted through a series of prisms (p.389). Gramsci's model of cultural influence here is still, in some respects, a 'totalizing' one. As such, it reflects an all-embracing conception of the party, hegemony and intellectual and moral reformation which is present in many other parts of his work. Nevertheless it is also clearly in intention an anti-bureaucratic, democratic conception because it bases cultural change in people's actual cultural experiences, capabilities and common sense, rather than seeing it as being imposed on them from without.

1 Ideological Material

A study of how the ideological structure of a dominant class is actually organized: namely the material organization aimed at maintaining, defending and developing the theoretical or ideological 'front'. Its most prominent and dynamic part is the press in general: publishing houses (which have an implicit and explicit programme and are attached to a particular tendency), political newspapers, periodicals of every kind, specific, literary, philological, popular, etc., various periodicals down to parish bulletins. If this kind of study were conducted on a national scale it would be gigantic: one could therefore do a series of studies for one city or for a number of cities. A news editor of a daily newspaper should have this study as a general outline for his work: indeed, he should make his own version of it. Think of all the wonderful leading articles one could write on the subject!

The press is the most dynamic part of this ideological structure, but not the only one. Everything which influences or is able to influence public opinion, directly or indirectly, belongs to it: libraries, schools, associations and clubs of various kinds, even architecture and the layout and names of streets. It would be impossible to explain the position retained by the Church in modern society if one were unaware of the constant and patient efforts it makes to develop continuously its particular section of this material structure of ideology. Such a study, done seriously, would be very important. Besides providing a living historical model of such a structure, it would accustom one to a more cautious and exact estimate of the forces acting in society. What resources can an innovative class set against this formidable complex of trenches and fortifications of the dominant class? The spirit of scission,[1] in other words the progressive acquisition of the consciousness of its own historical personality, a spirit of scission that must aim to spread itself from the protagonist class to the classes that are its potential allies – all this requires a complex ideological labour, the first condition of which is an exact knowledge of the field that must be cleared of its element of human 'mass'.

SCW, 389-40 (Q3§49)

2 Dilettantism and Discipline

Necessity of severe and rigorous internal criticism, with no lapses into conventionalism or half measures. There exists a tendency in historical materialism which stimulates (and supports) all the worst traditions of middle-level Italian culture and seems to correspond to certain traits of the Italian character: improvisation, 'flair', fatalistic laziness, mindless dilettantism, lack of intellectual discipline, moral and intellectual irresponsibility and disloyalty. Historical materialism destroys a whole set of prejudices and conventionalities, false senses of duty, hypocritical obligations; but it does not for this reason justify falling into scepticism and snobbish cynicism. Machiavellism had a similar result, because of an arbitrary extension or confusion between political 'morality' and private 'morality', between politics and ethics, though this confusion certainly did not exist in Machiavelli himself, far from it, since his greatness precisely consists in having distinguished politics from ethics. No permanent association can exist and retain a capacity for development if it is not sustained by certain ethical principles, which the association itself establishes for its single components in the interests of internal compactness and the homogeneity needed to achieve its ends. This does not mean that these principles are devoid of a universal character. Such would be the case if the association had itself as its end, if it were a sect or a criminal conspiracy (in this case only does it seem to me possible to say that politics and ethics are indistinguishable, precisely because the 'particular' is raised to a 'universal'). But a normal association thinks of itself as an aristocracy, an elite, a vanguard, and thus linked by a million threads to a given social grouping and through that to the whole of humanity. Therefore the association does not set itself up as something fixed and definitive, but as tending to widen itself out towards a whole social grouping, which in its turn is conceived as tending to unify the whole of humanity. All these relationships give a tendentially universal character to the group ethic, which has to be conceived as capable of becoming a norm of conduct for humanity as a whole. Politics is conceived as a process out of which a morality will emerge; that is to say, it is conceived as leading towards a form of social coexistence in which politics and morality along with it will alike be superseded. (Only from this historicist point of view can one explain the widely felt anguish about the contrast between private morality and public/political morality; this anguish is an unconscious and sentimentally uncritical reflection of the contradictions of contemporary society and of the absence of equality of moral subjects.)

But one cannot talk of elite/aristocracy/vanguard as if it were an indistinct and chaotic collectivity, into which, by intercession of a mysterious holy spirit or some other mysterious and metaphysical unknown deity, is poured the grace of intelligence, ability, education, technical preparation, etc.; and yet such a way of thinking is widespread. We find reflected here on a small scale what happened on a national scale when the state was conceived as something abstracted from the collectivity of citizens, as an eternal father who thought of everything, arranged everything etc; hence the absence of a real democracy, of a real national collective will, and hence, as a result of this passivity of individuals, the necessity of a more or less disguised despotism of the bureaucracy. The collectivity must be understood as the product of a development of will and of collective thought attained through concrete individual

effort and not through a process of destiny extraneous to
individual people; hence the need for an inner discipline and not
just an external and mechanical one. If there have to be polemics
and splits, there is no need to be afraid of confronting them and
getting beyond them; they are inevitable in these processes of
development, and to avoid them only means putting them off until
they indeed become dangerous and even catastrophic, etc.

SCW, 399-401 (Q6§79)

3 [Integral Journalism]

The type of journalism considered in these notes is one that could
be called 'integral' (the meaning of this term will become
increasingly clear in the course of the notes themselves), in other
words one that seeks not only to satisfy all the needs (of a given
category) of its public, but also to create and develop these needs,
to arouse its public and progressively enlarge it. If one examines
all the existing forms of journalism and the activities of newspaper
writing and publishing in general, one sees that each of them
presupposes other forces to be integrated or to be co-ordinated
with 'mechanically'. For a critical and comprehensive treatment of
the subject, it seems more opportune (for methodological and
didactic purposes) to presuppose another situation: that there
exists, as the starting point, a more or less homogeneous cultural
grouping (in the broad sense) of a given type, of a given level and
especially with a given general orientation; and that one wants to
use such a grouping to construct a self-sufficient, complete cultural
edifice, by beginning directly from ... language, from the means of
expression and reciprocal contact. The whole edifice should be
constructed according to 'rational', functional principles, in that
one has definite premises and wants to arrive at definite results.
Of course, the premises will necessarily change during the
elaboration of the 'plan' because, while it is true that a given end
presupposes given premises, it is also true that during the actual
elaboration of the given activity, the premises are necessarily
changed and transformed. One's knowledge of the end, as it
widens and becomes more concrete, reacts back upon the
premises, 'shaping' them increasingly. The objective existence of
the premises allows one to think of given ends, i.e. the given

premisses are such only in relation to certain ends that can be conceived concretely. But if the ends begin progressively to materialize, the initial premisses necessarily change, which in the meantime are no longer ... initial, and therefore the conceivable ends change too. This connection is rarely considered, even though it is immediately obvious. We see it manifested in businesses with 'planned' management, which do not function as pure machines but depend on a mode of thinking in which freedom and the spirit of enterprise ('doing deals') play a far greater part than the official mouthpieces of abstract (or maybe too 'concrete') 'freedom' and 'enterprise', stuck as they are in their present roles, would care to admit. This connection is therefore a real one, yet it is also true that the initial 'premisses' continually reappear, though under other conditions. Just because the new intake into a school learns its ABC, it doesn't mean that illiteracy disappears once and for all. Every year there will be a new intake which will have to be taught the ABC. Nevertheless it is clear that the rarer illiteracy becomes among adults, the less difficult it will be to get 100 per cent attendance in the elementary schools. There will always be 'illiterates', but they will tend to disappear above the normal age of five or six.

SCW, 408-9 (Q24§1)

4 Types of Periodical

Three fundamental types of review can roughly be distinguished, characterized by the way in which they are compiled, the type of reader they aim at, and the educative goals they want to achieve. The first type can be established by combining the editorial elements found in a specialized way in B. Croce's *La Critica*, F. Coppola's *Politica* and C. Barbagallo's *Nuova Rivista Storica*. The second type, 'critical-historical-bibliographical', by combining the elements that characterized the best issues of L. Russo's *Leonardo*, Rerum Scriptor's *L'Unità* and Prezzolini's *La Voce*.[3] The third type by combining some elements of the second type with the English type of weekly like the *Manchester Guardian Weekly* or *The Times Weekly*.[4]

Each of these types should be characterized by a highly unitary and non-anthological intellectual line; it should in other words have a homogeneous and disciplined editorial staff. Hence only a few 'principal' contributors should write the essential body of each number. The editorial line should be highly organized so as to make an intellectually homogeneous product, while respecting the necessary variety of styles and literary personalities. The editorial staff should have a written statute which, for what it is worth, can prevent incursions, conflicts and contradictions (for example, the content of each number should be approved by the majority of the staff before publication).

A unitary cultural organism which offered the three above-mentioned types of review to the various strata of the public (and a common spirit should in any case be present in all three types), backed up by a corresponding book publication, would satisfy the needs of a certain mass of readers, a mass which is intellectually most active, but only in the potential state, and which it matters most to develop, to make it think concretely, to transform it and homogenize it through a process of organic development that can lead it from simple common sense to coherent and systematic thought.

The critical-historical-bilbiographical type: analytic study of the material, carried out from the viewpoint of the reader of reviews who generally cannot read the works themselves. A scholar who examines a definite historical phenomenon in order to build up a general overview must carry out a whole series of preliminary investigations and intellectual operations of which only a small part end up being used. Such a labour would, however, be used for this average type of review, put in the hands of a reader who, in order to develop intellectually, needs to have access both to the overview and to the whole work of analysis which led to that particular result. The ordinary reader does not and cannot have a 'scientific' habit of mind, which is acquired only through specialized work. It is therefore necessary to help him obtain at least a 'sense' of it through an appropriate critical activity. It is not enough to give him concepts already elaborated and fixed in their 'definitive' form. Their concreteness, which lies in the process that has led to that form, escapes him. One should therefore offer him the whole process of reasoning and the intermediate connections in a well defined way and not just by referring to them. For example: a complex historical movement can be broken down in time and space and also into various levels. Thus, although

Catholic Action has always had a single and centralized leadership, it displays greater differences (and also contrasts) in regional attitude in different periods and according to the specific problem encountered (e.g. the agrarian problem, trade-union line, etc.).

In reviews of this type certain sections are indispensable or useful: 1) a political-scientific-philosophical encyclopaedic dictionary, in this sense: in each number one should publish one (or more) short encyclopaedic monographs on the political, philosophical and scientific concepts that come up time and again in the newspapers and the reviews and which the average reader has difficulty in understanding or actually misinterprets. In reality, every cultural current creates a language of its own, i.e. it participates in the general development of a determinate national language, introducing new terms, giving a new content to terms already in use, creating metaphors, using historical names to facilitate the understanding and judgement of specific contemporary situations, etc., etc. These monographs should be 'practical', related to needs that are really felt, and should be written with the average reader in mind. If possible, the compilers should be aware of the more frequent errors and should trace them back to their sources, which are the publications of scientific trash, like the 'Biblioteca Popolare Sonzogno' or the encyclopaedic dictionaries (Melzi, Premoli, Bonacci, etc.) or the most widely circulated popular encyclopaedias (Sonzogno, etc.). The monographs should not be presented in organic form (e.g. in alphabetical order or grouped according to subject matter), nor should they be allotted a pre-established space, as if a comprehensive work were already in view, but they should be immediately related to the subjects discussed in the review itself or in its more advanced or more elementary sister publications. The length of the treatment should be determined in each case not by the intrinsic importance of the subject but by its immediate journalistic interest (all this is stated as a general rule and with the usual grain of salt). In short, the encyclopaedic section must not be presented as a book published in instalments but, in each case, as a treatment of subjects that are interesting in themselves, from which a book might derive but not necessarily.

2) Linked to the preceding section is the one dealing with

biographies, to be understood in two senses: both in that a person's whole life can be of interest to the general culture of a given social stratum and in that an historical name can become part of an encyclopaedic dictionary because of its association with a particular concept or event. Thus, for example, one might need to mention Lord Carson in order to allude to the fact that the crisis of the parliamentary regime already existed before the world war and precisely in England, in the country where this regime appeared the most efficient and substantial. This does not mean that a full biography of Lord Carson has to be provided. A person of average culture is interested in only two biographical facts: a) in 1914, on the eve of the war, Lord Carson was in Ulster where he enlisted a very large armed corps in order to oppose, through an insurrection, the application of the Irish Home Rule Act, approved by Parliament which, according to the English saying, 'can do everything except make a man into a woman'; b) Lord Carson not only was not punished for 'high treason' but he became a minister a little later, on the outbreak of war. (It might be useful to present complete biographies in a separate section.)

3) Another section can include political-intellectual autobiographies. If these are well put together, with sincerity and simplicity, they can be of the utmost journalistic interest and can have a great formative effectiveness. The way in which one has succeeded in freeing oneself from a given provincial or corporate environment, as a result of what external impulses and with what internal conflicts, so as to achieve a historically superior personality, can suggest, in living form, an intellectual and moral course, besides being a document of cultural development in given epochs.

4) A fundamental section can be the critical-historical-bibliographical examination of the regional situations (meaning by region a differentiated geo-economic organism). Many people would like to know and study local situations, which are always interesting, but they do not know how or where to begin. They do not know the bibliographical material or how to research in libraries. One would therefore need to provide the general framework of a concrete problem (or a scientific theme) by listing the books that have dealt with it, the articles in specialized reviews, as well as the material that is still in a raw state (statistics, etc.), in the form of bibliographical summaries, with a special circulation for publications that are

unusual or in foreign languages. In addition to regions, this work can be done from various points of view for general problems, cultural problems, etc.

5) A systematic culling of data from newspapers and reviews for whatever is relevant to the fundamental sections: simply citing authors and titles, with brief remarks on their general tendency. This bibliographical section should be compiled for each number, and for some subjects it also needs to be retrospective.

6) Book-reviewing. Two types. A critical-informative type: on the assumption that the average reader cannot read the book in question, but that it is useful for him to know its content and conclusions. A theoretical-critical type: on the assumption that the reader has to read the book in question; therefore it is not simply summarized, but the critical objections that can be brought against it are voiced, its most interesting parts are stressed, points that have been sacrificed in it are developed, etc. This second type of book review is more appropriate to the higher level of periodical.

7) Critically presented bibliographical data, arranged by subject matter or groups of topics, on the literature concerning authors and the fundamental question for the conception of the world underlying the review published: for Italian authors and for Italian translations of foreign authors. This critical bibliography should be very detailed and meticulous, since one must remember that only through this work and this systematic critical elaboration can one arrive at the genuine source of a whole series of erroneous concepts put about without control or censorship. One must keep in mind that in every region of Italy, given the very rich variety of local traditions, there exist groups of different sizes characterized by particular ideological and psychological elements: 'each town has or has had its local saint, hence its own cult and its own chapel.'

The unitary national elaboration of a homogeneous collective consciousness demands a wide range of conditions and initiatives. Diffusion from a homogeneous centre of a homogeneous way of thinking and acting is the principal condition, but it must not and cannot be the only one. A very common error is that of thinking that every social stratum elaborates its consciousness and its culture in the same way, with the same methods, namely the methods of the professional intellectuals. The intellectual is a 'professional', a skilled worker who knows how his own specialized 'machines' function. He has an 'apprenticeship' and a 'Taylor system' of his own. It is childish and illusory to attribute to everyone this acquired and not innate ability, just as it would be childish to believe that any unskilled worker can drive a train. It is childish to think that a 'clear concept', suitably circulated, is inserted in various consciousnesses with the same 'organizing' effects of diffused clarity: this is an 'enlightenment' error. The ability of the professional intellectual adroitly to combine induction and deduction, to generalize without falling into empty formalism, to transport from one sphere of judgement to another certain criteria of discrimination, adapting them to new conditions, is a 'specialization', a 'qualification'. It is not something given to ordinary common sense. This is why the premise of 'organic diffusion from a homogeneous centre of a homogeneous way of thinking and acting' is not enough. When a ray of light passes through different prisms it is refracted differently: if you want the same refraction, you need to make a whole series of rectifications of each prism.

Patient and systematic 'repetition' is a fundamental methodological principle. But this must not be a mechanical, 'obsessive', material repetition, but an adaptation of each concept to the different peculiarities and cultural traditions. The concept must be repeatedly presented in all its positive aspects and in its traditional negations, arranging each partial aspect into the totality. Finding the real identity beneath the apparent contradiction and differentiation, and finding the substantial diversity beneath the apparent identity, is the most delicate, misunderstood and yet essential endowment of the critic of ideas and the historian of historical developments. The educative-formative work that a homogeneous cultural centre carries out, the elaboration of a critical consciousness that it promotes and favours on a specific historical base which contains the concrete premises for such an elaboration, cannot be limited to the simple theoretical enunciation of 'clear' methodological principles: this would be to proceed merely in the manner of the eighteenth-century *philosophes*. The work needed is complex and must be articulated and graduated. It requires a combination of deduction and induction, formal logic and dialectic, identification and distinction, positive demonstration and the destruction of the old. And not in the abstract but in the concrete, on the basis of the real and of actual experience. But how can one know what the most widespread and entrenched errors are? Evidently, it is impossible to have 'statistics' on ways of thinking and single individual opinions, with all the combinations of them found in larger and smaller groups, statistics that give an organic and systematic picture of the real cultural situation and the ways in which the 'common sense' is really manifested. The only alternative is the systematic review of the literature that is most widely circulated and most accepted by the people, combined with the study and criticism of the ideological currents of the past, each of which 'may' have left a deposit, combining variously with the preceding and successive layers.

A more general criterion enters into this same order of observations: changes in ways of thinking, in beliefs, in opinions do not occur through rapid, simultaneous and generalized 'explosions'. Rather, they are almost always the result of 'successive combinations' determined by the most disparate and uncontrollable 'formulas of authority'. The illusion that there are 'explosions' comes from a lack of critical penetration. Methods of traction did not develop directly from the animal-drawn coach to the modern electric express train, but passed through a series of intermediate combinations, some of which are still in existence (such as animal traction on rails, etc.), and railway stock which has become outdated in the United States is still used for many years in China and represents a technological advance there. Likewise in the cultural sphere the different ideological strata are variously combined and what has become 'scrap iron' in the city is still a 'utensil' in the provinces. Indeed, in the cultural sphere 'explosions' are even less frequent and less intense than in the technological sphere where, at least at the highest level, an innovation spreads with relative rapidity and simultaneity. The 'explosion' of political passions accumulated in a period of technological transformations, which lack correspondingly new forms of adequate juridical organization but which instead are immediately accompanied by a degree of direct and indirect coercion, is confused with cultural transformations, which are slow and gradual. Whereas passion is impulsive, culture is the product of a complex process of elaboration. (The reference to the fact that at times what has become 'scrap iron' in the city is still a 'utensil' in the provinces can be usefully developed.)

SCW, 412-9 (Q24§3)

XIV   ART AND THE
STRUGGLE FOR A NEW CIVILIZATION

Introduction

The discussions of culture and literature in the prison notebooks (1929-35) coincide in time with the great debates on the European left over realism and modernism, proletarian literature, popular frontism and socialist realism. At first sight they appear tangential to those debates, but on closer inspection they overlap with several of their key themes – most notably the relation between artistic freedom and political direction – as well as developing a quite distinct perspective.

This can be seen clearly in one of the most interesting notes, an indirect 'dialogue' with the French Communist Paul Nizan. In this note ('Literary Criticism'), which was written in 1933, Gramsci discusses Nizan's article 'Littérature révolutionnaire en France' (1932), which he knew not at first hand but only as it was reported and paraphrased by a hostile reviewer in *Critica Fascista*, one of the journals he was permitted to read in prison. Nizan was writing as a member of the Association des Ecrivains et des Artistes Révolutionnaires (AEAR), an international organization which then included among its members John Dos Passos, Anna Seghers, Louis Aragon and Luis Buñuel. The line pursued by the AEAR, Nizan argues, is so closely tied to the aims of the proletariat that, as the class struggle and the world crisis intensifies, as war draws nearer, the most honest of the 'pre-revolutionary' writers from the other literary currents will be drawn to it, whereas the unreconstructed petty-bourgeois members of those groups will show their true colours and go over to the fascist camp.

Gramsci's main objection to Nizan's position is that it is too 'cosmopolitan'. By 'backing' just one cultural line, that of the AEAR, at the expense of all the others, Nizan ignores the necessity for cultural change to start from below, from where people really are in cultural terms, and to move through a 'national' stage before it can become genuinely internationalist. In particular Nizan, for Gramsci, is too dismissive of popular literature, which he treats as a form of opiate foisted upon the working class by their bourgeois masters. In contrast to these positions, Gramsci insists that the strategies for a new culture must be multiple, that one must back several currents simultaneously, and that the new literature must 'sink its roots into the humus of popular culture as it is, with its tastes and tendencies and with its moral and intellectual world, even if it is backward and conventional' (p.397).

These arguments are related both to Gramsci's opposition elsewhere in the notebooks to cosmopolitan or pseudo-internationalist outlooks (for instance his criticisms of Trotsky) and to his opposition to a narrowly artistic approach to culture and criticism. He argues that literary criticism should overlap and fuse with social criticism, with the ideological struggle to form a new culture. He takes respectively as his positive and negative models of literary criticism the nineteenth-century intellectual Francesco De Sanctis (a left democrat who sought to connect artistic criticism to political and social criticism) and Benedetto Croce (a liberal-conservative concerned to separate aesthetics from history and practical activity).

Gramsci's discussion of artistic freedom and political direction is equally distinctive. Another of his arguments against Nizan's position of supporting only the most 'correct' political line in art is that artists and writers must 'necessarily have a less precise and definite outlook' than politicians. He also writes ('Criteria of Literary Criticism'): 'When the politician put pressure on the art of his time to express a particular cultural world, his activity is one of politics, not of artistic criticism.' These arguments, despite first appearances, do not add up to a defence of the autonomy of the individual artist vis-à-vis all forms of political direction. Indeed Gramsci is concerned precisely with 'the formation of specific cultural currents', which he sees as entailing 'rational' forms of conformism, in other words the voluntary acceptance and participation by artists in a progressive cultural tendency. What he does reject are merely 'factitious', 'external' and coercive attempts to create a new artistic style by political fiat. Against this he argues that when artists feel the historical necessity of a new culture, they will accept its rationality voluntarily and produce works which follow the curve of the historical tendency. The precise forms of

their works cannot be predicted in advance. All one can say is that
with the development of the economic and social forces, with the
rise of the working class (a 'new social group that enters history
with a hegemonic attitude', p.395) a new culture will be born
which will generate its own artists and its own works of art.

1 Art and the Struggle for a New Civilization

The artistic relationship brings out, especially in relation to the
philosophy of praxis, the fatuous naïvety of the parrots who think
that with a few brief and stereotyped formulas they possess the key
to open all doors (those keys are actually called 'picklocks').

Two writers can represent (express) the same socio-historical
moment, but one can be an artist and the other a mere scribbler.
To try to deal with the question just by describing what the two
represent or express socially, that is, by summarizing more or less
thoroughly the characteristics of a specific socio-historical
moment, hardly touches at all upon the artistic problem. All this
can be useful and necessary, indeed it certainly is, but in another
field: that of political criticism, the criticism of social life, involving
the struggle to destroy and to overcome certain feelings and
beliefs, certain attitudes towards life and the world. This is not the
criticism or the history of art, nor can it be presented as such –
except at the expense of creating confusion and a retarding or
stagnation of scientific concepts: in other words a failure precisely
to pursue the intrinsic aims of cultural struggle.

A given socio-historical moment is never homogeneous; on the
contrary, it is rich in contradictions. It acquires a 'personality' and
is a 'moment' of development in that a certain fundamental
activity of life prevails over others and represents a historical
'peak': but this presupposes a hierarchy, a contrast, a struggle.
The person who represents this prevailing activity, this historical
'peak', should represent the given moment; but how should one
who represents the other activities and elements be judged? Are
not these also 'representative'? And is not the person who
expresses 'reactionary' and anachronistic elements also representative of the 'moment'? Or should he be considered representative

who expresses all those contrasting forces and elements in conflict among themselves, that is, the one who represents the contradiction of the socio-historical whole?

It could also be said that a critique of literary civilization, a struggle to create a new culture, is artistic in the sense that a new art will be born from the new culture, but this appears to be a sophism. At any rate, it is perhaps on the basis of such presuppositions that one can best understand the relationship between De Sanctis and Croce and the controversy over form and content. De Sanctis's criticism is militant, not 'frigidly' aesthetic; it belongs to a period of cultural struggles and contrasts between antagonistic conceptions of life. Analyses of content, criticism of the 'structure' of works, that is, the logical, historical and topical coherence of the mass of artistically represented feelings, are connected to this cultural struggle. The profound humanity and humanism of De Sanctis, which even today make this critic so congenial, would seem to consist precisely in this. It is good to feel in him the impassioned fervour of one who is committed, one who has strong moral and political convictions and does not hide them nor even attempt to. Croce succeeds in distinguishing these various aspects of the critic which in De Sanctis were organically united and fused. Croce has the same cutural motives as De Sanctis, but at a time when these are in a period of expansion and triumph. The struggle continues; but it is a struggle for a refinement of culture (a certain type of culture) and not for its right to live: romantic fervour and passion have subsided into a superior serenity and an indulgence full of *bonhomie*. Even in Croce, though, this position is not permanent. A new phase follows in which cracks appear in the serenity and indulgence, and acrimony and a barely repressed anger emerge: a defensive, not an aggressive and impassioned phase, hence not to be compared with that of De Sanctis.

In short, the type of literary criticism suitable to the philosophy of praxis is offered by De Sanctis, not by Croce or by anyone else (least of all by Carducci).[1] It must fuse the struggle for a new culture (that is, for a new humanism) and criticism of social life, feelings and conceptions of the world with aesthetic or purely artistic criticism, and it must do so with heat and passion, even if it takes the form of sarcasm.

SCW, 93-5 (Q23§3)

2 Art and Culture

It seems evident that, to be precise, one should speak of a struggle for a 'new culture' and not for a 'new art' (in the immediate sense). To be precise, perhaps it cannot even be said that the struggle is for a new artistic content apart from form because content cannot be considered abstractly, in separation from form. To fight for a new art would mean to fight to create new individual artists, which is absurd since artists cannot be created artificially. One must speak of a struggle for a new culture, that is, for a new moral life that cannot but be intimately connected to a new intuition of life, until it becomes a new way of feeling and seeing reality and, therefore, a world intimately ingrained in 'possible artists' and 'possible works of art'.

Although one cannot artificially create individual artists, this does not therefore mean that the new cultural world for which one is fighting, by stirring up passions and human warmth, does not necessarily stir up 'new artists'. In other words, one cannot say that Tom, Dick and Harry will become artists, but one can say that new artists will be born from the movement. A new social group that enters history with a hegemonic attitude, with a self-confidence which it initially did not have, cannot but stir up from deep within itself personalities who would not previously have found sufficient strength to express themselves fully in a particular direction.

Therefore, one cannot talk about a new 'poetic aura' being formed – to use a phrase that was popular a few years ago. 'Poetic aura' is only a metaphor to express the ensemble of those artists who have already formed and emerged, or at least the process of formation and emergence which has begun and is already consolidated.

SCW, 98 (Q23§6)

3 Literary Criticism

See Argo's polemical article against Paul Nizan ('Idee d'oltre confine' [Ideas from across the border]) in the March 1933 issue of *Educazione Fascista*, concerning the conception of a new literature that should arise from an integral moral and intellectual renewal.

Nizan seems to pose the problem well by beginning with a definition of an integral renewal of cultural premisses, thus limiting the very field to be investigated. Argo's only valid objection is this: the impossibility of going beyond a national and autochthonous stage of the new literature and the 'cosmopolitan' dangers of Nizan's conceptions. From this point of view, many of Nizan's criticisms of groups of French intellectuals should be reconsidered: the *Nouvelle Revue Française*, 'populism' and so on, including the *Monde* group; not because his criticism is politically off-target, but because the new literature must necessarily manifest itself 'nationally', in relatively hybrid and different combinations and alloys. One must examine and study the entire current objectively.

Besides, one must keep the following criterion in mind when dealing with the relationship between literature and politics: the literary man must necessarily have a less precise and definite outlook than the politician. He must be less 'sectarian', if one can put it this way, but in a 'contradictory' way. For the politician, every 'fixed' image is *a priori* reactionary: he considers the entire movement in its development. The artist, however, must have 'fixed' images that are cast into their definite form. The politician imagines man as he is and, at the same time, how he should be in order to reach a specific goal. His task is precisely to stir men up, to get them to leave their present life behind in order to become collectively able to reach the proposed goal, that is, to get them to 'conform' to the goal. The artist necessarily and realistically depicts 'that which is', at a given moment (the personal, the non-conformist, etc.). From the political point of view, therefore, the politician will never be satisfied with the artist and will never be able to be: he will find him always behind the times, always anachronistic and overtaken by the real flow of events. If history is a continuous process of liberation and self-awareness, it is evident that every stage (historical and in this case cultural) will be immediately surmounted and will no longer hold any interest. It is this, it seems to me, that must be kept in mind when evaluating Nizan's opinions about various groups.

From the objective point of view, though, just as Voltaire is still 'current' for certain strata of the population, so can these literary groups and the combinations which they represent be, and indeed are. In this case, 'objective' means that moral and intellectual renewal does not develop simultaneously in all of the social strata. On the contrary, it is worth repeating that even today many people are Ptolemaic and not Copernican. There are many 'conformisms', many struggles for new 'conformisms' and various combinations of that which already exists (variously expressed) and that which one is working to bring about (and there are many people who are working in this direction). It is a serious error to adopt a 'single' progressive strategy according to which each new gain accumulates and becomes the premiss of further gains. Not only are the strategies multiple, but even in the 'most progressive' ones there are retrogressive moments. Furthermore, Nizan does not know how to deal with so-called 'popular literature', that is, with the success of serial literature (adventure stories, detective stories, thrillers) among the masses, a success that is assisted by the cinema and the newspapers. And yet, it is this question that represents the major part of the problem of a new literature as the expression of moral and intellectual renewal, for only from the readers of serial literature can one select a sufficient and necessary public for creating the cultural base of the new literature. It appears to me that the problem is this: how to create a body of writers who are, artistically, to serial literature what Dostoyevsky was to Sue and Soulié or, with respect to the detective story, what Chesterton was to Conan Doyle and Wallace. With this aim in mind, one must abandon many prejudices, but above all it should be remembered not only that one cannot have a monopoly but also that one is faced with a formidable organization of publishing interests.

The most common prejudice is this: that the new literature has to identify itself with an artistic school of intellectual origins, as was the case with Futurism. The premiss of the new literature cannot but be historical, political and popular. It must aim at elaborating that which already is, whether polemically or in some other way does not matter. What does matter, though, is that it sink its roots into the humus of popular culture as it is, with its tastes and tendencies and with its moral and intellectual world, even if it is backward and conventional.

SCW, 99-102 (Q15§58)

4 Criteria of Literary Criticism

Is the concept that art is art and not 'willed' and directed political
propaganda in itself an obstacle to the formation of specific
cultural currents that reflect their time and contribute to the
strengthening of specific political currents? It seems not; indeed it
seems that such a concept poses the problem in more radical
terms, those of a more efficient and conclusive criticism. Given the
principle that one should look only to the artistic character of the
work of art, this does not in the least prevent one from
investigating the mass of feelings and the attitude towards life
present in the work of art itself. Indeed, one need only consult De
Sanctis and Croce himself to see that this is accepted by modern
currents in aesthetics. What is excluded is the idea that a work is
beautiful because of its moral and political content and not for its
form, with which the abstract content is fused and becomes one.
Furthermore, one should examine whether a work of art might not
have failed because the author was diverted by external practical
(that is, artificial and insincere) preoccupations. The crucial point
of the polemic seems to be this: X 'wants' to express a definite
content in an artful way and fails to create a work of art. The
artistic failure of this work shows that in X's hands that particular
content was unpliable and refractory (since he has proven to be an
artist in other works that he has really felt and experienced). It
also shows that his enthusiasm was fictitious and externally willed,
that in that specific case he was not really an artist, but a servant
who wanted to please his masters. There are, then, two sets of
facts: one aesthetic (to do with pure art), the other politico-
cultural (that is, frankly political). The possibility of coming to
deny the artistic character of a work can help the political critic
proper to demonstrate that, as an artist, X does not belong to that
particular political world. And since his personality is prevalently
artistic, that world does not have any influence on him at a deep
and intimate level, and does not exist for him. As far as politics is
concerned, therefore, X is play-acting, he wants to be taken for
what he is not, etc., etc. The political critic, then, denounces him
as a 'political opportunist', not as an artist.

When the politician puts pressure on the art of his time to
express a particular cultural world, his activity is one of politics,
not of artistic criticism. If the cultural world for which one is

fighting is a living and necessary fact, its expansiveness will be irresistible and it will find its artists. Yet if, despite pressure, this irresistibility does not appear and is not effective, it means that the world in question was artificial and fictitious, a cardboard lucubration of mediocre men who complain that those of major stature do not agree with them. The very way of posing the question can be an indication of the firmness of such a moral and cultural world. In fact, so-called 'calligraphism'[2] is nothing but the defence thrown up by petty artists who opportunistically assert certain principles but who feel incapable of expressing them artistically (i.e., in their own proper sphere of activity) and drivel on about pure form which is its own content, etc., etc. The formal principle of the distinction and the unity in circulation of the spiritual categories, abstract through it is, allows one to grasp the actual truth and to criticize the arbitrariness and pseudo-life of those who are not prepared to put their cards on the table or who are simply second-rate individuals whom chance has placed in positions of authority.

SCW, 108-10 (Q15§38)

5 Sincerity (or Spontaneity) and Discipline

Is sincerity (or spontaneity) always a merit and a value? Only if disciplined. Sincerity (and spontaneity) means the maximum degree of individualism, even in the sense of idiosyncrasy (in this case originality is equal to idiom). An individual is historically original when he gives maximum prominence to social being, without which he would be an 'idiot' (in the etymological sense, which is however not far from the common and vulgar sense).[3] There is a romantic meaning attached to such words as originality, personality and sincerity, and this meaning is historically justified in that it springs from an attempt to counteract a certain essentially 'Jesuitical' conformism, an artificial and fictitious conformism created superficially for the interests of a small group or clique, and not for those of a vanguard.

There is also a 'rational' form of conformism that corresponds to necessity, to the minimum amount of force needed to obtain a useful result. The discipline involved must be exalted and promoted and made 'spontaneous' or 'sincere'. Conformism, then, means nothing other than 'sociality', but it is nice to use the word 'conformism' precisely because it annoys imbeciles. This does not mean that one cannot form a personality or be original, but it makes matters more difficult. It is too easy to be original by doing the opposite of what everyone else is doing; this is just mechanical. It is too easy to speak differently from others, to play with neologisms, whereas it is difficult to distinguish oneself from others without doing acrobatics. Today people try to be original and to have a personality on the cheap. Prisons and mental asylums are full of original men with strong personalities. What is really difficult is to put the stress on discipline and sociality and still profess sincerity, spontaneity, originality and personality. Nor can one say that conformism is too easy and reduces the world to a monastery. What is 'real conformism', what is the most useful and freest form of behaviour that is 'rational' in that it obeys 'necessity'? In other words, what is 'necessity'? Everyone is led to make of himself the archetype of 'fashion' and 'sociality', to offer himself as the 'model'. Therefore, sociality or conformism is the result of a cultural (but not only cultural) struggle; it is an 'objective' or universal fact, just as the 'necessity' on which the edifice of liberty is built cannot but be objective and universal. Liberty and free will, etc.

In literature (art), sincerity and spontaneity are opposed to calculation or mechanical procedures. This, too, can be a false conformism or sociality, that is, a tendency to settle down into customary and received ideas. There is the classical example of Nino Berrini who 'catalogues' the past and seeks to be original by doing what is absent from the files. Berrini's principles for the theatre are as follows: 1) the length of the work: determine the average length, basing it on those works which have been successful; 2) the study of endings: which ones have been successful and have won applause; 3) the study of combinations: for example, in the bourgeois sexual drama involving husband, wife and lover, see what combinations are exploited the most and, through elimination, 'invent' new combinations discovered in this mechanical way. In this way Berrini found that a drama must not have over 50,000 words, that is it must not last beyond a specific time. Every act or principal scene must culminate in a given way and this way is studied experimentally, according to an average of those feelings and stimuli that have been traditionally successful.

Undoubtedly, with these criteria a box-office catastrophe is impossible.[4] But is this 'conformism' or 'sociality' in the sense explained above? Of course not. It is an accommodation to what already exists.

Discipline also means a study of the past, since the past is an element both of the present and the future. It is not, though, an 'idle' element, but a necessary one in that it is a language, an element of a necessary 'uniformity' and not of an 'idle' and slothful uniformity.

SCW, 124-5 (Q14§61)

6 ['Functional' Literature]

What in literature corresponds to 'rationalism' in architecture? Clearly, literature based on a plan or on a pre-established social course, in other words, 'functional' literature. It is strange that rationalism is acclaimed and justified in architecture and not in the other arts. There must be a misunderstanding. Is it perhaps that architecture alone has practical aims? This certainly looks like being the case because architecture is used to build houses; but this is not the point: it is a question of 'necessity'. One might say that houses are more necessary than the products of the other arts, meaning by this that everybody needs a house, while the products of the other arts are necessary only for intellectuals, for the cultured. One should then conclude that it is precisely the 'practical' people who propose to make all the arts necessary for everybody, to make everybody 'artists'.

Social coercion again! How people do blather against this coercion! Nobody sees that it is merely a word! Coercion, direction and planning are nothing more than a terrain for selecting artists. They are to be chosen for practical purposes, in a field in which will and coercion are perfectly justified. As if there has not always been some form of coercion! Just because it is exerted unconsciously by the environment and by single individuals, and not by a central power or a centralized force, does it cease to be coercion? Ultimately, it is always a question of 'rationalism' versus the individual will. Therefore, coercion is not the issue, but whether we are dealing with an authentic rationalism, a real functionalism, or with an act of the will. This is all. Coercion is such only for those who reject it, not for those who accept it. If it goes hand in hand with the development of the social forces, it is not coercion but the 'revelation' of cultural truth obtained by an accelerated method. One can say of coercion what the religious say of predestination: for the 'willing' it is not predestination, but free will. In fact there is opposition to the concept of coercion because it involves a struggle against intellectuals, especially traditional and traditionalist intellectuals who are prepared at most to concede that innovations can be brought in little by little, gradually.

It is curious that in architecture rationalism is contrasted with 'decorativism', which is called 'industrial art'. Curious but correct. In fact, any artistic manifestation that is meant to satisfy the taste of individual wealthy buyers, to 'embellish' their lives as they say, should always be called industrial. When art, especially in its collective forms, aims to create a mass taste, to elevate this taste, it is not 'industrial', but disinterested: i.e. it is art.

The concept of rationalism or 'functionalism' in architecture seems to me to be rich in consequences and principles for cultural politics. It is no accident that the concept arose in the present period of 'socialization' (in the broad sense) and of attempts by central forces to organize the great masses against the remnants of individualism and the aesthetics of individualism in cultural politics.

SCW, 129-31 (Q14§65)

NOTES

I Socialism and Marxism 1917–1918

1. 'Servants of the Queen', in *The Jungle Book*, London 1894.
2. Giuseppe Prezzolini, 'Il processo della democrazia', *Il Popolo d'Italia*, 24 April 1918. The remainder of this paragraph reproduces almost exactly the text of Prezzolini's article.
3. This article in its full version starts by replying to a series of articles in *La Stampa*, the Turin newspaper linked to Giolitti, on the divisions in the PSI. The PSI reformists had argued that Socialist collaboration was necessary if the nation was 'to move, act and break with inertia' (SPW I, p. 43).

II Working-Class Education and Culture

1. Enrico Leone, revolutionary syndicalist. The article referred to is 'Democrazia in frantumi' ('Democracy in Smithereens') in *Guerra di Classe* (journal of the syndicalist union USI), 15 January 1916: 'The modern worker learns far more from his class organizations than from the official book of knowledge ... There is thus no salvation except in workerism, in the class with calloused hands and with brains uncontaminated by culture and the infection of the classroom ... away with politics! The road is open. Ignorance has discovered the method of the general strike and feeds upon it, making the idea grow great. Wars are just what is needed to root this idea in the minds of the ignorant and primitive class.'
2. *Avanguardia* was the journal of the Socialist youth federation FGSI. At its national congress at Bologna in September 1912 the discussion on youth education and culture had been opened by Amadeo Bordiga. Angelo Tasca, one of the delegates from Turin, had intervened arguing that the party needed a full-scale theoretical and cultural renewal and that *Avanguardia* should give priority to education and culture. Bordiga opposed this: 'No one becomes a socialist through education but through real-life necessities imposed by the class they belong to.' Tasca replied that Bordiga 'wants to "ignite", we want to "evangelize" ... We want to preach socialism in the hope or certainty that we shall "ignite", not to "ignite" in the hope or certainty that socialists will be produced.'
3. The reference is to a meeting of the Turin council in December 1916 to discuss a council-funded vocational training institute for young workers. Zino Zini was a Socialist councillor and teacher of philosophy who favoured a humanities element in the institute's curriculum. Francesco Sincero, one of the Liberal majority, argued that such an approach was

404 *Notes to pp. 62-122*

inappropriate to the low educational level of the workers and said that the institute's role should be restricted to technical education.

4. This article appeared in *L'Ordine Nuovo* in 1919 and is part of its discussions of factory councils and council democracy (see Section III). 'Council' here corresponds to the Russian word *soviet*.

5. The PSI reformists accused the *Ordine Nuovo* group of 'Bergsonian voluntarism'. Henri Bergson (1859-1941) had been one of the early intellectual influences on Gramsci. He criticized mechanistic theories and exalted the freedom of the will (voluntarism) and chance.

6. Lenin, *The State and Revolution*, in *Collected Works*, Volume 25, p. 471: 'It follows that under communism there remains for a time not only bourgeois right, but even the bourgeois state, without the bourgeoisie!'

III Factory Councils and Socialist Democracy

1. Filippo Turati (1857-1932), leading PSI reformist. Minos was famous in Greek legend as a pitiless judge.

2. This article appeared on the first Sunday of the occupation of the factories in September 1920.

3. The decision by FIOM to end the factory occupations was submitted to the workers' approval by referendum on 24 September 1920. A small majority approved the agreement.

4. *Umanità Nova* was the newspaper of the Unione Anarchica Italiana whose leading spirit was Errico Malatesta. The phrase 'the Turin communists' in this article refers to the communist fraction within the PSI; by the time this article was written, that fraction had, with others, split from the Socialists to form the Communist Party.

5. Giacinto Menotti Serrati (1872-1926), PSI maximalist leader. In October 1919 he had called for the PSI's affiliation to the Third International (Comintern). He refused, however, to comply with one of the key conditions of affiliation – expulsion of the reformists – set out by Lenin at the Second Comintern Congress in 1920. He thereby helped provoke the splitting of the PSI and the formation of the Communist Party in January 1921. He finally expelled the reformists only in 1922.

IV Communism 1919-1924

1. In *Le Père Goriot*, Goriot asks Rastignac whether he would still eat oranges if he knew that each time he did so someone would die in China. Rastignac answers that he would, since oranges are a familiar part of his everyday world, while China is far off and unknown.

2. This article was written just before the Seventeenth Congress of the PSI at Livorno (15-21 January 1921): see introduction to this Section.

3. Reggio Emilia in central Italy was a principal bastion of reformist socialism.

4. On 16 December 1920 *Avanti!* carried an article by Serrati (see

Section III note 5) which opposed Lenin's call for the expulsion of the reformists and defended party unity. The reformists, he maintained, were not counter-revolutionary, the bourgeoisie was strong and revolution was not on the immediate agenda ('Risposta di un comunista unitario al compagno Lenin': an edited version is in G. Manacorda (ed.), *Il socialismo nella storia d'Italia*, Bari 1966, pp. 488-501).

5. The Italian Popular Party (PPI) was a mass Catholic party founded by Luigi Sturzo in January 1919. It won 100 seats in the elections of that year (the first with both manhood suffrage and proportional representation) and became the second largest party in parliament after the PSI (155 seats). After Mussolini took power the PPI split over the stance to be adopted towards the Fascists and was progressively abandoned by the pro-fascist Catholic right (Vatican, Jesuits) before being suppressed, like the other opposition parties, in November 1926.

6. On 3 August 1921, the PSI parliamentary group signed in Rome a 'pacification pact' with the Fascist deputies, in the hope of securing an end to Fascist violence; in fact the raids barely abated, and the pact was annulled.

7. At Treviso on 12 July 1921, Fascist squads destroyed the premises of the local Catholic and Republican newspapers. At Sarzana on 21 July a small force of *carabinieri* dispersed an armed Fascist expedition of 600. At Roccastrada on 1 July a Fascist expedition wrecked the home of the Socialist mayor and later forced him to resign. A further raid was carried out on 24 July.

8. On Turati see note 1 to Section III above. Ludovico D'Aragona (1876-1961) was the reformist general secretary of the CGL.

9. Marcellus, during the Punic wars between Rome and Carthage, was the first Roman general to show that Hannibal was not invincible.

10. The reference is to the right-wing minority in the PCdI around Angelo Tasca.

11. Arturo Caroti was an important maximalist leader from Pisa, a parliamentary deputy, who joined the Communist Party when it was founded. His son Leopoldo, referred to here, had launched a journal called *Spartacus* at Livorno in 1919, while still a student.

V Fascist Reaction and Communist Strategy 1924-1926

1. Roberto Farinacci, 'intransigent' Fascist, party secretary 1924-26; Giovanni Amendola, Liberal parliamentarian, a leader of the Aventine opposition to Fascism in 1924; Luigi Sturzo, leader of the Catholic Popular Party; Filippo Turati, reformist Socialist leader. Gramsci's characterization here of the 'legalitarian' opposition to Fascism as 'semi-fascism' reflected a view becoming widespread in the Comintern in 1924. Bordiga had told the Fifth Congress in July that 'all bourgeois parties, particularly social democracy, take on a more and more fascist character', and Stalin was to call social democracy in September 'objectively the moderate wing of fascism'.

2. The Sicilian Fasci (*fascio* in the nineteenth century meant simply 'band' or organization) was the name of a movement of broad popular discontent in Sicily in 1893-94 which linked poor peasants, sulphur miners and elements of the urban middle classes around socialist and autonomist demands. The movement was violently repressed by Prime Minister Francesco Crispi. The same period saw the formation of the PSI (1892) and working-class agitations in many cities (1898), in turn put down by force, most brutally in Milan.

3. The *podestà* was the centrally appointed Fascist official at the level of the commune (the lowest tier of Italian local government), who replaced the pre-Fascist elected *sindaco* (mayor), communal council and executive.

4. Since 1922 the PSI had been split into two parties: a maximalist party (which retained the name PSI) and a reformist minority party (named PSU) around Turati (see note 1 to Section III).

5. Antonio Graziadei (1873-1953) leading PCdI right-winger, had published in 1923 a revisionist text (*Prezzo e sovraprezzo nell'economia capitalistica*) for which he had been attacked by Zinoviev at the Fifth Congress of the Comintern (1924). He was to be expelled from the party in 1928.

6. In August 1917 Kornilov (commander-in-chief of the Russian armed forces) assembled troops to march on Petrograd and forestall a Bolshevik seizure of power. Kerensky (head of the provisional government) ordered his arrest. The episode served to strengthen the Bolsheviks.

7. i.e. NEP (New Economic Policy) man.

8. The article from which this quotation is taken is in SPW I, pp. 146-9.

9. See note 2 above.

10. Red Week (7-14 June 1914) was a wave of demonstrations and a general strike sparked off by the massacre of anti-war demonstrators (three dead, fifteen injured) by troops in Ancona. The Gentiloni pact was a secret deal in the run-up to the 1913 general election between Catholic voters and Liberal candidates who promised to support Catholic policies (defence of Catholic private schools, opposition to divorce etc.) It was estimated that over 200 deputies were elected through the pact.

11. Sidney Sonnino (1847-1922) and Antonio Salandra (1853-1931), leading right-wing Liberals. In 1915 they had been jointly responsible, as Foreign Minister and Prime Minister respectively, for negotiating the secret Treaty of London which committed Italy to intervention in the First World War.

12. Camillo Prampolini (1859-1930), reformist leader of the PSI federation of Reggio Emilia.

13. Giustino Fortunato (1848-1932), important liberal conservative writer on the southern question (*Il Mezzogiorno e lo Stato italiano*, 1911). Benedetto Croce (1866-1952) was born in the Abruzzo region and brought up in Naples, where his intellectual circle was subsequently based.

14. Piero Gobetti (1901-1926) was a left liberal sympathetic towards the *Ordine Nuovo* group. He believed in an alliance between workers, peasants and intellectuals as a key to the 'democratic revolution' in Italy. He worked as theatre critic on *L'Ordine Nuovo* in 1921. He founded his

own publishing house and an anti-fascist weekly *La Rivoluzione Liberale* (1922-25). He died in exile shortly after the magazine was suppressed by the Fascist government.

15. Guido Dorso, radical writer on the southern question. His book *La rivoluzione meridionale* (published by Gobetti in 1925) called for the overthrow of the centralized Italian state and the southern ruling class.

VI Hegemony, Relations of Force, Historical Bloc

1. This debate, which lasted until the fifteenth century, centred around the so-called *filioque* clause in the Creed, in other words the argument whether the Holy Spirit proceeds 'from the Father and from the Son' (*patre filioque*) as the Western Church maintained or, as the Byzantines held, only from the Father.

2. 'The changes in the economic foundation lead sooner or later to the transformation of the whole immense superstructure. In studying such transformations it is always necessary to distinguish between the material transformation of the economic conditions of production, which can be determined with the precision of natural science, and the legal, political, religious, artistic or philosophic – in short, ideological forms in which men become conscious of this conflict and fight it out.' Marx, Preface to *A Contribution to the Critique of Political Economy*, in *Collected Works*, Volume 29, p. 263.

3. In the original the expression is '*rovesciamento della prassi*':: 'the revolutionizing (or "overturning") by (or "of") Praxis'. The phrase presumably translates Marx's expression '*revolutionäre Praxis*' in the third thesis on Feuerbach: 'The coincidence of the changing of circumstances and of human activity or self-change can be conceived and rationally understood only as *revolutionizing* practice'. (*Collected Works*, Volume 5, p. 7).

4. This is a short extract from a longer discussion of Croce's view of Marxism, in particular his recent (1925, 1930) reductionist characterizations of the base-superstructure model as a dualism of essence-appearance or noumenon-phenomenon, with the economy functioning 'behind the scenes' as a hidden god (*deus absconditus*). Gramsci observes that this view was far cruder than Croce's own youthful conception of Marxism (1900) as well as being at odds with his 'dialectic of distincts', namely the principle whereby two or more concepts or categories may be distinguished from one another while remaining equally 'real' and circulating together under a higher unity. Giovanni Gentile (1875-1944), philosopher and Fascist, opposed this system of distinctions with a modified Hegelianism (the philosophy of 'pure act') in which the family and civil society were subordinated to the state while culture and moral life were subordinated to action.

5. Sorel does not in fact appear to have used the expression 'historical bloc' which Gramsci attributes to him on more than one occasion in the prison notebooks. There are however two passages in the introduction to

Reflections on Violence (1909) which Gramsci probably had in mind. In the first, Sorel distinguishes between the facile optimist who believes in ever more progressive social advance and the active pessimist for whom the existing social order must be superseded by a redemptive break (*scission*) and recomposition: 'The pessimist sees social conditions as forming a system bonded by an iron law which it is necessary to undergo, such that it is given as a whole (*en bloc*) and cannot disappear except by a catastrophe which destroys it entirely ... What is most profound about pessimism is its way of conceiving the march towards deliverance. Man would not go far, in the examination both of the laws of his poverty and of fate ... if he did not have the hope of putting an end to these tyrannies with a struggle undertaken in common with a group of comrades.' (*Réflexions sur la violence*, 6th edition, Paris 1936, pp. 18-9). The second passage explains the concept of 'myths' as ideal constructions which produce real actions (the general strike, revolution as catastrophe, etc.): 'I wanted to show that one should not try and analyse such a system of images in the same way that an object is broken down into its elements but one must take them as a whole as historical forces (*il faut les prendre en bloc comme des forces historiques*).' (pp. 32-3). It should be noted that the concept of historical bloc in Marxist terms as a unity of structure and superstructure is Gramsci's own distinctive elaboration and does not have any direct analogue in Sorel.

6. For this attribution of the concept of hegemony to Lenin compare an *Ordine Nuovo* article of March 1924 which refers to Lenin's *Two Tactics of Social Democracy* (1905): 'Bolshevism is the first movement in the history of class struggle to have developed the idea of the hegemony of the proletariat.' *Two Tactics* criticized the Mensheviks' economistic theses that the bourgeois-democratic revolution must be led by the bourgeoisie as a stage towards the socialist revolution. Lenin argued by contrast that the proletariat must exercise 'hegemony', i.e. leadership of the bourgeois revolution and alliances with the peasantry and other exploited groups. Hegemony is distinguished from the dictatorship of the proletariat in that the latter is a form of state power exercised against opponents, whereas the former involves the proletariat as 'the ideological leader of the democratic forces'. (See on this Buci-Glucksmann 1980: 174-84.) The '1848 doctrine of the permanent revolution' refers to that formulated by Marx and Engels in 1850 (see note 10 to Section VII below). The slogan was taken up by Trotsky with reference to the 1905 Revolution, but was opposed in Trotsky's formulation by Lenin (see note 18 below) and – according to Gramsci – 'expanded and transcended' by a different formulation, that of hegemony (see VII.5). In some contexts in the notebooks Gramsci uses the term 'permanent revolution' in this positive sense; in others he uses it negatively with reference to Trotsky's conception.

7. Croce, *Materialismo storico ed economia marxistica* (1900), 6th edition, Bari 1978, p. 108.

8. Marx, Preface to *A Contribution to the Critique of Political Economy*, *Collected Works*, Volume 24, p. 263. 'Just as one does not judge an individual by what he thinks about himself, so one cannot judge such a

period of transformation by its consciousness, but, on the contrary, this consciousness must be explained from the contradictions of material life.'

9. Croce, *Materialismo storico*, pp. 86-7.

10. See *Capital*, Volume 1, Lawrence & Wishart 1983, p.65: 'The secret of the expression of value, namely that all kinds of labour are equal and equivalent, because and in so far as they are human labour in general, cannot be deciphered, until the notion of human equality has already acquired the fixity of a popular prejudice.'

11. See *Contribution to the Critique of Hegel's Philosophy of Law. Introduction, Collected Works*, Volume 3, p. 182: 'The weapon of criticism cannot, of course, replace criticism by weapons, material force must be overthrown by material force; but theory also becomes a material force as soon as it has gripped the masses.'

12. On the Action Party and the Moderates, see VIII.1 and the introduction to Section VIII.

13. Henri De Man, Belgian socialist, author of *Au delà du marxisme* (Beyond Marxism) published in 1929. Gramsci possessed an Italian translation of the book in prison and devoted several observations to it (see for example SPN pp.376, 418 and 430).

14. After 1870 (when Rome was annexed to the kingdom of Italy) the Church expressed its opposition to the new liberal state by requiring Catholics to abstain from voting in general elections. After 1900 this boycott broke down through a series of deals whereby liberal candidates were elected by Catholic voters after pledging to support policies favoured by the Church. Finally in 1919 Catholics formed their own party, the Popular Party.

15. Marx, *The Poverty of Philosophy, Collected Works*, Volume 6, pp. 210-11.

16. Letters to Josef Bloch and to Heinz Starkenburg, 21 September 1890 amd 25 January 1894. In the letter to Bloch, Engels writes: 'According to the materialist conception of history the determining moment in history is *ultimately* the production and reproduction of real life. More than this neither Marx nor I have ever asserted. If therefore somebody twists this into the statement that the economic moment is the only determining one, he transforms it into a meaningless, abstract and absurd phrase.' (*Selected Correspondence*, London 1936, p. 475)

17. Achille Loria (1857-1943), academic economist who put himself forward as an original thinker and enjoyed a certain vogue, not only in Italy, in the 1880s and 90s. Loria's theory, to which he gave the name 'historical economism', was a mish-mash of vulgar economics and vulgar Marxism, of no intrinsic distinction but interesting, in Gramsci's eyes, as an example of 'certain degenerate and bizarre aspects of the mentality of a group of Italian intellectuals and therefore of the national culture ...' to which he gave the name '*lorianismo*'.

18. Again Gramsci's discussion of hegemony refers back to the use of the concept on the Russian left. The 'development of the theory of the political party' is that of Lenin from *What is to be Done?* (1903) onwards. The 'theory of the permanent revolution' is that of Trotsky, who wrote in

1905 that the revolutionary provisional government of Russia would be 'the government of a workers' democracy ... with a social democratic majority'. Against both this position and that of the Mensheviks (who saw the revolution as necessarily bourgeois and said the Social-Democrats should therefore abstain), Lenin and the Bolsheviks put forward the slogan of the 'revolutionary-democratic dictatorship of the proletariat and peasantry', arguing that the only durable revolutionary government in Russia would be one in which representatives of the peasants and urban petty bourgeoisie participated alongside representatives of the minority proletariat. This 'hegemonic' approach meant political concessions by the Social Democrats to the 'constituentist' demands of these groups, i.e. their demands for a constituent assembly and constitutional reforms.

19. Boulangism was a right-wing movement led by General Boulanger, *revanchiste* ex-minister of war, in 1887-89. It called for a new constituent assembly, reform of parliament and 'military regeneration' of the nation. Elected with a huge majority, Boulanger appeared about to attempt a *coup* in 1889 but hesitated and fled the country. The Dreyfus case, which polarized French politics and public opinion, lasted from the first condemnation of Alfred Dreyfus in 1894 to his final acquittal in 1904. The 'classic work' on Napoleon III's coup d'état of 2 December 1852 is Marx's *The Eighteenth Brumaire of Louis Bonaparte*.

20. Georges Valois organized a movement aimed at 'national revolution', based on ex-servicemen and inspired by Mussolini. General Rudolf Gadja, discharged from the Czech army for plotting a military putsch in the 1920s, formed a fascist League for Electoral Reform which won three seats in the 1929 elections in Czechoslovakia.

VII The Art and Science of Politics

1. P.N. Krasnov, *From Two-Headed Eagle to Red Flag*, Berlin 1921.

2. 'Cadornism' is coined after Luigi Cadorna, commander-in-chief of the Italian armed forces until the defeat and retreat at Caporetto (September 1917) for which he was held responsible. Cadorna epitomized for Gramsci the kind of military (and, by analogy, political) strategist who forces reality into a preconceived schema, even if this means demoralizing his army, sacrificing troops in battle and provoking a mutiny. Gramsci elsewhere defines Cadornism as 'the conviction that a thing will be done because the leader considers it just and reasonable that it should be done; if it is not done, the blame is put on those who "ought to have ..." ' (SPN, 145).

3. This is presumably a reference to the failure of Communists in Italy between 1921 and 1926 to win more than a minority position within the trade-union movement.

4. The 'fourth meeting' is the Fourth Congress of the Comintern (October-December 1922). Trotsky said, during his report on NEP: 'It will hardly be possible to catch the European bourgeoisie by surprise as we caught the Russian bourgeoisie. The European bourgeoisie is more

intelligent, and more far-sighted; it is not wasting time. Everything that can be set on foot against us is being mobilized by it right now. The revolutionary proletariat will thus encounter on its road to power not only the combat vanguards of the counter-revolution but also its heaviest reserves. Only by smashing, breaking up and demoralizing these enemy forces will the proletariat be able to seize state power. By way of compensation, after the proletarian overturn, the vanquished bourgeoisie will no longer dispose of powerful reserves from which it could draw resources for prolonging the civil war. In other words, after the conquest of power, the European proletariat will in all likelihood have far more elbow room for its creative work in economy and culture than we had in Russia on the day after the overturn. The more difficult and gruelling the struggle for state power, all the less possible will it be to challenge the proletariat's power after the victory.'

5. i.e. the theory of permanent revolution.

6. Trotsky in *My Life* (London 1930) quotes Lunacharsky's remarks: 'Comrade Trotsky held in 1905 that the two revolutions (the bourgeois and the socialist), although they do not coincide, are bound to each other in such a way that they make a permanent revolution ... It cannot be denied that in formulating this view Comrade Trotsky showed great insight and vision, albeit he erred to the extent of fifteen years.' Trotsky replies to this: 'The question was not of the dates of the revolution but of the analysis of its inner forces and of foreseeing its progress as a whole.' (pp. 157-8).

7. On the united front formula see the introduction to Sections IV and V.

8. The text referred to appears to be Stalin's 'Interview with the First American Labour Delegation' (9 September 1927). Gramsci had in prison an edited translation published in the *Rassegna Settimanale della Stampa Estera* (Foreign Press Review) of 4 October 1927. His discussion here takes off from the delegation's first question concerning the relations between Marx's and Lenin's thought and does not relate directly to the content of Stalin's replies.

9. The first phase referred to is that of the Second International. The second is Trotsky's internationalism, invoked increasingly after 1924 against the notion of socialism in one country. Gramsci is arguing that this internationalism implies the expectation of the revolution spreading out from Russia in the way that Napoleon's armies carried certain of the ideas and achievements of the French Revolution across Europe.

10. The Jacobins were defeated in the reaction of 9 Thermidor (27 July 1794). Gramsci recalls elsewhere 'the Jacobin-type slogan was used in Germany around '48 by Marx: "revolution in permanence" ' (Q1§44, p. 53). The slogan is in fact used by Marx and Engels in the Address of March 1850 to the Communist League: 'While the democratic petty bourgeois wish to bring the revolution to a conclusion as quickly as possible ... it is our interest and our task to make the revolution permanent, until all more or less possessing classes have been forced out of their position of dominance, the proletariat has conquered state power,

and the association of proletarians, not only in one country but in all the dominant countries of the world, has advanced so far that competition among the proletarians in these countries has ceased and at least the decisive forces are concentrated in the hands of the proletarians ... If the German workers are not able to attain power and achieve their own class interests without completely going through a lengthy revolutionary development, they at least know that the first act of this approaching revolutionary drama will coincide with the direct victory of their own class in France and will be very much accelerated by it. ... Their battle-cry must be: The Revolution in Permanence.' (*Collected Works*, Volume 10, pp. 281 and 286-7).

11. Sorel developed right-wing sympathies around the First World War. The introduction to his *Reflections on Violence* took the form of a letter to Halévy. Charles Maurras (1868-1952) was one of the leaders of the fascist Action Française movement.

12. Ferdinand Lassalle, *Arbeiter-Programm* (1862): 'The bourgeoisie conceives the moral object of the state to consist solely and exclusively in the protection of the personal freedom and property of the individual. This is a nightwatchman's idea (*eine Nachtwächteridee*) ... because it represents the state to itself from the point of view of a nightwatchman whose whole function consists in preventing robbery and burglary.' (Lassalle, *Auswahl von Reden und Schriften*, ed. Karl Renner, Berlin 1923, p. 184). The term *Nachtwächterstaat* entered colloquial usage with the meaning of a state which imposes a minimum of duties on its members. It can be seen here that Lassalle uses it critically; he himself argued for a Hegelian form of ethical state.

13. Sorel explained his concept of myth in the introduction to *Reflections on Violence*: see also note 5 to Section VI above.

14. See note 19 to Section VI above.

15. The term 'organic centralism' was used by Bordiga in opposition to Gramsci during the preparation of the documents for the Lyons Congress (see Section V and introduction). He argued that in certain conditions the party centre could guide the party even against the will of the majority of members. 'Hence it would be necessary to replace the formula "democratic centralism" with that of "organic centralism".' See also Gramsci's note 'Knowledge and Feeling' (Section XI.3) and compare another passage: 'So-called "organic centralism" is founded on the principle that a political group is selected by "co-optation" around an "infallible bearer of truth", one who is "enlightened by reason" who has found the infallible natural laws of historical evolution, infallible even if only in the long run and even if immediate events "seem" to disprove them.' (Q13§38, p. 1650)

VIII Passive Revolution, Caesarism, Fascism

1. Victor Emmanuel II was King of Piedmont at the time of unification and became the first King of Italy.

2. On 'transformism' see Glossary, p. 430.

3. Neo-Guelphism was a liberal Catholic movement in Italy in the first half of the nineteenth century. Its aim was an Italian federation under the Pope. Among its leading exponents was Vincenzo Gioberti (1808-52). Other variants of federalism were those of the moderate liberal Massimo D'Azeglio, the radical liberal Carlo Cattaneo and the radical democrat Giuseppe Ferrari.

4. Vincenzo Cuoco (1770-1823) described the Neapolitan revolution of 1799 as a 'passive revolution' because it was the work of the enlightened bourgeoisie without mass participation (*Saggio storico sulla rivoluzione napoletana del 1799*, 1801). He subsequently argued that such passive revolutions were necessary in order to introduce moderate reforms and avoid revolution on the French model.

5. Marx and Engels, *The Holy Family*, *Collected Works*, Volume 4, pp. 118-24, Chapter VI, Section 3(c).

6. See for instance the Foreword to *The Phenomenology of the Spirit*, Section III, part 3 and *Lectures on the History of Philosophy*, Part III, Section 3.

7. From 1793-96 the Vendée region in western France was the theatre of a peasant guerrilla revolt against the Republic, fomented by royalists and priests.

8. The Le Chapelier law of June 1791 dissolved craft guilds, prohibited other associations of workers and employers and made strike action illegal. The law of the *maximum* fixed a ceiling for food prices and wages, and drove a wedge between the Jacobins and the workers.

9. Between 2 and 6 September 1792, when Danton was minister of justice, over 1,100 prisoners, many of them non-political, were massacred in Paris jails after rumours of a plot to release counter-revolutionaries.

10. See note 10 to Section VII above.

11. Quarto was the port near Genoa where Garibaldi's volunteers (the Thousand) embarked en route to Sicily in May 1860. Cavour initially tried to obstruct the expedition, but after Garibaldi crossed onto the Italian mainland at the Strait of Messina, Cavour's main concern was to engineer a moderate rather than a democratic outcome.

12. This paragraph refers to the debates around the 'Jacobin' slogan 'permanent revolution' in Russia. The slogan was used by Parvus and Trotsky (Bronstein) in relation to the 1905 revolution. The 'tendency which opposed it' refers to the Bolsheviks, who 'applied it' in a different form, that of the concept of hegemony of the proletariat. See on this note 6 to Section VI above.

13. Gramsci saw the French socialist-anarchist Pierre-Joseph Proudhon as having moved after 1848 from Jacobinism (in his sense) to conservatism, whereas he considered the Italian liberal Gioberti (see note 3 above) to have moved in the opposite direction. Before 1848 the example of the Jacobin Terror of 1793 had frightened Gioberti – like other European liberals – into moderate positions, whereas the severity of the repression after the 1848 revolution made him reconsider his judgement of Jacobinism and develop his own diluted version of 'the Jacobin "National-popular" ' (see on this SCW, pp. 247-9). Sorel, after working

as an engineer and holding a positivist outlook in the 1880s, developed anarchist sympathies around the turn of the century and elaborated a form of syndicalism that was highly influential in Italy, for instance on Mussolini. He moved onto right-wing nationalist positions around the First World War. The repression referred to is that against the Paris Commune in 1871.

14. See Marx, Preface to *A Contribution to the Critique of Political Economy*, *Collected Works*, Volume 29, p. 263.

15. For the three moments, see 'Analysis of Situations: Relations of Force', pp. 204-7.

16. The Italian Nationalist Association was a right-wing party formed in 1910. It played a major role in pushing for Italy's intervention into the war in 1915. In 1923 it merged with the Fascist Party.

17. Depretis, Crispi and Giolitti, Italian Prime Ministers over the period 1876-1914, were each widely considered by their opponents to have exercised dictatorships in the sense of managing elections and manipulating parliamentary clienteles to secure personal majorities. The Crispi government in the 1890s also became synonymous with colonialist militarism, anti-socialism and armed repression of popular protest. Gramsci himself, in his early writings, described Giolitti's rule as a personal dictatorship: see for instance 'Class Intransigence and Italian History' in this volume, p. 42.

18. i.e. the National Government formed after MacDonald's abandonment of the Labour Party in 1931.

19. October 1922 was the month in which the Fascists came to power (March on Rome, 28 October). The Popular Party split in 1923 over policy towards the Fascists and presented its own list of candidates in the April 1924 election. 3 January 1925 was the date when Mussolini introduced the 'exceptional laws' and marked the beginning of Fascism's 'totalitarian' phase. The attempted assassination of Mussolini in Bologna by the student Zamboni on 31 October 1926 was used as an occasion for a final clampdown and all opposition parties were outlawed on 8 November (Gramsci was arrested the same day).

IX Americanism and Fordism

1. Compare two paragraphs on Freud. The first dates from 1929 (Q1§33, p. 26): 'The spread of Freudian psychology seems to have resulted in the birth of a literature like that of the eighteenth century; the "savage", in modern form, is replaced by the Freudian type. The struggle against the juridical order is conducted through Freudian psychological analysis. This would appear to be one aspect of the question. I have not been able to study Freud's theories and I am not familiar with the other kind of so-called "Freudian" literature Proust-Svevo-Joyce.' The second (Q 15§74, pp. 1833-34) was written in 1933: 'The healthiest and most immediately acceptable nucleus of Freudianism is the requirement to study the morbid repercussions of each construction of "collective man",

of each "social conformism", every level of civilization, especially in those classes which "fanatically" make a religion, a mystique, out of the new human type that must be attained. It should be seen whether Freudianism did not necessarily mark the end of the liberal era, which is precisely characterized by a greater responsibility (and sense of this responsibility) on the part of selected groups in the construction of non-authoritarian, spontaneous, libertarian etc. "religions". [...]'

2. Vittorio Alfieri (1749-1803), the Italian poet and dramatist, recounts in his autobiography (*Vita*, Epoca Terza, Chapter XV) how in his determination to stop wasting his life and dedicate himself wholeheartedly to poetry he used to get his servant Elia to tie him to a chair at his desk, thus giving him no choice but to carry on working.

3. The militarization of labour was a policy which operated for a short time in the Soviet Union in the period of War Communism. Adopted at the Ninth Party Congress (1920), it was most closely associated with the figure of Trotsky. It met with growing opposition from the trade unions, particularly after the end of the Civil War, and was implicitly defeated with the rejection of the Trotsky-Bukharin trade union theses at the Tenth Congress (1921). Trotsky put the policy in these terms: 'Militarization is unthinkable without the militarization of the trade unions as such, without the establishment of a regime in which every worker feels himself a soldier of labour, who cannot dispose of himself freely; if the order is given to transfer him, he must carry it out; if he does not carry it out, he will be a deserter who is punished. Who looks after this? The trade union. It creates the new regime. This is the militarization of the working class.'

4. In 1923 Trotsky wrote a series of articles for *Pravda* dealing with popular customs, leisure and the family (English translation: *Problems of Life*, 1924) and also published *Literature and Revolution*, to which Gramsci contributed a note on Italian Futurism (translated in SCW, pp. 52-54). He discussed Taylorist methods in *Terrorism and Communism* (1920).

5. This expression, whose revealing 'tactlessness' instantly attracted the attention of commentators, occurs on p.40 of Frederick Taylor's *Principles of Scientific Management* (1911): 'this work [pig-iron handling] is so crude and elementary in its nature that the writer firmly believes that it would be possible to train an intelligent gorilla so as to become a more efficient pig-iron handler than any man could be.'

6. Horace, *Satires*, I, ii, 119: 'namque parabilem amo venerem facilemque'.

7. Henry Ford (with Samuel Crowther), *My Life and Work*, Garden City and London 1922, and *Today and Tomorrow*, ibid., 1926. André Philip, *Le Problème Ouvrier aux Etats-Unis*, Paris 1929. The 'educative initiatives' referred to are presumably institutions like the Henry Ford Trade School, created in 1916 for the further education of workers.

8. *Babbitt*, Sinclair Lewis's satirical novel about a middle-American real-estate man, was first published in 1922.

X Intellectuals and Education

1. Giovanni Agnelli, head of Fiat; Stefano Benni, head of Montecatini chemicals.
2. On Loria see note 17 to Section VI. The notion of 'unproductive labourer' in fact has its origins in Marx's definitions of productive and unproductive labour in *Capital*.
3. In the first decades of this century, Gentile and Croce had developed a wide-ranging critique of the existing school system, stigmatizing it as 'instruction' (imparting of knowledge) not 'education' (drawing out of the pupil's capacities). Under Fascism the Ministero della Pubblica Istruzione was renamed Ministero dell'Educazione Nazionale.
4. On the Casati Act see the Introduction to Section II.
5. The Gentile reform of 1923 provided for compulsory religious education in elementary schools, despite the former hostility of idealist philosophers like Gentile and Croce to clerical influence in education and their view of religion as pseudo-philosophy or dogmatic ideology. The motive was most probably a pragmatic one: to provide a conservative world-outlook for working-class children who would not go on to secondary school. As Gramsci points out elsewhere (Q11§1, p. 1367) Gentile's position 'is nothing other than a derivation from the concept that "religion is good for the people" (people = child = primitive phase of thought to which religion corresponds etc.) in other words it is a (tendentious) abandonment of the education of the people.'
6. Mnemonic Greek words used to memorize syllogisms in classical logic.

XI Philosophy, Common Sense, Language and Folklore

1. See 'Socialism and Culture': Section II.1.
2. See note 5 to Section X above.
3. See 'The Popular University', Section II.4.
4. The reference is to Mirsky's article 'Bourgeois History and Historical Materialism' in *Labour Monthly*, Volume 13, July 1931, Number 7, pp. 453-59. Mirsky was a former white Russian who emigrated to England, joined the Communist Party and taught Russian literature at King's College, London from 1922 to 1932.
5. Giuseppe Giusti, *Epigrammi*: 'Il buon senso ch un dì fu caposcuola / or nelle nostre scuole è morto affatto./ La scienza, sua figliola,/ l'uccise per veder com'era fatto.'
6. cf. 'Validity of Ideologies', Section VI.9, and the corresponding notes (10 and 11) to that Section.
7. See note 15 to Section VII.
8. I have followed Gerratana's critical edition (p.1860) here in inserting the word 'not'. This interpellation makes the passage correspond better to the letter from Sorel to Missiroli to which Gramsci refers here and elsewhere (Q4§44; Q10, II, 41.xiii).
9. The image of the Hegelian dialectic as a man 'standing on his head' is

frequent in Marx and Engels (Marx, Afterword to the Second German edition of *Capital*, Volume 1 and, earlier, *The Holy Family*, VIII, 4; Engels, *Ludwig Feuerbach*, 4). It is in fact a turning against Hegel of a phrase used by Hegel himself in the preface to *The Philosophy of Spirit*.

10. The character is Monsieur Jourdain in *Le Bourgeois Gentilhomme*, Act Two, Scene Four.

11. Matteo Giulio Bartoli (1873-1946) taught linguistics at the University of Turin and had supervised Gramsci's unfinished thesis on historical linguistics. He founded a movement known as 'neolinguistics' (later 'spatial linguistics') in which language change was seen as a process whereby a dominant speech community spread its influence over contiguous subordinate communities: the city over the surrounding countryside, the 'standard' language over the dialect, the dominant socio-cultural group over the subordinate one. Bartoli developed a set of 'areal norms' according to which the older of two given linguistic forms would be found in more isolated areas, in peripheries rather than centres. Using these norms, the linguist could reconstruct the direction in which innovations (new linguistic forms) had spread. It has been argued (see introduction to this Section) that Gramsci's conception of hegemony, insofar as it deals with relations of cultural and ideological influence between social groups, was influenced by this and related conceptions.

12. In line with its elitist and laissez-faire principles, Gentile's Education Act of 1923 had made no provision for specific teaching of Italian grammar. This meant, as Gramsci argues here, that 'the national-popular mass is excluded from learning the educated language' and remained confined to the ghettoes of their dialects.

13. See 'Observations on the School', Section X.2.

14. In Rousseau's *Emile, or Education* (1762) the young boy is schooled by nature (direct observation, experience, etc.) rather than artificially socialized, and is kept away from religious dogmas till the age of fifteen.

15. *La scoperta de l'America* (1894) by Cesare Pascarella is a humorous account in linked Roman dialect sonnets of Columbus's voyage. It ends with a praise of great Italians and their flair for discoveries.

XII Popular Culture

1. The linking of these two concepts in French political thought can be traced from Rousseau's concept of the sovereignty of the general will, inalienable and thus not delegable to representatives (*The Social Contract*, 1762), through the 1789 Declaration of the Rights of Man ('sovereignty resides essentially in the nation') and the unimplemented Jacobin constitution of 1793 ('sovereignty resides in the people') to the republican slogans of 1848.

2. Compare the similarly phrased remark in the note on intellectuals, p.303. Caro (1507-66) and Pindemonte (1753-1828) were Italian translators of, respectively, the *Aeneid* and the *Odyssey*. Their versions, done in a classicizing style very remote from modern colloquial Italian,

were used in schools until quite recently.

3. Camille Flammarion (1842-1925), author of popular books on science.

4. In the Risorgimento and following unification Alessandro Manzoni (1785-1873) argued that educated spoken Florentine should become the basis for the national language of united Italy. Ruggero Bonghi, a Manzonian in linguistic policy and Education Minister in 1874-76, had maintained in *Perché la letteratura italiana non sia popolare in Italia* (1856) that Italian literature was not popular because of the artificial and indigestible style in which most authors wrote.

5. *Maggi* (literally 'Mays') are traditional May Day festivals in central Italy in which people act out stories of popular biblical, chivalric or historical figures in a sequence of songs interspersed with refrains on the fiddle. The story of Pia dei Tolomei, murdered by her husband, was famous from Dante's *Purgatorio*, V, 130-36.

6. Giovanni Rosini's *La monaca di Monza*, published in 1829 and frequently reprinted, is a popular historical novel about a young woman forced into a convent against her will who takes a lover and commits murder. Gramsci discusses Dumas's *The Count of Monte-Cristo* (1844-5) at greater length in SCW, pp. 348-9, 353, 355-8.

7. 'Catharsis' here almost certainly has Gramsci's specific meaning of 'the passage from the purely economic (or egoistic-passional) to the ethico-political moment, that is the superior elaboration of the structure into the superstructure in the minds of men' (SPN, p. 366). The more conventional Aristotelian sense of catharsis with reference to tragedy (i.e. purgation of pity and terror) is probably not relevant despite the fact that Gramsci is talking here about theatre.

8. Alessandro Schiavi, *Labor. Fiorita di canti sociali*, Milan 1924. Schiavi was a socialist, Pietro Gori an anarchist. Togliatti's translations appeared in *L'Ordine Nuovo* in 1919-20.

9. Thomas Babington Macaulay, 'On the Athenian Orators' (1824) in *Miscellaneous Writings*, London 1870, pp. 56-63. The other observation recalled further on in this note is from the same essay.

10. In his essay 'L'ultimo del puristi' (1868), Francesco De Sanctis recounts how his former teacher Basilio Puoti used to be surrounded by a group of veteran pupils who had been with him for five or six years and to whom he jokingly referred as '*gli anziani di Santa Zita*' (the phrase is from Dante, *Inferno* XXI, 38).

XIII Journalism

1. The term 'scission' (sometimes translated as 'cleavage') is drawn from Sorel, who wrote in the *Reflections on Violence* (Chapter 6, Section 1) of 'the scission between classes, the basis of all socialism'. It derives from his analogy between socialism and primitive Christianity. For Sorel, Christianity made a distinct 'scission' or 'rupture' from Judaism while at the same time inheriting its compatible elements. In the same way socialism, in its scission from capitalism, would keep the heritage both of

capitalist science and technology and of the 'morality of the producers' (i.e. the proletariat), formed through trade union solidarity and struggles (see *Le Système historique de Renan*, Paris 1905, p. 71). Compare Gramsci's statement of 1920: 'Every revolution which, like the Christian and the Communist revolutions, comes about and can only come about through a stirring within the deepest and broadest popular masses, cannot help but smash and destroy the existing system of social organization.' (SPW I, p. 331)

2. Croce's *La Critica*, a highly influential review of philosophy, literature and history, was founded in 1903. *Politica* was started in 1918 by the nationalist Francesco Coppola and the national-syndicalist Alfredo Rocco. Corrado Barbagallo founded the *Nuova Rivista Storica* in 1917.

3. Luigi Russo, democratic Crocean, edited *Leonardo* from 1925 to 1929. *L'Unità* (not the Communist newspaper) was founded by the socialist 'southernist' Gaetano Salvemini (pen-name: Rerum Scriptor) in 1911 after he left *La Voce*, an innovative review of politics and culture edited by Giuseppe Prezzolini from 1908 to 1914.

4. The *Manchester Guardian Weekly* and *The Times Weekly* were among the periodicals Gramsci received in prison.

XIV Art and the Struggle for a New Civilization

1. Giosue Carducci (1835-1907), poet and critic. As a critic he concentrated on close textual analyses and opposed the historico-political criticism exemplified by De Sanctis.

2. The Italian word is *calligrafismo*: the term, which connotes a concern with style and form in writing for their own sake, became the label of a literary movement in the 1930s as well as of a somewhat aestheticizing style in cinema.

3. 'Idiot' and 'idiom' derive from the same Greek root, *idios*, meaning 'private', 'one's own'.

4. Gramsci reviewed several plays by Nino Berrini (1880-1962) when he was theatre critic on the Turin edition of *Avanti!*.

GLOSSARY OF KEY TERMS

Caesarism

A political opposition between two or more social forces is said by Gramsci to be resolved in a 'Caesarist' way when a third force arises to hold them temporarily in equilibrium. Caesarism is not really above the interests of both of the opposing forces and will in practice favour one or the other: it will be either 'progressive' or 'regressive'. A Caesarist solution may take the form of a personal dictatorship (Caesar, Napoleon, Bismarck) but not necessarily. In modern societies, Gramsci says, it 'may exist even without a Caesar'. Here a political crisis will be less likely to result in a Bonapartist-style military dictatorship and more likely to be resolved by an emergency parliamentary coalition, the intimidation of political opponents or the use of police. See Section VIII.

Civil Society

Gramsci uses this term to designate 'the ensemble of organisms commonly called "private" ' (p. 306), that is to say the sum of social activities and institutions which are not directly part of the government, the judiciary or the repressive bodies (police, armed forces). Trade unions and other voluntary associations, as well as church organizations and political parties, when the latter do not form part of the government, are all part of civil society. Civil society is the sphere in which a dominant social group organizes consent and hegemony, as opposed to political society where it rules by coercion and direct domination. It is also a sphere where the dominated social groups may organize their opposition and where an alternative hegemony may be constructed.

Common sense

Everyone, for Gramsci, has a number of 'conceptions of the world', which often tend to be in contradiction with one another and therefore form an incoherent whole. Many of these conceptions are imposed and absorbed passively from outside, or from the past, and are accepted and lived uncritically. In this case they constitute what Gramsci calls 'common sense' (or, in another context, 'folklore'). Many elements in popular common sense contribute to people's subordination by making situations of inequality and oppression appear to them as natural and unchangeable. Nevertheless, common sense must not be thought of as 'false consciousness' or as ideology in a merely negative sense. It is contradictory – it contains elements of truth as well as elements of misrepresentation – and it is upon these contradictions that leverage may be obtained in a 'struggle of political "hegemonies" '. For Gramsci it was important that Marxism should not present itself as an abstract philosophy but should enter people's common sense, giving them a more critical understanding of their own situation. See in particular Section XI and 'philosophy of praxis' in this glossary).

Economic-corporate

This term is always used, overtly or implicitly, in opposition to 'hegemonic'. 'Economic-corporate' interest means the collective interest of a particular economic category: for instance merchants, or engineering workers. For a social group to become hegemonic it must move not only from economic-corporate consciousness to class consciousness; it must also go further, since class consciousness is still founded upon collective *economic* interest. Becoming hegemonic may well mean sacrificing economic class interest in order to build 'expansive' alliances. See on this the description of successive 'moments' in the formation of collective political consciousness in 'Some Aspects of the Southern Question' (p. 174) and 'Analysis of Situations: Relations of Force' (pp. 205-6).

Economism

Economism means for Gramsci the theoretical separation of the
economic dimension from a social and political ensemble: more
specifically, the reduction of this ensemble to its economic causes.
Economism is epitomized in his view not only by the 'mechanical
historical materialism' of the Second International (1889-1914) but
also by revolutionary syndicalism and bourgeois liberalism (or
laissez-faire), which in this respect he assimilates to one another.
The former privileges the revolutionary transformation of
economic production at the expense of the winning of political
power and the transformation of the state. The latter sees the
economy as a self-regulating sphere of individual enterprise to be
separated from the interventions of the state. Yet in reality the
state is necessary to sustain a capitalist economy and bourgeois
society, and historically it increasingly intervenes in them. In
contrast with economism Gramsci develops the concepts of
hegemony and historical bloc (q.v.).

Hegemony

This term appears to have entered Gramsci's usage from the
political vocabulary of Russian Social Democracy and the Third
International (for a fuller discussion, see Anderson 1976-7: 15-20
and Buci-Glucksmann 1980: 174-85). In this context the word
meant leadership of a class alliance: in a first instance (referred to
the 1905 revolution) proletarian leadership of the bourgeois-
democratic revolution; subsequently (after 1917) proletarian
leadership of an alliance with the peasantry and other exploited
groups. This leadership is based on the economically central role
of the leading class but it is secured politically by that class's
making economic concessions and sacrifices to its allies. In
Gramsci's 1926 essay 'Some Aspects of the Southern Question', he
argues (p. 173 in this edition) that the proletariat can only become
hegemonic, a ruling class, if it can overcome its economic
self-interest and win the support of the poor peasantry and
southern intellectuals. This notion, which develops out of Soviet
debates in 1923-26, recurs in the prison notebooks (see for
instance VI.10, 'Analysis of Situations: Relations of Force'). It

becomes closely associated with two other concepts: 'Jacobinism' and the 'national-popular' and opposed to two others: 'economism' and 'economic-corporatism' (q.v.). Hegemony in this sense is necessarily rooted in an economically dominant, or potentially dominant, mode of production and in one of the 'fundamental' social classes (bourgeoisie or proletariat), but it is defined precisely by an expansion beyond economic class interest into the sphere of political direction through a system of class alliances.

In the prison notebooks this meaning of 'hegemony' remains but the term is extended in two ways. Firstly, it is applied not just to situations of proletarian leadership but also to the rule of other classes at other periods of history. Secondly, it is qualitatively modified: hegemony comes to mean 'cultural, moral and ideological' leadership over allied and subordinate groups. Hegemony in this sense (which Gramsci develops through the mediation of Croce's concept of the 'ethico-political') is identified with the formation of a new ideological 'terrain', with political, cultural and moral leadership and with consent (VI.5). Hegemony is thus linked by Gramsci in a chain of associations and oppositions to 'civil society' as against 'political society', to consent as against coercion, to 'direction' as against 'domination'. (X.1). These binaries draw on the coercion-consent opposition in Machiavelli and some other political thinkers. Gramsci's concept of hegemony also appears to have been influenced by historical linguistics in its accounts of the influence or 'prestige' exerted by one form of a language over another.

Hegemony in Gramsci is sometimes interpreted as a relation purely of cultural or ideological influence or as a sphere of pure consent; it is also sometimes assimilated to the notion of 'dominant ideology' (see for instance Hunt 1986:215 and Boggs 1976). Yet these interpretations seem to be mistaken. Gramsci stresses that 'though hegemony is ethico-political, it must also be economic, must necessarily be based on the decisive function exercised by the leading group in the decisive nucleus of economic activity.' (pp. 211-2) In cases such as that of the French parliamentary regime 'the "normal" exercise of hegemony ... is characterized by the *combination of force and consent* variously balancing one another' (VIII.2, my emphasis). He also insists that hegemony is dynamic (a 'continuous process of formation and superseding of unstable equilibria') and that 'the fact of hegemony presupposes that account be taken of the interests and the tendencies of the groups over which hegemony is to be exercised'. (p. 211) In other words it presupposes an active and practical involvement of the hegemonized groups, quite unlike the static, totalizing and passive subordination implied by the dominant ideology concept. It also seems incorrect to maintain that, since Gramsci applies the concept of hegemony not only to proletarian revolutionary leadership (as in the Russian tradition) but also to bourgeois rule, this means that he sees bourgeois and proletarian rule as being structurally assimilable to one another or as containing a sort of interchangeable core. Gramsci is in fact careful to distinguish different forms of hegemony according to the different historical situations and the class actors involved. Typical forms of bourgeois hegemony are 'passive revolution' and 'transformism' (q.v.) or that of the parliamentary regime. By contrast, Gramsci defines proletarian hegemony indirectly when he writes of the philosophy of praxis (q.v.): 'It is not an instrument of government of dominant groups in order to gain the consent of and exercise hegemony over subaltern classes; it is the expression of these subaltern classes who want to educate themselves in the art of government ...' (VI.7)

Historical bloc

This is a concept used by Gramsci to designate the dialectical unity of base and superstructure, of theory and practice, of intellectuals and masses (and not, as is sometimes mistakenly asserted, simply an alliance of social forces). It is a central concept in establishing a theoretical distance from economism (q.v.) and restoring reciprocity to the study of concrete historical situations. Indeed, it has been argued that the concept so reworks the base-superstructure metaphor as to supersede it and make it redundant as such, even though Gramsci himself stops short of taking this theoretical step. In VI.3 he writes 'Structures and superstructures form an "historical bloc". That is to say the complex, contradictory and discordant ensemble of the superstructures is the reflection of the ensemble of the social relations of production.' See also the important passages in VI.4 and XI.3.

Intellectuals

Gramsci defines intellectuals in the prison notebooks as those people who give a fundamental social group 'homogeneity and awareness of its own function'. Intellectuals are educators, organizers, leaders. 'Organic' intellectuals are those who emerge from out of the group itself: for instance a worker who becomes a political activist. 'Traditional' intellectuals are those who have remained from earlier social formations and who may attach themselves to one or the other fundamental class: for instance priests, who may have either a revolutionary or a conservative function depending on their class identifications. In the political party organic and traditional intellectuals come together. In Italian the term 'intellectual work' (*lavoro intellettuale*) also has the sense simply of 'mental work' or 'work by brain'. In both cases 'intellectual' defines a function as much as it defines the concrete individual who fulfils this function. Gramsci is thus able to envisage a situation in which, as part of the revolutionary transformation of society, the intellectual function is massively expanded – in other words more and more people share the tasks of mental activity, of organizing, deliberating and leading, both politically and within the sphere of economic production. For Gramsci this would also be a process of democratization and would inhibit the formation of bureaucracies, which arise precisely where decision-making is monopolized by a specialized elite of intellectuals.

Intellectual and moral reformation

Gramsci adapts this term, via Georges Sorel, from Ernest Renan (one of whose books was entitled *La Réforme intellectuelle et morale*) and applies it, by analogy with the Protestant Reformation and the French Revolution, to a wholesale transformation of conceptions of the world and norms of conduct brought about by the philosophy of praxis (q.v.).

Jacobinism

In Gramsci's early writings the term 'Jacobinism' has negative connotations of sectarian, mystical, abstract, elitist (see for instance III.2; also SPW I, pp. 32, 170, 309). In the prison notebooks, however, it is 'revalued' and acquires the positive meaning of leadership of a national-popular alliance in which the peasant masses are organically bonded to the leading class, country to city. It is likely that this revaluation was influenced by Lenin. In *Two Tactics of Social-Democracy* (1905) Lenin called the Bolsheviks the 'Jacobins of contemporary Social-Democracy' whose slogan is 'the revolutionary-democratic dictatorship of the proletariat and peasantry'. In July 1917 he wrote: ' "Jacobinism" in Europe or on the boundary line between Europe and Asia in the twentieth century would be the rule of the revolutionary class, of the proletariat, which, supported by the peasant poor and taking advantage of the existing material basis for the advance to socialism, could not only provide all the great, unforgettable things provided by the Jacobins in the eighteenth century, but bring about a lasting world-wide victory for the working people.'

National-popular

This term is associated with the concepts of hegemony and Jacobinism as well as being a recurrent term in Gramsci's cultural analyses. Politically, a national-popular movement is one in which a fundamental class becomes hegemonic at a national level by drawing subaltern social groups into an alliance. 'Any formation of a national-popular collective will is impossible unless the great mass of peasant farmers bursts *simultaneously* into political life.' (SPN 132) The term 'national-popular' reflects Gramsci's conception of the revolution in Italy as a *national* movement which fulfils under socialism the historical tasks which the bourgeoisie had abdicated after the Risorgimento. As he had written in 1919: 'Historically the bourgeois class is already dead ... Today the "national" class is the proletariat.' (*L'Ordine Nuovo*, 1919-1920, Turin 1975, p. 278). Culturally, the term (which was perhaps influenced by nineteenth-century Russian debates) designates forms of art and literature which help cement this kind of hegemonic alliance: neither 'intellectualistic' nor 'cosmopolitan' but engaging with popular reality and drawing in popular audiences. Italian intellectuals are historically *non*-national-popular (see XII.1, 'Concept of "National-Popular" ').

'Organic' and 'conjunctural'

For Gramsci, Marxist analysis must distinguish what is organic, that is to say of the whole system and relatively permanent, from what is conjunctural, that is to say specific to a given moment. It must know how to read the structural contradictions in the economy beneath the conjunctural conflicts at the level of the political system and of ideology. Gramsci's position here is different from that of economism (q.v.) with which it might at first sight be confused. For the latter, one must always look to the 'reality' of the economic base beneath the 'appearances' of the superstructures. For Gramsci, on the other hand, one must constantly *connect* the organic and the conjunctural moments to one another. This means understanding and seeing as equally real the terrain of the conjunctural, since it is precisely 'upon this terrain that the forces of opposition organize'. The error comes when one pays excessive attention only to one or the other. Overemphasis on the organic at the expense of the conjunctural leads to economism, just as overemphasis on the conjunctural leads to 'ideologism'. (See VI.10)

Organic crisis

An 'organic crisis' is a crisis of the whole system, in which contradictions in the economic structure have repercussions through the superstructures. One of its signs is when the traditional forms of political representation (parties or party leaders) are no longer recognized as adequate by the economic class or class fraction which they had previously served to represent. It is therefore a crisis of hegemony, since it occurs when a formerly hegemonic class is challenged from below and is no longer able to hold together a cohesive bloc of social alliances. Such an organic crisis opened, in Gramsci's analysis, in Italy before the First World War, when the bourgeoisie and the landowners, faced with the growing power of working-class organizations, lost confidence in the Liberal ruling elite to represent them. Organic crises produce a situation of rapid political realignments. In Italy after the war these resulted in the rise to power of Fascism. (See VI.12 and VIII.9 and 10)

Passive revolution

Gramsci adapts the term 'passive revolution' from Vincenzo Cuoco's history of the 1799 revolution in Naples, but it is 'completely modified' by his own usage (Q 15§17, p. 1775). It is used to describe any historical situation in which a new political formation comes to power without a fundamental reordering of social relations. He first applies it to the Risorgimento to describe the process by which the bourgeoisie, represented by Cavour's Moderates, achieves power without a revolution of the French type. He then extends it to other liberal movements of the post-1815 restoration and finally to fascism, which modernizes the economy 'from above' by breaking the political power of both the laissez-faire bourgeoisie and the organized working class. Gramsci describes these forms of passive revolution as manifestations of a 'war of position' by the dominant classes after a phase of war of manoeuvre from below (French Revolution; the period 1917-21). Although it has sometimes been asserted – perhaps because of this assimilation between passive revolution and war of position – that Gramsci also advocated a form of 'passive revolution' for the left, in fact he explicitly says that it is only an analytical tool, a 'criterion of interpretation', and not a programme 'as it was for the Italian liberals of the Risorgimento' (VIII.5). He also says that the 'dialectic of conservation and innovation' which constitutes passive revolution 'is called reformism' in modern terminology. (Q10 11§41.xiv, p. 1325). See in particular Section VIII.

Philosophy of praxis

This term is used in many passages of the prison notebooks in place of Marxism (Gramsci also refers to Marx as 'the founder of the philosophy of praxis' and to Lenin as 'the greatest modern theorist of the philosophy of praxis': VI.6). The expression, however, is more than a device to bypass the censor: it also conveys (as it did for the Socialist philosopher Antonio Labriola from whom Gramsci borrowed it) a specific *conception* of Marxism as a unity of theory and practice. For Gramsci the philosophy of praxis is both the theory of the contradictions in society and at the same time people's practical awareness of those contradictions. The philosophy of praxis is the 'self-consciousness' of historical 'necessity'. It involves the formation of a revolutionary collective will which can act in accordance with that necessity. Gramsci in other words sees the philosophy of praxis not only as a system of philosophical ideas but also as forming the basis of a mass 'conception of the world': 'the character of the philosophy of praxis is especially that of being a mass conception, a mass culture, that of a mass which operates as a unit, in other words one which has norms of conduct which are not only universal at the level of ideas, but "generalized" in social reality.' (Q10, II§31) 'The philosophy of praxis is absolute "historicism", the absolute bringing down to earth and worldliness of thought, an absolute humanism of history. It is along this line that one must trace the thread of the new conception of the world.' (Q 11§27, SPN 465, translation slightly altered).

State

Gramsci uses the term 'state' in at least two different senses in the prison notebooks. In the first (narrow) sense the state is a sphere of 'domination', the organ or instrument of the oppression of one class by another (see, for instance, X.1, p. 306). This corresponds to one of the uses of the term in Marx and to Lenin's use in *The State and Revolution* and it was also the main sense in which the term was used in the Second and Third Internationals. In the second (wider) sense (which seems also to be a later one in the composition of the notebooks) the state is an 'integral' state. It has the functions *both* of coercion and of consent. It contains *both* the apparatuses of government and the judiciary and the various voluntary and private associations and para-political institutions which make up civil society (q.v.). In this wider sense, the state possesses 'educative' and 'ethical' functions which will remain, indeed expand, under socialism as the state in the narrow sense (as an instrument of coercion and class domination) withers away: 'It is possible to imagine the coercive element of the state withering away by degrees, as ever more conspicuous elements of regulated society (or ethical state or civil society) make their appearance.' (VII.8) Within the integral state, the term civil society has 'the sense of the political and cultural hegemony of a social group over the whole of society, the *ethical content of the state*' (Q6§24, p. 703, my italics).

In the first sense, then, state is separated from civil society, as coercion against consent, domination against direction, dictatorship against hegemony. In the second sense, state includes both civil society and the state in the first or narrow sense (now called 'political society'). In both cases the distinction between two 'regions' (political society/civil society) is the same, and both together are methodologically separated by Gramsci from a third 'region' – 'economic society' or the economic structure.

Transformism

A term originally used in Italian political jargon in the late 1870s to describe loose alliances between factions of Left and Right (opponents were 'transformed' into supporters across the floor of parliament), Gramsci extends it to describe the characteristic form of bourgeois hegemony in Italy between unification and Fascism. With a system of transformism there is no real opposition or alternation in power. Instead there is a piecemeal absorption of the opposition by the ruling elites. Gramsci distinguishes two main phases: 1860-1900, 'molecular' transformism, in which individual exponents of the democratic opposition go over to the moderate-conservative centre; 1900-1918, transformism of whole groups of the left who go over to the centre or right: for instance, the Nationalist party is formed out of ex-anarchists and syndicalists (Q8§36, pp. 962-63).

War of Manoeuvre/War of Position

These military terms, used in relation to the First World War, meant, respectively, a war of rapid movement with a series of frontal assaults, and trench warfare backed up by reserves of supplies, munitions and soldiers behind the lines. In parallel with the state/civil society distinction, Gramsci applies the two concepts to politics. 'It seems to me that Ilyich [Lenin] understood that a change was necessary from a war of manoeuvre [frontal attack on the state] applied victoriously in the East in 1917, to a war of position which was the only form possible in the West.' (VII.2) War of position is linked to Gramsci's notion of hegemony in its various senses: class alliances, 'molecular' ideological and political work in civil society, consent. It should be noted, however, that he uses the term 'war of position' not only to designate a revolutionary strategy for the left but also to describe a phase of 'revolution-reaction' or passive revolution (q.v.) which follows upon a revolutionary offensive (war of manoeuvre): in this sense fascism is also a form of war of position (see p. 267).

FURTHER READING

The following is a selection of secondary works in English. The books by Fiori and Davidson are biographies. Spriano's is an account of Gramsci's relations with the PCdI during his imprisonment. Those by Boggs, Joll, and Simon are general introductory studies. Those by Cammett, Clark and Williams 1975 deal with the early period. The articles by Bobbio and Texier are two sides of a celebrated discussion on the question of Gramsci's 'superstructuralism'. Althusser's chapter is a critique of Gramsci's 'historicist' Marxism. Mouffe 1979a gives a post-Leninist interpretation of the hegemony concept; Laclau and Mouffe 1985 develop it into the basis of a 'post-Marxist' position. Anderson provides information on the history of the concept before Gramsci and suggests that he failed to confront adequately the question of state power. Femia is valuable on the concept of 'contradictory consciousness'. Buci-Glucksmann's is a dense but historically detailed and fascinating study. Sassoon 1987 contains a thorough discussion of Gramsci's conception of the party. Entwistle interprets Gramsci's educational ideas. Kiernan 1974 makes original observations on Gramsci's discussions of non-European societies. The subjects of most of the other works listed here are apparent from the titles.

Althusser, Louis, 1970. 'Marxism is not a Historicism' in L. Althusser and E. Balibar, *Reading Capital*, translated by Ben Brewster, London: NLB, Chapter 5.

Anderson, Perry, 1976-7. 'The Antinomies of Antonio Gramsci', *New Left Review*, 100, November 1976-January 1977, pp. 5-78.

Bellamy, Richard, 1987. 'Antonio Gramsci', in *Modern Italian Social Theory. Ideology and Politics from Pareto to the Present*, Cambridge: Polity Press.

Bobbio, Norberto, 1967. 'Gramsci and the Conception of Civil Society', in Mouffe 1979b.

Boggs, Carl, 1976. *Gramsci's Marxism*, London: Pluto Press.

Buci-Glucksmann, Christine, 1980. *Gramsci and the State*, translated by David Fernbach, London: Lawrence and Wishart.

Cammett, John M., 1967. *Antonio Gramsci and the Origins of Italian Communism*, Stanford: University Press.

Clark, Martin N., 1977. *Antonio Gramsci and the Revolution that Failed*, New Haven and London: Yale University Press.

Davidson, Alistair, 1977. *Antonio Gramsci: Towards an Intellectual Biography*, London: Merlin Press.

De Giovanni, Biagio, 1976. 'Lenin and Gramsci: State, Politics and Party', in Mouffe 1979b.

Eley, Geoff, 1984. 'Reading Gramsci in English: Observations on the Reception of Antonio Gramsci in the English-Speaking World 1957-82', *European History Quarterly*, Vol. 14, pp. 441-78.

Entwistle, Harold, 1979. *Antonio Gramsci. Conservative Schooling for Radical Politics*, London: Routledge and Kegan Paul.

Femia, Joseph V., 1981. *Gramsci's Political Thought. Hegemony, Consciousness and the Revolutionary Process*, Oxford: Clarendon Press.

Fiori, Giuseppe, 1970. *Antonio Gramsci: Life of a Revolutionary*, translated by Tom Nairn, London: NLB.

Forgacs, David, 1984. 'National-Popular: Genealogy of a Concept', in *Formations of Nation and People*, London: Routledge and Kegan Paul, pp. 83-98.

Hall, Stuart; Lumley, Bob; McLennan, Gregor, 1977. 'Politics and Ideology: Gramsci', *Working Papers in Cultural Studies, 10: On Ideology* (reprinted as *On Ideology*, London: Hutchinson, 1978).

Hall, Stuart, 1987. 'Gramsci and Us', *Marxism Today*, June, pp. 16-21.

Harman, Chris, 1983. 'Gramsci Versus Reformism', London: Socialist Workers Party pamphlet.

Hoffman, John, 1984. *The Gramscian Challenge. Coercion and Consent in Marxist Political Theory*, Oxford: Blackwell.

Hobsbawm, Eric, 1977. 'Gramsci and Political Theory', *Marxism Today*, July, pp. 205-13.

Hobsbawm, Eric, 1982, 'Gramsci and Marxist Political Theory' in Showstack Sassoon 1982.

Hunt, Geoffrey, 1986. 'Gramsci, Civil Society and Bureaucracy', *Praxis International*, Vol. 6, No. 2, July, pp. 206-19.

Joll, James, 1977. *Gramsci*, London: Fontana Modern Masters.

Kiernan, Victor G. 1972. 'Gramsci and Marxism', *Socialist Register 1972*, London: Merlin Press, pp. 1-33.

Kiernan, Victor G. 1974. 'Gramsci and the other Continents', *New Edinburgh Review, Gramsci Issue III*, No. 27, 1974, pp. 19-24.

Laclau, Ernesto and Mouffe, Chantal, 1981. 'Socialist Strategy: Where Next?', *Marxism Today*, January.

Laclau, Ernesto and Mouffe, Chantal, 1985. *Hegemony and Socialist Strategy. Towards a Radical Democratic Politics*, London: Verso.

Lumley, Bob, 1977. 'Gramsci's Writings on the State and Hegemony', Stencilled Occasional Paper No. 51, Centre for Contemporary Cultural Studies, University of Birmingham.

Merrington, John, 1968. 'Theory and Practice in Gramsci's Marxism', *Socialist Register 1968*, London: Merlin Press, pp. 154-76 (reprinted in *Western Marxism: A Critical Reader*, London: Verso, 1978).

Mouffe, Chantal, 1979a 'Hegemony and Ideology in Gramsci', in Mouffe 1979b.

Mouffe, Chantal (ed.), 1979b. *Gramsci and Marxist Theory*, London: Routledge and Kegan Paul.

Mouffe, Chantal, 1981. 'Hegemony and the Integral State in Gramsci. Towards a New Concept of Politics', in George Bridges and Rosalind Brunt (eds), *Silver Linings: Some Strategies for the Eighties*, London: Lawrence and Wishart.

Nairn, Tom, 1980. 'Antonu su gobbu' in Showstack Sassoon, 1982.

Salvadori, Massimo, 1976. 'Gramsci and the PCI: Two Conceptions of Hegemony', in Mouffe 1979b.

Showstack Sassoon, Anne, 1978. 'Hegemony and Political Intervention' in Sally Hibbin (ed.), *Politics, Ideology and the State*, London: Lawrence and Wishart.

Showstack Sassoon, Anne (ed.), 1982. *Approaches to Gramsci*, London: Writers and Readers.

Showstack Sassoon, Anne, 1987 (revised edition). *Gramsci's Politics*, London: Hutchinson.

Simon, Roger, 1982. *Gramsci's Political Thought. An Introduction*, London: Lawrence and Wishart.

Spriano, Paolo, 1979. *Antonio Gramsci: The Prison Years*, translated by John Fraser, London: Lawrence and Wishart.

Texier, Jacques, 1967. 'Gramsci, Theoretician of the Superstructures. On the Conception of Civil Society', in Mouffe 1979b.

Togliatti, Palmiro, 1979. *On Gramsci and Other Writings*, edited by Donald Sassoon, London: Lawrence and Wishart.

Williams, Gwyn, A., 1960. 'The Concept of "Egemonia" in the Thought of Antonio Gramsci: Some Notes on Interpretation', *Journal of the History of Ideas*, Vol. XXI, October-December, No. 4, pp. 586-99.

Williams, Gwyn A., 1975. *Proletarian Order. Antonio Gramsci, Factory Councils and the Origins of Communism in Italy 1911-1921*, London: Pluto Press.

Name Index

Engels, Frederick 189, 213, 215, 408, 409
Ennius, Quintus 316
Erasmus, Desiderius 352
Eugene of Savoy 375

Farinacci, Roberto 142, 405
Ferrari, Giuseppe 413
Ferri, Enrico 174
Feuerbach, Ludwig 351
Flammarion, Camille 368, 418
Foch, Ferdinand 229
Ford, Henry 275, 277, 278, 282, 290, 291, 296, 359, 415
Fortunato, Giustino 179, 182, 183, 406
Forzano, Gioacchino 372
Fontenay, Paul 364
Fovel, Massimo 282, 283, 285
Fracchia, Umberto 367
Francis of Assisi, Saint 333
Freud, Sigmund 414

Gajda, Rudolf 217, 410
Garibaldi, Giuseppe 247, 249, 251, 259, 413
Gentile, Giovanni 193, 224, 303, 311, 358, 359, 407, 416, 417
Gentiloni, Ottorino 176, 406
Giacometti, Paolo 372
Giardini, Cesare 372
Gioberti, Vincenzo 50, 212, 263, 413
Giolitti, Giovanni 29, 42, 44, 77, 105, 122, 175, 176, 177, 248, 268, 403, 414
Giusti, Giuseppe 346, 416
Gobetti, Piero 184, 185, 406
Goethe, Johann Wolfgang von 266
Gori, Pietro 374, 418
Gramsci, Delio 20, 22
Gramsci, Francesco 17
Gramsci, Gennaro 17
Gramsci, Giuliano 20, 22
Gramsci Marcias, Giuseppina 23
Graziadei, Antonio 154, 155, 406
Groethuysen, Bernard 338
Guerrazzi, Francesco Domenico 368, 369
Guicciardini, Francesco 228

Halévy, Daniel 233, 234, 412
Hegel, Georg Wilhelm Friedrich 234, 236, 255, 351, 417
Heine, Heinrich 49
Herriot, Edouard 252

Hitler, Adolf 219
Horace (Quintus Horatius Flaccus) 415
Hugo, Victor 370

Ibsen, Henrik 372
Invernizio, Carolina 368
Isgrò, Michele 21

Joan of Arc 371
Joyce, James 414

Kamenev, Lev 21, 137, 170
Kerensky, Alexander 164, 406
Kipling, Rudyard 31
Krasnov, Peter 226, 228, 229, 410

Labriola, Antonio 176, 258, 429
Lactantius, Firmianus 316
Lanzillo, Agostino 210
Lassalle, Ferdinand 235, 236, 412
Laviosa, Antonio 214
Lenin, Vladmir Ilyich 18, 19, 45, 46, 47, 49, 51, 73, 77, 136, 165, 166, 168, 192, 195, 228, 229, 230, 246, 404, 405, 408, 409, 410, 411, 426, 429, 431
Leone, Enrico 56, 176, 403
Leonetti, Alfonso 22
Lewis, Sinclair 298, 415
Linati, Carlo 296, 297
Longobardi, Ernesto Cesare 176
Lo Piparo, Franco 324
Loria, Achille 213, 215, 308, 409, 416
Louis XV 287
Lunacharsky, Anatoly 73, 411
Luxemburg, Rosa 77, 222, 225, 229

Macaulay, Thomas Babington 374, 375, 418
MacDonald, Ramsay 270, 414
Machiavelli, Niccolò 22, 224, 238, 239, 240, 241, 242, 255, 381, 423
Malatesta, Errico 404
Marinetti, Filippo Tommaso 73
Martinet, Marcel 374
Manzoni, Alessandro 368, 418
Martini, Ferdinando 368
Marx, Karl 17, 30, 33, 35, 36, 37, 39, 86, 102, 189, 190, 198, 200, 230, 246, 248, 346, 407, 408, 411, 429
Masaniello (Tommaso Aniello) 372
Massaja, Guglielmo 369
Mastriani, Francesco 368, 369
Mathiez, Albert 203, 208, 246

Subject Index

Action Française 412
Action Party *see* Risorgimento
Americanism: and European intellectuals 296-8; and hegemony 279; gangsterism 287; intelligentsia 298-9; labour unions 279; negro question 279; pioneer tradition 291-3; prohibition 287, 289, 291-2, 293-4; prostitution 293-4; puritanism 290-2; rational demographic composition 277; rationalization 279, 289; sexual question 280-2, 287-8; and the state 285
animality 286
architecture 381, 401-2
armistice (1918) 122, 123
Association des Ecrivains et des Artistes Révolutionnaires 391
Avanti! 17, 18, 176, 404, 419
Aventine secession 135, 153, 405

Banca Commerciale 149
Bank of Italy 149
Bolshevik Revolution *see* Russian Revolution
Bolsheviks 30, 51, 82, 131, 231, 410, 413; *see also* Communist Party of the Soviet Union, Social-Democratic Party, Russian
Bonapartism 268, 269, 289
Boulangism 216, 217, 410
bureaucracy 219, 269; expansion of after 1848, 271

Cadornism 227, 410
Caesarism 248, 268, 269-74, 420; and 'catastrophic' equilibrium 272-3; and hegemonic influence of fundamental classes 273; and organic equilibrium 271; progressive and regressive 269-70, 273
calligraphism 399, 419
catharsis 372, 418

Catholicism 198, 241, 243, 332-3, 340, 344, 352, 361, 369; Catholic Action 146, 386; Christian democracy 176; Church 54, 191, 241, 244, 330, 333, 342, 361; Counter-Reformation 370; and French Revolution 340; integralism 330; Jesuits 315, 330, 337, 360, 369-70, 405; popular 352, 361, 370; and popular literature 369; relation between intellectuals and 'simple' in 332-3
centralism, democratic 112, 412; organic (bureaucratic) 112, 133, 244, 301, 350, 412
charismatic leaders 219, 240
Christianity 287, 337-8; primitive 350, 418; *see also* Catholicism, religion
cinema 293, 356, 363, 364, 374, 376, 419
Città Futura, La 18
city and country 118, 119, 247; in Jacobinism 252; and sexuality 280
civil society 285, 313, 420; in advanced states 227; in East as 'primordial and gelatinous' 229; as ensemble of organisms commonly called 'private' 306; greater autonomy from state activity before 1848, 233; and hegemony 194, 306, 307; as one of two major superstructural 'levels' 306; and party 310; and political society 210, 211, 306, 307; and state 194-5, 210, 222, 224, 236, 306-7, 310; as 'the state itself' 236; superstructures of like trench systems 227; in West as 'system of fortresses and earthworks' 229
coercion 288, 289, 315, 401-2
collective man 232, 325, 348, 415
collective will 239-42, 382, 426
colonies 112-3, 233
Comintern *see* International, Third
common sense 244, 323, 324, 327, 332, 342-9, 421; as chaotic aggregation of disparate conceptions 345; con-

210-2, 422 and liberalism 176, 202, 210; theoretical 210, 212

Taylorism 275, 276, 288, 290, 294-6, 359, 389, 415
Third Republic (France) 203-4
trade unions 78-80, 83, 92-6, 97, 131, 141, 243, 278, 279, 415
transformation of quantity into quality 45, 335
transformism 247, 248, 250, 424, 430
Treaty of London (April 1915) 406
Tsarism 48

united front *see* Communist Party of Italy, International, Third

Vatican see Catholicism
voluntarism 30, 38, 404

war communism 415

war of manoeuvre (war of movement) 222, 223, 224, 225-30, 430-1; French Revolution as 267; and frontal attack 228, 229-30; March 1917 to March 1921 as phase of 267; theory of permanent revolution (Trotsky) as political reflection of 228
war of position 222, 223, 224, 225-30, 248, 430-1; nineteenth-century liberal era as a long 265; fascism as representative of 267
will: free 400; as operative awareness of historical necessity 241; rationalism and individual will 401
World War, First 29, 33, 34, 41, 48, 60, 73, 76, 87, 115, 118, 122, 124, 181, 226-7, 247, 248, 260, 406, 412, 414, 430

YMCA (Young Men's Christian Association) 284